We Wrote Letters Then

Vietnam War 1967 - 1968

This is a book about how a young couple caught in the stream of history, communicated with each other, family, and friends in the years 1966 through 1968. During that time, prior to the internet, e-mail and social media outlets, personal communication was limited to postal mail and the rare telephone call.

Bill and Elin Walker, Copenhagen 1961

Bill and Elin Walker, St. Maarten 2013

We Wrote Letters Then

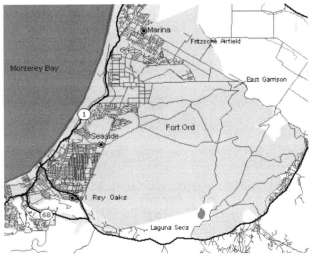

Fort Ord, Monterey Bay, California

Chu Lai, Vietnam

Odense, Denmark

We Wrote Letters Then

How family and friends stayed

in touch during the Vietnam War

Letters sent and received by

Bill & Elin Walker

1967-1968

Compiled and edited by
Joan Walker Miskell & William Alan Walker

w2m
WalkerMiskell Publishing

Photography enhancements by John Scull Walker & Joan Walker Miskell
Translations by Elin Rasmussen Walker

WM

WalkerMiskell Publishing
Beacon, New York

Copyright © 2015 by Joan Walker Miskell

ISBN 978-1-329-79892-2

First Hardcover Printing: December 2015

Paperback Printing: January 2016

Contact: wwalker7395@yahoo.com or jwmiskell@gmail.com

What's my doubt, what's my fear in the chaos of the world.
The house of love is firm, a courtyard to our heaven.

ELIN RASMUSSEN WALKER - 1961

* Elin Rasmussen Walker jotted down this statement while dating Bill in 1961. "I was contemplating marrying you, knowing there would be chaotic, uncertain times ahead for us, and major decisions would have to be made."

Bill had the quote engraved on a charm and gave it to Elin the morning after their wedding day – October 7, 1961.

*For all the military families who have
endured separation while serving their country.*

CONTENTS

In the spring of 1961, Elin met Lieutenant Bill Walker at an International Student Club social event on the Washington State University campus. After a short courtship they were engaged, and were married in Spokane in October 1961. They immediately left for his new assignment to Headquarters Fourth Armored Division, Goppingen, Germany. They left Germany in 1965, and after attending an Army school in Indianapolis, Indiana, Bill was assigned to Fort Ord, California in 1966.

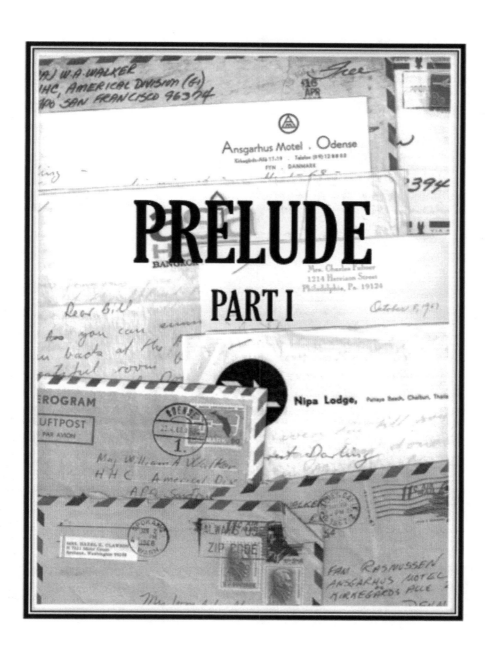

PRÉLUDE

PART I

Fort Ord, California
September 12, 1966

Dear Joan,

Finally getting around to writing to you to thank you for your last letter - and the fudge which we received afterward and devoured quickly, ah! Good old Copper Kettle! Thanks so much. We enjoyed it heartily.

How is everyone in Philadelphia? Are Mike and Kathy back from their honeymoon? We are continuing to enjoy it here. The weather on the peninsula is getting nicer now (27 days of fog in August). Of course inland a few miles and it's always sunny. We've had company start to roll in. The Morgans from Spokane were here for dinner last week with their daughter Claudia (who visited us in Germany) and son-in-law, Richard Phenneger, who live in San Francisco area. Also two different sets of Elin's old friends from San Francisco will come. We spent the weekend in San Francisco with friends who live there (the Reekies) who visited us in Philadelphia at Christmas. What a fabulous, beautiful city! The ultimate in America as far as I'm concerned. You wouldn't believe it!

Are you still at the bank? Kirsten is still working in the bank in Odense (she asked about you), but is talking about coming to the U.S.A. next year.

Write soon - hope all is going well - Elin says hello!

Love
Bill

Philadelphia, Pennsylvania
October 16, 1966

Dear Bill and Elin,

Please forgive me for not writing. I have been kept quite busy. I am attending night school Monday and Thursday nights – taking shorthand. I really enjoy it though I have an awful lot of written homework. I also joined the Robb Grange Chorale (Mr. Hamilton) and that meets on Tuesday and Wednesday nights. By the time weekends roll around, I am ready to relax. Janice Smith and I have become theater goers. We've seen two plays already and next week we'll go to another. The first one – "The Loves of Cass Maguire" wasn't very good. The second – "Walk Happy" was very good… a musical. Next week we will see "Holly Golightly". It doesn't have a very good write-up but we will see.

I also got to see Peter, Paul and Mary at the Academy. They were great!

Jack and his sergeant (whom I have been dating) came up one weekend, and we & Janice Smith went to New York for the weekend. We really had a fabulous time. Saturday afternoon we just walked around the city, visited Central Park, watched a German parade, and went to the Empire State Building. After changing clothes, we went to a French restaurant for dinner, and then proceeded to Rockefeller Center where a big political dance was being held by invitation only. Someone came up to us and gave us free tickets. We went down, danced awhile, when who should appear on stage but Nelson Rockefeller. I shook hands with him and got his autograph. It was quite a surprise. Then we went to the Village. We wanted to go to "Arthur's" (Sybil Burton) but it was a 4 hour wait. So we walked around and walked in some other clubs. The people were odd, but great! We topped off the weekend at a Yankee's game. A great weekend!

Your new home looks real nice. I'm sure you will be happy there. Oh yes! Happy belated anniversary! Write soon.

Love
Joan

At home – Rendova Drive, Fort Ord, California

Fort Ord, California
October 26, 1966

Dear Joan,

We were delighted to receive your letter and to gather from the gist of it that you have been having a ball recently - good - keep it up! The New York jaunt must have been great. I recall because the last time I was out on the town in New York was in 1959, and spent an evening (into the wee hours) traipsing through the Village spots - some fun.

We have been enjoying the most beautiful weather this month, and predictions are that it will continue into November - about 75-80 degrees in the day, cool at night as usual.

We've been going to the beach on weekends. You can't swim here because of the undertow, but you can get out in the surf a ways (we do our swimming in the Post pool - indoors).

We are really busy with many projects. Every night is taken up at the craft shops, the pool, or some project at home.

We had hoped to go to San Francisco last weekend, but I had to work, so it will have to be in early November. There is a city! You wouldn't believe it! We are already starting to think about the holidays. We haven't done any entertaining since we've been here, and are ready to throw some parties. Also, Hazel will be staying with us sometime during the holidays and we will entertain for her.

I seriously doubt if I will be here very long. Most captains who have been back from European assignments for six months are on orders for Vietnam and I've been back almost a year! When I do go Elin will fly to Denmark over the North Pole to spend the year, and I'll probably try to hop a flight back East before leaving. But we'll worry about that when it comes.

Take care, & write again soon.

Love
Bill

Big Sur

Elin basking in the sun at Carmel

Entertaining at home
Photo by John Burks

Fort Ord, California
December 4, 1966

Dear Elin,

    Ollie and I want to thank you for including us in your "after-Gala" party last night. Bill is a fabulous host, everything tasted so good, and the company was delightful. Thanks for a very relaxing and thoroughly enjoyable occasion, and it was nice to celebrate our joint effort which was an unqualified success. Thanks to you, Ord Art '66 has become an important event to Fort Ord and the civilian community, and perhaps a precedent has been set for future efforts. Congratulations!

Sincerely,
Carol

P.S. Also, congratulations to Bill on his entries in the show - I really got to see and appreciate them today - also in your beautiful home.

Elin Walker, Director "Ord 66" Art Show posing with paintings to be displayed

Page Three Panorama Friday, November 4, 1966

ENTERING HER PAINTING "WINDSWEPT CYPRESS" in the 1966 Ord Art exhibit is Mrs. George Knovick. Accepting the painting and marking it entry number one is Mrs. W. A. Walker (right). The exhibit is being held in conjunction with the Officers' Wives Club Gala, December 3 at Stilwell Hall. (U.S. Army photo by Wyatt)

Annual Holiday Gala Slated December 3

'Ord Art 66' Is Show Case For Works of Post Artists

FORT ORD, Calif.—A feature of the "Holiday Gala" held here December 3, was a segment entitled "Ord Art 66", under the direction of Mrs. William A. Walker.

The exhibit of arts and crafts offered amatuer and professional artists and craftsmen of the Ord community an opportunity to display their talent. The exhibit was open to all military, civilian and retired military persons.

Included were the works of four outstanding post artists.

Mrs. George C. Knovick, whose husband is assigned to the hospital here, entered a number of paintings including one titled "Windswept Cypress" done on the Peninsula. Mrs. Knovick is studying with a Carmel artist.

MSgt. James Stevenson, Hq Committee Gp, has been an amateur painter for 10 years. His entries were landscape oils done on his previous assignment in the Canal Zone, as well as some he has done while stationed here.

Water colors representative of the Japanese and Chinese schools were entered by Mrs. Edmond Fung, whose husband is with the Chaplain Section, U.S. Army Training Center. Mrs. Fung, a native of Nanking, China, came to the States as a young child, but later studied under teachers in Hong Kong.

Mrs. William R. Thompson, whose husband is with G-3 Section, USATC, specializes in water colors of children. She was recently selected to illustrate a children's book written by Mrs. Arthur Murray, wife of the dance instructor. Although she has had no formal art training, Mrs. Thompson has achieved professional status.

In addition to paintings, there were exhibits of sculpture, ceramics, woodworking, jewelry and leathercraft.

(U.S. Army photo by SP5 Jose Cardona)

Paul D. Lau, winner of the grand prize of "Ord Art '66" at the Fort Ord Holiday Gala, stands beside his bronze casting with Mrs. William A. Walker, chairman of the art display at Stilwell Hall last Saturday evening.

Holiday Gala At Fort Ord

Over a thousand soldiers, guests and Monterey Bay area townspeople swarmed throughout the vast edifice of Stilwell Hall last Saturday night when the Fort Ord sented the Christmas Holiday Gala.

Wreaths and decorated trees, featuring a 40-foot Christmas tree in the main ballroom, welcomed the guests.

Winning the overall grand prize for the best entry in the holiday table decorating competition was the table done by the 3rd Brigade, under the direction of Mrs. D. E. Hutter. This table used a black, white and gold oriental motif to depict the Eastern influence on Western culture.

The judges for the tables, Mrs. Robert (Virginia) Stanton, party editor of House Beautiful magazine, and Nell Currie, interior decorator, were so impressed with the quality of each of the table settings that they increased the number of first place prize winners from three to five.

Attracting a large appreciative crowd of viewers through the south rooms of the hall, "Ord Art '66"—under the direction of Mrs. William A. Walker—presented art work efforts of the Fort Ord community.

Nearly 350 individual entries from all over the fort, including soldiers, civilians and dependents, were judged by John B. Morse, artist; Robert Stanton, architect; Geza St. Galy, artist; and Barbara Tripp, interior decorator.

"The Crowd" by William Walker earned an Honorable Mention at the Art Show

"Bass Player" by William Walker also on display

Fort Ord, California
January 5, 1967

Dear Mother and Uncle Charlie

Realize that we haven't written since before Christmas, but the phone conversation in between account for that. Thanks for your call last week. Elin was happy to get your birthday greetings.

We had an interesting & rather different Christmas this year. Elin's Art Show dominated the scene until right before Christmas, so we didn't do too much entertaining. A late party for the people connected with the show, then right before we left for L.A. we had the neighbors (10) one evening for a hot German wine concoction. We drove to L.A. on the 23rd (5 hour trip). It's a beautiful trip, mountains, valleys and much of the highway right on the coast. Beautiful weather (was 74 degrees in L.A.) Everything green. We stopped in Solvang - near Santa Barbara. This is a small town settled by Danes, and it is quite a little bit of Denmark in the U.S.A. Windmill, gabled houses and all. Especially authentic Danish pastries and cooking, etc. All of the residents & shopkeepers speak Danish. Elin went wild! And we loaded up on goodies (we stopped there for dinner on the way back).

We stayed the first night in L.A. in a hotel in Beverly Hills. Drove through Hollywood, Sunset Strip, Wilshire Boulevard, etc. Then drove through Beverly Hills. The homes are absolutely fantastic, never seen anything like it. We were both flabbergasted. Thousands of beautiful show places. The next day we went to the Los Angeles Museum of Art, beautiful building, and went to the Farmers Market which is just like a European marketplace in many respects. We spent that night (Christmas Eve) and the next with Mr. Kalbfleisch and his daughter Ann in Fullerton (across L.A. about 30 miles near Disneyland). L.A. is so huge it takes hours to get through it going 70 miles an hour on the freeways! We had a cozy Christmas Eve and Christmas Day. Went to church in the morning & had dinner in the afternoon. On the 26th we spent 3 hours in Disneyland before driving home. Disneyland is just as wonderful as reputed to be. As appealing as Tivoli in Copenhagen - but in the Hollywood/Disney tradition. We could have spent several days there, and plan to return.

So, we didn't open our gifts until Elin's birthday on the 27th (the gifts from Denmark still haven't gotten here yet). We are delighted with your gift - only sorry that the store goofed - but we will enjoy it when the right pattern comes. Thank you very much. We've gotten to like our silver pattern more and more & it really looks elegant with Elin's beautiful table arrangements.

Went to two parties New Year's Eve. Nothing really exciting. Now back at work full time. I've been very busy. Elin was just offered a two day a week job in the Post thrift shop which is run by the Officers' Wives Club, which she took and started today.

We received a letter from Hazel today. She's in Arizona right now, will go from there to L.A. and from L.A. to here. Probably won't arrive here until late this month. We are looking forward to her visit. We should be getting some other company this month also.

It's been a little cool here, but the weather all through December has been beautiful. The days are always warm enough to be out in shirt sleeves, but at night you need a top coat. Quite a contrast to all the other winters we've spent, especially in Germany.

We've been reading about the tremendous snowstorms in the East & Midwest & find it inconceivable as we wallow in our delightfully mild winter. We went to a play the other night in "California's First Theater" in Monterey. The original adobe Spanish style building, built in the early 1800's for soldiers entertainment, has been kept completely authentic - down to the long, hard, wooden benches for the audience, and the shows are melodramas from the 19th century. Quite a panic & lots of fun. During intermission the audience sings songs to the accompaniment of a piano - very cozy atmosphere.

We just finished up the cookies you sent (the candy didn't last as long!). Everything was very delicious and we appreciated the time it took to make them.

We're wondering what this year will bring. Since I haven't heard anything by this time I am assuming that we will be here until summer at least - but that's pure speculation because people are still being reassigned with short notice. As Elin mentioned on the phone we are considering her staying in the U.S. &

getting education credits & teaching accreditation during the year I'll be gone. I think it would be a smart move. It's impossible for her to work in her field because there is a reluctance to hire military dependents who may be leaving at any time making it difficult to "walk in" to a good position without some longevity in an organization. On the other hand (had she had the credits) Elin could have taught any place we've been, either permanently or as a substitute. We shall see.

Keep well - and thanks again for the gifts -

Love
Elin and Bill

Solvang, California

Elin with Carl Kalbfleisch – Fullerton, CA

Elin at Disneyland

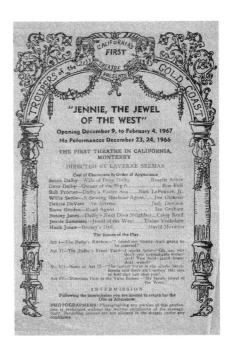

"California's First Theater"

Eislingen/Fils, Germany
January 9, 1967

Dear Elin and Bill:

It must seem quite unusual to you that I take so long for answering a letter. What it really was that kept me from writing to you for Christmas I cannot say exactly, I just know that there was so much to do before the holidays, that the evenings and days were going so fast and that I did not get all the mail out as I had intended to do. I was then hoping to be able to write between Christmas and New Year, but again, so many other things came in between.

Well, it is not too late yet to wish both of you the very best for 1967, happiness and health, and for you Bill, should you have to go to Vietnam, especially all the best. Thank you for your letter from November and for your Christmas message.

I am very sure that you had very nice holidays and that you did start the New Year well. Was it nice in San Francisco and Los Angeles? Did you celebrate Christmas the Danish or American way? Elin, what news do you have from home? Is everyone well? Is your sister still at home?

I had a very nice Christmas this year, got so many presents and so much mail as never before. Christmas Eve I spent with my relatives in Donzdorf. On the first holiday I worked in the Geislingen hospital (I do it now 1 or 2 Sundays a month since I saw how much work there is and how few nurses); on the second holiday I went skiing with Marianne. New Year's Eve I spent at home, and as a great surprise, had a 3 in the morning phone call from Helga and family. I have now a phone in the apartment since the middle of December. On New Year's Day was the General's reception in the afternoon. I had to introduce all the German guests to him. To welcome all the guests on the door of the officers' club, we had a real chimney-sweep with a little pig in his arm. Everybody enjoyed that. As the CG sent out 110 Christmas cards to German people, Lord Mayors and Mayors, Landrats and Chiefs of Police wherever we have troops stationed, and as I had to handle the German people for the reception (type invitations, etc.) I was very busy before the holidays, but it was all worthwhile.

News in the office: Actually not too many, as most of the people you don't know anymore. As of today, Capt. Romans (his wife is expecting in spring) is in our office as the XO or whatever this position is called, Capt. Hoots in Nuremberg, Capt. Bowling Chief of PSD. Lt Bischoff leaves the end of this month, to be a civilian again.

I had Christmas mail from Colonel James from Vietnam, Martha Pigeon, Strekers, Perrys. Colonel Hawkins should be in Hawaii now, or maybe he is already on his way to Vietnam. The new AG is real nice.

Right now we have lots of snow, ideal skiing weather, I don't know if I wrote you last year that I took up skiing. Marianne and I will go for 9 days to St. Moritz from 28 Jan to 5 Feb. The Headquarters is in Grafenwoehr right now, that is the best time for me to go.

So you see that I must feel well again or I could not do all these things. Truly, I feel real fine, and on New Year's Eve I was especially thankful that all had gone so well last year. Working now in the hospital I have seen more than one woman where things did not turn out as well as with me.

According to your letter it seems that you really have been busy in your favorite pass-times - art, sculpture, etc. Was the Art Show a success? I plan to go to the States from 7 June to 7 July 1967; Helga wrote she will start making plans only then when I land at O'Hare in Chicago. I sure hope to make it this year.

With best wishes and regards

Margarete

Fort Ord, California
January 10, 1967

Dear Jack,

Sorry you weren't home when we called Mother during Christmas week – hope you had a good leave and holiday.

Many thanks for your gifts! The pipe scouger (I hope that's what it is!) already has been very useful – and will revive some of my decimated pipes. Elin is thrilled with the wild towels – you know her taste. Thanks so much.

Joan writes that you may get orders in the spring (??) Do you think you may get out here? We certainly hope so – already have a thousand places we want to take you – weather is great (at the moment anyway) and so is the place.

Activity is a bit quiet after the holidays (not at work though). The Bing Crosby Invitational Golf Tournament takes place in a week – so will probably join the mobs at Pebble Beach to gander at the celebrities. Saw "A Funny Thing Happened at the Way to the Forum" at one of the little theaters in Carmel last Saturday – very good and quite hilarious. We're expecting Hazel for a visit any day now – she is presently in Arizona or Los Angeles.

We spent Christmas in L.A. with the family Elin lived with in California in 1956. Had a good time and saw something of that sprawling city. It's really fabulous. Drove through Beverly Hills and Hollywood.

Also got three hours in at Disneyland – wild!

So much to do and see out here – we love it, especially the Monterey Peninsula – great atmosphere everywhere.

I still haven't heard anything about a future assignment so guess I'll be here at least until summer, but never can tell.

Write your plans.

Love,
Elin & Bill

Philadelphia, Pennsylvania
January 10, 1967

Dear Elin and Bill,

Just can't tell you how surprised I was on Saturday to receive your lovely package. You shouldn't spend your money on me - I send the "taste of home" because most folks that are "Busy People" love to "nibble" and home made things sort of hit the spot.

We shall enjoy every morsel of fruit and cheese and think of you as we do. The pictures you enclosed are most beautiful. My one fondest dream is to see the Pacific Coast some day. I won't give up yet. The pictures make the dream more persuasive that's for sure. Poor old Philadelphia, with such mucky weather hasn't many redeeming features when we face such beauty as you are enjoying (only Independence Mall, Fairmont Park, and the Academy of Music). They had a beautiful salute to the "Old Lady on Locust Street" as the Academy of Music is named, on TV yesterday - and to anyone who has ever heard music sung or played there, it really gives you that "creepy spine" of thrill.

Many thanks to you both.

Fondly
Mrs. Sternelle

Fort Ord, California
January 18, 1967

Dear Mor, Far and Kirsten,

It was very exciting to receive the package from Denmark (it arrived two days ago). We had Jul all over again - and your gifts were all wonderful! Tusind Tak! I am very happy with your generous gifts, and thank you. The photo album is already filled with pictures, and I had desperately needed a new one so that was very appropriate. Also the ashtray is perfect in our living room.

I have been very busy at my work in the headquarters. But most weekends have been free, so we have been enjoying the many things to do and see here. The weather has been beautiful all winter - warm days and sunshine all the time. You can even sun bathe on the beach now, although we haven't done that since October. This coming weekend we are having guests from San Francisco - the Welters, whom Elin knew from her year in California in 1956-1957. They are a lot of fun so it will be an enjoyable time. We are also expecting Mrs. Clawson for a visit at any time. She is in Los Angeles visiting relatives and will probably come here at the end of the month.

My family is fine - Jack is still in the Air Force, he is expecting to go to Asia this spring, and if so will probably visit us before he goes. We are also hoping that my mother will come for a visit this summer. I still haven't heard about going anywhere so guess we will stay here in California at least until the summer. As Elin has told you we really love it here. This is one of the best places in the United States to live. But it is very strange not to have any winter at all. Elin planted bulbs for spring flowers last week - and they will bloom next month!

We are going to have a Dansk dinner for some of the Danish friends here soon, with akvavit and Carlsberg, and sandwiches and lots of "skoals" - Wish you could be here for it!

Thank you again for all of your presents.

With love, and best regards.
Bill

P.S. Write soon about the broken chessmen so that Elin can make replacements!

Enjoying life on the Pacific Coast

Philadelphia, Pennsylvania
January 21, 1967

Dear Bill and Elin,

Be prepared to get letters written on this stationery for a while because I received 200 pages of it!

Christmas was so strangely different this year. To begin with, the snow was so deep that no one came Christmas Eve. That really broke a record. Then for the first time, my brothers and with their wives, two nephews (Herb Williams, Jack La Bar), came, plus Nana Williams, Aunt Rachel, Mike and Kathy for Christmas Day dinner. It was fun but so different. The year before had been such fun that the contrast was painful. Los Angeles must have been a different Christmas for you both, too.

We all thank you for our gift which certainly must have taken many hours to make. Joan loves the slides. We have shown them about five times!

The silver came and I took it back. It takes more time to get small knives so the store will send the set when it comes. Joan gave me a ring set with garnets (lovely) and Jack gave me an electric knife. I didn't think I would like it but I do.

Several days after Christmas Nana Walker got here. Then Aunt Helen invited us there for dinner. Charlie couldn't go. The hills were beautiful there, covered with deep snow.

Now the holidays are gone and everyone is in the winter "swing."

Uncle Charlie has been miserable. He has headaches that require a prescription every four days. He complains constantly to anyone who will listen. He is weaker and lacks spirit.

We have big news about Jack. He has his orders to go to Thailand in early April. I hate to see him go so far but he seems anxious to make the change. He has been dating Vivian Robinson (the red-head) again. They look well together and we all like her.

Joan is continuing her studies at Peirce Jr. College and now can easily take 60 words a minute in short hand. There has been no further word from Gene Smith (the suitor who came here), but we know he went to Vietnam. I ask no questions but I'm sure she reconsidered and sent him away. I do wish she would meet a nice fellow.

We are both sewing like mad. Joan made a neat "jump suit" in plum and gold fine wool. It is special. I am making several things, I hope!

The house next door has not been sold. Did I tell you Mrs. Ellingsworth (the first floor tenant) died? The place is a lodestone around my neck.

Uncle Bob Williams has been in the hospital with internal bleeding from a duodenal ulcer which he never knew he had. He will have to rest at home now for a while. They say ulcers come from inner tension. Uncle Loren has had one for years.

Have you heard anymore from Cousin Phyllis? I assume she is with her son.

This letter is not very interesting but I can't seem to make it come out right. Guess I'm too tired.

At any rate, I think of you both every day and hope you are doing well.

My love always,
Mother

Uncle Charlie, Mother and Joan

Fort Ord, California
January 30, 1967

Dear Jack,

We were delighted with your call and the news of your assignment, but especially with the fact that you'll be visiting here soon. That is exciting and we have already started planning – or I should say plotting - things we want to do while you're here. We'll just play it by ear because it will depend on when you come and how long. Please be advised that we hope you allot a maximum of days here (although we realize you will want to spread your leave around). Anyway, there is much to do and see here, and we would like you to stay as long as possible.

Thailand should be a tremendous experience. We are very happy for you and will talk about it when you are here.

We've had some lousy weather recently – rain and fog – but up until two weeks ago has been beautiful.

Had weekend guests last two weekends from San Francisco.

Went to the theater last night – tremendous show. Hope to take you to at least one show when you are here. Guarantee that you will be enamoured with the Monterey Peninsula. This is the one place in America that we love and could be very happy living permanently. You'll see why!

Anyway, let us know your exact plans when they are formulated. If you do go to L.A., we may drive down and pick you up and drive back up the coast (a fabulous trip). Would all depend on the time frame of course.

Write soon and let us know your plan.

Bill
Elin sends her love

Fort Ord, California
February 9, 1967

Dear Mother, Uncle Charlie & Joan,

Guess we haven't written for a while. We enjoyed your last letter Mother, have been meaning to answer it before this but lots of company & work put it off.

Hazel is with us right now. She arrived Monday & will stay a few weeks, we hope. Naturally we are delighted to see her again. She is in good spirits & we've been doing lots of talking these past four days (she sends regards to all of you). Last weekend we had Claudia Phenneger (the Morgan's daughter) with us for the weekend. Her husband is a Pan American pilot & he was on a trip. Had a good time and went to a play ("Any Wednesday") in Carmel, & showed her a lot of the area.

Tomorrow night we are taking Hazel to a tiny theater-restaurant in Carmel - a delightful place that you would love - holds only 100 people. We had dinner at 7:00 p.m. then at 8:30 a play. Lots of fun. On Saturday we are having 10 for a dinner party here. Will have beef fondue. We also will have the 12 year old daughter of friends from San Francisco here as a houseguest this weekend, so will be a busy fun one. Weather has been delightful, in 60's and low 70's in daytime the past couple of weeks. If it is nice on Sunday will take a picnic to the beach. We've been reading about the tremendous snows in the East (and don't mind a bit!).

Joan, we were thrilled to get yours and Jack's call the other night. We are so excited to have Jack coming here. Have lots planned (I will try to take a couple of days leave - we would like to take him to Los Angeles). We are also excited about his orders to Thailand (I should be so lucky!). It promises to be a fabulous assignment.

Elin is working two days a week now in the Post thrift shop. It's a charitable organization run by one of the Generals' wives & Elin is doing bookkeeping for extra spending money.

My work continues to be challenging and interesting. Still no orders anywhere so I'm going to stop anticipating leaving, for a while. Sure wish you could come out so we could share this beauty and charming atmosphere with you.

We've both been on a diet & have done pretty well to get down to old weights. Consequently we feel great! Hope you are all well - write soon.

Love,
Elin & Bill

Denver, Colorado
February 9, 1967

Dear Elin and Bill,

We are in Denver. Keith is on the Post copy desk, sporting the only blue striped shirt and paisley tie in the lot, and on record is telling a somewhat startled audience he doesn't care a whit for baseball. The advantage of the paper may well be that it provides the needed impetus for us to do some wild, independent improbability for we do like the Rockies.

As for housing, we are ensconced in the whole five room first floor of an old house in an old district, emphasized by the three fireplaces (none of which works, but oh the "character"), the whopping dining room with all sorts of sideboards, a bedroom out of a tiny Grand Hotel, a country kitchen with a fridge that freezes everything at almost off (something to do with the altitude) and co-features a gas range with burner knobs like a choke–trial and error. The furniture is somewhat ancient and, I might add, one piece is in need of repair. The chair on which I was just sitting collapsed. That is a true story - not made up for effect.

Our oasis in the hills consists of old Europeanites (18 years of living abroad), a Stars and Stripes gal and her family. She's put us on to a Sing and Heist your steins keller in a small mountain village and says it's great fun. We'll see tomorrow. We're stopping in on our way to a skiing debut. Maybe we won't get back to the slopes. Since our main love is the mountains (notice the lack of data on Denver), we've tried to get there on every day off. Surprisingly, the snow is scant. It comes for a couple of days and then there's sun and 60 degree weather for a couple of weeks. The roads in the mountains are clear for the most part. We have yet to use our brand new chains, still boxed. Sad. Denver really isn't bad. As you well know, a lot of enjoyment is people and they always take time to cultivate, and more so here then say in San Francisco. So far most seem concerned with God, mother, and the flag and sports. But, there are five theaters (Albee and Beckett playing now, among others!), a chapter of the English speaking union, an opera association in Central City, quite a charming little art museum (sort of one of everything - two periods to a room) and even an international house which we've already inspected, so somewhere in the woodwork we'll find some spark, meaning un-suburbanites.

Now that I've rattled away a good portion of the page and let my ego show, what's new with you? I expect by now the art show has paid further benefits. And you're breaking the Carmel ice. Elin, how's the constitution? Health, I mean? We had quite a grand holiday. After Keith pinned his job, we sped down to Tucson for three days and Christmas Eve and then drove Christmas Day to Oceanside, in a truly diplomatic move, and quite enjoyable too, until the trip back when we ran into -15 degree weather and a snow storm in the mountains of Arizona. I found my youngest brother 3 inches taller than I am (that's when I stop beating them up) and my mother now into the swing of Tucson bridge parties. Keith's sister goes off to Europe for the first time, in March, and is awfully excited – she'll stop off here on her way.

I must end. Write!!

Carol

Elin with Carole Eardley Reekie
London 1965

Odense, Denmark
February 20, 1967

Kare Elin & Bill,

I'm coming, I'm coming. I am crazy with excitement to see you in California. I talked to the personnel manager today and got permission to combine 3 weeks vacation. I have talked to a travel bureau and I'll leave on the 29th of March and arrive San Francisco 29 March at 1600. I can stay 3 weeks and leave Tuesday the 18th of April. What do you say about that, will you have me? It's the only way it can work. By making it 21 days it makes the trip 800 kroner cheaper. Now I'm anxious to hear what you say. I hope it suits you. I'm looking forward to it and am very excited.

That is about as long as I can be away with a full time job. I hope you feel 3 weeks is enough because that is all I can get off at this time.

Write soon - loving regards to you both.

Kirsten

Fort Ord, California
February 24, 1967

Dear Kirsten,

A short note before we leave for San Francisco. We were very excited to get your letter tonight, with the news that you will be coming to visit us in March! And, we are especially happy that you can come for three weeks. This will give you enough time to really enjoy this wonderful place (we think that California is the best place in the U.S.A.) - especially where we are living. Many things and places to show you. We are looking forward to a good time - and you are very, very welcome!!!!!

Tomorrow morning we go to San Francisco to visit friends, and then meet Jack at the airport tomorrow night. We will stay overnight in San Francisco then come back here. Jack will only be here three days before he leaves for Thailand (exciting!). So we will have a cozy time together for three days.

So, please give my very best regards to Mor and Far - and lots of fun in your trip preparations!

With love – Bill

Ellen and Bernhard Rasmussen
(Mor and Far)

Fort Ord, California
March 3, 1967

Dear Mother, Uncle Charlie and Joan

Jack was here and is gone - it seemed so short. We all had a good time. He came into San Francisco and we stayed overnight with some of my friends, Claudia and Dick Phenneger. He is a Pan Am pilot, and we met the wives of several other pilots, all very enthusiastic about Bangkok and Thailand. I'm sure he'll have an interesting year.

On Monday we drove down the coast to Hearst's castle, San Simeon, one of the most beautiful drives in the U.S. Joan, we took the stove and cooked steaks for sandwiches, and it was fun remembering our cookouts. Tuesday we spent at the beach. Jack got a lot of color. He left here looking real healthy. He said the tan went well with his "baby blue" eyes. He is a ham. The last night we had a very festive good-bye dinner. Artichokes, avocados, beef fondue, Caesar Salad, condiments, cheese rolls and Peach Melba. Jack loved it.

We hope everyone is feeling better. Uncle Charlie, now with spring coming you're sure to get feeling better, we think of you often.

This weekend we'll stay home. I have to write checks for my new job. Quite a nuisance job that is, but the little (very little) extra money does help, especially with all the places we are going.

Kirsten comes on March 29th for three weeks, so we have to get some plans for her entertainment. We are looking forward to seeing her. Bill only expects to be here until fall. We'll see, I bet it will be longer.

We are both well. We treated ourselves to new spring outfits, the first time since we got married. Bill got a blue suit, Jack helped him pick it out, and I got a white knit dress. When we get all decked out will send a picture. It's funny, but our home always seem to come first, but it is fun to get some nice things for oneself once in a while.

Bill is real tan. He loves it here. I guess it will be hard for him to move away from the ocean.

We found a dream house and Bill is wild about it, but California prices kill you.

Write soon,
Elin

Jack at Big Sur

Picnicking on the beach at Big Sur

Randolph Hearst's castle - San Simeon

From left: Evelyn, Gwyneth & Hadyn Morgan; Claudia and Dick Phenneger

Odense, Denmark
March 7, 1967

Dear Elin & Bill,

Thank you both for your happy letters. I am so glad to know that you two also think it is exciting to have me come.

I am so excited I can't tell you. I am a little worried about the trip itself. You know how I hate traveling in trains and buses, planes and boats, oh well I'll try to enjoy it. You don't need to make any great arrangements just because of me. Don't forget everything will be new to me and when you have to work Elin I should be able to take care of myself. By the way I have the address of some people in San Francisco, an elderly couple who stayed here last summer for a couple of days, said to come and see them.   So far as I could gather they were aristocratic people, a very elegant couple. If I have the chance I could also look up the people.

I have a weight allowance of 20 kg, and that includes all my luggage, so that is not very much. I plan to bring as few clothes as possible. I haven't got my visa yet, it may take another week till it comes through, and

I have to go back for another smallpox vaccination, as the first one didn't show the way it is supposed to. It would be fine if Claudia could come to meet me at the airport, but please don't turn the world upside down to have someone come to meet me.

Elin you must tell me if there is anything you would want me to bring, not too heavy. I'll try not to forget my camera this time. I'd like to take some pictures of the place.

It is going to be so exciting to talk to you again, and tell you about things here, and Bill is going to have to listen to our "funny language" for awhile once again. So Ned is working for the State Department. I thought he was going back to school. The family is scattered pretty far around, isn't it.

Well so long to you-
Kirsten

Fort Ord, California
March 8, 1967

Kare Mor, Far og Kirsten,

Another beautiful day here in beautiful California - and Kirsten - we just can't wait until the 29th when you arrive! Very exciting! - and we have so many things that we want to do while you are here that we don't know where to start. At least if we don't go anyplace while you are here you will have seen one of the most beautiful and fantastic places in the United States right where we are fortunate enough to live, that your whole trip will be worthwhile! (We do hope to take you to see some more of California though!)

Jack was just here for four days on his way to Thailand. We had a good time together, picnics on the beach and trips around the area to see the beautiful scenery. The weather has been wonderful all winter. No coats necessary in the daytime at all, and most days fit for the beach in a bathing suit.

Elin is busy with her two day a week job. She is in very good health and spirits and as beautiful as ever!

Hope you enjoy these pictures. I have also taken some color pictures of our flowers, which have been in bloom during January and February. I will send them to you when printed.

This is such a beautiful spot in the world that it would be hard to imagine without seeing it. We think that it is the best place in America, and feel so happy to be able to be living here. Anyway - Kirsten will verify that after her visit.

Hoping that all is well with you and the motel.

Best regards and much love,
Bill

Fort Ord, California
March 8, 1967

Dear Mother, Uncle Charlie and Joan,

Mother - thanks so much for your letter which we received today. So glad to hear that Uncle Charlie is feeling better & is up and around. Uncle Charlie we've been thinking about you often. Just wish you could jet out here for a few of invigorating California sun and atmosphere! Anyway - we are very glad that you aren't "on your back" anymore, and hope that your health keeps on improving.

We so enjoyed Jack's brief visit. We tried to cram in as much as possible while he was here - and I think we convinced him in the few days that he was here that this really is "God's Country" here in America! Well in the four days that Jack was here we showed him San Francisco (that gem of a white city, set in the beautiful bay, defying description to anyone who hasn't seen it with their own eyes) and our own Monterey

Peninsula, which we love dearly. Every time we drive into Monterey at night and see the lights of Monterey and Pacific Grove twinkling on the bay, it evokes a gasping feeling. Well, we had picnics on the beach at Carmel and down the coast near Big Sur, and we ventured down 90 miles from here to William Randolph Hearst's castle, San Simeon, We toured that somewhat decadent but expensive and expansive example of American imperialism of the 1930s. A beautiful setting, but what bad taste! Nevertheless the coastal route is the most fantastically beautiful drive you could imagine. We had never been down the coast to San Simeon and the three of us marveled at the beauty at every turn.

So several ideal days and we put Jack on a bus to Travis Air Force Base. Very envious I might say, of his sojourn to Thailand. He is certain to have fantastic experiences. The many people we know who have been stationed in Thailand have loved it. God knows we're happy he didn't get stationed in Vietnam.

Hope you enjoy these pictures which I took while Jack was here. Will give you an idea of the magnitude of this place.

Kirsten is flying here from Denmark on the 29th of March - over the Pole - for three weeks. We are quite excited about her visit. Just found out about it last week. She pooled together all of her vacation time from the bank to take three weeks at once. We are really looking forward to her coming, and will surely have a good time showing her the area.

I still haven't gotten any word on future assignments, so I'm sitting fat and happy here. Don't expect that it will be too much longer, but then I've been saying this for almost a year now. So, will just bide time. (Uncle Charlie take care & we hope you are feeling a lot better). Hope to hear from you soon.

Much love,

Elin & Bill

Philadelphia, Pennsylvania
March 19, 1967

Dear Bill & Elin,

Sounds like you had a fabulous time with Jack out there. California must be a beautiful state. If you are still going to be in Monterey during the summer Mother and I would like to visit you. I'm trying to persuade Mother to go out for at least two weeks while I stay home with Uncle Charlie. Then maybe I can come out. I would like for her to go anyway, as she hasn't had a real vacation for quite some time. What do you think?

Is Kirsten there now? She must be quite excited with the trip! Please give her my warm regards.

Right now I'm looking into all the airlines. I'm reading the want-ads faithfully and have my name in an employment agency. I really would like to be an airline reservationist in a front office. I went to TWA, Pan-Am and American Airlines and each place told me it would be easier to become a stewardess first, as they reserve a lot of ground jobs for them. But in order for me to even apply, I must lose some weight. So, of course I'm on a diet. I've lost 4 pounds so far with only 11 to go! I never realized how difficult it was to go into the airlines.

Nothing really exciting happening around here. I'm just waiting for summer to come. At least then I'll have more to do. I'll keep in touch and let you know if anything comes of the airlines.

Write soon and take care.

Love,
Joan

Ford Ord, California
March 21, 1967

Dear Jack,

Received your letter yesterday and were glad to hear about your trip to Thailand. Bangkok must be fascinating. We hope that you'll have an opportunity to get there again before too long.

We can well imagine that you will have a demanding job there, and guess that the pressures and hours will be similarly to those in Vietnam. We'll keep our fingers crossed on the promotion! We'll be anxious to hear about your experiences, and especially about the Thais.

Called Mother the other night. She had gotten a letter from you. She sounded in good spirits and said that Uncle Charlie was downstairs and apparently not too bad. We told her about your stay with us and how much fun we had (also sent some pictures of you which I took).

We've been taking it easy the past few weeks. Kirsten arrives next Wednesday. We'll meet her at San Francisco airport in the afternoon and come right back here. Hope to get to L.A. one weekend while she is here. Anyway, we will have a good time while she is here no matter what we do.

The weather has been bad the past two weeks. First rain we've had all winter. It cleared up Sunday and we took a picnic to the beach, but proved to be too windy.

Tomorrow night we are going to the local premier of "Dr. Zhivago" in Carmel. It's a benefit showing for American Field Service. Will have champagne, caviar, etc. We made some posters advertising it – should be fun.

We finally broke down and got a TV, so have been watching the news shows and finding out with others that TV hasn't improved much in the past 10 years!

Are you working with any Thais at the base, or is it all American staffed? Is there a town or village near the base? How about any Thai military? Let us know all about it once you get acclimated.

We enjoyed your postcard from Travis – very apropos, considering one of the conversations before you left!

That's about it for now. Will write again after Kirsten gets here. Watch out for the snakes, rats, etc., etc., etc.

– and write when you can.

Bill

Fort Ord, California
April 11, 1967

Dear Mother, Uncle Charlie and Joan,

Many thanks for your phone call the other night Mother - and for your letter a few weeks ago Joan.

As you can imagine we have been so occupied with company for the past two months that the correspondence has slacked off. Nonetheless we think about you often and trust that all is well in Philly.

Uncle Charlie - hope that you are feeling yourself again. As we mentioned on the phone, Kirsten has been here since March 29th. She arrived in San Francisco after a 12 hour Polar flight. Unfortunately we have been experiencing the most miserable weather that we have seen in this part of the country while she has been here. An unusual amount of rain, hail & even snow in the mountains nearby. So far only four sunny days that one could spend on the beach. But nevertheless we have been having a wonderful time with her here.

A fellow she dated (& met) in Denmark two years ago (an American who was working for RCA in Greenland and vacationing in Denmark when they met) came out from Minneapolis for the weekend (and is still here!). An international, round the world romance! He is a very fine fellow & of course Kirsten has been happy to see him again.

We (Elin & I) are (or must be) getting old - this pace of entertaining is getting to us I guess. On Friday night after work, we three drove to San Francisco (two hours) to meet "Tom" at the airport. He came in at 7:00 pm. We four went to Chinatown in the City for dinner. They split up and Elin & I walked through the North Beach area & ended up in the roof-top lounge of the Mark Hopkins Hotel, which commands a fantastic view of the city. At midnight we met Kirsten and Tom, then all went to a Topless Club. Some fun (have seen a lot better and more aesthetic showings of the bosom in Europe & elsewhere), but once while in San Francisco I guess one must go to a topless joint. We saw Carol Doda at the Condor Club (the original topless) and her silicone enhanced "twin 44s" breasts (!), plus a psychedelic dance by a rather "turned on" couple. Rather educational - ha! In this age of "hippies" etc. we're beginning to feel our age. Anyway we had a ball in the City and arrived back at Fort Ord at 5 a.m. Next day & rest of weekend sightseeing - Carmel Beach for a picnic and lots of chatter.

You realize we have had a steady stream of company since before Christmas. Of course we never tire of showing guests the marvelous scenic sights around here, and taking them to the wonderful and unique theaters and nightspots.

We've had Phyllis for two weeks; several couples from San Francisco for weekends; Hazel for two weeks; Jack a week; and Kirsten 3 weeks. When are you coming? (!) Anyway it's been great fun & keeps us in touch.

We've received several letters from Jack in Thailand. I was surprised to hear on the phone that he had a sun stroke since he wrote both times that he was "enjoying" the pool every day.

My work is very demanding and interesting & the days slip by very fast. Can't understand why I haven't gotten orders for Vietnam yet. I've been here a long time compared to most - but I'm not asking any questions & will continue to enjoy it here while we remain.

How are Mike and Kathy doing? Do you see them frequently? Is Mike contemplating a move eventually or will they be in Limeport for a few years?

One thing that the rain has done here is bring out the wild flowers in all their magnificence. You would love it Mother, fantastic carpets of color. Especially along the coast in Pacific Grove (4 miles from Fort Ord). This is the town where the butterflies migrate from October to March (we took Jack to see them). It is a fantastic coastline, rugged rocks and beach with the surf ever pounding in a dramatic spray for several miles, and then the "magic carpet" as they call it here, of wild flowers right along the coast in grand profusion. It's magnificent. Also the fields of poppies (California's state flower) blooming in acres of fields along the highway to San Francisco. It is brilliant here at this time of the year, even with the uncalled for rain. A marvelous spot on earth, and one that we never tire of reveling in and truly appreciating.

Well, I've rambled on enough (When I had never experienced California before I couldn't understand the enthusiasm with which Aunt Ruth and Aunt Helen, etc. lauded it's virtues, but now know!).

Much love to you,
Bill

& Elin sends her love too!
  & Kirsten says hello.

The Condor Club – Carol Doda

Tom and Kirsten – Carmel

Fort Ord, California
April 12, 1967

Dear Far and Mor

Today it is Wednesday and Tom has been here since Friday and we have had some wonderful days. We talked and talked about marriage and discussed things. Tom is not a die hard Catholic, so that will not be a problem.

If we wait a couple of months it will be a wedding in Minnesota, just the two of us, so it is better in California where we have Elin and Bill to celebrate with. It will be half a year before Tom can leave his school in Minneapolis, and that is too long to wait, after all the time we have been apart.

I'm sorry that it won't be a wedding in Odense, but I am happy here.

The wedding will be tomorrow, Thursday, in a little church close by. Friday we fly to Minneapolis, and Tuesday I will fly home with a different plane than I had originally booked. I am quitting my job at the bank as of 1 June and will travel back to Minneapolis as quickly as I can get a visa after 1 June. So I'll have time to pack and get ready.

Tom is in a school where he has to study for ½ year. He gets a salary. It's about some electronic brains that his company builds and sells to different companies. They send mechanics with each machine for installation. That is what Tom is training for. We will go to Germany or England, so that will be close. I'm coming home to explain it all.

Tom is so sweet and I'm so in love and happy. Bill and Elin like Tom and we all get along great. This time, at least you have met your son-in-law.

Loving regards
Kirsten

Mr. and Mrs. Bernhard J. Rasmussen
announce the marriage
of their daughter
Kirsten
to
Mr. Thomas John O'Donnell
Friday, the fourteenth of April
Nineteen hundred and sixty-seven
Carmel, California

A Highlands Wedding

Capt. William Walker (USA) and Mrs. Walker of Fort Ord have announced the marriage of her sister, Miss Kirsten Rasmussen of Denmark, and John Thomas O'Donnell of Minneapolis.

The newlyweds, who met while Mr. O'Donnell was vacationing in Denmark, were married Friday evening, April 14, at Carmel Highlands Inn Chapel by Chaplain George L. Lutz.

The bride, daughter of Mr. and Mrs. Bernhard Rasmussen of Odense, Denmark, chose a traditional white gown and carried an arrangement of daisies.

The couple's home will be in Minneapolis until next fall, when the bridegroom's firm, Electrical Mechanical Research, sends him to Europe.

*Marriage of Kirsten Rasmussen & Thomas O'Donnell with
Elin as Matron of Honor & Bill as Best Man*

Mr. and Mrs. Thomas O'Donnell

Kirsten and Tom leave for Minneapolis
Bill in background

Ford Ord, California
April 20, 1967

Dear Jack,

This has been a turbulent month! Much to relate to you and I don't really know where to begin.

We were glad to receive your last letter and can imagine that you are deeply ensconced in work. A lieutenant who is working for me is just back from Thailand and he has been telling us about the country, and specifically how much better off is the Air Force than the Army!

Kirsten arrived in San Francisco on March 29th. We met her and came back to Ord. Then the following weekend Tom flew out from Minneapolis for the weekend. (He is the fellow she met in Denmark two years ago while he was on vacation in Denmark while working for RCA in Greenland). Well – he extended the weekend visit and the romance, which blossomed in Denmark two years ago, resulted in their getting married here – in Carmel! It was quick, but nevertheless we had an elegant little wedding at the Highlands Inn in Carmel – with a fabulous dinner afterwards at the Inn, which overlooks the ocean, etc. all very romantic. They left the next day for Minneapolis. Then two days later Kirsten flew to Denmark (she will come back to the States as soon as she can resign her job and emigrate – she hopes in a month).

Tom is working with computers and is presently going to school. His firm will send him to Europe (Germany) in the fall. We really like him very much, and they are extraordinarily happy together!

So, on top of all this excitement, I get orders this week. Will go to Fort Hood, Texas in July and join a new unit activating – and then to Vietnam, probably in the fall. It looks like a real good assignment for me, and I'm quite excited about it. Tentatively, Elin will go to Texas with me, then go to Spokane in the fall for school to get her teacher's accreditation. She will then go to Denmark next June and presumably I could meet her there next year coming back to Europe from Vietnam.

Called home last night to give Mother the news. She says that now she will come out here before we leave in June (we will take a leave before going to Texas – probably to Mexico). Anyway, we also talked to Joan who announced that she has been accepted by the airline school in Minneapolis and will report there in

June. So, by coincidence, she will probably meet Kirsten and Tom there. We are delighted that she is going (I'm sure that you are too), and glad to see her finally getting out of the bank and away from Frankford for a new glimpse of life.

So Jack – hope that you are weathering the heat, snakes, etc. Maybe we can meet in Bangkok or someplace next year!

Write soon and best from Elin.
Bill

Note from Elin:
I am about to give up on the cookie business. I've already baked 3 times only to have it been eaten by one – your brother. We love him though. Elin

Odense, Denmark
April 28, 1967

Dear Elin

Thank you for your letter. I think like you that it will be hard for you to be here a whole year. It would be a long row of days to go and wait and wait. And it's right about the everyday Dane's attitudes about the U.S. people. They pretend to know something they have no idea about. The idea about going to Spokane I like. Then you would do something productive with your time. I think your plans are very good, and then we will get to see you and Bill here. You can also follow along what is happening better, most of the time.

But as you write, plans can be changed. We are very excited to see pictures from the wedding. Kirsten will write to you one of these days.

Loving regards
Mor

Fort Ord, California
April 30, 1967

Dear Far and Mor

Today I received the first proof picture from the wedding. Bill and I chose what we wanted and sent most of them off to Tom. Then, he can choose and mail them on to you. They are small but when they are made up in the finished size they will be nice. Some are really good, and there are also failures.

My plans as of today, are as follows - it's still loose because we don't have a date for travel to Texas. It can happen with very short notice. Bill is going to Texas in the middle of the State, at least 3,000 kilometers from here on the 15th of July. He only gets 5 days for the trip and two weeks vacation. We will vacation together, load the car with things that will be most useful for the 2-6 months in Texas. I expect that Bill will leave for Vietnam about October.

I would like to become a teacher so I could go to Spokane to start a semester in September and stay with Mrs. Clawson nine months or as long as it would take in school. After 6 months in Vietnam the Army will fly the men to Hawaii so we could have a week together there. So next July I could come home and stay the last 3-4 months, and Bill could get permission to be sent home via Europe. We could meet in Odense and he would visit you.

It is only preliminary planning. Everything can change 20 times yet, but one has to start thinking about possibilities.

I would prefer to be home with you the whole time, but I can't just sit and do nothing for a whole year, and it would be a bit hard among all those Danes who are so anti-American, and who don't understand what it is all about.

If I ever am going to be a citizen of the U.S. I'll have to stay or start an immigration registration for beginning again. This is a very confusing family by now, but at least we are all happy and in good health so a little travelling does no harm.

I quit my small job, it's only been a headache with all the visitors we have had this year.

To Kirsten:

Kisser, Joan is going to Minneapolis from June until next March for a stewardess and travel school - the Humboldt Institute. She is looking forward to it and is excited to know that you will be there.

I have sent a lot of announcements out (I am including the list). It was easier than sending them to you. I sent a bunch to Tom, about 50, so he could send them to his family. Write and tell me what all the different people said when they received them. They must have been surprised.

What about your papers? If you think you can stay with your health insurance it's not very expensive and you never know when you'll need it.

Kis, I'm thinking about sending a box to Minnesota with a bunch of kitchen and other various things. Now that all of my things shall be stored one year or more, and since I am getting rid of a lot of things you might as well use what I would send for a half year, and then throw them out. Can you use an electric frying pan, small grill, throw rugs, towels, dish towels, sheets, iron, etc. These are not my good things but stuff I would have sold in the Thrift Shop. Write what you can use and what there is no use sending.

Railway express is not very expensive and it could be a savings for you, but I'm not sure you want hand-me-downs so I would like an honest reply.

I'm running now - so much to take care of. I'll write next week when I know more about everything.

Karligste Hilsner
Elin

                                                    Fort Ord, California
                                                    May 1, 1967

Dear Mor and Far,

In all the excitement I haven't thanked you for the gifts you sent with Kirsten - and for which I am very grateful. Kirsten can tell you how much I appreciated the glasses from the farm. They will always be significant since I'm sure that many "skoals" were raised by them, and many more will be - to good health and cozy memories. And the purse & it's contents and the elegant silver and ebony coaster I very much appreciate. Tusind Tak for these gifts from the heart!

I do not know too much about my job in Vietnam but it appears as though it will be a very responsible one, with an opportunity to use all of my military experience and knowledge. As Elin has probably told you although we leave for Texas soon, I will probably not go to Asia for several months afterwards.

I just wrote a letter to Tom and sent him the newspaper clippings of the wedding. We get along very well and I am very glad that he is a member of the family now!

Thank you again for the gifts - and my best regards

Bill

Bloomington, Indiana
May 4, 1967

Dear Bill and Elin,

What a jolt! Not only a wonderful letter from our two favorite people but (for me) such disappointing news. I really am upset - I was so looking forward to being near you. I'm afraid I just can't help it but my devious little mind has already started hoping that if your unit leaves from the West Coast that Elin will come with you and then spend as much time as possible with the children and me. (Maybe she might even come back to Monterey to live - Sorry, I can't stop hoping, and I guess, daydreaming).

We will be leaving here on the 13th of June and I imagine we will arrive in Monterey on the 18th or the 19th - how I hope we will see you!

Kirsten's wedding is a delightful surprise and knowing Elin it must have been beautiful. Please send the newlyweds all our best wishes.

Events here are beginning to pick up with the end of school so near. Mike of course is doubly busy and I have just decided that I had better get at least a bit organized if I expect to get everything done.

How delightful Acapulco sounds.

May 11 -

Had hoped to finish this before the rush of the past week started - but obviously didn't make it. So will try to finish this off so I can get in the mail.

Mike just received word that he passed the French proficiency test. He was very worried about it because without it he wouldn't get his M.A. He's just on cloud nine now that the degree is assured.

Tara and Gar are fine, very excited about the upcoming move. We take Gar back to Dr. Garceau next week - we're keeping our fingers crossed that there has been some improvement!

Must stop now - let us hear from you soon, hoping we'll be able to see you!

Karen

Mike and Karen Urette

Minneapolis, Minnesota
May 6, 1967

Dear Bill,

Thanks for the newspaper clippings, I've sent them on to Kirsten. This waiting for the immigration department's approval seems interminable, although if I look at a calendar it's only been two weeks. Well 2 down, and with luck only 2 to go.

Will you and Elin be going up to Philadelphia before leaving - when my school ends, sometime in July? I thought to take a trip to New York so Kirsten can meet my folks. Maybe we can all get together in Philadelphia.

Tom

Elin - here is the check for the photos. Remember to get the negatives. If he wants more money for them, it's OK to pay him.

Fort Ord, California
May 11, 1967

Dear Far, Mor and Kisse

Today, Bill came home and said we have to move next week, instead of having a month to organize. Now I only have 8-9 days.

It is so hard to know what is the right thing for me to do this next year. If only I knew. What do you think? It would be possible for the Mulvads to come over here, but I don't think I'll have time to organize something. Will see.

Bill still wants to go to Mexico, so on next Saturday or Sunday we'll go, on the 20th or there about. Bill has to be in Texas June 15. We have to do something with our furnishings, they have to go someplace.

Mor, shall I go to Spokane or Philadelphia or stay here? I'll come home for 3 or 4 months. There are advantages and disadvantages with each possibility.

I love this area but it is hard to get a good job for such a short time. If only I knew what to do.

Loving hellos
Elin

Odense, Denmark
May 13, 1967

Dear Mrs. Fulmer - Dear Family,

Thank you so much for your note, and thank you very much for the cheque. I was so happy to get it. I can't wait to buy something with it together with Tom when I return to Minneapolis - it is a problem getting things shipped from here.

I really had a wonderful stay at Elin and Bill's. California is very beautiful. I know you will enjoy it if you go out there this spring.

Well Joan! I hear you are also going to be in Minneapolis for the same time. I hope to see a lot of you. I like the twin cities because of all the lakes and the green you see all of the time.

Do write me and tell me what your plans are, when will you be going? I expect to be there middle or end of June. I'm waiting for my immigration and it takes long.

This is our address –
35554 Emerson Ave, Apt 26, Minneapolis, Minnesota 55408
Telf. 823-2110

I do thank you again for the cheque. We'll spend it on something very special. I look so much forward to going back and meeting Tom's family in New York. We are very unhappy about Bill having gotten his orders for Vietnam. I keep hoping they will stop it.
My best regards to all of you.

Love Kirsten

In Flight - American Airlines - Over Colorado
May 18, 1967

Dearest Elin

This time Tuesday we were leaving your house!
Wanted to tell you again what a delicious luncheon you had - really do not know which I enjoyed more, the food or your beautiful house with all the "interesting" things. You have such good taste and I might add ability.
The fog got us this A.M. on our departure - Instead of our flying non-stop from Los Angeles to Memphis we had a longer delay in L.A. plus have to go into St. Louis & then to Memphis. Have a delay in St. Louis - all in all will make us late reaching our destination if the plane does not go down! (Have lots of insurance so think I am safe - ha).
Have a nice vacation / because or whatever & I'll see you back at the "Blaue House" commonly known as the Thrift Shop.
Again thanks for a lovely luncheon.

Always Audie

Bloomington, Indiana
May 18, 1967

Dear Elin & Bill -

Again, thanks for the call tonight - now I'm going to set aside my books for a moment to pass on a few "second thoughts!"
Please realize that I am "in the blind" on the housing situation having only the ambiguous ads in the paper to go by, but I think it's important for you to know how we're thinking anyway. Being very truthful, I tend to feel that a 3 bedroom, 1 bath house or apartment would probably be a little inconvenient for the four of you for a year - but that's not to say it couldn't be done!
Still think that the idea on all grounds (psychological, safety, enjoyment, financial, et al) is great!

All our best -
Mike and Karen

Fort Ord, California
May 20, 1967

Dear All

Every day is so hectic that I hardly can follow along. I have finally gotten a new girl trained in my small accounting job. She was the third in a month. The two others said "no thank you" after a couple of weeks. I was given a nice silver tray as a goodbye gift.

We are looking at a house around $30,000 or 200,00 Danish Krone. Quite expensive but apartments are also expensive, about 1,000 Danish Krone a month.

I have gotten an offer about a job as assistant manager for a dress shop.   I would start at $400 a month. But it involves long hours and lots of work. The man who owns the store has called twice and really wants me to start, but we had plans to go on vacation. I don't think our lives have been in such chaos ever. Everyday something new that it's impossible to know how it will turn out.

Karen Urette is coming here with her two children. Mike has to be in Vietnam the 15th of June. So, we could live together.

Bill and I have received permission for me to stay here until 10 September. Bill has to be in Texas by 15 June, in about 3 weeks. He expects to be in Vietnam in late summer.

The house we found yesterday would be our dream house, but it will be quite expensive in the beginning until we pay off the second mortgage. What do you think, it's a form of forced savings? I have looked at houses all day and there are several interesting ones in this area.

How are Kisse's plans coming?

Loving regards- Elin

Fort Ord, California
May 28, 1967

Dear Mother,

These have been turbulent times! Too much happening all at once. Too many decisions to be made on short notice - changes in orders, etc. I guess that you could gather all this in our phone conversations!

As I mentioned the last time you called, Elin has been offered a very good job here. After much consideration & discussion, we decided that it would be best financially & move-wise if she accepted it and stayed here until next year. Then she will be able to fly to Hawaii to meet me on my R&R (after 6 months in Vietnam I can go to Hawaii for a week's leave). Next spring or summer she could fly to Philadelphia to spend a month with you, then go to Denmark for a month or two before I get back.

I also mentioned on the phone that we have been looking for a house ever since last year. Real estate here on the Monterey Peninsula increases 4% a year & the area is growing so fast & is such a desirable location that you can't go wrong. Anyway last week we found a house in Pacific Grove that we are trying to get into. It is very cute but needs some paint, etc., which would keep Elin busy in addition to the job. If the deal doesn't pan out we'll have to come up with another plan.

Elin can stay in our government quarters until September. I am flying to Texas on June 13th. I assume that I will be there through the summer, but don't have much information about the unit yet. Once I get there & see what the situation is, Elin might fly down for a few weeks later on. I hope that I'll get a few weeks' leave before going overseas. Later on, how much and when is speculation until I get to Texas and get the "straight poop." Then I'll plan on going to Philadelphia or, if the timing is right, maybe you could still come to California.

I finished work last Thursday & am now on leave. We gave up our plan to go to Mexico & will wait to find out about the house before taking off someplace. May go to Las Vegas & L.A. if anywhere.

I guess that Joan is getting ready to go to Minneapolis. Kirsten hopes to be there by the first week in June, as soon as her visa is approved. We haven't heard recently what the status is. We are concerned about Mike's back. Just what is the condition & what is his status now? I guess that you are embroiled in "end of term" affairs at this time, which is always hectic. Are you going to work this summer? I hope not necessary.

Hazel writes from Spokane frequently. I think she is disillusioned with Spokane, living there alone & she hinted that she was looking for a place, or considering moving elsewhere. Will write again soon. We have to cut down on phone calls (last month's bill was $91.00!) - that should make Uncle Charlie feel glad that we're not using his!

Much love,
Bill

Support Units Joining 198th

By a Times Staff Writer

WASHINGTON — Makeup of some of the support units for the Army's newest separate brigade, the 198th Inf, at Fort Hood, Tex., was revealed this week.

Officials said the 198th, which was scheduled for activation in May, would have a cavalry troop, engineer company, support battalion, maintenance company, supply and service company, two truck companies plus a host of detachments.

The latter will include signal and military police elements.

Forming the new Vietnam-bound brigade are designations—if not the men and equipment—of the 1st and 2d Armd Divs.

Coming from the 1st are the 1st Bn, 6th Inf; 1st Bn., 46th Infantry, and the 1st Bn, 52d Inf.

Contribution of the 2d Armd Div. is the 1st Bn, 14th Arty.

Reports from Fort Hood indicate the 1st Bn, 46th Inf, is training without armored - personnel carriers and has become a foot soldier unit.

Army special orders have identified the 5600-man brigade as a mechanized infantry unit but the official Washington announcement on formation of the 198th labeled it regular infantry.

New Infantry Brigade Forming at Hood

WASHINGTON—The Army is forming a mechanized infantry brigade, the 198th, at Fort Hood, Tex.

Special Defense Department approval for the new brigade apparently was received since it is not specifically funded in regular or supplemental military budgets.

Sources said the unit will be a separate ROAD brigade with about 3500 men.

Three separate infantry brigades are already fighting in Vietnam.

ARMY TIMES   **MAY 24, 1967**

Two Hood Divs Form New Unit

By a Times Staff Writer

WASHINGTON—The 1st and 2d Armd Divs' loss will be the new 198th Inf Bde's and Vietnam's gain.

Pentagon officials say they're taking the 1st Armd Div's 1st Bn, 6th Inf; 1st Bn, 46th Inf, and the 1st Bn, 52d Inf to form the latest separate Army brigade, which is scheduled to be activated at Fort Hood, Tex., this month.

The 2d Armd Div is giving the 1st Bn, 14th Arty to the 198th.

The Pentagon has announced the creation of the 198th at Fort Hood, saying it will have an authorized strength of about 5600 men. It was incorrectly reported here last week that the unit would have about 3500 men.

Officially, the Army says manpower to replace men drawn from the armored units will come "from existing resources."

Officers here said, however, that it was a "good guess" that the two armored divisions were over-strength and could make up the losses quickly. New units are being activated to replace the losses, they said.

*   *   *

THE TWO HOOD divisions have been in the "train and retain" and "train and pass" business for many months, taking recruits, giving them basic, AIT and passing them off to other units going to Vietnam or holding on to a smaller number for their own use.

Officers who have served at Hood recently say that a lack of skilled manpower has caused havoc with armored vehicles at the post. There simply were too many vehicles for the number of mechanics available.

*   *   *

THE PENTAGON announcement on the 198th described it as an infantry unit. However, Army special orders in April assigning men to the 198th said it was a mechanized unit. Officials here agreed that a change was made. They declined to say why, however.

In a background briefing Pentagon officials confirmed the obvious, saying the 198th will go to Vietnam. It will join other separate brigades there but will differ from the 196th Light Inf and 199th Light Inf in its make-up. They are light units organized on airborne tables of organization with about 3500 men.

Army Chief of Staff Harold K. Johnson is known to feel that a ROAD infantry brigade is better suited to Vietnam operations than the light or airborne type of unit.

Sources in Washington said that the 198th is not specifically funded and will "be taken out of the Army's hide."

POSTCARD
Las Vegas, Nevada
June 1, 1967

Dear Mother & Uncle Charlie,

We finally decided to take off on a little trip the other day. Spending two days in Vegas amidst all the tinsel & superficial glamour. Quite an experience & part of the U.S. that one shouldn't miss.

Last night we saw Della Reese at the Sands Hotel and tonight will see one of the spectacular follies shows at another big hotel. We may head for the Grand Canyon tomorrow, but our plans are flexible.

Love
Elin and Bill

Norwalk, Connecticut
June 9, 1967

Dear Beth & Charlie

This morning has been terrific. We are gradually getting straightened up. This is a cute place right along the water, the tide goes in and out. We have a very attractive tree that hangs over our enclosed porch, the screen goes all the way to the floor, the water at the end of a small yard. In the tree are two bird houses. We watch many birds and squirrels. Helen buys food for them.

We have a glass sliding glass door all across the porch. All the walls are white. I have a room with two glass doors that open up to a small porch. I have all my plants on it. The rooms aren't nearly as large as Valley Forge. Sliding white doors go across each room at the closets. There are some nice houses around this section. Joe's mother and father were on vacation. They are here now. They stayed all night. We are going out for a ride and see if we can locate some stores.

There is a clubhouse here. A man came to visit us. He brought his son to meet Jeff. They have a boat, they will take us for a ride sometime. They are very nice.

I wrote to Mike at the hospital. Write and tell me how he is. I hope much better. I am glad Kathleen is going to have a baby. When is Bill going? Let me know his address when he does. How is Charlie? How does Joan like being away from home?

When we left Valley Forge it was 1 o'clock in the morning. Then we stayed at night at a very nice motel. Arrived there at 4 a.m.

Write to me once in awhile and let me know the news. How is your brother who had the accident?

Our number is 21 Cannel Road, S. Norwalk Conn.

Love
Mother Walker

Mother (Nana) Walker

Fort Ord, California
June 10, 1967

Dear Jack

Long time since we've heard from you, but imagine that you are probably working full time. We've been in somewhat of a turmoil for the past two months, but now things are settling into place.

I'm leaving Tuesday for Fort Hood. We are buying a small house in Pacific Grove (not the one we showed you) – it is high up in the center of the Monterey Peninsula – only five minutes drive to beach – "rustic charm." Needs lots of work but has lots of possibilities. Even has studio in back with view of bay! Elin won't be able to move in for a month or so, so will stay in our house at Ord until then. She was offered and accepted a job at a women's apparel store here as sort of an assistant manager. Sounds like a very good job that will be interesting and lucrative.

As far as we know, Kirsten is still in Denmark, although she is ready to fly to Minneapolis as soon as her visa comes through which will be any day now.

We spent two days in Las Vegas last week, then drove to San Diego for several days on the beach, then to L.A. to visit friends and back here.

Weather is miserable here right now and will be for rest of summer. Hot in the interior of California and cold and foggy on the northern coast.

We talk to Mother on the phone frequently. She sounded chipper last week when we talked to her, although Mike was in hospital for tests on his back. Haven't heard outcome yet. We called Mike and Kathy last month

I don't know exactly what I'm getting into at Fort Hood, but I do know I'm going into a good job in a new unit scheduled to go to Vietnam – when and where I don't know yet, but should find out when I get to Texas.

Thought for a while last week that I might be going to Middle East instead! – but thank God that crisis appears to be under control for a while and it doesn't appear likely that we'll be involved.

Take care and let us know how you are doing. My address after 14 June will be:
9th Support Battalion, 198th Infantry Brigade, Fort Hood, Texas

Bill

P.S. Congratulations on your promotion!

Fort Hood, Texas
June 14, 1967

Dear Elin - Darling - (Elskling!)

At 8:00 tonight it was 90 degrees - and now at 10:00 it hasn't dropped much. This place is hot, and big, and hot, and desolate - and I have been sweating like a pig and not liking it for the past 24 hours I've been here. A warrant officer, noticing my sweaty face, matted down hair and generally uncomfortable looking appearance told me that I would get acclimated to the heat in a few days. I hope so.

My footlocker arrived OK & everything was in it including my pictures of my honey (most important). After a miserable night in a makeshift BOQ (I was up at 5:30 am) I got into a better BOQ - small sitting room, bedroom with sink, and share shower and toilet with some unknown person next door. I am going to try to move into the main BOQ complex near the club tomorrow. This place is two miles from the club and not too desirable.

Well, you remember ROAD and the 4th Armored Division? This is it all over again. A bag of worms. They don't even have an office for me - half of the Brigade is set up, some of the AG section in one of the Armored Division's PSD. Work is cut out & I know already what the problems will be. My PSD Chief has been here two weeks, a Captain Dove, & he seems pretty sharp. Has already done some groundwork and has his section half organized. The rest of the officers should be in this week. The departure time is, as I was told, and we will most likely get two weeks leave in September.

Even though this adds a few extra months to our separation, I'm very glad we decided on the plan in effect. You would be absolutely miserable in this godforsaken place (and consequently so would I worrying about it) and I feel much more happier about you being on the beautiful Monterey peninsula. How is your job???? Probably frustrating at first. We'll both be going through the trials & trauma of adjustment to new people, work, environment, etc. at the same time.

In addition to those reasons I'm glad you didn't come here. I found out that in a month we are moving 20 miles from here on the reservation.

I really am impressed with the Bergs, and I'm sure that your experience working for them will be very rewarding, both for you and them. Don't get depressed when little things go wrong! I've got to tell you now because it will happen and I won't be on hand to set you straight!

For the time being you can write to me at:

Company A
9th Support Battalion
198th Infantry Brigade
Fort Hood, Texas

Once I get oriented I may come up with a better address. I am in Room 17, Building 2210, Post BOQ on Headquarters Avenue. There is a phone in the hall, extension 4661 - but I wouldn't trust getting too much response from it. I'll call you periodically.

Do write all the news. Anything new on the house, etc. I love you!

Good night darling - Bill

Fort Ord, California
June 14, 1967

Dear Mother and Uncle Charlie

I just said goodbye to Bill yesterday. He left here at 8:30 in the morning and called at 7 at night after a good trip. It was hot there. I started work at 9 o' clock a.m. Only gave me 10 minutes to cry. My job will be nice and guaranteed to keep me busy. I got home at a quarter to seven last night.

The loan on the house hasn't gone through yet but I do hope to hear news soon so I can make arrangements for moving.

How is Mike doing? We wrote him. I'll write too now.

Two days ago I received these pictures from Denmark. I would like to share them with you, but ask that you please send them back as I have no duplicates.

I hope everyone is doing fine, in the east. I keep getting cards from Phyllis. She is touring in California. Wonder what that means.

Much love
Elin

Cousin Phyllis Hague with Elin at Carmel

Fort Hood, Texas
June 15, 1967

Dear Elin,

A long day - that seemed like two - and an overwhelming sense of the problems immediately facing the job. It's all from Scratch, no buildings, little equipment, etc. The people are just about all here as of today (I have 7 officers and 78 enlisted men) but no place to start operating! This I hope will be solved by tomorrow, but at the moment things are confusing.

The Brigade CO came back this afternoon, so I hope to meet him tomorrow & get some things squared away. I got two second lieutenants in today, so will have to break them in. I suspect that in a few weeks the dust will have settled & we will be operational, but right now it's confusion. I was up at 6 this morning & I got back to the BOQ at 8:00 pm. No lunch. Took a shower to get the Texas sweat and dust off and walked two blocks to the club annex. Alas, they had a go-go band there tonight & the place was mobbed with 2nd lieutenants (there is a preponderance of them here). Took me an hour to get some food & I had a few beers while waiting. No place to cook in the BOQ although there is a refrigerator outside the door. But I have not had an opportunity to get anything - food, beer, or booze yet. Everything is too far away & I have been going to briefings or in meetings all day. Still didn't get to Finance today but determined to do so tomorrow morning before I go to another briefing at 10:00 am.

Some of the people I've met who will be in the Brigade appear to be well qualified, however since the majority of the officers weren't due in until today I haven't met most yet. It's all going to be quite an experience.

I got a Life Magazine today so my mail is coming through (at address I wrote yesterday). I will change addresses on magazines to P. G. once you move.

So it's off to bed for another hot, sweaty night. They say you get used to the heat eventually (in addition to the heat this is a very noisy place - occupant across the hall has a loud stereo).

So my honey, hope you had a good day at work today. Am anxious to hear how the job is going & anything on the house. I love you!

Bill
& write

Fort Hood, Texas
June 18, 1967

I feel like calling you again tonight but will wait a few days & write this instead. It's now 7:00 pm. Spent all day with my PSD officers & NCOs finding out about personnel situation. Things very hectic. Worked all day yesterday too. This will probably be the routine.

I dislike Hood intensely! Big disadvantage not having transportation & I may get a bike or a used scooter. The club annex near my BOQ is closed Sunday, Monday & Tuesday. No place to eat within walking distance. Even when you do get to the main club, you can't eat in the dining room without a tie. The informal bar-restaurant only serves steaks (which even I can get tired of steak for every meal!). There is no place to cook in the BOQ & I haven't been able to get to the commissary yet for snacks for the refrigerator.

I finally got an office & found places to set up the AG section (scattered all over post). Most of my people are here & they look pretty good. Captain Dove, who I mentioned, for PSD chief; two warrant officers for PSD - Mr. Young & Mr. Harmon; a 2d Lieutenant Yates for the PSD; 2d Lieutenant Goertel for Admin Services; and 2nd Lieutenant Brown for Postal section. Still to come in are Captain Payant - executive officer and Lieutenant Bean - Replacement Detachment. Then there are 68 enlisted men (mostly PFCs).

Nothing is organized in the Headquarters yet, but the units are. It's very harassing because we are being expected to come up with statistics & figures & aren't even moved into offices yet. However, by the end of next week I feel that we'll that we'll be more or less operational.

Am starting to meet some officers in the Brigade (outside of the AG officers). The Brigade Commander, Colonel Waldie, seems to be a very fine, intelligent man & I was very impressed by him on our first meeting. Many of the staff officers won't be in until July, however.

I'm glad you got a dog! I wish I had one! He will be good company & I know you'll feel a lot safer with someone around to "bark."

It seems like I've been here two months instead of 5 days. I miss you honey (there is a possibility my leave will be before September - but too early to speculate on that now). I'm glad the job is going well, only wish that the house will get settled soon. (Enclosed - $400.00)

Good night darling - I love you
Bill

Fort Ord, California
June 22, 1967

Hi Love

Sure wish you would follow that impulse and call - can't you call from your office? I think the phone is bugged. There is a funny buzz on it.

I am seeing if an appraiser - Mr. Appelton - will look at the house tomorrow, Friday afternoon for $35.00. Worth it though.

June 24 - 67

My how time flies, I hardly have time to think. I am at my usual place in the kitchen with a cup of coffee. It seems I only sit when I am home. I went to the house yesterday. Met Mrs. Herd. She is an older woman and quite uncoordinated - was sick or something. Mr. Appelton, the appraiser, looked at everything. One comment was "You sure will have a lot of work done," and "Do you need all this room." He is to let me know today what he estimates it at. Mr. Ryan and I are going over there on Sunday to discuss the heating arrangements, if I'm still interested after the new appraisal. The bank had an adjusted appraisal at $20,400, splitting hairs, they are. It still is a cute place, but the neighborhood questionable down below.

I paid the insurance bill and here is the statement that our loan is paid off. Kirsten wrote that she will be in Minneapolis on June 22, so I should get a call from her tonight, Saturday. Mor wrote - I think they are sad to be alone - she only said they had to fix her room up and get a girl to live there so they wouldn't be so tied down. I sure hope they will come over this year.

The Bergs received your letter and were pleased. They think you are just grand. Thanks for the money orders. My balance now after paying bills is $372.17. How are you doing?

Please don't get too excited about me coming to Texas. I don't see how I can swing it financially as well as time-wise. If I have to move and get organized plus working. So far I haven't even cleaned this house once. By the time I have eaten and fed the dog it is usually after 8 o clock. That doesn't leave much time for letters, papers. Only had the TV on once for ½ hour.

Duke is a good boy - very patient and obedient. Last night he sneaked up on the bed on your side at the foot. You'll love him. So good-natured, it is some work but not bad. Mor also wrote that they think of you often, even if they don't write. Now that Kirsten is gone it is hard for them to write in English. She sends regards to both of us and I send oodles of love. Please honey, don't get too lonely, just think of how much everyone loves you and thinks of you. Promise now. I do think all this will be the hardest on you, but chin up, this too will pass. Who knows, they might just end this war.

Love Elin

P.S. What insurance shall I get? What is your zip code?

Spokane, Washington
June 23, 1967

Dear Elin and Bill,

Are you in California or Texas? In Texas, I bet. Let me know where and also when Bill will be leaving for Vietnam.

I went to Yellowstone and Tetons and to Sun Valley with Alice Wooley. We had a wonderful week. At which place in Yellowstone did you work, Elin and did you like it a lot or not, and were you able to save money? Foods and everything there is so expensive.

If you two have not seen Sun Valley, I hope that some day you will go there, for it is really lovely and different from Yellowstone. I liked Jackson, Wyoming so very much that some day when I sell this place, I think that is where I will move. It is absolutely the most picturesque little town I have ever seen.

When I got home I had a big blow. The Red Cross and the Fairchild Air Force Base MARS station had been trying to locate me ever since the morning we left here. Joan was seriously ill in the Wiesbaden Hospital–with acute asthma and has been kept in the oxygen tent and fed intravenously. She is a victim of the military socialized medical practice. Last winter when she had pneumonia and was so ill she was treated by a Turkish doctor at our hospital for several weeks for allergies to the smog, then when she became so much worse they demanded another doctor and he said she had double pneumonia and had it for several weeks. Then she was so run down and thin it took so much more antibiotics to cure her. On top of that the doctors have continued to give her shots for her allergies to the smog there. Recently Tim had a virus and it went into a bronchial infection and of course Joan got it from him and again they gave her the antibiotics. Then recently she had asthma and they gave her shots for that and also for allergies. It was enough to kill her and it nearly did.

I called Tim's sister Elita in N.Y.C. who has an exec job with the telephone company and can call anyplace all over the world and also get her calls put right through. Within 15 minutes she had called and talked to Tim and called me back. Now Joan is out of the oxygen tent part of the time and can get out of bed some, but they do not know when she will be able to go home. Tim had asked for a 30 day leave to take Joan to Italy as though that climate and the sunshine might do good for her. So he is taking the leave now to stay with the children instead. If she should get worse or if they do not hold their own and let the doctors fill her full of all those medicines, then I will fly over and see that they get straightened. I just had to learn over the years just what I can tolerate and just to throw them down the stool when I start to get reactions to them, and evidently Joan has my allergies to drugs and medicines.

I am slaving over the garden and yard and am always so full of aches and pains from it all. It is just too much manual labor for me to keep up, so much as I dearly love this home and perhaps become neurotic without it, I can see the handwriting on the wall sometime in the not too distant future.

Terry Kim's husband is finishing his PHD this summer and will teach in a college in Colorado. He is getting his PHD in International Gov. and Far Eastern History. Is Kirsten back here with her husband yet?

Do let me know where you are and when Bill will be leaving.

Aren't you glad that you went to Beirut when you did?

When are you planning to come to Spokane too, Elin?

Much love,
Hazel

Bill and Elin with Hazel Clawson at Elin's parents' 25th wedding anniversary
Ringe, Denmark 1963

Waukegan, Illinois
June 24, 1967

Dear Elin and Bill:

I don't know where this letter will reach you, but I try at least to get in touch with you. I talked to Omer Pigeon this week on the phone - I had written to them too and he called me and told me that you are presently changing stations. Does that mean Vietnam, Bill? How are you both? I read that you are being promoted to Major Bill, congratulations. What are your plans, Elin?

Since 8 June I am here in the States, I finally made it. Time just flies by. There is so much I and we would like to do and never get around doing it. Helga and her family - three children now - are fine, the children are real cute, but they sure keep their Tante Margarete going. I am alone with them this weekend. Helga and Larry went for a 3 day well-deserved R&R. So far I have been twice to Chicago. On 12 and 13 June I was in Buffalo, resp. Geneva, NY, to attend the wedding of General Sutherland's daughter, had a lovely time and got to see a lot of the state of New York. Next week, from Monday to Wednesday, I will go to St. Louis, to distant relatives, Thursday once more to Chicago. Next weekend we plan to drive up to Wisconsin to see the cottage where Helga with her family will go in August for one week. On 5 July I will fly to Washington to Nona and Jack Stewart. (He was promoted to full Colonel on 17 May, do you know it?). On 7 July I will leave D.C. early for New York, from where we will fly back at 2200 hours, arrival time in Stuttgart on 8 July at 10:40 hours. On 7 July I will take a (preferably harbor boat) trip in New York, as I have been there 4 times before, I know most of the interesting places. Maybe I can meet Jack and Mary Brown, will write them after I am finished writing to you (it is midnight by the way, but that is the only time I can get something done, have written several letters already). This is roughly my schedule - I did not want to do too much, my main purpose for coming here is visiting my sister.

Do you have any news for me? I had a letter from Colonel James, he is presently in the States for the graduation of Lois-Ann from Nurses School, but he will be going back to Vietnam to a job equivalent to the AG in USAREUR. I will write to the DeNios too. Is Jean back already? How is your family back home, Elin? I guess you had a very nice good tour in Fort Ord and hate to leave there.

Just in case this letter does reach you, maybe I will hear from you while I am still here. Helga's phone number is: 623-5771.

Let me come to an end now.

All my best wishes to you both with best regards
Margarete

P.S. Bill, did you ever get the matter with Rechtsanwalt Maenner settled?

Fort Hood, Texas
June 24, 1967

Dear Jack,

What happened to you? Unless Elin got a letter within last two days, last we heard from you was in March. Everything OK?

As you can see, I'm at Fort Hood. Elin back at Ord. I'm trying to get my section organized in this new brigade – things are hectic but shaping up. I've got a large section – 8 officers and 68 enlisted men. Biggest and most demanding job I've had yet. We are a Brigade Special Staff section, and right now helping to organize the brigade. Fort Hood is miserable. Hot as hell and humid (a prelude to Vietnam!), and out in the middle of nowhere. I'm living in a BOQ – bedroom and sitting room, and not air conditioned.

We get 2 weeks leave before going to RVN. Hopefully it will be when Mother could go to California to stay with us for a while.

I called Mother the other night. I guess she wrote you about Mike's operation on his back – which was successful?

Well let me hear from you, or are you all "Thaied" up?

Bill

Philadelphia, Pennsylvania
June 26, 1967

Dear Bill,

What a hectic life your mother leads! Remember the fable of a mother in a rocker with a shawl around her shoulders uttering wise sayings in a contented fashion, and munching sweets? Forget it!

I have Nana Williams here, I have hired a housekeeper as of tomorrow morning, and I am going to run a convalescent home on the side! Be careful of what you say when you write because Nana and Uncle Charlie must hear every word you boys write and then read the letters again at their leisure. Nana's heart is in bad shape and we can't get a housekeeper up in the mountains. However I am going to hire help in August (in addition to the day help) and either come to see you or be free to "trot" if you come East.

We sold the property at 1212 and now I must be very careful of the money ($7,000 clear) as that is the sum total of Charlie's money. With my income, we should make out. I am so happy to be rid of the gigantic headache it involved.

Mike was so very pleased to get your letter. He is convalescing and seems to be improving daily. His spirits are good.

Joan left and I dare not think too much about her or I shall weep. Not because I didn't want her to go, but because the life went out of this house. I like youth!

Her address is 2300 Nicollet Ave., Apt. 35, Minneapolis, Minnesota.

She called Kirsten but was disappointed to learn that she had not arrived in U.S. Isn't Tom good looking?

I will write to Elin this week. She sent me a lovely letter and the beautiful picture of your home. I love the picture of you both where your head is atop hers! I hope you know the one I mean. I am returning them to her as she only has one set. Your home is elegant.

I could write about the world situation, but I'm too tired tonight. Enough to know that we are holding our own here and spirits are good!

My love always,
Mother

Fort Ord, California
June 26, 1967

Dear Mor and Far

Thanks for your letter. Yes it's a shame you are alone - but that's how life is sometimes. I hadn't thought that I would sit here all alone, but I'm so busy that I barely have time to think.

Did I write and tell you I got a dog? "Duke" is a 5 year old poodle, very obedient, neither barks or does other impossible things. It is nice to have him at night. It was a dog that a neighbor had. He was being sent to England, and it takes six months of prior quarantine to get authority to bring a dog to England, so I bought Duke. He has already gotten used to me.

Bill calls every three days. It is hot where he is 30c to 35c. He says he is sweating constantly and it's hard to get something to eat since because the main place to eat is 2 km away. He says he walks, walks, walks. It's the biggest base in the USA. It takes 1½ hours to drive from one end to the other.

I'm still negotiating about the house. It will take at least 3 more weeks if I definitely decide to buy it. It's a big decision.

I'll run now, have to go to work.

I love you both and constantly have you in my thoughts.

Elin

Fort Ord, California
June 27, 1967

Dear Bill

I can't remember what I have told you and what I haven't.

I am going to get my money back. Had a meeting at Vergas' office.

Yesterday I saw a small house in Monte Vista, on Monte Vista Drive. It has two small bedrooms, one bath and a kitchen. A small area for a washer and dryer. Small garage, Nice wooded lot. Fireplace, living and dining room. About the size of our present place. Beamed ceiling. Price $23,500. It is right by the gate to Skyline Forest. The owners are selling themselves. No yard work, all shrubs. It seems rather perfect for me now, and I'm sure you could rent it in that area which is a choice location. I only saw it for 10 minutes. Am going back tonight to look more.

I am working too hard at Bergs. I doubt I can last one whole year. I should have stayed with the Thrift Shop. This is just ridiculous. At least 10 hours a day. I must run now.

Much love -Elin

Fort Hood, Texas
June 28, 1967

Hi Darling

Miss you - would have called last night but just couldn't trek over to the office again to use Autovon, so will write instead. I received this letter from Mother today, and am returning the appraisal form.

I have too many thoughts on the house to come to a logical argument for or against. Unless we get a real bargain (now that we can get out of the deal) it may cause more headaches than pleasure.

I'm into somewhat of a routine now, up at 6:30 am, in the office by 7:15 (first one in the headquarters - the only people with a sense of urgency about this seems to be in my section. This is bound to change in two weeks when the rest of the staff arrives). Lunch at the Snack Bar or my clerk, PFC Berry, goes out for a hamburger. On Monday & Tuesday the Club Annex (within walking distance) is closed, so eat hamburgers at the Snack Bar. On Wednesday, Thursday, Friday I eat at the Annex. On Saturday & Sunday eat at the main Club (approximately 3 miles away - last Saturday I walked home, good P.T!) I've been going to the office at night, or sitting in my room doing work. There is a pool not far from the BOQ & I've gone for a swim twice (hope I do more after work). There are 7 swimming pools on post.

I called Maria tonight, she wasn't home & I talked to her husband. Sounds very nice & they will call back. Another lieutenant invited me for dinner next week - and he's the one who had me out last week - wants to feed me again (the equestrian).

As I mentioned on the phone I'm giving a little cocktail party at the club this Sunday night for my officers. It's important to establish unity - especially when we're going to be living and working together in Vietnam & it's up to me to start the ball rolling. Will only be 15 people and we'll have some hors d'ouevres & bartender in a small room. The three lieutenants are all from Fort Hood & have wives here, & two others are settling their families here while they are in Vietnam (can't conceive why anyone would stay here unless compelled!).

Maria just called & they asked me to dinner tomorrow, so will go at 7:00 pm. They will pick me up.

Off to bed with Time magazine.

Be good - I love my honey!

Bill

Fort Ord, California
June 28, 1967

Dear Love

I had a "hell" of a day yesterday, almost quit. I got our check back from Jody. I'll destroy it. What shall I do with the money, put in a savings here?   If I do decide to get the house the bank likes for you to have an account with them.

I cried a lot yesterday. It all seems too much, and for what. All my money will just go to live.

We can get the house almost at our terms now - all cleaned up and all. What do you say. Unless you give some firm guidance I'm going to be very put out. I'll not have another "I don't know" answer. How much do you like the house and are you willing to put money into it, or have you worried about that.

Your mother has never written to me. The people around here - not one has ever called me, and I get a cold shoulder from most. Sometimes I feel "all" Americans are only interested in you when they think it's politically right. I'm fed up. Fed up with it all and ready to skip town, house, and even you. Your family couldn't care less about me. What if something should happen to me, or you. Do you think they would aid me?

I have to run –Elin

Fort Hood, Texas
June 28, 1967

Dear Mother, Uncle Charlie, and Nana,

Glad to receive your letter today Mother - and learn that all is well on Harrison Street.

This is the hottest place I've been - and I haven't really been comfortable since arriving, however you do get used to the constant heat & I guess we'll be able to stand Vietnam better. These have been frustrating days, trying to organize a brand new section as well as handling the personnel requirements for a brand new brigade (5,500 men). It is a big job, and it's not that my section & myself don't know what to do - we are somewhat hampered at the moment by people inexperienced in our type of operation which is not normally found at the brigade level. It will all work out in time, when the rest of the staff arrives in a few weeks. Right now I am completely immersed in my job - all waking hours either at the office or scribbling notes in my room.

Really miss Elin's good cooking - if there were cooking facilities in the BOQ I would cook for myself. The officers' club is about 3 miles away from where I am staying (this is a fantastically large post) so I only go there on weekends. They do have a small annex within walking distance where I eat the rest of the week. The Club has a nice swimming pool, also there is an open pool a block from my room. So I have plans to relax there after work when possible.

Haven't seen anything of Texas since I've been here, except on the ride from the airport. It appears to be only flat, dry and hot. One of these weekends I would like to go to Dallas or San Antonio to see the sights.

I have some fine officers in my section, which is good because we're going to be together for the next year. Two captains, three second lieutenants and two warrant officers. Also some outstanding sergeants, who of course make or break an outfit. So, I'm not at all worried. Basically what my section's mission is:
  - maintaining all personnel records for all 5,500 brigade members;
  - handling all personnel management (getting right people into right jobs);
  - processing, writing, etc. all awards & decorations (which will be very busy in Vietnam);
  - handling all casualty reporting (also big in Vietnam);
  - providing complete postal service to the brigade;

- processing and controlling all incoming and outgoing correspondence for the brigade headquarters, and control and publish regulations.

To do this we have 9 officers and 68 men (I didn't know if you knew what we did so thought this little run down might be useful).

In Vietnam we will set up a base camp, and most likely remain in one place, along with a lot of other support services (Quartermaster. Maintenance, Finance, etc.). We are already getting equipment together, plus a lot of extras, to take along. From talking to many Vietnam returnees, the most comfortable situations and working conditions are created by good old American ingenuity.

Have been following the news sporadically since in Texas. Hopefully the Glassboro Summit talks will pave the way to closer realistic relations with the Soviet Union. I bet there was some excitement in Philadelphia with the Summit just across the river a bit in New Jersey.

What do you hear from Jack? I've written him but haven't heard from him since before Kirsten got married. I'm sure he's very busy. I'll drop Joan a line. Kirsten arrived several days ago. Elin is involved with her job, which she enjoys, but is taking a lot of time.

I won't know for a while yet exactly when I can take leave, but it will be end of August first of September in any event.

Much love to all –
Bill

Fort Ord, California
June 30, 1967

Dear Far and Mor

Yesterday I had a very depressing day. I can't follow along with everything at work. But I'll learn everything if I only give it time. I don't think I'll buy that house. I don't know if it is right, it would be a lot for me alone, also it is hard to rent something because it's so expensive and then one gets nothing out of it.

Maybe I should come home next year. What will I do here, only work and struggle with a house. What do I get out of that? I have not heard anything from my mother-in-law, for now three months. Hazel writes every week. Her daughter, Joan, is very, very ill. She has been in an oxygen tent in the hospital being fed intravenously for over a week. It has to do with her lungs - asthma, bronchitis and pneumonia. She had it too long with a cough. It's been a hard time for Mrs. Clawson.

Dori (Sigelkow) Matson had a son. If I stay here will one of you visit here? I'm well, have lost a bit of weight and gotten some nice clothes so I look nice.

Bill is fine but we miss each other.

Stay well –
Elin

Philadelphia, Pennsylvania
July 2, 1967

Dear Elin,

This is not my usual typewriting paper but it was a gift from a dear little girl so I will use it by writing to my sweet girls, you and Joan!

These pictures are lovely and I have showed them to many family and friends. Your home is indeed elegant and you and Bill are justly proud to show it off. I too, like the picture you titled your "favorite".

Thank you for sharing them with me.

Is Kirsten's Tom as cute as he looks? His eyes and smile are lovely and I surely wish Kirsten great happiness. I know Far wanted a Danish son-in-law and I hope he learns to like Tom as he does Bill.

Joan is adjusting to life far away from home and I surely hope she makes the most of this opportunity. She lives in a small apartment with other girls instead of a dormitory. Her only complaint thus far is that the girls are generally younger than she!

Your job sounds most interesting. I would guess your dynamic personality and business sense would be perfect for this position. I could tell that Bill was very proud of you. He tells me he misses you so much. And I am so happy that you make him so happy! That is the fondest wish of every mother. I know you miss him dreadfully but keeping busy is the best medicine for that.

Jack is teaching English two days a week in a Thai school. He heard an announcement over the radio asking for volunteers so he called and gave them his name. Last week he was chosen. A car drives him, in his civilian clothes, to the school and returns him to camp. He is very excited about it. I doubt if Jack would stay in the service. He has the days counted until he gets out. He also hates the hot weather.

Uncle Charlie is poorly and now my mother is here with us. I have hired a housekeeper as I couldn't take the extra work. Both are old with the debilities that seem to go with old age. Nana Walker, Aunt Helen, and family have moved again. This time they are north of New York City in Connecticut, right on the beach! Uncle Loren and Uncle Lacey have again been given promotions. Uncle Loren celebrated by buying a new Mercury and they both are going to Canada this week to fish!

The big meeting at Glassboro was just across the river from Philadelphia and of course we were all excited about it. I do hope the results are good ones but our papers gave little hope. Now I must write to my other "girl". I know she looks for letters. Don't work too hard but be sure to let me in on the new styles. It is a dress shop, isn't it? Maybe you can get a pale orchid knit (or blue) in 14B or 14½ for fall for me! Let me know the prices if you want to.

Love,
Mother

Fort Ord, California
July 8, 1967

Karre Far og Mor

First - Happy Birthday on your 55th year. I had not forgotten it - it is only that my life is so confusing at this time that time gets away from me.

My job - I gave notice. It was all too much, almost 10 hours a day, and I soured on it all. I quit on Saturday and on Monday I went to the transportation office. I made arrangements to move out this week. On Wednesday my clothes and some small things were packed. Yesterday and today all of our things were packed and will be put in storage. Now the house has to be cleaned to be ready for inspection. Then I go to Texas.

I miss Bill much too much. I'll stay there until he leaves, and I'll come home (now I know it would never have worked staying here alone). It won't be until October or later. Don't think I'm coming tomorrow. A lot can happen, what does one know day to day? I'm with my neighbor now, and worried about the long trip by car, but will have to figure something out.

I'm happy to be seeing Bill again. He has not found an apartment yet, but it will surely work out. We can always find a motel room. I'm well now that I have decided not to sit here all alone a whole year. It doesn't suit me. I'll write with more details as I find out.

Loving regards from Elin
Bill prefers that I go home.

San Francisco, California
July 11, 1967

Three postcards from Elin:

Lombard Street –

Dear Bill, Enjoying the 55 degree weather here. Sure wish you were here. With Marge & Warren Welter.

Elin

Fishermen's Wharf –

Had wonderful meal here. Also a bottle of Liebfraumilch. Don't know what to do - please advise.

Love Elin

Fishermen's Grotto –

Hi - Max, Warren & Marge & Susan miss you very much. Leaving for Texas tomorrow - by way of Oregon - we found a short cut.

Love Elin

En route on a Flight to Dallas, Texas
July 13, 1967

Dear Far and Mor

Oh how much has happened these last two weeks. I am on a flight on the way to Dallas and then on to Killeen, where Bill is waiting for me. He has found a small two room furnished apartment, so we will easily manage the next two months.

On Wednesday my clothes were packed. I can send them where I want in the USA. On Thursday our furniture was packed and on Friday put in large wood crates, the size of a room, and are now in storage. I paid a sergeant and a soldier to clean the house to be ready for inspection. Everything has to be shining and in tip top shape.

On Saturday I went to say goodbye to the Welters in San Francisco. On Monday we went to town so I could become a member of an Automotive Club AAA. They help you get home if you have an accident when driving. By chance I found out that there is a firm where one can arrange to have someone drive your car to another location. So I arranged that for the move to Texas. I drove back to Fort Ord, worked in the yard all of Tuesday, again for inspection. Wednesday came and it all went fine. I only had to pay $9.50 for some holes - 50 cents for every nail hole, so on Wednesday evening I went back to San Francisco. It's about 200 kilometers, and now this morning left the car, it was a very decent man, about 40, who is going to drive it to Texas. I had the car completely gone over, brakes, oil, etc. on Tuesday. I'm sure it will go well. It is better than my shaking for 5 days over the roads. It is about 3,500 kilometers over mountains and through the desert. I'm fully insured through the firm that arranged this. I hope it goes well, but before I did this I was beside myself thinking about the drive. It's so hot - over 30 degrees C, almost the whole way.

Bill is very happy that I am coming. Now we will see what I will do when he goes to Vietnam, but I guess I'll take a boat to Bremerhaven. What about taking the car to Denmark? I feel fine.

Elin

I hope you are doing real well. We miss you.

Killeen, Texas
July 16, 1967

Dear Far and Mor

Yes, now I have arrived in one piece. Bill had found a nice small apartment, bedroom, nice bath with blue tiles, & kitchen with all modern conveniences, a living room with nice furniture, blue & green, and a small terrace outside. It is very cozy and comfortably cool with "air-conditioning." He had it all arranged with flowers and bought the most necessary things to eat, so we will do fine here. I'm glad I came. Maria and her husband Gus came over one evening. They are fine and look to be a happy family. Maria is still small and so sweet. Their son is full of pep. They were a big help when Bill was here by himself. Our car should arrive tomorrow.

Saturday we were at a party in the open with Bill's new brigade. They're over 250 officers so it is a big group when everyone is together. Tuesday I am going to a ladies luncheon. Luckily Maria has done my hair. She is very good at it.

The base is so fantastically big that you can't imagine it. There are 100 streets in a row. The base is as big as Odense in population so it is a bit different from what we are used to. We live about 10 minutes from where Bill works. I have walked to the town of Killeen. It has about 23,000 inhabitants and a very "dead" village - but it's only for a couple of months. It's cool right now with around 25 degrees C, they say. Bill says just wait - it will really get hot. He sends his regards.

Loving hellos
Elin

Philadelphia, Pennsylvania
July 16, 1967

Dear Bill,

Today the Inquirer noted on the front page that your 198th Brigade was the largest being readied for Vietnam. Then it told in detail the attack at Da Nang last night and I surely didn't enjoy my breakfast.

There is big trouble with race rioting in Newark and tonight it has spread to Plainfield where Uncle Lacey lives. He doesn't know if he will have a store in the morning. It is sickening. Newark is just about destroyed with many civilians dead. Which situation is worse! We have big trouble here in our cities.

Mike is still improving nicely and the encouraging letters from you, Jack, and Joan helped his morale. He will always have to be careful about lifting or pushing heavy objects but his recovery is better than I had hoped.

Joan seems happy in Minneapolis but said no one writes to her. It is impossible for me to write more often but I guess I will have to try. She had the second highest mark in the class in political science. She also has had numerous dates! That is good for a girl who hasn't had many in a year.

Kirsten called me a week ago and said she was coming to visit us but called the next day and acted surprised to find herself in Connecticut! I was surprised to learn her husband is a computer expert, I guess I assumed he was a service man.

What would you like from Philadelphia for your birthday? If you can think of anything special telephone me collect. In fact I would call you tonight if I thought I could reach you.

Mike said you gave a party at the fort. How was it?

I bet you do miss Elin's good cooking and miss her, too. I wrote to her but feel sure she is very busy as she hoped to be. Do you ever get a chance to have a weekend together? Also, I've wondered about your house you told me about. Did you get it?

Nana Williams is still here and slightly improved. She is reading Manchester's book about Kennedy and likes it. Uncle Charlie is not well. Between the two I am getting jumpy! Did I tell you I hired a housekeeper? If only I can keep her!

Uncle Loren and Uncle Lacey went fishing in Canada two weeks ago. They brought us quite a few beautiful big northern pike and bass which I have stored in my new refrigerator. I bought a copper colored one with a freezer top. Nice.

My Indian student from New Delhi is now a PhD in chemistry and has taught a year. Tonight he telephoned and asked if he could come to see us (it's been at least three years since I've heard from him). So I invited him for dinner and then called Bob Hamilton, Larry Shallcross, and Vivian Robinson, Jack's girl. They are coming to help get the conversation ball rolling! It should be fun if I can keep my invalids well. Uncle Charlie's table manners are deplorable but my friends will have to understand that he is advanced in years and sick.

Dick Jones was promoted to Asst. Treasurer of Frankford Trust Co. and Michael, after getting his Master's degree, left teaching and entered the business field.

Mr. Pfeiffer, Mrs. Jones, and the Cutler brothers all send their best wishes to you.

Summer school is a drag and a bore but as three weeks have gone by I guess I can go two more! Mike, Kathleen, and I hope to go to visit Uncle Loren and then go up to see Joan around August 7th. Of course whether or not I go depends on the condition of my people here.

Wish I could see you more often. I surely do miss my family! How many years have you been gone? I count eight! Too many. If only you weren't so far away! And soon you will be going half way around the world. Life is complex. Do take care and know that I love you very dearly.

As ever and ever,
Mother

Los Angeles, California
July 17, 1967

Dear Elin,

We have thought about you two a lot – Bill is gone by now? I'm really sorry we couldn't get together for a proper send off. I suspect we might have been in Las Vegas at the same time, since that's the week we came through from Denver. Perhaps we were even at Oceanside when you came through. Anyway, let us know how everything is going, about your house and job.

Right now, we are settled in L.A. Keith is working on the National Foreign desks of the Times, and I am pounding out resumes, thus the erasese paper! We're ensconced in a temporary apartment just off Wilshire near the Ambassador Hotel, a bit of old but not without charm and fairly descent furniture.

Keith has been in the hospital for a bit of minor surgery, so our activities since arriving here have centered primarily around medical and housing matters. But he's fine now, or at least on the way to full spirits. He horrified the nurses by watching television through the late shows and even talked the doctor out of an extra day at the hospital. I'm really glad to be relieved of the role of "official nag" of the "are you sure you should do that" variety.

Of course there's smog, but we're attempting to ignore it. Otherwise, for all it's reputation and suburban sprawl, this city has many of the attributes of urban life — great restaurants, flicks, etc. And, even some good "walking" areas. The people are wild: we saw a very old man with no hair, wearing Bermuda shorts, high socks, and what looked like a fraternity blazer; and downtown one midnight, a woman of similar age – pushing a supermarket cart full of what appeared to be rugs, and trying to keep in tow a couple of dogs on a leash. Too much.

Enough ramble. I must return to those resumes – this a relief from having to type and spell perfectly – hate it! Within a month, we'll have a bigger apartment and you know you're welcome if you feel like a change of coast view – I doubt we'll be up your way for a while, but you never know.

Take care. Can we write Bill? Let us know how things are progressing.

More later AJ (After Job!)

Cheers,
Carole

Minneapolis, Minnesota
July 18, 1967

Dear Elin,

I meant to write sooner, but was waiting to hear from Kirsten. As it is, we have not been able to get in touch with one another. I am really disappointed, because Mother told me that she won't be in Minneapolis now, but in Connecticut. I do hope that we can at least get together once when they come back for their things. I guess it was all to good to be true that we would be so close.

I love the city of Minneapolis and enjoy school very much. I have had the opportunity to meet so many new people and go to new places. My courses are quite interesting, and I have already learned a lot about the airlines. I am taking English, psychology, political science, airline ticketing, reservations, travel tour, typing, and charm. It keeps me busy but I'm glad for that. I've also considered getting a part-time job. The extra money would sure come in handy.

So far since I've been here I've gone to hear the Minneapolis Symphony, went to a Minneapolis Twins baseball game, saw a play ("Shoemaker's Holiday") at the famous Tyrone Guthrie Theater, and went swimming at a few of the many beautiful lakes right here in the city. I'm never idle. I don't have a chance to be.

During this week and next, Minneapolis is the center for a huge Aquatennial celebration......parades, water shows, dances, and all sorts of different events. Many celebrities and officials are here, including Vice-President Humphrey. I took his picture at a parade on Saturday. It's really been a blast!

I wrote to Bill, but have not heard from him yet. I imagine he's being kept quite busy. And you, Elin ... how is your job? You must be busy too. Please write and tell me just what you are doing. I'd love to hear from you. Mail is scarce around here.

Take care and keep well.

Love,
Joan

Limeport, Pennsylvania
July 22, 1967

Dear Bill,

....."A day comes when a man notices or says that he is thirty. Thus, he asserts his youth. But simultaneously he situates himself in relation to time." So has Albert Camus written in The Myth of Sisyphus, and so you are thinking. I'm sure. All kinds of thoughts are probably running through your mind in arriving at this "formidable" age - of the length of life, of maturity, of accomplishment even of the purpose of existence itself. I wish you all of these things on your thirtieth birthday, and a continued life of fullness and depth.

About my little hospital bout. The operation is what is called a laminectomy which involved the removal of most of one of my spinal disks. I had been having a pain in my left leg for well over a year. The pain was caused by the pinching of the nerve at the point of the faulty disk. I have recovered rapidly from the operation, hoping now that the matter is finally over.

I am glad that you see in this Vietnam tour of duty a bit of challenge - otherwise it could be sheer drudgery. After you get back, Kathy and I will have to visit you and Elin in sunny California. By the way, as you may or may not know, Kathy, Mother, and I are planning on a trip to Chicago and Minneapolis starting August 7 - by car. We'll be visiting Joan and Uncle Loren and Aunt Kay. Mother, however, is not totally certain if she can make the trip because of Uncle Charlie and Nana Williams - neither doing very well. Mother has hired a housekeeper during the day while she is at school. She surely needs a vacation! If she goes why don't you fly up to Minneapolis or Chicago!! It's a thought anyway.

I am happy to inform you, if you are not yet aware of this bit of news, that you are to be an uncle! Kathy is expected to have the child some time in late December or early January. If it is a boy, I am seriously considering the name Jonathan Isaac!

Jack is becoming quite the amateur photographer! Some of the shots he has sent home to Mother are very good. He is hoping to see you when you go over. And he is counting the days of his tour.

Well it's sermon time tomorrow - preparation that is - and quite late now. I'll write again, and you do so too. Do a good job on your new assignment. Would like to be addressing you as Major Walker.

Mike

P.S. Kathy and I are learning a bit of bridge. You'll have to give us a few pointers.

Mike and Kathy

Fort Hood, Texas
July 24, 1967

Dear Jack,

Bill sure was glad to hear from you. We are now together again till Bill leaves.

Too many things were wrong with the house we were buying. I felt it was too much to take on by myself, so I got out of it and packed everything up. It will be stored for the next year.

Bill found a little cute furnished apartment. Is all air conditioned or I'm afraid I would melt away. I arrived with 3 suitcases, so I've been playing newly married again, buying necessities for a household.

Bill is forever working some nights til way after midnight – weekends too. So I guess I'll get lots of reading in and other small chores done. This town is "dead", "dead" – after the Monterey Peninsula, this is like a prison.

Jack, I keep baking cookies and never get them to the post office. I'll try again, but my life has been in such a turmoil lately.

I'm glad to hear that time is flying for you. Maybe you can see Bill in Bangkok before you leave. He wants to take his R&R there, and if the timing is right you could possibly see each other. I'm not looking forward to my year of being alone. I do think it will go slow, but that too will pass.

Much love,
Elin

Philadelphia, Pennsylvania
July 26, 1967

Dear Bill,

Did you enjoy the Geographic? I hope so because I am sending it to you again for another year as a birthday gift. Be sure to send them the new address.

Remember, although this birthday is "staggering", (so was my 30th!) each of us is also a year older and your age seems mighty young.

Thank Elin for her newsy letter. We wondered what she meant by you being "extended".
Jack is going to Bangkok on the 2nd.

Love always,
Mother

Killeen, Texas
August 1, 1967

Dear Far and Mor,

A thousand thanks for all your letters. Here everything is fine - except that Bill works without breaks. Yesterday on his birthday he came home after midnight. I hope that one of these days it will be less, but I doubt it. Bill is on the list to be promoted to Major. I hope it happens while I'm here. It should be about September or October.

About the car. I would like to have an explanation from Far why he says it won't be practical to bring the car along. How am I getting to and fro doing the things I'll want to do. I prefer to be independent. It only costs $208 to ship it over, not a lot.

Kirsten and I have talked a couple of times. She is a bit nervous about being all by herself for the first time, standing on her own. She is very happy with Tom but there are so many new things to get used to. He said they will live on the east coast around New York, so I'm planning to stay on the east coast a couple of months so I can see them. I can stay with Bill's family for a week and visit friends in Washington, D.C., that way Bill's family can't say I just blew through. They are disappointed that I'm not coming for the year, but that would never work.

Bill is leaving about the first week of October. Please don't mention it to anybody. So, I think I'll come home in the beginning of December, or at least before Christmas. Here it's warm, about 35 degrees C, and up so I stay inside most of the time.

Kierlig Hilsen
Elin

Killeen, Texas
August 3, 1967

Dear Mother, Uncle Charlie, and Nana -

Bill was so happy to get your birthday cards. He did moan about that this was one he would have rather forgotten, since he did turn 30, but we all do get older. A cute young private saved his day though by asking if he was 24 or 25, because he and his buddies had a bet on and they felt he was a terribly young captain. Little did they know it was his birthday. Well. I'm not going to be that vain when I get older (ha ha ha!). That day was no different than the rest here. He came home at midnight. I've never seen him work so hard before. He jokes and says that they are going to Vietnam just so they can rest a bit.

We got a very long letter from Mike with the very exciting news. Mike has a boy's name all picked out. I'm going to remind him that people do have girls too. I do think that is cute - he is no different than any other expecting father. Mother, how is it to be an expecting grandmother?

If you will all promise not to tell the world - it does embarrass Bill - he is now up for promotion to Major and should make it around October. I hope he gets it while we are together. It will mean more prestige, a very little in extra money and with a new tax bracket we will be no better off. But it does mean a lot in the Army. This is the big jump to field grade officer. Bill joked and said Mother would grow two inches in the chest! (He would die if he knew I'm telling you all this). Bill has put in for leave in September - the last part - and we will drive East. He has to leave for Vietnam from here. I will visit with everyone up and down the coast for a couple of months and I hope to get on an Army ship for Europe before Christmas. I'm not planning anything as so much is constantly happening to change our plans. You asked about Bill being extended beyond what we first thought. An officer is generally never extended and he does not reenlist. For better or worse Bill is now and has been a career officer. I have accepted that and I guess everyone else might as well. No need to count years gone, or for me to count moves. I count six homes in six years of marriage and that is what it is going to be like.

Dear Mother - I didn't choose the Army and I really don't think Bill did either, but that is how it is turning out. My pleading to get out has been to no avail so let us resign ourselves to support what he is doing, not what we wish he was doing.

We are both well. Haven't seen Texas at all, and doubt that we would like it. Isn't it terrible to be so negative about a place, but it is hot and large. About those weekend trips to California, you asked if we saw each other on weekends - we are 1,000 miles into Texas and 2,000 miles from California.

Hope you are all well,

Love
Elin

Fort Hood, Texas
August 3, 1967

Dear Jack,

Thank you so much for your letters and for remembering Bill on his birthday. Since it was his 30th, Bill would have rather forgotten, although he was happy to hear from everyone.

I'm enclosing 3 pictures from "cool" Monterey. Our hearts really ache to be back there. This place leaves much to be desired.

We are very excited to hear about your Bangkok jaunts – should be fascinating.

I have taken over the letter writing since Bill is forever working, but that you are quite familiar with. He is often not home before midnight and still gets going at seven the next day.

I was staying at Monterey, but after a month soured on everything – not the place, but just being alone, and decided to come here. This stay here was longer than anticipated.

We will go to Philadelphia in September, and then Bill leaves in October. I'll stay up and down the east coast for a couple months visiting whoever will have me. Kirsten and Tom are moving to the east. I hope to get a space available on a boat to go to Europe before Christmas. I shall stay home for the remainder of the time.

Bill is the AG of this new outfit – huge job, and he is on the promotion list for Major. Should make it around October. I hope to be home together with him when it happens, but who knows.

Hope all is well with you. We talk of you often.

Much love,

Elin and Bill

Minneapolis, Minnesota
August 5, 1967

Dear Bill and Elin,

I was glad to hear from you once again. It seems to make the day complete when you go to your mailbox and there's a letter in it for you. From the way you talk, Killeen doesn't exactly seem to be the most exciting town to live in. Am I right? It's too bad you can't come up to Minneapolis to see me. Maybe if you don't go back to Denmark right away, Elin, you can come out to see me. I know it's not around the corner, but thought I'd just ask.

School is going along very well for me so far. Our first set of marks come out two weeks from now. As it stands, I have a high average in all my subjects. However I still have quite a few more tests to take before the marking period is over. Here's hoping!

I can't believe how many unattached members of the opposite sex there are around the twin cities. I never had this many dates with different fellows in a whole year in Philadelphia. It's great!

I just got a part time job, working for my landlord as a bookkeeper. I will be in charge of collecting the rent from the girls, writing out receipts, and such. I'll only be working a few hours a week at $1.50 an hour, but that will give me a little spending money, of which I don't have much.

I have just finished cleaning my apartment. UGH! Now I must do my laundry with my roommate. Just about everything I own is dirty.

Write soon and take care.

All my love,
Joan

Pullman, Washington
August 7, 1967

Dear Elin and Bill,

Your lovely wedding announcement, that is Kirsten's, was received with pleasure. We didn't know where to send a reply or gift, since she was to go home to Odense first. Besides, I have had to concentrate on keeping myself up and going, to maintain even a toe hold in the swift currents of recent events around me. Edward, 16 years, and Kathy, 13, this month came out in the middle of June, Ed to attend music high school camp on campus. He's a good cellist. Kathy plays the flute well, but isn't old enough yet to register for the camp. Laura Lee and Kevin (8 years July 26) came out for the last week of programs and concerts. The fresh pure air here did them lots of good. They all stayed a week after camp was over so that Ed could play in a trio at church, and in University of Idaho orchestra music festival. Now they're packing for their moving to Princeton, N.J. where Don will be at the University there. Though very satisfied with the conditions of his work at University of Chicago, he finally was forced to see that Laura Lee could no longer live - literally - in the poisonous air there. He had a number of offers, but Princeton is giving him everything that Chicago did, in salary, number of rooms, and equipment.

I wish Kirsten the greatest of happiness in her new venture, and am sure you must have helped her in her choice. Am anxious to know more details, but knew you and she both had numerous details to attend to. Anyway we'll hope to see all of you one day. Our plans for either fall or winter vacation are vague at the moment. Doctor wants me to take a leisurely trip, perhaps a cruise, and I would like to remain a month or so near Phoenix, Arizona, if possible would like to see Carmel, California once more, too.

Laura Lee would have liked to invite Kirsten to stay with them in Chicago, but dangerous conditions in the area prevented, and she felt that Kirsten couldn't circulate freely enough to enjoy herself. It has been a great strain to keep the children safe and still leading as normal a life as possible.

   We're now enjoying the delightful Pullman summer climate: mostly warm in daytime with blue, blue skies, and cool at night.

   I hope you're both well and enjoying that part of our country. I never hear from Hazel Clawson - since a letter telling me how her house was a shambles when she returned from Germany. Poor dear. I would love to see her again.

With love to you both

(Mrs. A.W.) Edna S. Thompson

P.S. The church is that of President Woodrow Wilson's father. It also was historically connected with events of the Civil War.

Edna and Albert Thompson

Odense, Denmark
August 7, 1967

Dear Elin

Thanks for your letter. It was nice that Kirsten got to talk to you. Yes, she will learn now to get along and cope, but with Tom's help it will work. I'm convinced that they will mature, and everything else is minor.

It is outstanding that Bill is being promoted to Major. I hope also that it will happen while you are there. We are very proud of our sons-in-law. Far will look into what it will cost to rent a car in the "Tax Free Harbor" or buy one there. But it becomes a problem for you if you prefer to bring your car along. American tourists seldom arrive in their own cars like they used to. They rent one, or buy one. It's about the same. Far is going to investigate if it also applies to you. Of course you need a car, otherwise it becomes hopeless to go places like here in Denmark. But your car has to be someplace, so you might as well bring it.

It will all work out.

Loving regards to you both
Mor

Killeen, Texas
August 17, 1967

Dear Mother

Thank you for your letter and your card from Minneapolis. I do hope it was a nice trip for everyone.

We are looking forward to coming to Philadelphia in late September. I can't give you a definite date yet but it looks like the last week of September.

Bill was just in the field for several days. He is very busy and I only see him a couple of hours a day. In your last letter you wrote about "poor lonely Bill" when I was still at Fort Ord. Let me explain - Bill has a driver, wherever he wants to go he can. He has an executive officer, a captain. Bill can snap a finger and he will get things for him. He has several soldiers who type and take care of other things. In other words Bill is constantly surrounded by people, and all of the officers are in a great "fraternity" with high spirits and a buddy-buddy feeling. They are looking forward to this "adventure," Bill included. He is so bustling with activity and very happy in his work (someone please explain men to me, I don't understand!). I really think there is something about war, armies and the like that appeal to men.

Now we have the wives. They are uprooted, asked to pack - by themselves - find new homes, take care of the kids, buy and sell homes, drive the car to new locations, and in general run the house, usually miles from close friends or relatives. It isn't always easy.

We will drive back and Bill will have to fly back here. He leaves from here the beginning of October.

One of Bill's former bosses, Colonel Hawkins, is the Secretary of the General Staff for General Westmoreland, and he has written Bill that he will help him. Bill will look him up to get lined up for a good job the last six months. Usually they are one half year in one job, and one half in another.

Just remember that Bill is not a field soldier, he is on a staff and works in an office just like he would in a big firm. If anything happens to him it would be in a freak accident. In all of WWII only four people from his branch were killed, and they were in jeep accidents. So far in Vietnam no one in his line of work has gotten hurt.

We were thrilled to get to talk to Nana Williams and hear about the big family reunion, it must have been nice. I always get a good feeling at family reunions.

We went riding yesterday, but got two lazy horses so it wasn't as fun as we had expected. Better luck next time. Then we went swimming in the officers' club pool, and at night played bridge with our upstairs neighbors. Saturday, Maria and Gus (they have been so nice to us) took us out for dinner in Austin to a converted farm house. Quite the place to go around here and it was lots of fun.

Next Saturday the Brigade is having a formal, and I didn't bring any clothes for that. Wonder what I will do, I don't feel like buying a new dress that I won't need for a year, when I have things packed up. Last week I had a luncheon for some of the girls. We made Mexican flowers. I learned how to make them and the apartment is full of them. I thought the other girls would enjoy making them. It was fun. Also went to a coffee where we saw movies of Vietnam at base camps where Bill will be. It isn't too primitive. They have good food, large tents, each a hole to crawl in, and even TV.

I do hope they don't declare war. Then all our soldiers lose many rights and it will be an even worse hardship - on the families.

We are fine and very happy for every day together.

Love
Elin

Fort Hood, Texas
August 20, 1967

Dear Far and Mor

How are you, here all is well. Yesterday I went horse riding, played cards with our upstairs neighbors and swam. It was the first Sunday Bill was off since we have been here. We called Philadelphia because Bill's grandmother turned 80. There had been 69 together for a family reunion and dinner. Saturday Maria and Gus took us to Austin for dinner at an unusual restaurant. It was an old barn made into a restaurant, very cozy. We are only 100 kilometers from Johnson's farm, and our phone company is owned by Lady Bird Johnson.

Kirsten called a couple of times. I'll get to see her next month. I hope they find a nice place to live. Tom is good at figuring things out.

I won't buy a new car in Europe. What we have is only one year old, and in tip top shape. We can't afford to buy a new car again. All the moving has been bad enough. It sounds so simple to travel but oh what it costs! Our expenses weighed against income here in the U.S.A. make it almost impossible to save, especially with all of the moves we have had.

Bill will get vacation from September and will leave in the beginning of October.

We will drive to the east coast maybe we will get to see Mexico which is only 300 kilometers from here so I would like to see it. We are well.

Loving regards
Elin

198th Infantry Brigade

BRAVE and BOLD

PRESENTATION OF COLORS

AND

BRIGADE REVIEW

****

SADOWSKI FIELD

0830 Hours

26 August 1967

SEQUENCE OF EVENTS AND MUSIC

Formation of the Troops

Inspection
"French National Defilade"
"Men of Ohio"
"Washington Post March"

Presentation of Command
"Riders of the Flag"
"National Anthem"

Presentation of Colors

Posting of Colors
"Grand Old Flag"

March in Review
"Infantry Kings of the Highway"
"Dog Faced Soldier"
"Colonel Rogers March"
"Army Goes Rolling Along"
"Stout Hearted Men"

198TH INFANTRY BRIGADE

COL JAMES R. WALDIE . . . . Reviewing Officer
Commanding Officer, 198th Infantry Brigade

LTC TOMMY P. TREXLER . . . . . . Commander of Troops

BRIGADE UNITS

UNITS	COMMANDERS
1st Bn, 6th Inf	LTC William J. Baxley Jr.
1st Bn, 46th Inf	LTC Jack A. Henson
1st Bn, 52d Inf	LTC Paul A. Roach Jr.
1st Bn, 14th Arty	LTC William H. Embley
9th Spt Bn	LTC Frank P. Clarke
HHC, 198th Inf	CPT Charles D. Ebert
H Trp, 17th Cav	CPT Walter E. Reasor Jr.
555th Engr Co	CPT John M O'Connor

Music by 1st Armored Division Band
WO1 John J. Russell . . . Bandmaster
SSG John W. Schanck . . . Drum Major

INSIGNIA

The spirit and readiness for combat of the men of the 198th Infantry Brigade is illustrated on the unit's insignia. The unit's insignia depicts a "Reverse S" of flames crossed with a portion of a rifle at fixed bayonet emblazoned over a blue shield arched at the top and bottom.

The tongue of flames allude to the brigade's fire power and the bayonet, a basic infantry weapon, is symbolic of carrying the fight to the enemy. The flame and bayonet together thus refer to the unit's spirit and readiness to engage the enemy in fire fight or in hand-to-hand combat with the bayonet.

Presentation of the Colors

198th Receives Official Colors

The newly formed 198th Inf. Bde. received its official colors Saturday at Sadowski Field.

Approximately 2,000 officers and men of the 198th turned out in full battle dress, sporting their shoulder sleeve insignia, jungle fatigues, and carrying M-16 rifles with fixed bayonets.

Colonel James R. Waldie, brigade commander and reviewing officer, inspected the infantrymen and Captain William A. Walker, adjutant general, read the history of each unit of the brigade.

Col. Waldie was then presented the brigade's official colors by Brigadier General Ralph L. Foster, assistant commander for support of the 1st Armored Division.

In a brief speech, Col. Waldie stated, "It doesn't seem possible that just three months ago there was no such thing as 198th, and now we are ready to go. The road has been long and hard but well worthwhile."

"We received fine support from all Ft. Hood units, particularly the 535th Avn. Bn. and the 3rd Bde. of the 1st Armd. Div.," he added.

"My thanks and congratulations to the brigade for a job well done," he concluded.

The order was given to pass the 198th in review, and Lieutenant Colonel Tommy P. Trexler, brigade executive officer, led the infantrymen past Col. Waldie and the reviewing dignitaries to conclude the ceremony.

Special guests attending were: Lieutenant General and Mrs. George R. Mather, III Corps and Ft. Hood commander, and Major General Joseph P. McChristian, 2nd Armored Division commander.

PRESENTING THE COLORS—Colonel James R. Waldie, left, commander of the 198th Light Infantry Brigade, receives the brigade colors from Brigadier General Ralph L. Foster, 1st Armored Division assistant commander for maneuvers, during ceremonies at Ft. Hood Saturday. Also shown is Sergeant Major Samuel Smith, brigade sergeant major. (Temple Telegram Photo)

198th March in Review

Fort Hood, Texas
August 29, 1967

Dear Mother,

Hope that you have a nice birthday. We'll bring your gift with us in the car.

We're flying to Mexico City for a few days next week, then driving to Philadelphia via Houston, New Orleans and up through South, Expect to arrive in Philadelphia about September 14th. I couldn't get my leave when I wanted it, so this is a hurried up plan. Only get a short time.

Hope everyone is well. We're looking forward to seeing you in a few weeks.

With love,
Elin and Bill

Chu Lai, Vietnam
September 16, 1967

Captain Walker,

A quick note to let you know that I have been "on the job" for a day and to pass on a couple of problems. First off the Americal Division is in a state of confusion as to what they are going to do. In my discussion with the Division AG the only real impression I could get was that they are unsure of how things will be organized and what we will retain. As of now the AG hopes to organize along the same lines as ROAD Divisions. The only problem here is that no guidelines have been received from higher headquarters. I'm going to go ahead based on retaining the AG section.

In talking to the postal officer today he suggested very strongly that we go ahead and establish an account with the San Francisco Postmaster. It is recommended that a fixed credit of $30,000 be established and 20,000 blank money orders be obtained. This is in addition to the 6 machines and 3 scales. I'm told that the Killeen Postmaster can render assistance in setting this up.

Also because of the requirement for immediate issuance of PX ration cards, suggest you bring along with you unit rosters with name, rank, serial number and company so advance party can at least start preparing the cards for issue.

Any other information to be passed on immediately I will send to you by message. I don't think there will be any great problems here. The main one will be getting set up and ready to operate.

Captain Dove

This address is only a temporary arrangement for us to receive mail.

Philadelphia, Pennsylvania
September 18, 1967

Dear Far and Mor

Yes, now I have just said good-bye to my Bill for the next 12½ months. It's hard to imagine that I won't get to see his happy smile for so long. Now we hope all goes well.

We didn't get to Mexico. The consulate had told us that we could get visas at the airport. When we arrived on Sunday morning the 3rd of September we were told that only American citizens could get visas there, and the consulate was closed until Tuesday. We got tickets refunded and started to drive. It rained the next 6 days without stopping. We drove over New Orleans, Florida and up the east coast. It was beautiful, but too bad we didn't have better weather. We arrived here last Sunday. It has been a very hard week here. Mr. Fulmer had fallen. He is lame on one side, practically an invalid. He can't always remember things and is starting to develop dementia. Now, today, he is being moved from the hospital to a nursing home. It is so stupid here in America that you have to pay for most of the expenses for care. It will be $80 per week, so Bill's mother is beside herself.

I have to stay here until Christmas, but then I'll see Kisse, they are supposed to be here on the east coast around November.

I'm fine - stay well
Elin

Motel Tamanaca, New Orleans

Philadelphia, Pennsylvania
September 19, 1967

Hi there Lover Boy - I'm in a very peculiar mood. It seems with all the complaining going on around me I'm determined to stay cheerful - I will - that I promise you. I guess my favorite telephone company is giving you a hard time or I would have heard. I'm dying to hear all the gossip you'll have to relate.

We took Charlie to the home. Now I find that a very depressing place. Two ladies across the hall from Charlie are yelling all the time for their mother. If he stays like he is, I'm going to suggest he come home. We could easily take care of him if only your mother would simmer down a bit. She makes even little tasks difficult.

Say hi to Maria and Gus and to Beery and Captain Lancaster. I sure wish I was back there with you.

How's the weather? It is glorious here. Did you get a room? Did the keys fit, or did you find yours?

Much love and thoughts,
Elin

Philadelphia, Pennsylvania
September 19, 1967

Dear Jack,

Remember this? I get a small tear in my eye when I remember beautiful Monterey Peninsula., but we'll get there again.

Bill and I never made it to Mexico. The airline and the Mexican consulate told me that I could get a tourist card issued at the airport. When we got there only U.S. citizens could get it. It was Sunday, and Monday was Labor Day, so we couldn't wait until Tuesday. Bill only had 2 weeks leave, so we started driving – for the next 2500 miles. Then we came up the Atlantic coast and stayed at Myrtle Beach – had our only sun there, so stayed an extra day. Really swell there, then on up over the Chesapeake Bay Bridge – some bridge – huge, and then up thru desolate Delaware. Really surprised Bill that it is so deserted, and on home. Got a dozen fresh white sweet corn and mmm, are they good. I never had them before.

Mike and Kathy cook just great. Kathy is blossoming out – real motherly looking.

We were here one week and Bill flew off to Texas yesterday, and in a couple of weeks he will go on further. I'll miss that great smile of his everyday, but I think of you and it seems you only left yesterday and I tell myself – a year goes fast – ne ce pas (sic spelling) – ha ha ha!

Loved your tape – sounds like you and yet is sounds more like a man. I guess one grows up in the type of things you are involved in. I'm getting a box ready for you, but things have been hectic for some months now.

The morning Bill flew off Charlie was transferred out of the hospital to a nursing home. He is steadily improving from a week ago when he looked pretty bad.

I'll be here for a couple of months and help work something out. It will all work so don't you worry – OK?

I think about you all the time. We got the pictures developed and I'm anxious to see them.

Take care now.

Love Elin

P.S. Would you like some soap for cold water? You need anything?

Fort Hood, Texas
September 20, 1967

Dear Elin,

How's my honey? Things are relatively placid here. Uncle Joe & Terrible Tom both on leave, and things in AG running smoothly. Payant did a good job of controlling things & now it's just a few last minute items to resolve.

I got your travel pay and dislocation allowance today - $281.00!! So - here is $200 of it toward your fare to Denmark. I am keeping the rest so I won't need much out of next month's pay. My pay for this month will go to the bank as usual (should be $500 +. I will let you know exact amount). Starting on 31 October there will be a check to the bank for $600.00. I am doing this initially until I get over there. Then will see about Soldiers Deposits (10% interest). This is what I'll be getting as a Major:

Base pay	$656.00
Subsistence	47.88
Quarters	140.00
Hostile pay	65.00
Family Separation	30.00
Total	$938.88
Out of this comes:	
Insurance	$27.76
Social Security	27.87
*Bond	6.25
	$61.88

*I cancelled the $50 bond & will get a $25 bond every 3 months.

The advance pay won't be paid until October so I will start getting $877.00 on 30 November. You'll have to see how much you'll need & I'll put the rest in Soldiers Deposits and get 10%. We should easily save $5,000 to $6,000. I figure that after November we should be able to put away $500 a month. Let me know what you think.

We (Payant & I) went to Browns for dinner last night. Jane is home & must be off her feet for 6 weeks. She asked to be remembered to you. Payant just took off for a few days in Florida (I relented & let him go since he did such a good job while I was gone). So Brown let me use his other car, which Payant had been driving. A jazzed up 1967 Chevrolet with air conditioning, etc.

On Saturday I am going to the Youngs for dinner.

They expect high winds resulting from the hurricane to hit Austin tonight, so we may get a little backlash here. I am in a tiny BOQ room, but it doesn't matter. By this Saturday I have to have my two foot lockers packed & taken in. So there won't be much left except what I'll carry.

I am really intrigued with Eric Hoffer (I mentioned that we watched a TV special on him last night) and will try to get hold of his books. His philosophy is right along our lines, & he makes more sense about all issues than anyone else I've heard recently.

Got a Club bill for $51.75 - which I am writing a check for tonight.

Got into a battle with Bittrich as soon as I got back. Seems he had been conniving to get Berry as his company clerk. I just about told him to go to hell and he threw a "temper tantrum" - this guy has problems. He reacts like a child when he doesn't get his way. Thank God he'll be transferred out when he gets promoted.

It's so delightful around the Headquarters with Major Hurt gone, I can't believe it. Colonel Waldie sits in isolation all day and never says a word (both good & bad!). But - many are on leave now & things are packed and gone - so there's not that much to do (except for AG!).

How is Uncle Charlie reacting in the home? Tell him I was asking for him.

Give my love to Mother. I'm sure that you will get along now! Anyway I know you are trying.

I'll probably call this weekend - Take care -

Love
Bill

Minneapolis, Minnesota
September 21, 1967

Dear Elin,

I was glad to hear from you and happy to hear you would be staying in Philadelphia for a while.

Last Saturday afternoon Kirsten and Tom came and picked me up. We went to Lake Calhoun right here in the city. We walked around for a while and munched on vanilla ice cream cones. Then Tom dropped Kirsten and I off at their apartment while he went back to fish a little. Tom is a real sweet person. I think Kirsten made a good match. Kirsten and I sat and chatted for a while over coffee and cake. Kirsten looked so different to me after not seeing her for five or six years. It was wonderful seeing her again. The two of us thought how great it would be if you could come out to see us.

This weekend I am going to a rodeo. I'm really looking forward to it after getting my first glance at the one we went to in Montana. It should be fun.

My studies are still coming along fine. The longer I'm here, the more interested I become with the airlines. I only hope I will be able to get a job upon graduation.

Well, dinner's just about ready. Tonight we're having beef stew, and I'm starved!

Take care.

Love,
Joan

Minneapolis, Minnesota
September 21, 1967

Dear Mrs. Fulmer,

So Joan and I finally got together and it was fun talking to her. I think we both felt it was strange being here in the same town, she really looks good, and she seems to be happy about being here. The rules in the school sound very much like my time in Heidelberg.

I'm awfully sorry that Uncle Charlie is so ill, give him my best regards. I had a letter from Elin and Bill has left now. I hope Elin will still be there when we get back East.

We bought a Japanese tea set with your present, so when you come to our house some day you can see it. The cups have no handles. They are ceramic and double on the sides so they don't get too hot to hold, also the bottom does not get hot, so you can put it right on the table. I have even used them for soup and ice cream because they don't look like a cup.

I hope to see you when we get back so you can meet Tom. Joan and I have already made plans about her visiting me in New York at Christmas time.

Best regards
Kirsten

Fort Hood, Texas
September 22, 1967

Dear Jack,

Well, here I am back at Hood – after two weeks of leave – the last spent in Phila. Elin may have written you by now so this may be repetitious. We drove the Southern route to New Orleans – then along the Gulf Coast, through Mississippi. Ate lunch in Biloxi and thought of you. Stayed in Florida a few days (all of this in the rain!). Finally found sun for a few days in Myrtle Beach, S.C. – then drove to Phila.

Uncle Charlie had been in the hospital for two weeks when we arrived. Has just a gradual deterioration due to old age – arterial sclerosis. He is almost paralyzed on one side and wanders in his mind. Anyway we decided that the best thing to do at the moment was to put him in a nursing home, which was done last Monday (the day I left). He needs constant care and is too much to be handled at 1214 H. Mother has been quite upset by all this but I think we got her calmed down and accepting the fact that he is better off outside the house and with nursing care as long as he is incapacitated. I doubt if he will ever get better.

Elin is going to stay in Phila. until December when she plans to go to Denmark. I hope she and Mother will get along!!! It should be interesting. We didn't do much or see many people in Phila. I didn't feel like it. We did see Mike and Kathy (they came to Frankford and stayed overnight) and we had a good time together. Then Mike came down again the night before I left, and he drove Elin to the airport with me. He seems a lot better after his operation, and Kathy is doing well and getting bigger.

Went to Bob Hamilton's one night with Mother. The Pillers were there and we had a good evening of conversation.

I've got about 2 weeks, then will fly over. Hopefully I can get an R&R or leave to Bangkok before you leave next year and we can get together. I realize that the chances of both you and I getting off at the same time will be slim – but we'll see.

We heard your tape, and enjoyed it very much. Also enjoyed your letter and the pictures. You must be turning into a camera bug. Some of your pictures are excellent I think. I'm still plodding along with my Kodak Instamatic, but may get something good in RVN. What kind of a camera did you buy? I also got your slides developed. We looked through them hurriedly (not on the screen) and they look terrific.

Things are rather quiet here in the brigade right now – everything packed and ready to go. After the hectic pace of the past 3 months it's a welcome change.

Talked to Joan on the phone and she sounds great. I think this stint in Minneapolis is the best thing that's happened to her. Kirsten and Tom just got back to Minneapolis and Kirsten was getting together with Joan for lunch last week I think.

You sounded great on the tape – I'm sure you're having quite an experience there, both with your position and all the emotions and ramifications attached, and by virtue of being in Thailand.

Well, I probably won't write again until I'm about 10,000 miles closer – so take care.

Bill

Fort Hood, Texas
September 28, 1967

Dear Elin,

Happy first anniversary of the week! "The Lost Week." We'll make it up next year!

Been working like a dog all week - midnight hours again getting things finalized to leave next week, much coordinating, etc. Haven't even gotten to celebrate my promotion yet - but don't really care. These things here are really going so fast (got to find time to mail my suit back).

Actually things in the section are in good shape considering the tremendous effort & mountainous task the men have had to go through to get ready. It will be a relief for them to get on the boat or plane out of here. A lot of our (AG) problems will be left behind. As I said on the phone, went to the Youngs for dinner on Saturday & really enjoyed it. They have a lovely home & we had a good conversation & dinner. Stopped by Maria's and Gus' on Sunday and stayed for dinner. Will try to see them once more before leaving. Also saw Alice Miller in the PX parking lot. She & Ed wanted to have me over but don't think I can. It's been great with Major Hurt gone! I get along real well with Trexler but "Uncle" Joe will be back tomorrow.

I dyed all of my underwear green, now I've got so much green underwear I don't think I'll ever use it.

How are you getting along - really? I worry about it. I won't stand for you getting into an emotional state by thinking you have to stay in Philadelphia longer than planned & I mean it! Take heed! You owe it to Mor and Far to spend some months in Denmark. As long as Uncle Charlie is able to help himself a bit and is not restricted to a bed, but otherwise he should be under care (I think however, he'll do more with you around than before!).

This is an uninteresting letter because I'm tired - will do better later. You know what the routine is here anyway.

I love you honey and miss you & I know you are putting up with the whole situation tremendously.

Love
Bill

Washington D.C.
October 1, 1967

Darling,

We are at the DeNios' getting ready to go to church. Yesterday we saw "Funny Girl" with Carol Lawrence. I saw Mount Vernon and the city by night. I wouldn't mind being stationed here. Jean's parents had us over for a lovely dinner yesterday. I'm really having a good time - only I do wish you were here. Well my love, we made six years in the next six days. If the next six fly as fast we will be old before we know it. Really we do have something great and outstanding going for us. Isn't love great.

I'll stay here a week and might see the Painters and Duncans, etc. Will visit Karen and Mike tomorrow. The Pentagon is huge. This city is beautiful.

Take care now and remember I love you.
Elin

Spokane, Washington
October 1, 1967

Dear Elin & Bill,

Where is Bill now? I feel so badly you have to live apart - life is much to short for that. My prayers for his safety will be said every day. Somehow the year does pass - for now we just live one day at a time.

It is good you are staying on at Beth's for support for her now with Charlie ill. Age is such a sad state but we all must face it. Is Joan living at home now? Maybe Bill & Jack will get to see each other. Tim was in Thailand twice that year he was in Vietnam. Joan seems to be improving & thus, now no more troubles, but she is being very careful & not going to do a single thing outside her house this year, & Tim and the boys help her with her work.

We've been having some bad dust storms - it is still pretty dry in the Northwest and they cause hay fever trouble for me.

I'm teaching six weeks of foreign foods classes right now. It is much work but I enjoy it. I am with Suzie Jack often. They are very good friends. But for the first time in my life I am not making new friends. It seems everyone is either far left or far right - so I do not want anything to do with either - and feel if I just keep away I won't get involved with either group. I hope. I've never seen so many mixed up people as today. Of course this is not just in America - but all over most of the world. I do wish I could help straighten out things.

Write to me soon and do send Bill's address.

Much love,
Hazel

Elin with Hazel Clawson in Carmel

The following letter was started in Philadelphia on September 27th,
but not finished until after Elin arrived in Washington.

Washington D.C.
October 4, 1967

Dear Bill -

Things have really picked up - Friday and Saturday we were out. Friday night we drove up to your Nana's in Trucksville. She is just fabulous and except for being a little thinner, she looks great. Still does Justice of the Peace work. Not the really nasty cases, but easy ones. I got a chamber pot in white porcelain that she had behind the furnace in the basement. Real wild, I love it. Also got an old canning jar, large and still had juice in it from about 1920.

On the way back we stopped and had dinner at Mike and Kathy's. They have a real cute place, fixed up nicely, and she set a lovely table. She is not too much of a cook, but time will teach her. The dress I bought didn't fit her so I brought it back and on Tuesday had my first trip downtown. Took the el, it is all right but I wouldn't want to do it every day. I found another dress and found two pairs of shoes for me. Also ordered a fake hair piece for me - a fall. If you can get one, I'd love a wig.,. if anyone goes to where you can buy them. I'll send a lock of my hair later on.

Mel and Jean picked me up on Thursday. I really am enjoying seeing them and seeing the Urettes. They both have nice places. I miss you a lot and was very frustrated to think I couldn't talk to you while you were still in the States.

I do hope we can celebrate our next anniversary together, but I'm not sure we can, is it 13 months or an even 12 months?

Love you
Elin

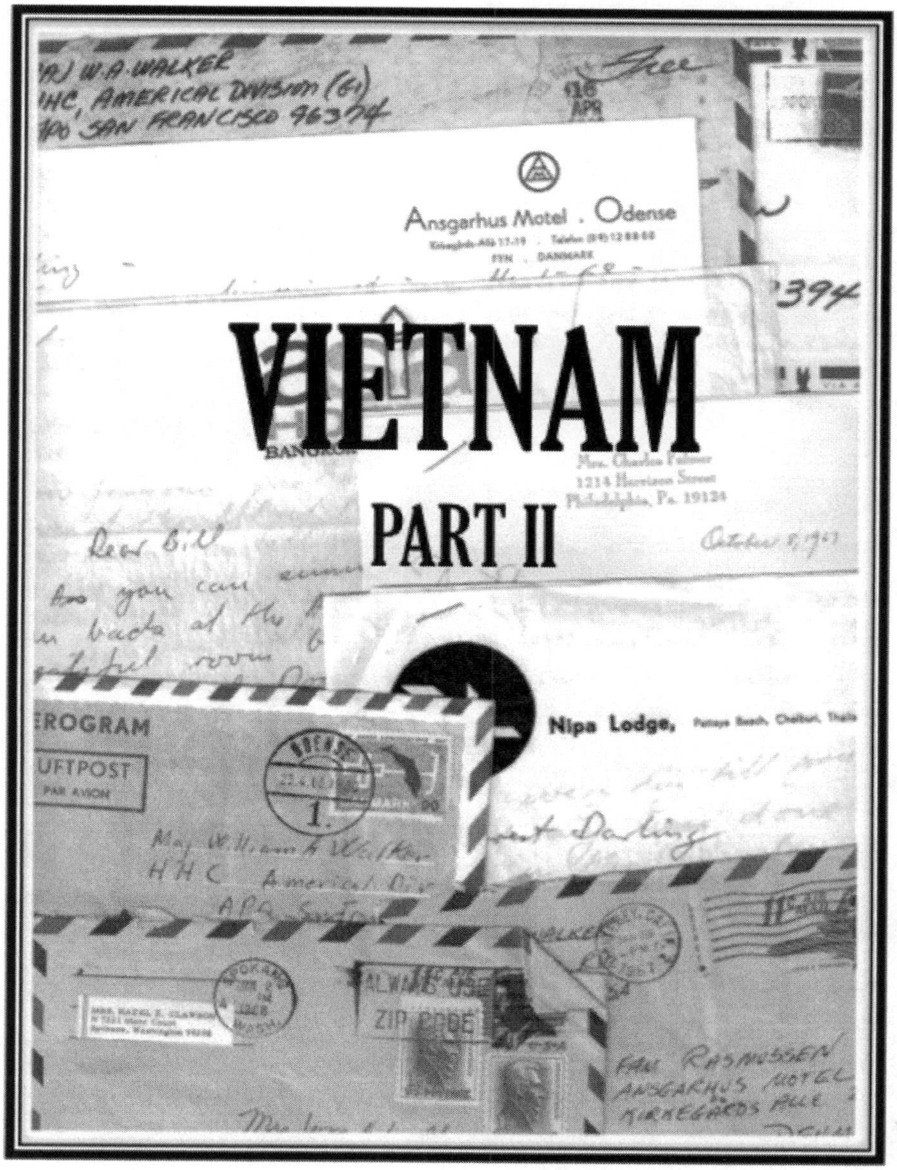
VIETNAM
PART II
Ansgarhus Motel . Odense
Nipa Lodge,
ZIP CODE

Enroute to Vietnam
Travis Air Force Base

Lieutenant Yates on right

Washington, D.C.
October 6, 1967

Dear Bill,

When you receive this you will already have been in Vietnam one whole week. Yesterday we visited Kennedy's grave - it is done beautifully and there were huge crowds there. I cried to think how different things would have been had he lived. Then we had a quiet night at home. Today we are going to the ballet.

I was very upset about my visit to the Urettes'. She is still sweet, but Mike ignored me, and was griping about gnats, the Army, etc. It sure was discouraging, and until he changes, they can sit and stew in their unhappiness.

I called Kirsten and Tom last night. They want me to come visit them. It seems they don't know for sure when they will be back here. I sure am enjoying my new clothes, especially traveling around. It's nice to look right all of the time. I got two new pairs of shoes, and I'll get new slips, etc.

Jean really shopped wisely in Vietnam - all very tasteful and nice things that look nothing too oriental. He got a modern teakwood screen that is just fabulous. He also bought some plain brass flatware, real nice, and some every-day stainless. He got an old fashioned phone from Hong Kong that I just love.

I think I'll write almost every day if you want a lot of chi chat, or maybe you would rather I didn't tell you about all of the little traumas of every day living. Bill, I'll really miss you and I think about you constantly. This, I guess, will be the hardest year of our marriage.

Next Sunday Mel and Jean are having a party -- the Painters who are in D.C., the Coops, Lyndy, and the Duncans, so I should get a lot of poop on how it is to be an AG officer over there.

I must run now - love you dearly and miss you.

Elin

Wake Island, Pacific
October 7, 1967

Dear Elin,

14 hours of flying so far & we've gained 9 hours. Next, brief stop in Philippines - then on to Nam. Called the Welters when we stopped at Travis.

Love Bill

Wake Island, Pacific
October 7, 1967

Dear Mother,

We're flying in a huge Air Force jet - C141. Anxious to complete this long trip. Say hello to Uncle Charlie.

Love Bill

Washington, D.C.
October 8, 1967

Dear Far and Mor

I am behind with my letter writing.

Bill was made Major on September 26, and October 7, our wedding date, he flew to Saigon. He should be there by now. I cried the last time I talked to him, but by now I have regained my composure.

I am in Washington, D.C. visiting friends from before - the DeNios. We have known them since 1961. He is a Major, just returned from Vietnam. Bill and he went to school together in Indiana. Now after dinner, we are going to the ballet. Last week we saw "Funny Girl." Next week we are going to visit the White House and Congress. It is all very interesting.

I called Kirsten and Tom. It looks like they will stay longer in Minneapolis. They want me to visit but it is so far, I don't know about that.

Mor I have sent a package. The red grapes are your birthday gift. I have made them from scratch. There are also two old dresses, and some spices. Don't pay customs on the spices. If it presents a problem let them confiscate them, but not your present. It's a pretty big box so I hope it arrives in good condition.

Would you prefer I come before or after Christmas? If Kirsten doesn't come to the east coast, I better visit them, or what do you think?

I feel fine and my health is glowing, only a little too heavy,

Yesterday I visited Kennedy's grave. It is so sad that he is not President. It seems like it would be easier if he were directing the war.

Stay well and I'm sorry I'm so slow with my letters.

Loving regards
Elin

Philadelphia, Pennsylvania
October 8, 1967

Dear Elin,

Washington is a great place and I can see you have fallen under its spell! It is really one of the outstanding cities in the United States. To be there and get into the White House and Congress, is the only way to really appreciate it. Your host and hostess are giving you the best.

Bill called me Friday night after he had talked to you. He said you both cried and then we both wept and it was all very sad. I cried most of the night and I was thinking probably you were doing the same thing. He said several times that he was glad we weren't there to see the troops go because it was so emotional. Do you know I can remember seeing the long troop trains taking soldiers to France in 1917? Then it was very exciting because the men sang and laughed. The young boys didn't know what they were getting into. But today our youth know well what lies ahead. Due to radio and television, they see graphic examples of war.

On Thursday afternoon, I visited Charlie and then drove to Limeport to see Kathy and Michael. I took the dresses and they both fit perfectly. In fact Kathy wore the blue the next day when we drove up the mountain to see my mother. She loves the dresses. It was very kind of you to get them for her.

Now it is Sunday evening. I have just returned from spending two hours with Charlie. He looked well and was dressed in a clean white shirt and a striped tie. He was listening to the football game alternating with the Cardinal and Red Sox baseball game. He has made friends with the white haired gentleman who sits across from him. Last he introduced me to him, a Mr. Evan.

You have mail from Kirsten, Hazel, etc. If you want me to forward it, please advise. I am sorry I didn't have your address to congratulate you on your anniversary. I shall make it up to you later.

Tuesday night I am going to dinner and the theater, "How Now Don Jones." It is the first of the season for my Theater Guild so I am hoping it will be good.

Janice spent last weekend in Minneapolis with Joan. They had a great time. Joan had several dates lined up for them, then Janice stopped off in Chicago to visit Uncle Loren and Aunt Kay. You know she likes Tom Williams. She also reported that Uncle Herb is feeling better but still hospitalized.

You are very welcome to have your friends here. In fact, if you need my bedroom, I can sleep with friends. It surely must be interesting and fun to meet again after an interval of being in other places. Have a good time and see all that you can.

Love,
Mother

                                        Chu Lai, Vietnam
                                        October 10, 1967

Dear Elin,

Well Honey, I'm here. Too short a time to assimilate any profound theories or statements on anything, except that it is a unique atmosphere so far. At present we are staying right on the beach at Chu Lai. A beautiful beach I might add. However the air is filled like birds with helicopters and jets. This area is quite secure. A huge complex, however not so nice in the mountains, which we can see, are supposedly infested with VC. Haven't seen many Vietnamese except for small groups of laborers, under guard within the complex.

As I suspected, the Americal Division is going to absorb the AG, Finance, and SJA sections, along with some other things and make a big Division headquarters. The Division AG seems very nice. At the moment they think I'll be the PSD chief, with Dove as assistant, and about 250 men. Actually I'm not sorry about that at all. The Division headquarters is about 4 miles from here, on the coast in a well built up American military area. Uncle Joe is of course very upset by the whole thing (he needs "experts" around him all of the time because he can't function too well alone). But after talking with the Division G1 and AG there is nothing more to be said. This is just all in the planning stages - will write more about developments as they come.

We had a long uneventful trip over. Stopped at Travis AFB, Wake Island & Clarke AFB in the Philippines. Didn't see anything any else then flew directly here to Chu Lai & haven't been outside the base. Will probably have to go to Da Nang & Saigon in the near future for coordination & information, etc., but I don't anticipate moving around any more than I have to.

We are not in tents but in frame, makeshift buildings with screened sides and metal roofs - "hooches." It's relatively cool at night right on the ocean. The real hot weather is finished until January. Of course it is still hot. Also the northern monsoons are about to begin, which will deluge this place with rain. Actually it should be bearable. Once I find out & get settled in a permanent place will start looking for ways to set up some comforts.

Hope your stay in D.C. was (is) fun. I didn't want you sitting around moping!! So it's good to be with friends & have some fun this year. I'll be very busy once things get started & won't have time to get that lonely - but you know I miss you very much & love you the same!

Love
Bill

South China Beach

View of South China Sea

Our hooch on the beach

Chu Lai, Vietnam
October 10, 1967

Dear Mother,

It always amazes me - even with all the traveling I've done that you can be transported physically & mentally into such extremes. I haven't been here long enough - 30 hours - to make any assessment (that will come later) but we are right on the beach at Chu Lai, part of a huge U.S. base. The coast is beautiful but the long beaches are filled with planes, trucks, tents, etc. The air is full of planes and the coastal mountains, which look so scenic, of Viet Cong! Nevertheless this is a very secure area and as far as my section is concerned we will remain in relative security. Not so for the infantry units which will sooner or later be in the surrounding areas.

This will be just a short letter - to let you know I got here, etc. Will write more details when I find out and observe more.

Hope things are going well. Say hello to Uncle Charlie.

Love
Bill

Washington, D.C.
October 10, 1967

Dear Bill,

Yesterday we did the Capitol. Saw Congress in session and the Senate. The most interesting was seeing the Supreme Court, all but one judge were on the bench. A bunch of smart judges they are, they ask very penetrating questions.

I taught Desiree and Dione how to make Mexican flowers, and even little Desiree made real pretty ones. Really surprised me.

Today it is rain and drizzle. Tomorrow we are going to a lunch with Jean's mother at some fancy restaurant, lunch and a fashion show.

Remember Gene Brown, married to Jane. They had three beautiful boys. Well they got a divorce when he was in Vietnam. Quite shocking. We will see him Sunday. Painters, Duncans and Coops are coming too. Maybe Ned and Bridget if they get back in time from Philadelphia. They are going up to celebrate Josephine's birthday, and they are moving into a new apartment.

I really, really could be happy in Washington. A fascinating city. I have already picked out a couple of neat areas - one is Georgetown, right next to downtown and within walking distance to American University. But Ned did say that the small town houses there start at $40 thousand. I guess that won't be the place then. This town has to be the neatest on the East coast. It's very clean and neat. They are really moving here on urban renewal. Why not try for this place after Vietnam. Please not some distant place. I'll never become a citizen then. Lots of interesting jobs around here.

The DeNios are hanging pictures and curtain rods. Kind of a homey feeling remembering how often we have done that. I am eagerly awaiting word about where you are going. Jean thinks he knows exactly. We have wild arguments over that.

On the radio they said an additional 40,000 men were going into the Marine area around the DMZ. It sounded like maybe they were talking about the 198th.   How is everyone taking things - how is the heat - how is my love adjusting to war. I get a stomach ache thinking about it.

I think of you constantly.

Love Elin

Capitol Building, Washington D.C. - 1967

Jean and Mel DeNio

Chu Lai, Vietnam
October 11, 1967

Dear Elin,

Seems like we've been here longer than 3 days. Still not in any routine yet. Things still somewhat unsettled as to just where and when the Division deal will take place.

Went to the 196th brigade headquarters - about 5 miles from here - today. They are responsible for securing the Chu Lai area. It's really very pretty, with the exception of the tremendous evidence of U.S. presence all along the beaches. Vehicles, ammunition dumps, etc. Saw lots of Vietnamese today all along the roads going to the 196th. Mostly younger children tending cows, etc. The heat is stifling and this is the cool season. Just before the Northeastern Monsoons. They say in the summer it gets up to 135 degrees F! I guess you get used to it, however everything is damp all of the time. They were right about the water. It has to have so much chlorine in it that it tastes unbearable. You'll have to keep me stocked in kool aid. My foot locker has some in it and I should get them tomorrow. Although these buildings we are in have electricity from a central generator, it is even more sophisticated at Americal Division Headquarters where I'll probably be going.

Next day: Not much happening today. Now going over to Division in the afternoons to do some coordinating.

- at night: 12 Oct 67

This is a disjointed letter! Now I'll finish it. Had a good afternoon. Went to Division and made arrangements to begin phasing in. Bittrich and his 4 men here are moving over tomorrow to start getting ready to receive our troops when they get off the boat. Actually it's a good set up. Fairly nice facilities -

flush toilets and showers in all the areas, just like a village. Well secured. The Deputy AG is Major Russ Powell. We went through the basic course together at Fort Harrison. A fine guy. I'm moving into his hooch - there are other majors in it and plenty of room. I've got to get a refrigerator when I get situated over there. I may be able to pick one up from someone who is leaving. My foot lockers arrived today - all OK, but I'm not setting anything here because I'll be moving probably in a week or so.

Dove and I may go to Saigon next week. I have to go to Cameron Bay on postal business & will include Saigon to do some coordinating. Also anxious to see all of the people I know there.

Think I'll go to bed early tonight. Will write more later. I guess you are still in D.C. & I don't have DeNio's address. Hope everything is going well. Much love honey - I miss you.

Bill

Movie theater

Showers

Washington, D.C.
October 11, 1967

Dear Bill,

Last night Mel, Jean, and I sat up till 3 o'clock gabbing mostly about VN. Jean had more tales to tell. One of his friends got malaria. He threw his netting away and I guess the mosquitos are microscopic, and he was bitten. He had two attacks stateside. Not a thing to do for it either. Apparently it resists all medicine. One fellow was at a drunk party in a hut, given for him. He got so drunk and involved in some unbecoming behavior that he had to get out of the Army. He was considered a security risk, and in his branch he had to be in on the top. It seems a shame that one night of drinking can ruin an otherwise fine officer.

Also Jean said that the people who were most likely to get hurt were those treating Vietnam like a game, not taking everything seriously, and letting their guard down. I hope your men will look out for themselves.

Jean has changed a lot. He is very calm now and quite interesting to be with. Their home is also the loveliest and most tasteful it has ever been. I'm glad I could be here these first weeks. Somehow it helps to talk about all of the changes, and face them. And, you know Mel is good for one as she is calm and not sensational.

Wasn't your mother's letter to me nice? I really think my yelling once has cleared the air. I really think we will become great, great friends. We do have a lot in common you know.

Kirsten and Joan want me to go to Minneapolis. What do you think? I'll write more later. I'm making a short timers calendar. Would you believe I'm 5 down and 360 to go.

Love always - hugs and kisses.
Elin

*Elin with Jean and Mel DeNio & children (Dionne, Desiree & David)
in their Washington D.C. apartment*

Chu Lai, Vietnam
October 14, 1967

Dear Mother,

Instead of being thrust into the midst of a war, we seem to be in some sort of relaxed recreation area! Not that there isn't a tremendous amount of activity here. The Chu Lai base camp is extensive with thousands of troops here within the perimeter. Many go out on operations from here and there is a continual flux of units. Nevertheless here we sit on the beach. This of course will change considerably once the main body of the brigade arrives next week. My section is apparently going to be integrated with the Americal Division Headquarters. So it appears that I'll be right here in Chu Lai. The division headquarters area is built up and living conditions are good. Flush toilets, showers and wooden buildings for working and living and a beautiful beach down the road.

Saw Martha Raye today. She and a troupe put on a little "Hello Dolly" extract. She's quite a trouper and the thousands of troops here in the outdoor amphitheater really cheered her on.

I haven't seen anything of Vietnam except a 5 mile area here by the coast. Next week will try to get to Saigon and Cameron Bay to do some coordinating. Have many friends stationed in Saigon who I am anxious to see. Lots of lizards around here - some quite large and colorful. Also many rats, not so colorful!

The monsoons are about to begin - today we had torrential rain for about an hour or so. They will get worse. The day before I arrived they had a typhoon here that washed out roads, buildings, etc. Went swimming in the ocean today - beautiful.

Anxious to hear how everything is working out. How Uncle Charlie is doing and whether he'll be at home or remain in the nursing home. This year will go fast for me. Once we get settled and go through some changes in configuration it will be half gone!

Take care - and much love.
Bill

Martha Raye with the troops

Chu Lai, Vietnam
October 14, 1967

Dear Elin,

The monsoon rains started this evening - torrential rains lasting about an hour - more of this to come. Very difficult to adjust to what is going on. Tremendous amount of activity here. Thousands of troops, much equipment, vehicles, planes, etc. But a very loose atmosphere, very unlike the strictly disciplined bases we've been familiar with.

Went swimming in the ocean today - really delightful & plan to do it every day while we are here on the beach.

The biggest thing anyone has done here so far is alleviating the beer & soda crisis, and then Major Hurt got involved in it and fouled everything up. Seems beer is in short supply because of a dock strike someplace. Since we don't have an account with the PX yet, the Brigade couldn't get credit for beer when a ship did come in with a load the other day. So the officers and NCOs put up $1,300 in cash to buy a load. Then Major Hurt got into it and held up the sale because of some hair-brained scheme and it wasn't until today - two days later that we were able to buy it. However, a lot of the Brigade personnel moved out of here today before they could get the beer. Now some of the backers are left with about 300 unsold cases!

Saw Martha Raye today. She was here with a "Hello Dolly" show. The troops really seemed to appreciate it. If it doesn't seem like I'm in a war, you're right; however there are VC not too far from here, outside the sector, although it is so huge that we are virtually isolated from the outside. The rest of the Brigade is going to another area for the present which does have a lot of VC activity. Before long some of the units are bound to get into some firefights. We can hear mortars at night off in the mountains & occasionally see flares, etc. We have some Vietnamese laborers in the camp. They are hired by the day for various clean-up work, mostly old men and women and young girls. Also the barbers are Vietnamese. Sgt Helford took Beery over to Americal Division headquarters to get a haircut, but when Berry saw the Vietnamese barber sharpening his razor, he wouldn't get a haircut!

There are all kinds of rats and lizards here. The lizards are huge and quite colorful (I'll try to get a picture of one). They crawl all over the tin roof at night. In the morning there are rat tracks in the sand everywhere. They are going to try to eliminate the rats. There was a plague epidemic here several months ago. In fact the diseases here are a serious problem and you have to take malaria pills every day and watch cleanliness. We have an outdoor shower right near the hooch. They burn out the contents in the crappers daily with diesel fuel. One sergeant, who is in charge of the burn detail said "When my children ask me years later if I was in the war - I'm going to say "Yes son, I did my part" - and when he asks "what did you do?" I'm going to have to say "Son, I burned shit for a year!"

I bought some booze at the PX and had martinis last night. Incidentally my September pay went to the bank - $542 - I wrote a $50 check at Fort Hood before I left and another $50 here yesterday. This month's pay will go to the bank ($600 I think) and I'll put the rest in Soldiers Deposits. Then you'll have to decide how much you will need each month. I'll be drawing a gross of $943.00 a month. The only deductions are $27 insurance; FICA tax - about $26 and bond $6.00 (I cancelled the $50 bond). I don't have to pay income tax on the first $500 of base pay. I'll pay what I owe on income tax at the end of the year and let the money get interest now. We should make out good financially.

Anxious to hear from you. We haven't gotten any mail in yet for the Brigade but expect some soon. Starting to rain again so will get to my hooch.

Much love- Bill

Young day laborers at camp

Chu Lai, Vietnam
October 14, 1967

Dear Jack,

Made it here last week, and at the moment we are ensconced on the beach at Chu Lai. Only a small portion of the brigade came by plane. The rest arrive by boat in the near future. I'll probably stay right here in Chu Lai – not at all bad. The coast is lovely. Of course there is a tremendous amount of activity. This sector is relatively secure and we are in the middle of a huge U.S. base camp.

I expect to go to Saigon and Cameroon Bay next week to do some coordinating and see quite a few people I know.

Right now we're feeling the beginning of the northeastern monsoon – high winds and torrential rain, but the weather is sporadic. Went swimming today – delightful.

Hope everything is going well over there. I'll try to take my R&R in Bangkok and maybe get to see you before you leave next year (March, I believe?).

I'll make this short and write more when I find out what in the hell I'm doing (things are continuing work-wise at the moment – all everyone is concerned about is the beer supply).

Bill

Bill near main officers' club

Outside main officers' club on bluff overlooking the sea

Washington, D.C.
October 15, 1967

Hi Honey,

By now I'm eagerly awaiting news from you. I figured I should have a letter next week.

It is Sunday and we are all ready, awaiting 36 people for open house. The table looks beautiful. Jean got lots of brass in VN - a tall brass candlestick, several lovely brass pots, and we are doing the whole table in brass. I made huge Mexican flowers that we have arranged going up the large candlestick. Our colors are orange, yellow, turquoise and blue. Real colorful and very effective. Jean is making one hot punch - glogg - and one cold champagne punch, something like yours. We have made sweet and sour meatballs, cream puffs filled with tuna, my crab mold dip, hot bean dip and Danish blue cheese vegetable dip. Is this all making you sick? Well honey I'm sick too that you are not here.

I have slept very badly this week. I keep waking up all tense, something I've never done before. I don't allow myself any self pity, but I do so miss you. It even hurts to watch love scenes on TV. How bad can it get.

Friday, Mel and I went to the National Art Gallery, a fabulous collection they have. I saw a picture by Salvador Dali, one of The Last Supper. Very moving. Also a picture called "Music" painted in 1910, in mood and style it reminded me of yours. We also visited the National Archives. Saw the original Constitution, Declaration of Independence, and The Bill of Rights.

Honey please write and tell me what all you are interested in me telling you. I'm giving you lots of tiny details, but what else can I write about if this bothers you. I can write more broad letters but I don't know what you would rather hear about.

We had a skaal the other night in Akvavit to you. You are very much here in spirit, believe me.

The Urettes aren't coming. Seems we have a real rift. Also she said he has to tell tomorrow how he decided whether or not to take a two year assignment with family in the Congo, or go to Vietnam in June. Some choice. Both are undesirable.

Must close now, we have to get ready. All my love - hugs and kisses.

Love
Elin

Philadelphia, Pennsylvania
October 15, 1967

Dear Bill,

I received your card from Wake Island (you wrote as though tired and I remembered my tiredness after flying 13 hours) and then I read the Atlas to find that obscure island. How marvelous is the navigation today that one can fly over the vast Pacific Ocean and find a tiny spot to land - such as Wake Island! Of course it is probably a fairly good size island when you see it but on the map it is barely a pin point!

I thought of you for days after you telephoned, wondering where you were at a given moment and also where you were going! That sentence is poor! But I'm sure you get the trend of my thinking!

Today has been a quiet Sunday. No roast in the oven for one person. Instead I ate a hard boiled egg salad for my dinner! Isn't that gruesome? But Michael called toward evening and I called Joan later so I have talked with family!

Elin returns Wednesday and I will be glad to have company again. I will try to plan some excursions for us so she can meet some of our relatives and friends. Major DeNio and his wife will stay here Wednesday night.

Uncle Charlie enjoyed the World Series and now listens eagerly to the Eagles football games. When I visited him this afternoon he barely said anything to me except facts concerning the game which he had tuned in during my time there. It was really funny but now I realize that he always did that. Joan used to fuss on Sunday afternoons when the T.V. had one game on and the radio broadcast another! Charlie would follow them both.

Jo Walker called and invited Elin and me to dinner on the 24th of this month. She has an apartment right across the street from school in Radnor.

Aunt Rosabelle called and said Dale has had a baby girl and Aunt Helen has gone to Texas to be with her a while. Nana was going to stay with Aunt Ruth if they can find room for her! Aunt Rosabelle thought they should take her to their home and I agree.

No news from Jack for several weeks. His Bangkok pictures are great.

Do take care, dear. Don't trust everyone! Guess I'll say good night and go sleep under that gay bedspread you bought me. Do I ever dream! Could it be the birds communicating!?!

My love always,
Mother

Washington, D.C.
October 17, 1967

Darling,

I'm down to 355.

Last night I spent having dinner with Ned and Brigit. You know how much I like him, well she is just great. We'll probably have more in common with them than anyone else. She was an AFS'er in 1960, has a great outlook on things, looks great, looks nice and intelligent. She has excellent taste and designs and makes her own clothes. Ned enjoys refinishing furniture. It wouldn't surprise me if they would become some of our best friends. I hope so anyway.

She lives in a tiny Georgetown house with two other girls. It is decorated with hand me downs. Georgetown has the Carmel atmosphere, and quite the place to live if one could afford it. I called the real estate agent about a modest looking place that was for sale - $79 thousand. Kind of kills you. Mel and I went to the White House today. We went through it twice - the first time there were thousands of New York high school kids, all very well dressed but loud, pushy, with no reverence for the place. Made me mad. Then we watched the official receiving of the Premier from Singapore. The gun salute and flags, the Marine Bugle Corps and all very, very colorful.

We leave for Philly tomorrow at 4 in the morning so I'm going to say good night to my love. I sure miss you.

When I have a whole day to myself I'll sit and write you pages and pages of thoughts, but I'm waiting for your reaction to Vietnam. I should have a letter tomorrow for sure, so far none, but it takes time I know.

Are you hungry for anything yet (other than me) - please send the SOS and I'll mail it pronto.

Love you deeply,
Elin

Chu Lai, Vietnam
October 18, 1967

Dear Elin,

Guess that you are back in Philadelphia by now. We have not gotten any mail in yet for the Brigade. Am anxious to hear from you, but will probably be another week before the mail starts reaching us here.

Today it is really blowing - sand all over everything. We expect a big storm tonight, ocean real rough. Have been going swimming every afternoon, except today and sitting around and drinking beer at night. Last night played bridge. The whole thing is rather frustrating at the moment. The Division AG expects us to come there as soon as the first of my section arrives on the 21st, but Hurt is insisting that I stay here for a period, and it is making things difficult. I told the Division AG 4 times that the Brigade commander would have to be told what the plan was. But so far everyone has been wishy-washy about the move. It's inevitable and I'm sitting here wasting time not accomplishing anything. Dove's ulcer acted up - bleeding, etc. and he is being evacuated to Japan for treatment or operation. This is unfortunate for all.

I'll be glad to get out of this brigade quite frankly. Most of the staff officers are out of it & the whole approach of the advance party is wrong. Most of them act rather petty.

After dinner:

Going to play bridge again tonight. Might as well take this interim period to relax a bit. Once things get going it's going to be back on the all day - all night routine. I'm going to have to organize a 300 man PSD & it's not going to be all roses. But I'm happy with this area (the Division headquarters is on a bluff overlooking the China Sea!). A lot of the infantry officers on the advance party are going out with units in VC infested areas on patrols, etc. So far we haven't had any injuries - even accidents but they are bound to come. I haven't been anywhere off the compound yet - but will get around later.

Well - off to my bridge game. Hope the mail comes in soon.

Much love
Bill

Chu Lai Beach – Brigade Surgeon with driver

Philadelphia, Pennsylvania
October 19, 1967

Dear Bill,

I guess I better reserve Darling, lover, etc. to the end in case you have to read letters in front of people. I'm answering 4 letters and one post card plus a package. Quite a lot all at once. Needless to say I'm thrilled to hear that you are well and in Chu Lai. Jean had told me all about it but I didn't believe it till you wrote. Sounds better than some places, but is it?

First my sweet thanks so much for the lovely gift. It will be perfect with my new black dress. I had it at Hood but never used it. I had to borrow some of Mother's jewelry for the dress -- now I don't need to anymore. It really is an exquisite pin and carving, very genuine. Who said you never gave me anything frilly. Your anniversary gift will have to wait till you come back. I found it down on Market and 40th Street. Mel and Jean and Desiree had to go down there about for Desiree's arm. We had left DC at 4 o'clock in the morning and arrived there at 9 o'clock. I didn't feel like asking Jean to drive me all the way to Frankford so I stayed with them. What an experience - Jean and I went junking. You wouldn't believe the characters, all half drunk. One woman wouldn't sell to us because the husband wanted to go to the races. He was leaving at 1 o'clock, and she told us to come back after 1 because he would try to sell us stuff and take the money with him, but she wouldn't let him. What a scene. We left them in a violent argument. Then we walked way down the street, many, many neat buys. I got a picture for you for the bedroom. Very Victorian. It is of a lovely lady - in fact it is a lovely drawing, only thing is she is topless. It is an oval mat and very elaborate frame. It's up to you to change the picture. One place had a lamp I'm very tempted to go back and get. It's $20 and of a baby boy angel holding a big white crystal bowl. Cast iron, very elaborate and big. But would we ever have a place for it in the bedroom? Also saw a very "camp" telephone stand and chair for $15. Jean really wanted to get it so we went to get Mel. She just about died, and poo-pooed the whole thing.

It's late at night and I'll finish off tomorrow. Good night my love.

October 20, 1967

Hi Love,

Back again. Well we left 40th Street. We saw two old wagons drawn by horses - right in Philly, can you imagine. One wagon looked 100 years old. On the way home we stopped at Independence Hall. They are really restoring it nicely. It was most interesting.

We got to Mother's house and I fixed lunch. Then I took the DeNios food shopping on the Avenue. Really reminded them of Europe. The butcher, Taddi's vegetables, the baker and all. We really enjoyed it. We went to the State Store and I asked for a bottle of Pinot Noir wine, and when I described it further the little man waiting on me said "Oh you mean Peanut Mir."

To home and I was all eager to have a festive Harrison Street dinner. Your mother had made arrangements with Rachel to go shopping for a coat. They left at 6 o'clock in torrential rain, and promised to be back by 7 o'clock. At a quarter to 8 we were starving and we started to eat an overcooked dinner. Jean mentioned that Western and Eastern hospitality sure differed. At 8:30 the sisters returned - no coat. We were through dessert by then, but it all got heated up. No one was too interested in questioning Jean on Vietnam. You see they know it's terrible and that is that. The next morning I had a nice breakfast. Your mother joined us for 10 minutes. That noon - she and Bob Hamilton went out for lunch. One really feels loved when I'm sitting here in solitude two blocks away.

I saw Uncle Charlie and he looks and acts his old self again, real cheerful and healthy looking. He can use a walker now and sits out in the front room all day and watches TV at night. The nurses aides are real good to him. He was moved to a nicer room with healthier people. They all get out of bed and get out of the room.

Yesterday your mother had a 15 years old boy point a loaded gun at her and the class. She got it away from him, and took the bullets out. That failed to convince her that life can be as dangerous in any place. She wants to send money to Jack because she thinks he needs it. He told her about his camera equipment, so he must be broke. I told her that he loaned his savings to a buddy. Won't these Walkers ever learn?

We acquired a $35 old chair that will take $50 to fix. It's ridiculous, but your mother felt sorry for the poor woman. Her son who is a doctor in the Navy, is getting married and she needs money for the wedding.

Bill - well I got it all off my chest. I got a letter from home, and they really want me to come and I feel I have to. Mor wants me home for Christmas. I feel I'm going. I can't handle myself around here as much as I try. Your mother is terribly upset about your being over there. She really was impressed with the DeNios. Desiree was real sweet and well behaved. She played with Joan's dolls. (The color TV was fixed for $220).

Please Honey, just burn this crummy letter, but I want you to help me. You never told Mother that you wanted me to go home, or did you? She wants me to get a job here and stay the winter. She doesn't say it outright, but she hints that I should get a job.

I transferred $1,000 to our savings, and paid all the bills. I also transferred some to an account here and closed out the one in California. That leaves $1,132 in savings, $578. In the Spokane account, and $200 here in Philadelphia. With the six next months I'll be in fine shape. Just send me $200 every month from then on and promise not to have lots of loose cash around. I'm sure there is a lot of stealing over there.

I'll write another long letter tomorrow. I'm really fine and in good spirits. The weather has turned nice and we might go to the mountains for the weekend.

Your description of "Uncle Joe" sounds typical. Maybe you will be much better off when you get away from him - or will you get away?

Actually love, this part of town is quite charming really. I love the atmosphere on Frankford Avenue. Real unique. Your mother looks great. She is relieved that Charlie isn't home, and guilty that she enjoys her freedom. But this is the best for her, since he bothers her so much.

Joan loves Minnesota. Kirsten and Tom are very active. He is studying Danish and she is taking a course about antiques, and swimming and exercises at the university. They go bike riding and celebrate the 14th every month. Kirsten wants me to come there. She even wants to send me the money. Out of the question, it's only $60. What do you think? I think she is lonely all day long by herself. I remember my first year and how horrible it was, just trying to adjust to my new routine. I'm glad that I did, because I never could find anyone I could be as happy with as you. You and I are just very, very special, and I feel we have something most people never achieve. I really should end this letter, but I get going and I don't want to stop.

We are moving a desk into this bedroom, the front that will give me a nice place to sit and write. It's almost like the one we have - the small gold one. Someone gave it to your mother.

The trees are all turning beautiful colors, and the wind is crisp. I imagine it couldn't be more remote than that to Vietnam. I feel for you in all that heat and rain. I really, really do, and I have you on my mind constantly.

Love - kisses and a million huge hugs –

Elin

Frankford Avenue

Philadelphia, Pennsylvania
October 20, 1967

Hi Darling,

I should warn you to disregard yesterday's letter and today's, since I'm having my monthly friend. Yesterday it was so bad I was in bed a lot. Almost like a miscarriage. I lost so much blood I thought I would faint.

Mother had invited Bob Hamilton for dinner, but wouldn't let me shop for food or cook. Then she got home and announced that she was taking us out to that little fish place. Bob was disappointed and we stood and waited 45 minutes for a table. The food was fine. Mother and Bob had lots of fun talking about people they knew. I wanted to tell Bob where you were and he said "Don't tell me about Vietnam. I don't want to hear." We came home and I had bled all through my clothes. Terrible experience. I guess it's because I'm all upset that I'm that way.

Today Mother went to a luncheon and I went to see Charlie. He is still well. By the way so far they are just giving them half Medicare. That is a help I guess.

Tonight Mother took me to a movie. She won't ever let me pay for anything, makes me mad. Also won't let me do any work. The movie was about middle-aged couples and how to cheat on each other. Very, very boring. Mother's cronies had said it was hilarious. I fail to see the humor in seedy motel scenes.

We came home to watch TV about the rallies on the Pentagon. Huge peace rally. I happened to say that I felt that dissent was part of the strength of this country, and that a great man once said "This is a rotten system, except it's better than any other." Well did I get shot down. I came upstairs just shaking and my heart pounding. Your mother almost dislikes me and it is not covered up very deep. This can't go on very long, and they are having huge demonstrations in Denmark too. Where am I going to go for a little peace?

Want to hear a good joke - "Why are there more Democrats than Republicans?" Answer "Have you ever heard the price of an elephant?"

I have your picture up and I look at it each night and say good night. Oh how I love you honey.

What's my doubt
What's my fear
In the chaos of the World
The house of love is firm
A courtyard to our heaven

Still is here isn't it. My only strength comes from the knowledge that you and I love one another and I know you are there in spirit, solid as a rock, but how I pray that your mother would only give me a chance to explain myself. But it is very hard. By now I open my mouth very little, and I'm very bored. I sit home all day and then at night I can't discuss anything with anyone. I'm for sure going home for Christmas. I had planned to stay longer, but for whom? Your mother, in her heart, thinks she is doing the best for me, but all these little things are beginning to add up. Please, please tell me how to be nicer and more accepting. I really want to have a good relationship. But how can I when like tonight I was treated to a lecture on that I shouldn't have too much meat and fat, it's bad for the heart. All we have around here is candy. Tell me what that is good for.

I'm very excited to hear about your trips to Saigon, etc., etc. I do hope this won't be too bad on you. Please eat right so you don't get an ulcer. Please, you are so marvelously calm though I think you will weather it all right.

Also honey, please destroy these letters, I beg you. I don't want you to re-read them, and all I want to do is to talk to you. I'm fine down inside and it does help to talk to you. I'm not complaining, just explaining, so you'll understand. But you do don't you. I'm afraid you would react just like I am. What a pity.

I love Frankford - real neat and loads of atmosphere. I'm taking the car in to have it fixed on Tuesday. I guess we better sell it, or what is your word? Ruins a car just to sit, and I can't see spending a fortune taking it to Europe. Well, we will see.

Love you much. Good night.

Elin

Chu Lai, Vietnam
October 21, 1967

Dear Elin,

Big day yesterday - we received our first mail - quite a load and Lt. Yates, Sgt Helford, Beery and I spent all day breaking it out and making an improvised post office. Got five letters from my honey and the morale count was high. It was real good to have contact again. It sounded like you had an outstanding time in D.C. Wish I could have been there.

The days just melt into one another here and you lose all conception of what day of the week it is. The past two days have been beautiful - the ocean has calmed down & beautiful skies and fairly cool (75-80 F) prevails. The coast is lovely. Tonight we have the grand opening of the officers' club - which is a grass roofed structure high on a sand dune overlooking the whole bay. I got a TV today from Special Services to put in it and must get it hooked up this afternoon. Also got a pool table, radios and games for a day room. You wouldn't believe the Special Services supply here - anything you want. Also got $4,000.00 of sports equipment to pass out.

My bridge game is improving. Four of us have been playing every night all week. We've got a good supply of beer and I doubt I've lost any weight. Two days ago a jet crashed right up the beach from here. A Lt. and a major were in it and they just found bits and pieces of the plane all over the beach.

The first ship isn't in yet - is 2 days late and we expect the first troops to arrive Monday 23 October. General Westmoreland is supposed to come down to welcome them in.

Major Hurt is as manic as ever. I've given up trying to do anything and am just floating along until Division directs that we go there. Actually it's been a vacation here on the beach. I'll send some film when the roll is finished. Been trying to get a picture of a lizard but they're elusive.

Anxious to hear how things are doing in Philly. Tell Mother I'll write to her in a day or so.

Much love honey – miss you
Bill

Philadelphia, Pennsylvania
October 21, 1967

Dear Bill.

This is a hodge-podge of things. Hope you have time to read it all.

Today I feel great again and have my strength and spirit back.

Mother is taking me out to dinner again. This makes about the 5th time. She feels very responsible for entertaining me! The weather is still beautiful and we are going out to see the leaves, in all their glory and splendor. Bill you wouldn't believe the gorgeous homes one can buy around Philadelphia for $20,000, and they are just out of this world.

This year might be all worthwhile if we can look forward to having a dream house. I plan to put $500 in savings in a couple of months, when I have my ticket all paid for, but I must admit it's easy to spend money here. Kind of a loose atmosphere.

Tomorrow I get my hair fall, will send you a picture of my self improvement program. It is hard to lose weight here though, and with the drinks in D.C. it was impossible.

Tomorrow I should have a newsy letter from you.

Do tell me if you don't have to have a daily dissertation of inertia. I'll stop then, but this is kind of my only outlet.

Take care, much love
Elin

Philadelphia, Pennsylvania
October 22, 1967

Hi Bill,

How is everything going? Here all is well - and I feel it might work fine. Yesterday I flew off my handle and said some things to your mother. She got very upset. I really didn't mean to hurt her, but at least we did get to talk out our differences. She thinks I hate her and I'm not as gentle as the people she has known. No one has ever yelled at her before. Well I've never had some of these experiences with other people either. We are just like opposite poles. I do sincerely feel that this storm has cleared the air. Your mother is really great inside, if only she could simmer down with me. Maybe this stay will smooth things out once and for all. I do pray it will.

Charlie is much improved. If he keeps this up he'll be home in a couple of weeks. I might try for a part time job between now and Christmas. All the stores need extra help now.

We are going to see Nana Williams on Friday and Mike and Kathy on Saturday. I'm really looking forward to seeing the country. I just adore Nana Williams. She made chili sauce the other day. She wants to drive - what spirit. My spirits much to my surprise are very high, everything considered.

I'll miss you - but I'll make it OK.

All my love dear
Elin

Chu Lai, Vietnam
October 22, 1967

Dear Elin,

The ship is in Da Nang & the first troops arrive here tomorrow morning. Gen. Westmoreland is coming down here to welcome them & there will be some sort of ceremony. I found out that Mr. Harmon was taken off the boat in Okinawa because of an eye ulcer. He is expected to join us later, but this really strips down the PSD officers - only Lt. Yates left at the moment! Hurt is still playing games & I'm in a very frustrating position right now. This man is sick & I'll be happy to get away from him. He has intimidated everyone here. I've reached the end of my rope with him. If things don't improve within the next few days I'm going to call Colonel Hawkins for a job. Although I would like to stay here in Chu Lai at Americal Division - it is really beautiful here - & I'd much rather spend the year on the ocean than be stuck in a huge headquarters in Saigon.

We've had beautiful days this week - water real blue & not too hot. Then - the mountain range to our rear is imposing, especially when you know those mountains are filled with VC. Most of the air strikes & the DMZ are out of here & and we drive by the jets loading bombs twice a day.

3 days later - 25 Oct 67

Inconceivable that three days passed and I didn't finish this letter. Time here has no meaning whatsoever.

The first ship arrived. I went to the port when Westmoreland came in. Quite an impressive individual, as you can imagine. Got some good pictures. The "landing" of the brigade was something else. The ceremony - covered by ABC, NBC, & CBS, plus foreign press - consisted of the first LST (a boat that holds about 900 men and took two days to come 150 miles) and you can only imagine how cramped the men were. Anyway, the boat docked but no one could get off until Westmoreland arrived. Then Colonel Waldie and the staff, plus the commanders who arrived two weeks ago. Got onto the boat with all of the units' flags. When Westy arrived with two 3 star generals (one Vietnamese), the band played and all marched off. Big show! Still - Westmoreland made an impressive speech. There were mobs of people (including me) taking pictures of the whole affair.

"Landing" of the Brigade

Troops are lined up coming off the boat

General Westmoreland welcoming the troops

Got two more letters today from my honey & one from Mother. Morale is high! To answer - I enjoy anything you write & the little things and thoughts are just as important to hear about anything else. I'm glad you had such a good time in Washington. It sounds like we would really enjoy a tour there. What's with the Urettes? Is Mike really off on a separate tangent - hope that they work out their life.

The food is terrible - the weather clammy. And I'm always dirty and sandy - but it's bearable & all things considered not bad at all. You know how much I enjoy being near the ocean, so under any circumstances that compensates for a lot.

I blew my stack the other night & told Major Hurt that I'd had enough of the harassment & pettiness, etc. He's calmed down considerably since. I'd just about reached the point where I didn't give a damn what happened.

Things are still hectic because I'm operating in three locations & Dove and Harmon are gone. We've been lucky with the weather. The monsoons should have begun two days ago - but nothing but beautiful days. The month of October averages 22 inches of rain normally.

Watched TV tonight & had some cold beer at our makeshift officers' club on the sand dune (I took some pictures which I'll send when I get them developed.

It's a strange atmosphere here & I still don't have any feeling for the total operation. This is partially because I haven't gone anywhere or had any contact with Vietnamese.

The letters I got today were postmarked October 19 - not bad. I presume that by this time you have gotten some serious mail.

I miss you honey & hope that things are going smoother in Philly.

Good night love,
Bill

Philadelphia, Pennsylvania
October 23, 1967

Dear Bill,

Today I got a nice letter from you. Nice because it's mostly about playing bridge and swimming. I bet by the time this gets to you that will all be changed. Today on the radio they told about the large troop movement into I Corps.

Well here goes my daily dissertation about the trivia of daily living. It's trivial really without you. Took the car to Mr. Gunning on the corner - down on Oxford Avenue. He wanted to be remembered to you (I don't really think he remembers you). He is a nice man, and for $7.72 I got the oil changed and my points cleaned. Runs smoothly again. He does not think we need a new carburetor.

Here is the joke of the day (this one is from Mother's school teacher crowd). "A woman was bringing her three children to school to register them. The secretary said, "What are their names, please?" The woman said, "O.I. Jones, M.J. Jones and D.C. Jones." "I beg your pardon," said the secretary, "you can register them with their full names, not initials." "Must I?" "Yes." "Well OK - this is O.I. - Outraged Innocence, this is M.J. - Misplaced Judgment, and this is D.C. - Damned Carelessness." (I guess it isn't funny written down).

I took the El downtown. Got my new fall - really long hair from Hong Kong. Maybe you can get me a wig sometime this year. Well, about my new hairdo - either it's very natural looking or so hideous that everyone is sparing me, because your mother hasn't mentioned it at all nor did Uncle Charlie. When I get someplace where there is a camera I'll take a picture for you to see. I have my hair parted in the front and a long ponytail in the back. I'm sure you really care - Ha, Ha. Tomorrow we are going to Josephine's for dinner. I bought 3 guest towels as a kind of housewarming gift. I hope it is all right.

The leaves are turning and are very beautiful. Yesterday we went to New Hope for dinner. The place you have been to, too - kind of like Carmel. Loads of antique shops and restaurants, gift shops and art colony.

I'm so anxious for you to get my letters so we can get some real communication established. I really enjoy your letters, and from now on I promise only cheerful ones from here - except for once a month. Is that allowed? If not please advise.

Mrs. Sternelle called tonight to get your address so she can get a package off in time for Christmas. She truly is a dear person.

Well love - so long for tonight. I feel quite guilty having so much leisure when I know how hard you work. Uncle Charlie asks about you. He is fine now.

Much love
Elin

Philadelphia skyline - 1967

Takhli, Thailand
October 23, 1967

Dear Bill,

I received your letter two days ago, and was glad to hear that you had arrived safely in Vietnam. I am sure that you could feel the change in environment the moment you stepped off the plane. I know that I did. Did you land at Ton Son Nhut before going up country? I have many friends scattered all through Vietnam. From the description of your camp, it sounds great! I have come to like Southeast Asia, but I don't know how your opinion will turn out. It is different over here in Thailand. Do you have any idea if you will stay where you are, or does it depend how the war goes? Things are running smoothly over here, we are just getting through with the monsoon season, as yours is just beginning over there. Really weird weather. The temperatures are dropping here also. It got down to 68 degrees the other night, and I thought that I would freeze. I am very tired of living conditions here. The communications sq. got the shaft as far as quarters go. I am very seriously thinking of going in with a friend of mine, and get a bungalow downtown for the remainder of my tour (four months). It would just cost each $20 dollars for one month, two bedrooms, bath, a large living type room, with a great big porch (on stilts). I could have a lot of needed privacy, something that I haven't had for eight months now! I'll let you know later what I decide. It would be a great place to get some painting done.

I guess by now, you have heard of the new Air Force directive, making E4s NCOs. I am now officially Sgt. Walker. It sounds weird but nevertheless that's me. Out of about 6,000 people here at Takhli, I would say over 2,000 are E4s. This base is crawling with Sgts. Unfortunately there is no pay increase to go with it. C'est la Guerre. I have been working straight days now, for the past three weeks. Two of us were put on days to help out with the recoveries every day. Most of other crews haven't had too many qualified Radar people. We are like a back-up crew. The hours are long though. I go to work at eight in the morning and am never out of here at night till after seven. The time has been flying though. I will have my assignment within 35 days. I can kick myself in the butt for not putting in for a consecutive overseas tour to Europe, but I didn't know what I know now back in July when I forecasted. I'll get back to Europe some way!

I've been having some clothes made for me these past two months, and I'm very happy with the results, and the price. Prices around the Takhli area are getting higher all the time. Most of the Americans don't even try to bargain for a price, therefore the Thais just set high prices. I am thinking a three day pass in November, and go up to Chaing-Mai. It is a city in Northern Thailand, in the middle of teak country. It is called the Bangkok of the North. I understand that it is a fantastic city.

As far as your coming to Bangkok I will be able to get off any time that I request (Politics - Ha!) I will probably leave Thailand for the states at the end of February. If you can manage to get an R/R at that time, or before, let me know the dates, and I will set up the hotel reservations, etc. Bangkok is really out of this world ! I know that you will see a great difference between the Thais and the Vietnamese.

I am at work now, and have got to get over to the operations trailer, for our recovery is about to begin. I will write again soon. You write to me when you have a chance. I haven't heard from anyone at home recently.

So take care -
Sawadee – Jack

When you landed in Vietnam, did your pilot say - "I hope that you all had a good flight, the temperature in Saigon is 91 degrees, with light to moderate ground fire." ?? - Ha!

Jack at Takhli Air Force Base, Thailand

Havre de Grace, Maryland
October 24, 1967

Dear Elin,

I received your lovely note so many weeks ago. Do forgive me for not writing sooner.

Much has happened since you left Killeen, Texas. After Juergen returned from Jungle School in Panama, he came down with a very high fever. It lasted for almost 5 days before the doctors decided to put him in the hospital. At first they thought it was pneumonia, then malaria. After that the flu. The doctors never did determine the cause, although they ran several tests. Apparently, the best guess is that it was a Jungle fever carried by a tick. After four days in the hospital, they felt he was feeling well enough to leave. He is in perfect health now.

We left Killeen three days later. When we arrived in Aberdeen we were very lucky to find an apt. so fast. Of course it isn't as nice as the Connally Apts. but will serve as a good home for eight weeks.

We went to New York City for three days last week. We both had a grand time. Of course we had to see all the normal sights. Our hotel was on West 45th Street and Broadway. We were in walking distance of all the action, and we certainly did a lot of walking. I have two terrible blisters on my heels to prove it.

One weekend we hope to see Washington D.C. Here Juergen works only 5 days a week, so we will have plenty of time to see several of sights of interest around this area.

I don't know how busy you are, but I would very much like to see your town and visit with you. I can have the car any week day, so if you would like a visitor, let me know the day and I will drive up. We will be here until December 14th. Anytime that it is convenient with you, it is fine for me. Also give directions as I will certainly get lost.

Our address: 413 Congress Ave. #3
                Havre de Grace, Maryland 21078

Fondly,
Mary Schleicher

Philadelphia, Pennsylvania
October 25, 1967

Hi Honey,

Got a real cheerful letter, the one where you had broken down the mail. I'm so glad we are finally in full communications. Your letters only take 4 days - I guess that will change when I get to Denmark.

Guess what I'm doing, baking things to send. Sure hope they all get there all right. It's some recipes out of the Army Community Service Center that are supposed to travel well. Last night we spent (Mother & I) a delightful evening with Josephine. She was genuinely interested in what you were doing and what was it like. About the first person who has shown genuine interest other than Mother. She adores you - and I must say she is a gem herself. She has a beautiful new apartment right across the street from where she is a counselor. She just turned 30 Monday and said it was quite traumatic. She had some lovely old things from her house. Beautiful old Biedermeier dining room chairs that Uncle Ed had repaired and she had upholstered in blue and green paisley. She has a Walker taste for things, for sure. Also last night your mother said I looked ten years younger with my hair down. She didn't even know it was my new fall. It really looks natural, so I'm very pleased. Got to get a camera.

Kirsten called and they are coming to Connecticut in two weeks. I'm very excited to see them both again.

Did I tell you that your mother is getting half Medicare. So far so good, I wonder how long they will continue that.

Love
Elin

Philadelphia, Pennsylvania
October 26, 1967

Hi Doll,

How are things panning out today. According to your stars you could achieve in a project to which you give your earnest endeavor. I guess that means that you have been transferred to the Division (ha, ha, I read the stars with tongue in cheek you know). I went to the small Navy Depot, and they don't have much of a commissary or PX, just the barest of necessities. So I guess that is out. I did some food shopping today - $30 - I figure this is one way I can help a little. Your mother always wants to treat. I'm cooking a small leg of lamb for us tonight. How is the food over there. You haven't said anything so far. I hope you are with a mess hall with good cooks. How did the grand opener of the O. Club go. I'm so glad you have enough beer. I got so thirsty for some I just bought a six pack.

Your mother and I get along famously now. I keep quiet and we have a minimum of conversation. Even the subject of how the Jews eat upset your mother. So now I just chuckle inside and let her rattle on. What is the use - she will never see things my way, and I'll forever be the "strange foreigner." She told Rosabelle on the phone "It isn't easy to warm up to them." Whatever that means - either daughter-in-laws or foreigners, she's also told me that it's hard to change after 40. So my love, fear not I'll attempt the impossible. She is very sweet, and oh she tries so very, very hard, but still she dislikes many of my ways.

I'm writing all this with a smile on my lips. I am really not upset about it anymore and just thought I would let you know. I love her dearly and hope you will always be close to her because she has always tried to do all the best things for you.

The weather is very glorious and considering everything I'm surprised how well I'm doing.

Mary Schleicher wrote. I invited her to come here and she just might. Would be nice, because believe it or not, I so miss the military. People in it are so much, much more broad-minded, one cannot even compare.

Honey I so miss you but in my heart I know that you are safe and sound. I have wonderful dreams about you, always at some party. I also know that your love is genuine, and I only have to wait for you to return and we shall lives happier ever after, just like a fairytale.

I'm going to run, seeing Charlie. He almost looks like his old self - lean and thin - but still well looking. Much love - hugs, kisses, etc., etc. (Just saw The King and I)

Love
Elin

Spokane, Washington
October 26, 1967

Dear Elin,

I heard on the radio Monday that an Army Group (that sounds like Bill's) had arrived in Vietnam on Monday.

I've thought about you so very much dear & I know how hard it is on you. Strauss was in Korea during the Korean War and then I remember the year Tim was in Vietnam. But it is just something we have to find strength within ourselves to go through it. It takes lots of prayers & faith just like so many other trials in life.

Send Bill's address to me.

I am working now for 2 weeks. The job was even offered to me. There is a private school here - the Autovian School for Special Children - and they've just opened a downtown office and I'm the only one in the office. Last summer I applied for a job as Supervisor over the credit & insurance offices at a new hospital. The Personnel Director and the Comptroller wanted to add the job & hire me, but were voted down & the job was not added. The Personnel Director had sent for my records & experience, liked them, and so he recommended me to a children's dentist. The dentist's secretary decided not to quit after all. The Personnel Director and the Dentist are on the School Board - so when this office was to be opened they called and asked me if I'd be interested. They recommended me and I got it! I can't believe that I can do this work. Right from the first day I took dictation & typed good business letters, the minutes of meetings also. I also do the accounts.

Hazel

Philadelphia, Pennsylvania
October 27, 1967

Hi Love,

So disappointed that I didn't have any letters today - but I figured 4 days ago this would be your big day, so I'll be patient and hope for one soon. How did the troop movement go - well I hope.

Just wrote Ann & Terry - told him he should marry, and said I hoped the Jesuits at Gonzaga didn't get him too. Many men that graduate from there are afraid of marriage or have weird ideas about it anyway.

Tonight Mother is going to play bridge so I'll be alone all day. They are reviewing Charlie's case and talk about bringing him home. He thinks I can take care of him. Bill, I have terrific guilt feelings, like I really should help. But, I would be very miserable here 4 hours a day, because the climate between Mother and Charlie isn't right and it has nothing to do with me. It goes way back, and there are many hurt feelings involved for me to get involved in the middle. Of course I can't give this as a reason. I also feel Mother would rather not have him home. Oh it's hard to know what real help is at the moment. Don't you worry about it, also please burn any of my letters that have any reference to the family, such as this one.

I washed the car today inside and out and it really looks nice. I'll write one whole letter about the car soon. We really must decide what to do with it. I'm not so sure I'm hot to spend $500 on getting it overseas and back. Jack is in the market when he returns in February. He mentions a V.W. but for the same money he could get ours and be better off. But maybe it's better not to get too involved. Mike sure wasn't interested. He has ordered a new Malibu '68. I did teach him a thing or two though and he got it for $100 more than the second hand one he looked at would have been. It does pay to look around.

I'm fine. Hope you are too.

Much love and a big juicy kiss,
Elin

Philadelphia, Pennsylvania
October 28, 1967

Hi Love,

Three weeks and it seems oceans since you left. I called Kirsten last night and guess what - they are packing up in Minneapolis. Tom is going to Sunnyvale, California and Kirsten is flying here on Tuesday. Tom said it would be boring for her to sit in a motel room for a month. He will fly back to Minneapolis and drive the car east the first week of December. I am sure excited to see Kirsten. She said we had to find them an apartment. I said where, and she said "anywhere, they have airplanes don't they." They will be here for a year. He has a large territory.

Well Mother and I are on our way up to Limeport. It's Mike's birthday on Monday so we are taking them out to dinner tonight.

I figure this week was a busy one for you, with the troops coming in. I have my fall on and feel young. Kirsten said she gained 17 pounds so maybe the two of us can lose some weight together.

I think of you day and night. I only take time out to sleep.

Love you dearly
Elin

Philadelphia, Pennsylvania
October 29, 1967

Bill,

It is just great to hear that you are in an area such as you have described in your letters. It is presumed that by this time the activity has been accelerated to a high degree with little time to photograph lizards! We could picture you doing the candid camera bit!

The weather here is good with gradual coolness moving into Philadelphia. Because of this, we put in the storm windows today and I noticed that I can't scramble in and out of second floor windows to the roofs as easily as heretofore!

Elin seems much more content since returning from Washington and now she is happy because Kirsten is coming. She does not have enough to do so I too, will be glad for her to have a young companion. Jo Walker entertained us at her little apartment last Tuesday evening. We enjoyed her very much. It is unfortunate that she lives so far. Jo looks well and is highly interested in teaching. She also likes Ned's fiancé and has encouraged her parents to accept her.

On Friday evening we have been invited to have dinner at the Edward Walkers' as Nana will be there and Aunt Rosabelle thought it a good time to see her. Aunt Helen is in Texas to help Dale with her newly arrived infant, a girl.

We celebrated Mike's birthday yesterday by taking him to dinner. The 4 of us toasted Mike and then Elin toasted you and Jack by wishing for a fast year! Of course Kathleen isn't too gay these days but we all enjoyed being with family. Mike was very happy to have received your letter as he shared it with us.

Louise Webster popped in today and said "Little Bill" (6 ft. 4".) is a lance corporal in the Marines now situated near the DMZ line in Vietnam.

Today I sat with Charlie for an hour and a half and he is not only better physically but much improved mentally. My opinion is that he will go along for some time and then unexpectedly, will suffer another stroke. Whether to bring him home or not will depend upon his condition. He asks about you and Jack daily and worries about you. He is getting excellent care and is content to be where he is.

Jack must be very busy because we don't hear from him - only a radiogram 10 days ago.

The theater guild here has been most enjoyable for me. I can't believe that I'm actually attending! This Thursday Melvin Douglas stars in a drama. The theater has always fascinated me, and I would have loved being involved in it more than I ever have. It rubbed off on you, I think. Right? Well, now I will write to Jack, Joan, and send a note to my mother. Until I write again remember that I love you dearly and pray for your safety and good leadership daily.

Hugs and kisses,
Mother

Los Angeles, California
October 30, 1967

Dear Elin,

I have just about exhausted the William or W. Walkers of Monterey - Carmel (said the information operator) - none is you. Where are you? We have been wondering and wondering, especially since we may come up that way before Christmas and would like to pop in.

Keith is on the Times and although not particularly promoting it, being pushed along the "young executive" trail. I am about to work. I am also dabbling in creative writing.

Our eyes run, and smart daily, and we can't see the hills for the smog, but we are finding L.A. quite bubbling - and beach happy. We are tan!

Can you visit - perhaps for the holidays?? What and where are you?

Cheers,
Carole (THAT ONE - Eardley Reekie)

P.S. Can we write W.A.?

Philadelphia, Pennsylvania
October 30, 1967

Dear Bill,

So happy to have your letter today - postmarked 26 October.

I so hope that you get yourself resolved with Hurt. Just play it cool. I have a feeling they would choose you over him and who knows, he may get shipped out. I shouldn't ruin a good set-up right away till you see what is up. I realize it's trying when another person is not on the same beam - even little things become irritating. I know of what I'm speaking. I got a lovely letter from Hazel - there is a person with compassion. She asked about you and I sent her your address. I'll send her letter in a big envelope. Did you get my last big envelope?

I now know that I have the strength to go through this year. I'm going to do what I feel is right. Other people might not know the reason for doing things I do - but I know what is right. My health couldn't take living under pressure for a year so I won't. As of now I plan to leave the middle of December or just before Christmas. We will see. I need a sailing permit, & the income tax returns for the last two years. I sure hope I have them someplace. I am thinking of leaving the car - renting it to Kirsten and Tom - because if we get the US for our next assignment we will want two cars. Where are we going to get a good car like what we have got. Then you can get a more sporty model for yourself. I just happen to like this model. If you get an overseas assignment we can sell it to Jack. You should know by March what you are going to do, don't you think? I would think you have to get your application in for graduate school this next month if you still want to go. Please let me know what you think about the car, then I'll need two new tires. I've given up the idea of shipping it to Europe. If you get a European assignment I'll have Kirsten ship it over. I just don't feel like shipping it now - seems like a waste of money. I might change my mind. Let me know what you think on the subject.

I'm mailing my summer things home this week. It's cheaper to mail things than to pay excess baggage at $2 a pound. That runs up fast. By mail it's $1 the first pound and 30 cents every other pound.

We haven't heard from Jack in a long while. Seems he is real busy. I guess this big bombing push is still going on & I believe they are preparing for a halt in the bombing. Sure hope some talks come out of it. But we surely are winning by now. I just feel we are.

I have to laugh at your statement that you don't have any feeling for the place, because you haven't gone anywhere or had any contact with Vietnamese. As far as I'm concerned that is just terrific. Remember this is not Germany where it's fun to get out and mingle. The less contact the better, I feel. You haven't missed things yet - when you do let me know. Remember I only have another month to mail stuff, so speak up now, OK?

If you get a thing from the finance office please clue me in too. I'm very cautious with my money till I see how it comes through and how much. I'm sure from now till Christmas I'll have to spend some money. My trip will be at least $300.00, and then I have to get gifts for everyone. I thought of giving Joan $50.00, to help everyone. She has two weeks vacation and wants to fly back here. That way your mother wouldn't have to send her as much. Is that OK? Otherwise I'm going to buy very modest gifts. I refuse to get in the rut of big elaborate gifts.

Bill I feel real close to you despite the distance. In spirit we are true companions and that is what counts.

Much love sweetheart –
Elin

                                                    Philadelphia, Pennsylvania
                                                    October 30, 1967

Dear Jack,

I've been so busy writing to Bill that it seems I've fallen behind in writing you. I assume you are extra, extra busy. We read about the big air push and raids on North Vietnam – must be trauma for you. I pray for you and all our men involved. Believe me, we think of you all the time.

Kirsten is coming tomorrow for a month. I'm so excited. Tom is going to Sunnyvale, Calif. for a month, then they are moving to Connecticut.

I'm on my way over to see Uncle Charlie. He always asks about you and Bill. He is real alert now and sits up all day. They take very good care of him there.

More news later. Just wanted you to know we love you.

Elin

Chu Lai, Vietnam
October 31, 1967

Dear Mother,

Enjoyed your long letter - & the Kool Aid. The days here melt into one another & already I've been here a month. Really haven't gotten started yet on a routine operation. The brigade is spread in several locations initially & a pending change will consolidate personnel activities at Division level - so presently my section is operating in three locations.

Haven't had any real contacts with the Vietnamese. We are secluded inside a huge defense sector that houses Marine and Air Force bases, along with Army, from which many air strikes are launched against the North. There are lots of Vietnamese who come in from nearby villages every day for daily hire, under guard, as laborers. Young girls & old men and women.

3 November 67

Well, never got this letter finished - been real busy all of a sudden and the past few days flew by.

Saw the Vice President the other day here in Chu Lai. He "sneaked" in unannounced & they had a small ceremony at Americal Division Headquarters. Quite frankly wasn't too impressed. Humphrey wore a shirt - outside pants - and a baseball cap pulled over his eyes. He gave a short speech & said that we shouldn't believe what we read about Americans protesting against the war.

The monsoons have started - torrential downpours occurring at any time. If you're caught outside it's totally drenched. This really is an incompatible arena of situations. Here at Chu Lai base we have movies, TV, clubs, beaches & about three miles away are fire fights every night & a blazing conflict goes on. Many of us can't acclimate ourselves to the picture - total - & I guess no one really can, whatever is his commitment.

The important thing is that those of us in support roles don't lose sight of the ordeals the combat units and men we are supporting are going through. Most of my men are now ensconced at Division headquarters (hot & cold running water, showers, flush toilets) & I'm afraid they don't have an appreciation yet of the situation that our units are in.

How is the theater season - have you seen any good plays so far? Well, into the rain for a drenching on my way to my hooch - in fact I think I'll take a shower in it. Tell Uncle Charlie I'm glad to hear he's feeling himself again. Hope all is well with you.

Love Bill

"This Day in History"
Vietnam War
October 21, 1967

100,000 people march on the Pentagon. Demonstrators including radicals, liberals, black nationalists, hippies, professors, women's groups, and war veterans march on the Pentagon.

The rally in front of the Lincoln Memorial started peacefully enough though Dr. Benjamin Spock - baby specialist, author, & outspoken critic of the war - did call President Johnson "the enemy." After the rally the demonstrators, many waving the red, blue and gold flag of the Viet Cong, began marching toward the Pentagon. Violence erupted when the more radical element of the demonstrators clashed with the soldiers and U.S. Marshalls protecting the Pentagon. The protesters surrounded and besieged the nerve center until early hours of October 23. By the time order was restored 683 people, including novelist Norman Mailer and two United Press International reporters, had been arrested. This protest was paralleled by demonstrators in Japan and Western Europe, the most violent of which occurred outside the U.S. Embassy in London when 3,000 demonstrators attempted to storm the building.

Vice President Hubert Humphrey's visit to Americal Division HQ
November 1, 1967

Philadelphia, Pennsylvania
November 1, 1967

Dear Bill,

We had a nice Halloween night. I took Mother to Becks, and then we drove to the airport. At Becks they had flags all over from Denmark. They are having a big Danish festival celebrating the 800th birthday of Copenhagen. We asked and got three Danish flags so we had those at the airport. Kirsten looks well - only marriage has made her chubby, like me, and we are discussing ways of losing all our excess weight. What a dumb thing always to have to worry about one's weight.

Yesterday I had a sandwich at Robert's Delicatessen on the avenue, and I plan to take Kirsten there before we go to see Uncle Charlie. He asks about you always and wants to be remembered to you. Kirsten and I are catching up on all the things that have happened. She sounds very, very happy, and Tom just called.

He is leaving today for California. What a shame we are not still there. I'm so homesick for our place in the sun in beautiful California. Weren't we happy there - I don't recall any sad days there, only happy, gorgeous, sun filled days. Remember all our hikes.

I am taking Kirsten to the avenue now for a good rye sandwich. We are talking about you constantly.

Much love,
Elin

Hi Bill,

I just came here to Philadelphia. I miss seeing you here too. Elin has been telling me what you have written home. Tom and I talk about the time when we all meet again.

Kirsten

Spokane, Washington
November 1, 1967

Dear Elin & Kirsten,

When did Bill make Major? I did not notice it as I read your letter but when I started to copy it down how wonderful & congratulations. He's doing so good at his career!

I was so very glad to see Kirsten's picture & her handsome husband. Thank you for sending it.

Wish I could help you two junk shop. It is so much fun. I love everything in my house & I think it is all so much more interesting than new & more expensive things.

The Crescent has opened a new Import Shop Department. I have much lovelier - genuine things & oh their prices are shocking. I figure I have a fortune in my things after I attended the antique show here last month. I felt like a millionaire for a few days.

I'm so sorry about Charlie - it is hard on the whole family. Where is Joan now? I think you should go home, Elin, at least for a while. You could always come back if Beth needs you.

My job is getting more interesting. They all tell me I'm doing a very good job & I think I am too. I have two rooms all to myself. The chairman of the executive board calls me & gives me things to do. Another board member comes in a few minutes each day when he's in town (he was just gone a week) & I call the head of the school each day & go out to the school sometimes. They rent a place for me in a storage garage near the office.

I'm having Alice Woolley & her husband & some of the AFB - ARC - F. Det. & the Moo's (wheat ranchers at Edwall) here Sun. P.M. for fondue dinner. I had 2 Sukiyaki (a dinner & a luncheon) before I started to work & they were big hits. I want to do an India dinner sometime soon.

I'll send your Xmas pkg. to Phila. early so you won't have to bring it back from Denmark. You may open it and then leave it at Beth's. What on earth can one send to Bill for Xmas?

Bye now & hello to Beth & Charlie.

Much, much love,
Hazel

I'll say a prayer each night for our Bill.

Chu Lai, Vietnam
November 3, 1967

Hi Honey,

Guess it's been a few days since I wrote - the days just merge into one another & I lose all track of time & date. I've gotten many letters from you & clippings, Kool Aid & other letters - which have been great. Sometimes I get three letters (all mailed on different days) in one day.

How about Ann being engaged - real happy for her - she is a fine person and deserves a good life. Also happy to hear (today) that Kirsten will be able to be with you for a while. Is she there yet? Anyway that will make Philadelphia more exciting & I'm sure that both of you can have some adventures.

Tell Uncle Charlie that I am thinking about him & very glad to hear that he is back off the sick list (I still don't want you to get burdened into a nursemaid situation there!!!).

On the car - I am against family financial deals & I feel they can only lead to problems. I feel it would be best to advertise in newspapers (if you can sell individually would get better price than with car dealer). In the long run the expense of shipping the car to Europe and back - with insurance required, probable customs questions, etc. that it would end up equal to the loss we'd take by selling it in Philadelphia.

This month $600 went to the bank. I drew $224 cash & put $100 of that in Soldiers Deposits. Now what I'd like to do is put $200 a month in the bank & $500 in Soldiers Deposits at 10%. You can draw whatever you need in excess of $200 from savings. What do you think? There is nothing to spend money on here except booze & that is so cheap that it's no great expenditure. I am going to buy a little refrigerator once I get to Division, and I'm going to start ordering things by PX mail order (like the punch bowl) & have them sent to Philadelphia.

Well it looks like I'll be going to Division in almost a week. I've been spending half a day there now. Plenty of confusion, & trying to get the postal & special services set up here at Brigade. The rains have started & it's messy here on the beach now.

We had our first casualties in the Brigade this week & it's been very sobering to everyone. A lieutenant and a sergeant were killed by VC and several wounded at Duc Pho. Unfortunately there will be more. Also unfortunately, as I predicted, it takes the first casualties to knock some of the "boy scout" adolescent attitudes out of some of the staff members and commanders.

The rain is really coming down now - we were lucky in that the monsoons normally extend all through October, November and December and we just got our first yesterday & today.

Once I move to Division I think I'll do some painting & hopefully some writing, but so far have no feel or much imagination for what is really happening here.

Bill

Philadelphia, Pennsylvania
November 3, 1967

My love,

Soon it will be a month and with Kirsten here, this next month will fly. I sure hope it's flying for you too.

I'm having many, many thoughts on Vietnam - and there are lots of discussions going on in this country. Having, as a child, experienced the German occupation of Denmark during WWII & the Danish resistance I feel I know more what you are really faced with. I've seen bombed places, people killed, and people returned home after being maimed and starved in concentration camps. I too have heard mortars off in the distance and spent fearful nights in a basement. I remember there was a whole night of shooting right by my home. Now, that fight was right because it liberated most of Europe, and for that reason Vietnam is partly right too. They too have a right to live free. Now, if American boys have to fight & die for the Vietnamese freedom - that is the issue, and shall we risk even further war? - that is an issue, and are we really doing it right is another issue. I know for sure that some of the hoods demonstrating are just gutless junkies who know not of what they are speaking. Then there are others who sincerely are against the war, and dissenting does not necessarily mean being a disloyal American. Often the two are classed together. I'm very encouraged by the amount of thinking going on. It will ensure that we don't drift in and out of things. I'm only sorry the serious thinking didn't start two years ago. I for one believe we should push in and get it over with and then try to put the pieces together. But, I can imagine the chaos created there when you impose Western culture on a French colonial one that was imposed on an Oriental culture. Three layers of thinking on top of an oxcart of cultures. It's such tremendous odds against the people really knowing what they want, that to expect them to know is folly.

Don't get discouraged by it all my love. I for one know it's very frustrating for you, and I too would be upset by pettiness. You wait until you see the face of "The Ugly American" and you'll be even more disgusted. But war has always brought out the worst part of the beastly man, be he Asian, European, or American. So don't feel responsible for them all. Just act as a higher example for your men to look up to. In these troubled times we need strong individuals like you - not fanatically moral but with standards that they stick with and uphold. Let me give a cute example. Kirsten and Far threw out the Mayor of Arrhus from our motel because he was too drunk. Now Far is a man of convictions and strong enough to stand by them. I don't think he was ever compromised of his ideals.

Bill, you are constantly in my thoughts and I feel very close to you. Please stay level and keep your head above water. God will give us the strength to endure. Somehow he never gives a situation without the necessary strength to take it.

I'll close for now,
Elin

P.S. 10 kisses and 50 hugs

Philadelphia, Pennsylvania
November 4, 1967

Dear Bill,

First about that telephone bill. I found a bill in our papers that had been mailed to you at Fort Hood. I guess we both overlooked it in the rush and confusion. It was with a bunch of orders and other junk. I had paid 20 dollars when I left Fort Ord. Anyway I sent a check and explanation today. It has to go by registered mail so don't worry, I have taken care of it. By the way, have you written any more checks because there is only $450 in there now, and I'm waiting for a notice about a new deposit. I guess it will take time. I'll be paying $60 on two new tires, and I need to pay $300 to get to Denmark, so I'm not getting my ticket 'till I get a notice about a new deposit. What arrangement are you making now? Did you have them send $600 and then start next month with the allotment or what? If I get in a pinch I'll get some taken out of savings again, but you know I transferred a thousand just because I hated not to carry interest on it.

How are you doing? How much do you find it is running you to live now that you have been there a month. Monday I'm going to Strawbridge's and pick out things to send to you and Jack. It should get there before Christmas. Food stuff and the like. Do you want me to give gifts for both of us, and then next year you can give stuff from Vietnam. But please advise as I still like to do things as a couple. Jack only wants food. I thought I would send Joan a check. I'll get Mike and Kathy something for their new house or the nursery. Also Tom and Kirsten for their new apartment (she by the way wants some things out of the catalogue. I'll elaborate later.) Can you use that mail order service or what? This is all petty things to worry about, but life must go on and these household problems make it all easier to get involved in. The big picture I can't change so I worry about the details which I can change.

How long does it take my letters to reach you? Yours arrive in four days. I think I'll start telling you which letter I am answering so we can get continuity. Your letter today was written on the 29th of October, mailed the 31st and is here on November 4th. Not bad.

Joan just called. She is fine. I'll send her your address. She doesn't have it, and hasn't heard from Jack in a month. We haven't heard from him in three weeks and Mother is a bit nervous about it. I'm sure he is only extremely busy with the big air push we read about.

Just had a knock down drag out with your mother about telephone rates on Sundays. She is a riot when she thinks she is right. We get along swell, and I'm very happy I came here. At least now I'm not afraid of her anymore, and things are in better perspective. She really is adorable if one can laugh a bit, so I'm just laughing now. I did take everything too seriously before - too sensitive. I realize that now.

Honey I hope you are well and just remember I'm here rooting for you. Much, much love.

Your sweetheart,
Elin

Chu Lai, Vietnam
November 6, 1967

Dear Elin,

A quick letter in the middle of the morning. Things still confusing as to my status & when we break from the Brigade. Uncle Joe still fighting everything, so I'm just sitting back and waiting for the fireworks.

We've had some more tragedy - another man killed by mortar fire, two men burned to death in a chopper explosion at Duc Pho, and 4 men including a lieutenant missing during a patrol.

Had some heavy rain, but today is beautiful again. Is Kirsten there now? If so tell her hello for me. Wish I were there so we could go traipsing around. As soon as the PX gets some in I'll buy two of those little Japanese tape recorders ($22 each) & send you one. I'm anxious to see a picture of you in your "fall" - sounds exciting.

Did you read that we're going to get a pay raise? Let me know if the financial arrangement I wrote about is OK - so I can change the allotment before next pay day.

Well must go to Division now so I'll get this in the mail.

Much love - & miss you.
Bill

Philadelphia, Pennsylvania
November 6, 1967

Dear Bill,

So much has happened since my last letter. It seems with Kirsten here time just flies.

Sunday was a gorgeous day so we decided to go to the Danish exhibit down at The Civic Museum. It's by the University of Pennsylvania. Mother had lots of homework so she stayed home. I found the place all by myself. It was a lovely exhibit and all of our things were there. Our lamp, the little orange & black one. The swan chair, our dining room chair, the bar, our silver, etc., etc. Quite something to realize our things are of museum quality. Also the chairs I've always wanted for the dining room - the tall high back ones.

As we walked by a line of people, someone said "Hello Elin" - it was a girl named Kirsten who had lived a block away in Odense. She went to the same school and I played with her older sister. She married an American guy from Bryn Mawr, Oliver Gildersleeve. Anyway we saw the exhibit and had coffee with another Danish girl and her husband. He is a PhD from Mexico City, and is studying at the University of

Pennsylvania. A very nice couple. They have one boy 16 months old, and one on the way. They have an old apartment on 30th Street. Real neat with loads of room.

Then we went to the Main Line with Kirsten & Oliver Gildersleeve. Oh you wouldn't believe the setup. Mother Gildersleeve is divorced and remarried to a doctor. She moved out and this young couple moved in. They inherited 2 dogs, a cat and a $80,000 home. Old English Tudor type. Oh what you and I could do there. But this couple has no "real class." She is very young and not that experienced. She has a maid's room or wing - and a maid to go with it. This young Danish maid calls them by their first names and watches TV with them every night. She stayed all the time we were there. I would not like to be that young Danish wife (she is 24). She has no background to cope with the class of people she is thrust into the middle of. I would adjust, but I wouldn't like to inherit someone else's horrible taste in furnishings, etc. It was interesting seeing them in their very unnatural surroundings. She was, as were Kirsten & I, very happy to reminisce about our childhood.

Today we visited a couple up off Herrog Avenue - the Adams. They travel all over the world and stayed at the Motel twice. He always goes by freighter. He had many ideas & I can get to Bangkok for $450. Then I need $100 extra. It will take me 30 days but I don't care, so we'll see. If you still want me to come meet you there I will, or any other place.

Tomorrow we are going to Media and visit some of Kirsten's friends. Wednesday I'm taking Charlie for a drive to Elmer's, and on Thursday we are going to New York and staying with Roger & Carol. I just called them. I got a deposit slip from the bank today for $600, so I'm in grand shape. I got snow tires today.

Elin

Chu Lai, Vietnam
November 8, 1967

Dear Elin,

How's my love today? This is a beautiful day here. Sitting in the office looking out at the ocean - very blue and calm today.

Yesterday we had fireworks. Hurt directed me to reassign Company A's mess sergeant to the Brigade Headquarters, in the continuing "rape of the Company" before we go to Division. However, Bittrich is already at Division with most of our people and the mess sergeant is running the Division's consolidated mess. Well the Division Chief of Staff directed that the mess sergeant not be moved. Then Hurt said that he was taking all of the Company's equipment. Colonel Clarke got into it and ran off Hurt. But Hurt is still scheming and dealing under the table, It got so bad yesterday that Bittrich put in a written request to Colonel Clarke asking to be relieved of his command and be slated to be reassigned because of what the Brigade (mainly Hurt) was doing to the Company. Colonel Clarke put a note on it saying he agreed with Bittrich & sent it to Terrible Tom. Now we'll wait and see. The Division AG is so furious at Hurt that he can't even talk about him without blowing up. He wants to transfer all of us to Division immediately. I've just been hiding out today until they resolve it. I've been in the middle and I won't operate that way any more, so consequently I'm not doing much of anything.

Hey - I got the cookies today. Very good! Also your letter philosophizing about the war. I agree with you. It's difficult for me to make any assessment here, because you probably know more about what is going on through news & TV & newspapers than we do.

Must take off for Division and I want to get this in the mail.

Love you and miss you very much.

Bill

Chu Lai, Vietnam
November 11, 1967

Darling,

I love you! tremendously & miss you every day. Got a sweet letter from Mor today & it made the whole week bright. She is a wonderful person. I admire your parents so much & feel very close to them.

Also got a "care" package from Mrs. Sternelle & I know how much thought & preparation went into it. She is very dear to think of me over these years & to take the time and effort to be thoughtful this way. Actually she sent a large box with many homemade cookies, fruitcake, a little Christmas tree with candy, Kool Aid & canned goods. Am saving most for Christmas. I'll write her. Haven't had any letters for five days - but then we haven't had mail deliveries into Chu Lai this past week - only sporadically.

Things have happened so fast here that I don't remember where I left off in the great conflict. Well - Uncle Joe played his part to the hilt, trying to keep his empire & succeeding in annoying the Division Chief of Staff to the point that two days ago Division assigned all of us (Admin Company) to Americal Division Headquarters. So, I packed up bag & trunks & moved out in the middle of the night (Joe had gone to Duc Pho). Haven't seen him since (although have spoken on the phone). Anyway, we are now ensconced at Americal Division Headquarters & I am in the throes of trying to organize a Division Personnel Services division. Unfortunately the Division Adjutant General & his deputy have never worked with a PSD before (shades of Germany & don't know what they are in for). Will be a lot of problems & harassment but it makes the days go faster.

We are living pretty good up here. All of us from the 198th who were transferred are in one hooch and each has a little cubicle about 7 feet by 5 feet to ourselves. We are going to get a refrigerator & some other niceties soon. I've got my rug (the one we bought at Gibson's) on the floor & the little teak table & once I get some paint I can make it cozy. I went to the village yesterday (reminded me of Lebanon) & bought some grass straw mats which I'm going to put on the walls. The village is something else - but the people are so warm & sensitive you can't help feeling with them, always smiling and making friendly gestures. I can see how many Americans have felt more strongly about our commitment here after serving in Vietnam and knowing the Vietnamese.

I wrote a letter to you last night after coming back from the officers' club but I re-read it this morning and ripped it up. Last night I had made up my mind to get the hell out after this tour (I'm really fed up with a lot of it after this 198th bunch). But today I'm thinking a little more logically, but still sure that I can't last another 12 years in this Mickey Mouse game (to a large extent).

We've had a little rain but still nothing like expected. Had a barbeque the first night I moved in here. Delicious steaks - I had three! We've got a barbeque grill, plenty of booze & steaks are easy to get through the Marines (trading). Only lack a refrigerator & we're trying to get a full size one for the hooch.

Unfortunately what's going on around us is not so pleasant. A number of civilians including children & water buffalo have been killed by 198th Brigade people in misjudgments or accidental fire. The Army makes "payments" to families when a member is accidentally killed, to soften the blow. Of course the big thing to the commanders is the number of VC killed. But I was told by a reliable source that even the innocent civilians accidentally killed are counted as "VC Killed" in the statistics. This wouldn't be surprising in view of the power and personality play that make up an Army. But it is still disgusting.

I'm just getting fat drinking beer each night & eating two huge meals a day. Of course this is winter & the temperature is in the 70's & low 80's so we are not sweating it off like we will be in the hot weather.

One of these days I'll write to Hazel & all the other friends I want to write to, but I just haven't felt able to express anything worthwhile to anyone else but you at the moment.

Say hello to Mother & Kirsten & Uncle Charlie. I'll write soon to them & take care my love, I wish you were beside me now - as always.

Love
Bill

Valley Cottage, New York
November 11, 1967

Dear Bill,

Kirsten and I are at the Baretz's in Valley Cottage. Their three kids are adorable, but is it ever hectic - like a 24 hour circus. Poor Roger gets up six times in one night. I just couldn't last. I don't know how Carol makes it. Yesterday we went to Ridgefield Connecticut, where Kirsten and Tom will be moving with his new job. It is beautiful there, and the people are very friendly. It's a very small and very wealthy town. Huge old mansions, etc. I think they will be very happy here. There is a zoning law against apartments so it's hard to find rentals. We got an idea of what is all about but it will be hard to rent a place cheap. They want $200 or more a month. We will have to come back next week. Today Carol and I are going to Manhattan.

Hope you are fine. We talk about you all the time.

Love Elin

Elin with Carol Baretz and children

Chu Lai, Vietnam
November 13, 1967

Hi Honey,

Received a letter today dated 4 November. We've had some delays in mail here recently but when it comes in there is usually a three day backlog.

Things are moving rapidly. I'm in the middle of setting up a 250 man PSD. So far I've been completely on my own (which I like) & the AG hasn't even been around. Much to do but many fine people to organize an outstanding section with. It's going to be fun to get it organized and running & I'm quite optimistic about it even though there is a lot of confusion right now. I can visualize the end result & will just keep working toward it.

We've had some delightfully cool days & sporadic rain that comes in torrents when it does. The days just melt into one & now that we have a substantial definite goal will do so even faster.

You haven't written yet about the amount I should send to the bank - will $200 a month be enough? Now it's $600 and I want to cut that down to put the maximum in Soldiers Deposits. I'll go ahead & do it for December & if you need more ($600 will go into checking account 30 November) you can always go into savings.

How are you going to Denmark? I assume by air. I don't plan on sending any Christmas presents to anyone. There is nothing available to buy - not even cards. We can order from the catalogue here & I will start sooner or later when you let me know specifically what you want (I know the punch set). I'll get things for next year when I go on R&R so I think your gift plans are fine. I am not spending much money at all. I drew $120 on pay day & have $85 left today. The $35 I spent includes meals & booze & some grass mats I bought in the village, plus toiletries & laundry..

I am still trying to get a refrigerator & will put out about $50 for one when I get a contact.

Well love - that's all for tonight. Hope all is well in Philadelphia & glad you are getting along.

Love you - as you know
Bill

Brooklyn, New York
November 13, 1967

Dear Bill,

Poor honey - I have been so busy I haven't gotten to write you every day like I like to do.

Today - Monday - we went from Valley Cottage to Brooklyn. I went all down Manhattan and under the tunnel, didn't get lost and found Roger's mother's store. We bought several things & I got most of my Christmas shopping done. Yesterday I bought a beautiful big platter in your mother's pattern at an antique shop. I sure hope she will like it. I also got a spice shelf for her, and several other small things too. Kirsten started to get her things. We've had no luck in finding an apartment for Kirsten and Tom, but maybe we still might. Tonight we are at the O'Donnells. Really a nice family. Tom's brother, Mike who is twelve, just beat me in chess. Just kills one. He is just the cutest boy one can imagine, and very bright.

I called Mother and told her we are coming home tomorrow. She said she had been ill all the time we were gone. She has a bad cold. We are spending Thanksgiving with her & Mike and Kathy too.

Today I saw Corine Fung. Chaplain Fung is stationed at Fort Hamilton at the career school. They live right at the ocean. I got on the wrong side and ended up in New Jersey. I went over the new bridge - cost me $1.00 to see the view. I had to turn around and come back. Corine wanted me to come back and do the museums together. This really is some town. Carol and Roger were very nice to the two of us and pressed us to keep staying longer with them.. We really enjoyed everything. The kids are darling and very active. They get up very early. Poor Carol is always doing something. Everyone tells me to send you their regards. It doesn't seem right without you here. I am excited to get your letters tomorrow. I understand there are several there for me.

By now I have most of my Christmas shopping done. What is your thinking about what I asked about Joan's gift?

I sure miss you more and more. I just had a sip of Cherry Heering and we proposed a toast to you. I'm very happy to be with Kirsten this month. We are enjoying each other's company.

My thoughts are very much with you and I pray that time will fly and that we shall soon know peace.

Much love
Elin

Philadelphia, Pennsylvania
November 15, 1967

Dear Bill,

Well we arrived home yesterday and I had three letters waiting for me. I had only been gone five days so what a treat. I understand you are getting mixed experiences - war is a mess. I sure hope you are settled in your new job by the time this reaches you, and I also hope Joe gets out of everyone's hair, period. Can't they ship him out instead of making it hard for 10 people around him. You always seem to pick some dunces.

I'm baking brownies now for you and Jack, and also I am sending today a small box with canned food for you. Nothing much, just a bit of cheese.

Yesterday we had a very good day. We stopped at Princeton and took Kirsten's girl friend out for lunch. She is a lovely girl, just newly married and we had much fun. Then we dropped in on the McClures. They just moved into the most gorgeous home, just a dream palace. The kids have the whole upstairs and the parents are downstairs, an ideal situation. Everyone was excited to see Kirsten. Only Teddy recognized her. We will have to go back soon. The Thompsons might come before I leave, around December 15. I have a plane reservation for December 19. I wish it wasn't so soon. So much more to do now that Kirsten is here.

Bill, I found a big platter for Mother's dishes, so that's her Christmas gift, along with some other little things. I think I will give Mike and Kathy a high chair. Kirsten and Tom's gift I have. I also sent Jack a big food box from both of us. So now I just have to get gifts for the grandmothers. So this year don't try to send things. Too much work at this time. Later on you can shop with next Christmas in mind. Should I send a check to Joan? I really think we could help her if we gave her $50. I am doing just fine money wise, and all I need is $200 a month, so please go ahead with your good plans. I'm quite excited to think we might save all that money. It should be 10 months times $500. It will give me plenty and you plenty too. Even with the $1,000 back in savings I still have a $500 cushion and that should be enough once I get Christmas over with. I won't spend so much anyway so don't worry about it. I even plan to get more money put back in savings. But I'm waiting 'till I get back to Denmark.

Am sending my love two small boxes today. Hope they get there in fine shape.

Much love- Elin

Minneapolis, Minnesota
November 15, 1967

Dear Elin,

Thank you so much for the stockings. They fit perfectly and match my dress quite well. And believe me, I'm going to need them with the cold weather we're having here. It was down to 18 degrees this morning.

My roommate Sandy and I are going down to Chicago for the Thanksgiving holidays. I talked to Aunt Catherine and Uncle Loren last night. They invited us to stay with them, so we will. It should be fun and a nice change. Herb will be there, too. I know they will show us a good time.

I still don't know Bill's address. Would you either tell Mother to send it to me, or would you send it to me? Thank you. I'd like to write to him, especially now that he's so far away from home.

I'm so sorry I'll miss you at Christmas time. It's a shame my vacation time doesn't start a little earlier.

My school work is coming along just fine. I guess Mother told you I made the honor roll. My social life is great, too. I'm getting to date a variety of fellows. The mid-westerners are quite different from the easterners, however. They're so much more casual. I'm just beginning to get used to it now.

Please write if you get a chance and thank you again for the stockings.

Love Joan

Chu Lai, Vietnam
November 16, 1967

Dear Elin,

Well, we're finally getting organized after a few frantic days of moving in the rest of the personnel. I have about 200 men and 11 officers in the PSD, with more to come. Some real fine people and believe it or not it's shaping up fast, although there will be many headaches. But it's fun to set up something this big & the time disappears. To top it off a new AG colonel reported in today, much to the surprise of the present AG who didn't know about it and had expected to stay here.

I got your letter today mailed on November 6 - 10 days. So by now you've probably been to New York and back. Sounds like you and Kirsten are having a great time. I'm really glad that she was able to spend this time with you. I think this is an excellent idea with the car (Did Kirsten ever get a license?).

Did you ever get the film I sent? I don't remember what's on it except pictures taken at Travis and the Philippines, and the beach where we first stayed. I'll take some more pictures of this place when the weather gets better. Been raining periodically and cloudy most of the time.

I have a real bed now (someone scrounged it for me) and a small mattress (must get a better one), plus a big wardrobe locker and am quite comfortable. We have someone scouting for a big refrigerator which is the only comfort item needed. They are trying to reconfigure the officer billeting so we will get more space. There are 8 of us in this hooch and it is rather cramped. But it's 100% better than before and I really don't care. Am spending every night at the office now anyway. Although the big workload & crash projects haven't started yet, there is much to straighten out.

How's my love doing? When do you plan to go to Denmark? It's too early to tell now, but I will definitely try to leave here through Bangkok & India, etc. so you can meet me somewhere. I don't know where to go on R&R (long time off). Either Bangkok or Australia. If I'm going to Bangkok anyway I may go to Australia. A lot of people are getting two R&R's here. Been here a month and a half already and soon it will be Christmas. We are saving up our booze rations for a big Christmas party (lasting a week!).

Well Honey - will write more later - take care & I love you.

Bill

Philadelphia, Pennsylvania
November 16, 1967

Dear Bill,

Today is extremely cold and we are bundling up in furs and gloves. Seems weird to think of you way over there in the heat.

I'm very happy with Kirsten here. We are having more fun talking. We had a liverwurst and bacon sandwich on the Avenue today.

Westmoreland wants more men in Vietnam. There is talk about a short stoppage in the air bombing - like 24 hours for Christmas. I wrote to Carole Reekie a long letter. It's nice that he (Keith) got on the Times. I hope he settles a bit. Some day we will see we have very nice and interesting friends. I love them all and draw much life from knowing we have so many friends.

Mother went back to school today and I feel her cold is mostly gone. I hope I don't get it, but I don't think so.

I'm buying my ticket for December 19. I will be home on December 20. Joan comes here for two weeks, and then Jack returns in two months so your mother shouldn't be too alone. She is kind of frightened to be by herself, and a bit immature about it. But I tell her one gets used to being alone, at least never get scared. She could get a dog too. It must be hard but it is to be expected.

Must close now. Hope you have settled in a better job. I'm excited to hear what all was resolved.

I miss you and send much love.

Elin

Philadelphia, Pennsylvania
November 18, 1967

Dear Love,

Received two letters - don't quite understand why you are not getting more of my letters. I usually have mailed one a day.

About money. I don't need anymore than the $200. This is my fifth time I have reconfirmed this. In fact I'm enclosing the bank statements because I think the Army over paid us $509.05, but I want you to check on it. I am exactly $509.05 off with what the bank shows. Maybe it's the bank's mistake. Please see what you can find out - or did I forget to enter $509.05 in my books. If so what was it in payment for?

Also please return the bank statements again as I want to keep continuity in my bookkeeping. The $1,000 I transferred to savings, and when I get to Denmark I will transfer more but first must get that $509.05 straight.

Please start that Soldiers Deposit business. Unless you start now it will be hardly worth it.

I am flying home on December 19th and I will pay for my ticket this week - $252.50. That will leave me with $500, and most of my Christmas shopping is done so I don't anticipate any extra expenses so you can see I'm doing fine. In January I plan to put $500 more in savings and eventually get back what we took out in July. That was just a loan you know, and we really should live off of it. I have helped with the groceries a little bit here, and I pay my upkeep and the cars, but really I have few expenses and few desires for anything without you around.

I am so happy for you that you finally got your job squared away. It seems like a mess to me, but then I guess it was to be expected. I wish you much luck with this job. I'm glad the days are going fast for you and hope that will continue. It's Saturday and Mother is out playing bridge. Kirsten and I just shopped for the turkey dinner. We both paid for part of it. Your mother is hard to help - she wants to do it all. Charlie is fine. He is quite happy at the home. We are going to see him now. He is off medicine as of next week, so it will be harder for your mother from now on. I think he as a person is better off in the home. There are constant activities there. He played bingo and won twice. He also knows the gossip about everyone there. He is cheerful and eats three meals a day.

I'll close now. Love and miss you as always.

Elin

Philadelphia, Pennsylvania
November 18, 1967

Dear Far and Mor

Now I have finally ordered my ticket for Denmark. I'm flying with SAS the 19th of December and will arrive December 20th at Kastrup at 9 in the morning. Then I can get a connection to Bildringer (Odense) at 12:10. I'm not too excited about the trip with Falck. Is there a chance I can get picked up? Now be honest, can Far fetch me in Bildringer?

Kirsten and I are sitting here and having a cozy time. She is embroidering her bell pull, and only has one more picture to finish. Unfortunately my bell pull was packed and I am missing yarn to finish it.

Bill writes constantly. He got a letter from Mor, and he said it made his week. He also said he admires both Far and Mor a lot, and looks up to you. He is probably OK, but is irritated over the pettiness among the officers he has to work with.

Next week it is Thanksgiving and after that we are going to Connecticut again to find an apartment for Kirsten and Tom. Now Kirsten and I have decided that she can drive my car the 9 months. That way it will get looked after and I won't have to sell it. It's too complicated to ship it to Denmark, and also expensive. Kirsten can't drive Tom's Porsche with all its gears, etc. so our small green Ford will suit her fine. I just bought new snow tires and I called the insurance company and it is no problem if she drives it. Now she has to get an American driver's license. Then Bill can get a sports car if he wants when he comes back. I want a four door car , so it is stupid to sell it and lose all that money. Don't you think that sounds OK? It will help both Kirsten and me.

Kirsten and I have been to town to shop. She is almost finished with her bell pull so she bought a new embroidery, a bedspread. It will be very elegant when finished. It is a cross stitch so I told her if she get tired of it she can send one part to me and a part to Mor. Unfortunately my embroideries are all packed away.

I have my ticket now. I bought a ticket all the way to Bangkok..... now we'll see if I'll need it. Bill writes letters now, he has gotten a regular bed and mattress and a bigger closet. He has a small space about 7 x 5 meters in a "hooch" shared with 8 officers. He is organizing his office.

We are having fun and when we find an apartment we will write.

I am looking forward to a happy reunion. Now, there are not even 9 months left.

Elin

Chu Lai, Vietnam
November 20, 1967

Hi Honey,

Just got your letter mailed from Brooklyn. And I'm glad that you and Kirsten had the opportunity to gallivant around New York. Must have been fun.

We are in the middle of organizing and reorganizing and getting ourselves organized and it's some mess, but actually fun and quite a huge challenge. I'm getting used to the routine (After 4th AD, Fort Hood and now this I think I could organize anything). A lot of good people in my shop but will need a lot more. I've been putting in long days all week - 'til about 10 P.M. But the days and weeks go fast. Almost have two months in already and that doesn't seem possible. Haven't been out of the headquarters since I was moved up here. But have to visit some of the units pretty soon.

We finally got a refrigerator in the hooch - a big full size with big freezer compartment. The "Judge" - Captain Springer - has been doing some legal work for some Navy people and in return is getting steaks, food, etc. So tomorrow night I think we're having a barbeque. Weather has been nice & cool. Very comfortable sleeping. Not much rain lately.

Thanksgiving already next week. Maybe I'll make some martinis,

Well not much more to write about right now, except work & I have enough of that.

Love you!
Bill

Nha Trang, Vietnam
November 21, 1967

Dear Bill,

Please excuse the delay in answering your letter but I do have a reasonably good excuse this time. I had the operation on the 13th and things have been pretty much a fog from then until yesterday. Except for being quite weak and hungry everything is looking up now. I still have quite a bit of discomfort but time will take care of this. I finally had a small amount of food today and was the most delicious I ever had.

I'm glad to hear that things are looking up there and hope that by the time you receive this letter things are really on the move. I have tried to get a definite answer from the doctor regarding my future status but still no definite answer. He did tell me that I would be hospitalized for 6 more weeks, 3 weeks minimum at Camp Zama for getting back into shape and then a leave if I wanted it. Based on the time involved I doubt that, even if I'm allowed to return, I can get back to Americal. I think I would be thrown in the replacement stream or an assignment from here to USARV headquarters.

I'm very doubtful of it but I will daydream a bit and hope I make the next promotion list.

So far I haven't received any of the bundles of mail you sent to Nha Trang and hope my foot locker is on the way. Give my warmest regards to everyone and still hoping I can make it back there,

Bob (Captain Bob Dove)

Philadelphia, Pennsylvania
November 21, 1967

Dear Bill,

Yesterday I got a real good letter from my love - you sound so much better now that you are out from under pettiness. I do pray the year will fly by for you without too much suffering mental or physical problems. I got your letter before going down town for my ticket so guess what I did. One way to Copenhagen is $252. One way Copenhagen Bangkok is $660. I save $100 by buying them together, so my love I splurged and bought the ticket all the way. I can have the ticket converted to anything else, or refunded. It's good for one year so I can't see how I can lose anything. Now if I do meet you in Bangkok I wonder how we will get back, but we shall cross that bridge when it comes. We sure better start putting pennies aside. I now have $100 in Spokane checking and $150 in Philadelphia. I'm not counting the $509.05 'till I know what it is all about. And I should get $200 on December 1 so I'm in grand shape.

I have a stomachache over excitement about Bangkok. If I can cook something up I might even go there for a couple of months if you think you can get there more than once.

All the Giandalias are coming for Thanksgiving, which is Thursday. Tomorrow is Wednesday. Mother is taking 27 kids to a play in the afternoon. Kirsten & I are going to help chaperone. The play is "John Brown's Body." It should be nice. Uncle Charlie is coming home just for dinner on Thursday.

We plan to go back to Connecticut on Monday and hope to find a reasonable apartment. Most rent for $200 which is a bit steep.

I do hope you are getting along fine. I do worry at times but other times I know you are fine - I just have that feeling.

It's getting cold here now and they predicted snow maybe soon. Must seem odd with you being so hot. Just now we are talking about the Christmas when Jack, Ned and Kirsten had Christmas with us in Germany. That was a fun one.

Much love and affection. I'm dreaming of you now - they are all happy dreams.

Love Elin

COMMANDER'S MESSAGE

On this traditional Thanksgiving Day, as we find ourselves half way around the world from home, we should pause for a few moments to count our many blessings as Americans. We should never forget that in Vietnam, our actions are defending free men everywhere. We pray that peace will come to all the world and that all of us can return to our loved ones in the not too distant future.

W. C. WESTMORELAND
General, United States Army
Commanding

Philadelphia, Pennsylvania
November 21, 1967

Dear Jack,

I'm so excited to think you are a sergeant – few people get to be that as rapid as you. I do hope you eventually get the pay that goes with the rank.

Jack, about buying things – I personally think if you have the money to spare, you should get yourself a set of Noritaki china – something like "Blue Dawn" or "Gold Lane" are nice. You can hardly get everyday dishes that cheap here. Mother doesn't need any, and no one else in the family needs dishes now. So why don't you get a set for your future home. If your "chosen" doesn't like them, use them for every day. I guarantee you'll never regret it. Almost everything in the catalogue is a good buy. Stainless is, the crystal is, but only get things you really like. You might even have a bachelor place for a while and would enjoy having nice things. Steer away from things that have oriental designs on them. One tires of it in the end, and don't get too many touristy things.

The brass candlesticks are excellent buys, so are most of the brassware. Only choose simple looking things. Remember, plain things mix with almost everything. Don't worry about getting things for Bill and me. We can do our own bargain shopping now. Mike and Kathy might appreciate something practical for their new home, like a cherrywood salad set. Those are very expensive here – it's 8.75 in the catalogue for 11 pieces, or a nice Lazy Susan – 3.25 F. Bill and I have the stainless steel dinnerware – B – on page 124. I paid $100 for the set. In the book it's $33.95 – you compare. I have a catalogue so if you have specific questions I'll be happy to give my opinion. Hope this has all been of some help.

Hope you are fine. I wish you a fine Thanksgiving. I'm thankful you and Bill are healthy.

Love
Elin

Philadelphia, Pennsylvania
November 24, 1967

Dear Bill,

It's the day after Thanksgiving. Everything went fine. Uncle Charlie was home 6 hours and got up the stairs by himself. He was very happy to be home but he was tired when we took him back to the home. He is gaining weight and isn't complaining as much as he used to.

Mike and Kathy were here. She looks cute now and had on the white dress I gave her. Her parents were here with her brother Jimmy. After dinner Charlie showed his pictures. Kirsten and I did the dishes.

These months here have taught me a lot about the family I married in to. I have not changed my views on it, only now I have learned to live with it. I now realize the uselessness of arguing or even trying to change anything, and I feel free of an enormous burden. I realize that you are not like that and that you and I have a life all our own. I only hope that we will keep growing and not fall into other traps of living. It's easy you know. Remember how many nights were wasted when we would have a couple of beers, etc. I also hope you and I will learn to have real arguments where real understanding evolves. Sometime you are afraid of being truthful because of what used to be a reaction. But Bill, without discussion how can one have real understanding. Only when we say words do we convey ideas. Oh - I'm so excited to talk, talk, talk to you again. We have so much yet to explore in the world. My heart is bursting to go see it all and experience it all. Even to hear about all of the atrocities you now are learning about and seeing - that too is part of life.

Just think I might see you in Bangkok. Who would have ever thought of that.

Are you still getting out of the Army? If you are I guess we should conserve even more of our funds. Where would you want to settle then? California or the East, the South - the North, and, what would you now like to go into? I have made up my mind to become a teacher. Of that I'm sure, and if I had only known you were getting out I never would have planned to go to Denmark. Maybe we could both teach, or maybe you would stay and get a degree and teach, or maybe you'll become a great TV star - Johnny Carson and you could be twins.

How are some of the people you live and work with? You never mention any. Is Beery still with you or did you lose him in the shuffle? How are your new bosses? Nice I hope. How was Thanksgiving over there - depressing?

Honey, don't get too worked up about Christmas. It's just another day in the year and there will be so many good ones later that you can miss one. It sure isn't worth a week of headache.

I hope we have luck in Connecticut this time. We are leaving Monday. Tom should be home the following Monday. They are so in love, it's just wonderful to see Kirsten. She is so sweet and Tom is so good to her. I hope they will always be that happy.

I send all my love and I feel very near to you because I know you too have me in your heart. You know that knowledge makes it all easier. Somehow I know we are together and everything is all right.

Bye now
Elin

Philadelphia, Pennsylvania
November 24, 1967

Dear Bill,

Thanksgiving Day is over but not as it used to be. Of course we had a turkey and I invited Mike, Kathy, her parents, because the girls were here. We brought Charlie home and had all the trimmings but at the pit of my stomach I had a strange ache. Why do we change in life as we do? Why do families break apart, move, migrate, go to war, etc. I remembered holidays with the Walkers, Auntie Jule, Ruth, Rube, Dave, your father, and it all seemed so gay. But Mike said to me Thursday night, "Mother, this is the first year I've ever seen you so calm, lacking nervousness, and you ate your dinner." I told him it was the frozen daiquiris he fed me but really I think I was so introverted with the past, that I wasn't worrying about the present! A switch!

Your letters sound better - as though you are adapting after a frustrating start. I do hope all goes well and that your danger is at a minimum. I tacked the Geographic map on the cellar door and I watch for all the names mentioned. I have your area circled. The last battle for hill 875 was a bitter one according to our news reporters. It saddens and sickens me.

Mr. Haynes, my neighbor several houses below Ritchies, has a son on the coast near Chu Lai but I forget the name of the town. He is 1st Lt. Paul Haynes and his father is mighty proud of him.

Michael, Kathleen, Joan, and I are going to spend a quiet Christmas at their home. I cannot have parties and crowds here while you boys are over there in a war. I'll celebrate when you come home. Also, with Charlie ill, I have no desire to have a gang here.

Uncle Ralph surprised me by calling and asking me to go to dinner last night! I accepted and he came with his new girl friend, whom he hopes to marry some day. She was very chic and very different from Jean. She is a private secretary at Du Pont in Wilmington, has been divorced and is the mother of a seven year old girl. I had a good dinner and we came back here talking (also Elin and Kirsten) until one this morning. I like her. She is the kind he should have married years ago. He is trying to straighten himself out with the income tax bureau and then pay back all his debts ($25,000). What a mess! He especially wanted to be remembered to you.

No more thoughts tonight. It is late and I need sleep so I'll dream of you

My love always,
Mother

RALPH WILLIAMS

Ralph Williams entered the Marines the day after he graduated from high school in June 1943. He was with the Marines in World War II during the invasion of Guam, Tinian, Saipan and Iwo Jima where he was wounded.

Chu Lai, Vietnam
November 25, 1967

Dear Elin,

Realize that it's been a few days since I wrote to you - Although I have absolutely no conception of time - or days here. I don't know whether today is Friday, Saturday, or Sunday! I received quite a few letters from you this week - all happy ones - and I'm glad that everything has worked out so well these past weeks. Also got your package today which I very much appreciate. Some things are easy to get here, but others are impossible. The work is tremendous now as you can imagine, but I am enjoying it & things are rapidly pulling together. It's quite a challenge for everyone involved and most are reacting accordingly.

Enclosed is a menu of our Thanksgiving dinner. Believe me it was delicious and old Sergeant Santiago, the mess chief, put his heart into it. So I got stuffed.

I went to Finance on the $509 deposit. It wasn't made from here, but there have been several instances where Fort Hood has sent deposits of that month to banks of officers who left the 198th Brigade! Wrote to the bank for the check number and who prepared it. I changed the allotment to the bank but it won't be effective until January. Nevertheless this will put in money you can transfer to the savings account, and have available if necessary. Once you put money in Soldiers Deposits you can't get it out until you are back in the States. So starting in January I'll have $2900 going to the bank, $550 to Soldiers Deposits, and $125 to me. I expect to save enough out of the $125 for the R&R & also to buy things.

I think it's a good idea to send Joan $50. Why don't you just go ahead and write the check. The other gifts sound great. There is nothing to buy here. I'll get things in Bangkok (or wherever I go). May be able to get two R&Rs! I'd like to go to Australia. I've talked to people who have been there and they say it's fantastic.

We are going to be able to get our data processing machines soon. All I need to get them are personnel with experience, so I'm on a campaign. I already snagged an infantry lieutenant who has worked in data processing and we are trying to get some more men in the Division who have experience and schooling. I have to go to Saigon soon to coordinate this and some other things. I'm going to try to get Colonel Jame's help.

Well Honey, much love to you, I'm fine and the year is already 1/6 gone. Only 10 more months!

Much love –
Bill

Chu Lai, Vietnam
November 25, 1967

Dear Mother,

I was glad to receive your letter - and card (which I set out in my office) and am especially glad that the arrangement with Uncle Charlie has worked out so well - both for him and you. Elin writes that he is happy there - making friends - and enjoying the attention. Did he come home for Thanksgiving? I know it is the best thing for you to have some freedom, and as long as it can be financed, is the best solution.

The days and weeks go fast here - I'm quite busy now & working every night until about 10 pm. I have a big section, 11 officers and 250 men, 7 cover a vast area of actions. It's really interesting and a great challenge to set up - in view of the combat situation of the units & men we are servicing. Living is Spartan but quite comfortable & I have no complaints whatsoever. Not much time for leisure, but then there is no need for it.

Got a Thanksgiving card from Uncle Loren and Aunt Kay, which I appreciated. Also got a box of goodies from my old friend Mrs. Sternelle. She is a dear person to do that.

I'm glad that Kirsten was able to come to Philadelphia this past month. I know that she and Elin must be enjoying their time together. How are Mike and Kathy doing? Elin wrote that you had dinner at their place.

Well, nothing too exciting - war stories or anything - to write about. Just the paper war that is the same anywhere in the Army. So will close for now.

Much love,
Bill

Philadelphia, Pennsylvania
November 27, 1967

Hi Darling -

Just a quick note. I'm in the car, waiting for Kirsten to say goodbye to Uncle Charlie. We are going back up to Connecticut to look for an apartment for Tom and Kirsten.

Friday night Vivian was over for dinner. She is very sweet. On Saturday Uncle Ralph and his girl friend Blanche took Mother out for dinner. His girl friend is a very stunning divorcee. Quite good looking, dyed blond, high piled hair and the latest in clothes. They looked like they were very much in love.

On Sunday Kirsten and I drove to Limeport. Heard Mike preach and had dinner at their house - roast and macaroni. We again inspected their new house. They will move in Saturday.

Darling I miss you, but the somehow the time does go. And it seems like soon we will start 1968 and then it will be downhill.

I have a feeling you are only getting half my letters because I've had several (not important) specific questions and never heard anything. Also it seems like you are not getting as many as I write. Often I send a letter a day.

Much love and affection and remember I'm right with you in thoughts.

Love- Elin

Minneapolis, Minnesota
November 27, 1967

Dear Elin,

As you may imagine, I was flabbergasted when I opened your letter today. I can't thank you and Bill enough for your generosity. But I can't write to Bill yet as I still don't have his new address. I have decided to send him some pictures, and I'll find some other little things to send him. As you were a student away from home, I'm sure you know how handy that check will come in.

My roommate Sandy and I had a wonderful, relaxing holiday in Chicago. Aunt Catherine cooked some wonderful meals for us. It was the next best thing to being home. We went downtown the day after Thanksgiving, and tried to shuffle through quite a crowd of people. I think everyone in the Midwest came to Chicago for the parade and to begin their Christmas shopping. But it was fun to be in a big city. We flew back from Chicago as it only cost a dollar more. We had a wonderful flight back with a delicious luncheon on the plane.

Now that I'm back in Minneapolis, I'm trying to get in the swing of studying again. I had two tests today, one paper to write, and am looking forward to a psychology test on Thursday. I'll probably have a lot to do before the Christmas holidays.

It's beginning to get really cold out here. Last night it went down to 8 degrees below zero. But we still haven't had any snow. I really hope we don't get much, because then wouldn't be able to go out too much.

Write soon and tell Mother I'll probably write to her tomorrow.

Thank you again for your check. You are, without a doubt, a most wonderful sister to me. I'm only sorry we don't get to see each other more

Take care – love,
Joan

Chu Lai, Vietnam
November 29, 1967

Dear Elin,

The past three days have been busy, hundreds of things to be done & not enough time to do them all. It's good to be so busy though, and see a full 10 months of planning & work ahead. Actually I'm enjoying it (the work). After Hurt (he calls me at least twice a day) this is heaven. Tonight we barbequed steaks at the hooch & had steaks, pickles & beer and hot bread fresh from the Army bakery - excellent! The "Judge" has been scrounging food & now we have a freezer of steaks (at least 75).

Today I got a package from Uncle Loren & Aunt Kay. Really nice - different cheeses, Danish sausage, nuts, crackers, kippered herring, etc. I'm saving these goodies for Christmas.

I'm really excited about your buying a ticket to Bangkok. I'm sure that I'll be able to go back that way. Also I'll get an R&R, so there is a possibility of getting there if you went there early. (What do you have in mind? I know that there is some plan brewing!). Everyone who has been to Bangkok says it's fantastic. The AG went to Tokyo on TDY for three days after he got here. Wish I could get a TDY trip like that.

Is Kirsten still in Philadelphia? How was Thanksgiving dinner with the Giandalias? I haven't gotten any letters for 5 days, but that's not unusual. Often I get 3 or 4 from you on one day.

The weather has been nice, not too warm & little rain. Went to the officers' club last night instead of working & watched the ocean below. This area will most likely be a big resort some day. Have you heard from Jack recently? I haven't written to him.

Well good night Honey. I love you & miss you.

Bill

Ridgefield, Connecticut
November 30, 1967

Dear Bill,

Elin and I are having some very happy days. We looked and looked for an apartment for Tom and I, and finally found this, which is small and cute. We have been shopping and pretty soon we will have it quite in shape. How are you Bill, I'm hearing about some of the things you write from Elin.

I so hope that time will go not too slow for both of you, till you meet. Today was a pretty messy snowfall for the first in the season. A truck up ahead of us today couldn't make it up a hill and hundreds of others sat waiting for more than ½ hour.

There are flies in this apartment (this time of year?) We have been spraying them, now they are all buzzing around dying.

I really had a good time at your mother's house. I like the 3rd floor, it looks real cozy. Elin has started me thinking of color coordinating the different rooms here. She gives me good advice, so it worked out real good that we can spend this time together. I wish she was staying longer with me. Tom is coming back from

California December 10th. I wonder how he will like the apartment, it is real odd. Tom went to the wine place where all four of us went wine tasting , and he ordered us a case of the kind of wine we bought with you. We might have a chance to get transferred to California one day. Maybe we can get together all four of us, in Denmark next. That will be a great experience for Mor and Far.

Take care of yourself,
Kirsten

Ridgefield, Connecticut
November 30, 1967

Dear Bill,

It is Thursday already and I have only written my honey one letter this week.

Our trip from Philadelphia to Connecticut went smoothly. We looked at the map and saw that Nana Walker and Aunt Helen lived 20 miles from where we wanted to rent an apartment, so as soon as we reached Norwalk we called them. They told us to come on over. We bought a local paper, and drove over. Kirsten had called about an apartment. We were to see it at 5 pm. It was 4:15 pm so Jeff (your cousin) and two of his friends - all long hair hip looking, piled in the back to show the way and we drove off. I kept my usual speed but all three youngsters asked that I slow down. What a switch! We found a small two room apartment atop a store, with no windows in the kitchen so we said no thank you. We took the boys back and Aunt Helen asked us to stay for dinner. Joe came home early at 6:45. He drives 1½ or 2 hours a day. What a drag.

We had a lovely meal. Nana Walker looked great. She has a nice bedroom fixed up very modern. The candlestick we gave her is very prominent and she loves it. The house is a converted summer house in a swamp. A German added on to it himself (it looks it) and they are paying $265 a month - unbelievable. One bath - tiny - and three small bedrooms, one large living/dining and kitchen. Aunt Helen and Joe have very good sense for making nice things, but the whole house is filled to the point that one cannot see the results properly. Helen was making some owls out of tin cans and stones when we came, and Joe is making a stereo component cabinet. Nana was making a Christmas wreath and sewing pot holders; and, four cats were making themselves at home on tables, etc. What a menagerie. We had more fun - they are very refreshing to talk to and one could learn a lot about what to make and how. All wanted me to remember them to you, especially Nana. She looks great and she only has good to say about everyone. I like that.

We checked into a motel - $16 - and hardly slept all night for the noise in the walls. We then started looking again the next day and saw more dumps. One $200 a month apartment converted in an old home even had built-in mice in the loft. We then called about a small furnished place. We drove out on a farm road, all suburban by now, and came to this charming farm. The apartment was the third floor - a loft. It has a center staircase that comes up into the kitchen, with a room on either side, and a bath. The rent is $100 a month all inclusive, so we took it. We had to put a deposit on it and the owner drove home from New York office - 60 miles away. He is in real estate and sells hotels and motels. The downstairs is just filled with antiques and they have a housekeeper, a very comfortable place. Also, Kirsten would be safe when she is alone. The people are very sweet and I feel Tom and Kirsten will be happy here.

Carol (and Roger Baretz) had called me in Philadelphia before we left and insisted we stay with them so off we went. It was a one hour drive from here and we had dinner with them and stayed. They are very concerned about you, and have proved to be very good friends just like the DeNios. The next day we (Kirsten, Carol and I) went to Manhattan. I drove and we shopped all day. We had much fun and I didn't buy anything. Kirsten found a beautiful ceramic lamp that she bought and a long hanging lamp. We went to Bloomingdale's - very exciting things. Nothing else in the world equals their furniture department. At least I have never seen anything that equals it. We also went to the decorator centers. You must have a decorator along to buy anything. The prices of the antiques are unbelievable. A biedermeirer mirror was $1,000. I wonder if they get it. We took Carol back and went shopping for cleaning things for the apartment. I remembered every time I went out and shopped and was sad that we were not shopping for our new place.

We are now cleaning out the loft. It reminds me of Barefoot in the Park. The refrigerator starts with a bang, the cooking is on hot plates, the water is from a well and all is very primitive and cute. This will be fixed up to be darling. One can really use one's imagination. There are doors leading out to rooms under the roof so there is lots of storage space. The furniture consists of very simple, straight uncomfortable things. One double bed and one single bed. A table and two chairs will do fine until their things arrive.

We called Tom and he is coming home next Sunday instead of this Sunday, so I'll have to stay longer. She can't stay here alone without a car or anything. I hope Mother understands. I'm sorry I only have such short time until December 19. Just not time enough. Friday Mother is going up to Mike and Kathy. They are moving and their place is a gem. I sent Joan a $50 check. It should help her as well as Mother, without giving your Mother money.

I'm very upset over the shifts in the Defense Department. Something is brewing - one wonders what. One wonders how this whole thing will end. I'm taking one day at a time and keeping super super busy. Fixing up this little place together with Kirsten is taking my mind off lots of things.

I miss you a lot, especially when I go to New York and do all these exciting things. It just seems like you should be here with me. So much to talk about, so much life to live, so many ideas to share - and writing is just too slow.

Hope to get your mail forwarded here. The address here is c/o Pollack, Bennet Farm Road, Ridgefield, Connecticut. We are going shopping again for more food and stuff.

Hope all is well with you.

I love you dearly.
Elin

Elin and Bill with Carol Baretz in Germany - 1963

Valley Cottage, New York
December 2, 1967

Dear Bill,

I miss you so. Last night I saw a one hour TV program filmed in and around Chu Lai. It was "Same Mud, Same Blood," a very moving and realistic view of the war, and I felt so sorry for all the men over there sweating. Getting wet - drenching in the mud - being shot at. It all seems so endless and now Mr. MacNamara is gone. I wonder what all is going on. Kirsten is sewing blinds for her new apartment. We are back at the Baretzs' and Kirsten and I have many fabulous ideas for fixing up the attic. I think that it will be a real cute love nest. I just called Mike and Kathy. They are moving. Also called Mother, she is going up to help move today. It snowed all over so she was afraid to leave until Saturday. She received your letter dated 25 November - said you were fine.

The weather is unusually beautiful - white snow and brilliant sunshine. Couldn't be prettier. Connecticut is beautiful too. You would love where Kirsten & Tom are. Tom isn't coming till next Sunday so I have to remain up here so she isn't stuck without a car. On Monday she gets a phone put in.

I sure wish Tom had seen the before and after of that apartment because it is really going through a change. One can buy such fun things in this country, not at all like when we started in Germany. Kirsten and I haven't slept well since last Sunday in Philadelphia. By now I'm almost dizzy from not resting. There are so many new noises to get used to.

This month will fly for me. So much happening - sure hope it will fly for you too. Don't get too depressed around Christmas. Just remember it is only another day and we will have many lovely days together soon. I have done most of our Christmas giving already. I found a big platter in Royal Danish porcelain in your mother's pattern. I gave it to her already so she could use it for the turkey on Thanksgiving. She is very pleased with it. I also bought her a nice spice rack - she liked it. I mailed Joan her $50.00 check. Jack, I sent a box of food. Mike & Kathy - I have several ideas, and I'll get your two grandmothers something nice. I'm signing all the gifts Elin and Bill. After all it's your money that's paying for it all. I'll take a bottle of Scotch for Far and I mailed a dress for Mor.

Honey I'm going to close. Hope you are well and in good spirits.

Love
Elin

Chu Lai, Vietnam
December 3, 1967

Hi Love,

I'm sitting here in the hooch by myself - sipping some Cherry Heering & thinking of you. Got four packages today - two from you, cookies from Kirsten and some goodies and tobacco from Mike and Kathy. I really was happy to get all of it. Especially my honey's little gourmet items - great! I'll have to lay out a spread at Christmas for the guys in the hooch. Everything arrived OK except some of the crackers broke. I've got a whole shelf full of goodies now and have cheese in the refrigerator.

Things have been hectic here - crash projects, trying to get systems established, etc. We have a new AG - LTC Chung - appears to be real sharp. There has been a lot of action around here this week, in the Division area. Apparently a lot of North Vietnamese regulars are in the sector. A 198th Brigade Captain was killed this morning when his jeep hit a mine. The 198th has lost about 15 men so far.

I've got some good officers in the section. Captain Shivar is my assistant - real fine person. He is about 38 years old, from North Carolina, has a real Southern accent. Then there is LT Jaquez. He is from Mexico and his wife is Dutch. She is in Holland now. LT Nichols (a bit stubborn) I do not know well yet. Also LT McMahon (who just got here). Then there are four warrant officers - CWO DeValle (an outstanding person - real sharp), WO Tipton, WO Buxton & WO Lilly. Of course LT Yates is here and WO Harmon (who is now on the hospital ship - he has been having much trouble with his eyes).

I got your long letter yesterday and read it several times. I'm glad that you have made peace with yourself over the fact that you are not going to change my family. You should never get trapped in pettiness & static situations.

Next day - 4 Dec 67

We have so much fun together & I mostly miss sharing feelings & ideas with someone.

Next day - 5 Dec 67

Well - you see I didn't get this finished yesterday. I lose all track of time & things have been so hectic here. So much to be done and it takes time but it's expected to be done.

By the time you get this I will have been here two months. The first month seemed like an eternity but now the weeks fly - the days just merge into each other. I've been sitting here eating brownies and raisons! - and everyone in the office enjoyed the French strawberry drops! I bought a bottle of Cognac & around Christmas will have to fix a gourmet spread with all the delicacies you sent.

Well love - I'm going to sign off just to get this - finally - in the mail.

Love you very much,
Bill

Ridgefield, Connecticut
December 4, 1967

We just returned from New York where we spent the weekend with Carol and Roger. Kirsten was very busy and she got most of her curtains and drapes done for the small attic. We made cloth shades in wild colors. Really a great idea - now we hung everything and are making final adjustments on hems, etc. Tom called yesterday (he made five calls before he located us) and he was flying from San Francisco Sunday night at 6 o'clock. Picking the car up in Minneapolis today, Monday. Kirsten is terribly excited to see what he thinks of this place. We sure hope he approves. After all the elbow grease we are putting in to the place he better like it. It's very cheap and for the money, very cute.

I just called Mother. She was having a bridge group in. Had a nice letter from you and said I had three. Can't wait to read them all. Time this last week has flown - so much to do up here - almost wished I had longer to stay here. I do hope the four of us will get together. If we get to Denmark Tom and Kirsten plan to fly over too. Would be fun.

I'm upset by reading that Vietnam is ripe for a plague. Seems that when much foliage is destroyed the wild rat migrates to populated areas and gives disease to domestic rats and the fleas from the carcasses carry the plague. Sure hope they get the rats in Chu Lai under control soon. At this point I'm hoping for the next 10 to go quick and for a peaceful future. You and I have much good life together and single just doesn't cut it. I'm relatively content but far from happy. I know it's much worse on you - in fact I feel guilty when I have fun or when I'm comfortable. I think of how hard you are working to provide that comfort and peace of mind (material goods - peace of mind) that I have. It just doesn't seem fair. Seems like I should carry a heavy burden or load of the burden.

Tonight I hope the two of us will sleep.   The last night we slept here, neither of us slept - the old refrigerator goes on and off with a loud noise. How do you sleep - I guess you are so tired you just pass out. Does the heat or humidity bother you? I hope not too much.

I saw a TV special - scenes from Chu Lai. Beautiful beach – what it looks like - and what rains, what mud and slush.

I'm going to close for tonight. I do hope you are getting all your mail. I have given your address to several people. Nana Walker sent her box to you today. Everyone asks about you and are very concerned. The American public seems to be more aware of everything all of a sudden. Many mixed feelings and opinions. Kirsten is making good night tea. Sure wish you would be right here to enjoy it with us.

Good night my love. I'll have many pleasant dreams about you.

Love
Elin

Ridgefield, Connecticut
December 5, 1967

Hi Honey,

Today it seemed like we earned our keep. I scrubbed a wood floor down and waxed it. The house is from 1783 so the floor is old. We really got it looking nice. Then we went shopping again. Kirsten has spent $1,000.00 setting up this house, and there is so much more to go. She hasn't bought any furniture either for her money. I sure am glad we have all that behind us. We bought Carol a nice sewing basket as a thank you for all their hospitality.

Tom is supposed to show up tonight. Kirsten is busy finishing the curtains and after 5 weeks separation she is excited to see him. We just wrote out a list of the things she bought as an explanation for all the money used. I should be going back to Philadelphia at the end of this week, then I can answer your letters. Now I only have 2 weeks left in this country. Seems awfully short time. I still don't know how I will manage to get all my stuff to Denmark. 44 pounds just isn't enough for 10 months living. I think I will take your suit along so when you need it I'll mail it to you or bring it to you.

The weather is very beautiful here and I'm enjoying the Connecticut countryside very much. I hope you are still doing fine. I have a feeling you are all right. I'm doing very well and I'm looking forward to next year.

Love
Elin

Kirsten O'Donnell, Ridgefield, CT

Chu Lai, Vietnam
December 8, 1967

Dear Elin,

Tonight I'm on staff duty. Nothing to do so a good opportunity to sit & write lots of letters. Something I haven't done except to you and Mother. I wrote to the Welters & Bob Dove (was operated on in Japan) and will write a few more.

Things are starting to shape up in the PSD, although I'll be busy until I leave. Something new every hour. Still it's best to be extremely busy. Col. Chung is back from Tokyo. He is really fine - will be a pleasure to work for. Major Batts is the Deputy AG. (He was the AG of the 196th Brigade) - and a real character. He is a Negro & has a slow clipped accent. Quite intelligent but has some mannerisms that break everyone up. I really like him & it makes the tremendous workload much more bearable if there is a good working relationship with the bosses.

The weather continues to be cool - with sporadic torrential rain that lasts 5 or 10 minutes. If you're caught in it (and it comes quite unexpectedly) you're immediately drenched. Every time I look at the sea or sit at the officers' club at sundown - right over the ocean & watch the surf below I get the most nostalgic & the closest to getting melancholy. That brings back the most beautiful moments and most peaceful and warm times - and that's when I feel such an overwhelming love for you. I want to go back to California and live the way we should - in our hearts and in the depth of understanding and appreciation for all of the beauty of nature and ideas and people and just love of everything. It's simple and grand at once - and you and I loved each other more there because we had found a setting and an atmosphere that we fit into like a missing piece of a jigsaw puzzle.

I am so tired of mediocrity - it drags you down and it becomes more difficult to maintain your individuality as the years suck you into the routines of the social and working atmosphere. And all of a sudden you find that you've let little bits of yourself and your personality go to the system & you can't retract them within the system. It's been rewarding in many ways but I've learned all I need to know about it. The same situation and the same mundane people appear throughout it, and I'm not going to find anything else in it. I've looked & examined it and my place in it very deeply - and I want out. I'm sorry for my past indecision. I know they have been frustrating, even exasperating to you - and probably will again. More later on this.

I'm going to write to Jack now & hopefully to Hazel and the Reekies. But I feel drained of things to talk about. My whole days and nights are tied up in the PSD and there is no exciting experiences, etc. to relate.

So good night love - wish I were crawling into bed with you right now.

Bill

Chu Lai, Vietnam
December 8, 1967

Dear Jack,

Don't recall whether I ever answered your letter weeks ago. Things have been moving fast here. Now I'm stationed at Americal Division headquarters and head a 200 man Personnel Services Division - am still in Chu Lai - right overlooking the South China Sea - so it's a nice spot.

Things are hectic getting organized - working day and night - but it's shaping up - no time to get nostalgic.

Have been few places outside this area and I don't really intend to go anywhere - really tied down to my section. The work is interesting though I'll be ready for an R&R.

Exactly when do you leave Thailand? If I can swing it (doubtful) I will try to get an R&R to Bangkok if there would be any possibility that we could meet there. Still doubt if I can get away this soon.

How has your work been? Busy I imagine. I haven't seen much of Vietnamese life - went to the village of Chu Lai several weeks ago and it reminded me of sections of Beirut and Damascus but hardly as prosperous.

Jack let me hear from you and I'll promise to write sooner. Elin leaves for Denmark on 19 December.

Bill

Chu Lai, Vietnam
December 8, 1967

Dear Mother,

I was glad to receive your letter last week. I'm sure it wasn't a Thanksgiving like those past. You can never really recreate those wonderful situations or occasions in the past - just retain fond memories of them. But, you always have to look forward to new similar times.

Life here is somewhat a routine now - although a hectic one. But I enjoy the work & enjoy being constantly busy with not enough time (ever) to get all done that should be. This doesn't leave any time for melancholy! Already have been here two months. The rest of the time will go fast.

I'm glad that Joan will be home for Christmas & you should have a cozy time in Mike & Kathy's new house. Elin writes that it is a real gem, and it will be fun for them to have their first Christmas in a new home. Maybe you'll be able to spend some Christmases with us in the next years.

There is so much tragedy over here - but even that you become immune to when you process reports and statistics every day on casualties.

We've got Christmas decorations all over - even trees. I'm saving all of the delicacies that Elin, Uncle Loren, Aunt Kay and Mrs. Sternelle sent for Christmas to spread it all out for a celebration.

I don't have any real needs for anything material here. We have all of the essentials & a few luxuries & you really don't need extras. We have it so much better here at the headquarters than the troops in the field - although even in the base camps you'll find TVs and refrigerators! It's a strange war - full of many contrasts.

Tell Uncle Charlie that I send my regards. I'm glad that he is happy at the home. I know it was the best move as far as you are concerned. Well, will write again soon.

Take care & much love.
Bill

Ridgefield, Connecticut
December 8, 1967

Dear Bill,

We went over the two month mark.

Yesterday we had a grand time. Tom arrived from California Wednesday night about 9 o'clock and we were very excited to hear his judgment about the attic. It is quite rustic so he wasn't too enthusiastic. But the next day we showed him what is available and he decided it's OK. I guess they will buy a home if they are to live here long. Their new address is Bennet Farm Road, Ridgefield, Connecticut.

At 3 o' clock yesterday we went to Manhattan and exchanged their lamp and got the kind like Carol and Roger's. It's going to look great. Then we walked down and happened upon the lighting of the Christmas tree at Rockefeller Center - magnificent. We then had the "Kolde Bord" at Copenhagen Restaurant. $7.00 a dinner but well worth it. It was Tom's treat. We will go there when we are all in Manhattan again. (I had a stomachache all night from too much lobster, caviar, herring, liver paste, etc.) All Danish waitresses and nice atmosphere. Real treat. We then went down to the Village and walked the streets. Great book stores. Had a nightcap beer at the White Horse Tavern, favored by Dylan Thomas. Great characters in there. Looked like Europe.

Yesterday, Saturday, Tom worked and Kirsten and I saw "Taming of the Shrew" with Taylor and Burton. Great movie.

I called your mother and she and Rachel were going to Nana Williams' for the weekend. Your mother had a cake sent to the home for Charlie's birthday. Joan and your mother were thrilled with the check I sent Joan. Monday Kirsten and I are driving to Philadelphia. Tom just happens to have to go to Atlantic City, so he will come back via Philadelphia and pick up Kirsten. They might stay overnight.

Bill I'm really beginning to miss you more and more. Frustration is building up over things and events and no one to really discuss things with. Tom is a real great person - he thinks like we do - and he and Kirsten are unbelievingly happy together.

I'm looking forward to getting my mail tomorrow. It has been well over a week since I've been there and I'm longing to hear from my honey. I hope all is well - or as well as it can be under the circumstances.

All my love,
Elin

                                                                    Frankfurt, Germany
                                                                    December 9, 1967

Dear Elin and Bill,

I do hope that this card will be forwarded to you, in case you are no longer living in Fort Ord. We are also hoping that you will write and tell us what happened to you during this last year and where you will be stationed next.

Did you notice our new address on the envelope? Tom accepted a job with the 3rd Armored Division in Frankfurt, and is now working at the Drake Edwards Kaserne. We hated to leave Goppingen, but felt that we ought to see something of a different section of Germany. Frankfurt is so torn up right now with a new subway which is being built, that we decided to rent an apartment in Oberursel, a rather charming little town twelve miles northwest of Frankfurt at the beginning of the Taunus Mountains. We had to choose between taking a small modern home or a large old-fashioned one, and took the old-fashioned one. Consequently, we now have tremendous rooms with ceilings 10 feet 8 inches high and our heating bill is terrific, but the crystal chandeliers look lovely and our furniture in general shows off much better. Furthermore, we have wonderful views of the Taunus Mountains from most of our windows.

Have you heard from Hanna and Martin Frank this year? He resigned his job in Offenbach about a year ago and spent the next few months job hunting. Hanna came to see us right in the middle of this period and she promised to write and let us know as soon as they knew where they would be living, but we never heard from her. Last summer I called the Hageles to see if they could tell me anything. They reported that they had called Offenbach the week before but that the whole Frank family was on vacation in England. Some friend of Hanna's was in the house and said that Martin did have work but they would be moving to a smaller apartment in a few weeks. I've been busy myself getting settled here in Oberursel that I didn't have any time to write to the Hageles until a few days ago, but I'm hoping that by this time Hanna has gotten in touch with them and has told what their new address now is.

I do hope that Bill has not been sent to Vietnam, but in case he has, is there any chance of your coming back to Denmark to live, Elin? Please let us know if you ever come through Frankfurt; we'd love to see you. So do keep in touch with us.

Much love from Emma

                                                                    Chu Lai, Vietnam
                                                                    December 11, 1967

Dear Elin,

Today it got cold - about 60 degrees - in fact had to use a blanket for the first time. The sea is very rough - high winds. I don't mind the weather change - a bit like Monterey weather in July and August. Got two letters from you today from Connecticut. Kirsten's place sounds cute & I'm sure you had fun fixing it up.

I've been trying to fix up my office this week to make it more cozy since I spend most of my time here. Beery stained the plywood mahogany. I took some of the pictures from the photo album & put them on black mats with plastic coverings & arranged a series on one wall. I have a green paper Christmas tree. Then I went to the village today and bought a gong. It is not old but decorative. Then I found two old Vietnamese (I think) coins - very heavy and large (5" diameter). Each set on a carved stand. They are terrific & I have them on my desk. You will like them. I also have grass mats on the floor so it is at least "friendly" looking.

Things are going a lot smoother in the PSD - in fact by comparison we had a quiet week. On Saturday night all the PSD officers went to the officers' club. They had a Country & Western group from the States. It's the first time since I've been here that they have had any live entertainment & the place was packed. We all had a good time & got rather boisterous. Anyway, it was agreed that it was worth it to relieve tensions, etc.

Well, you'll be leaving a few days after receiving this so the next letter I'll send to Odense. Have a good trip & give my love to Mor & Far when you get there.

I love you deeply.
Bill

Philadelphia, Pennsylvania
December 12, 1967

Dear Bill,

I received your very moving letter today - the one you wrote while on Staff Duty, and about how your soul has to fly and get away from the system. Some day you and I will find our "nice" own nook, the place we will fit into. I'm sure you will decide on something and I'll root for you all the way.

Life has many strange ways. On Sunday I called many different friends - let me start.

Called Hazel - she is fine, sent us a book published in 1903 about Denmark, Norway and Sweden. Some American traveled there for 3 months and wrote his impressions on it. Very humorous. She also sent a book to Kirsten and Tom. Very sweet of her.

Then I called the Kalbfleishes. The young boy answered. His mom and Mr. Kalbfleisch were out for the evening. Ann and Art had gotten married the day before in a beautiful candlelight service and were off on a secret honeymoon.

Then I called Barbara and Tom Romans on Long Island. They have an 8 month old baby girl named Cynthia and are very proud of her. They miss Eislingen. Seems things are high here. How I remember our adjustment. She had much gossip about Goppingen, and I hope to sneak a visit in before I leave. Time is running short though.

Called the Fungs. Barbara Prince is coming.

(George Golden's younger brother is in your mother's class - she just informed me)

So here is the news -

The Princes are flying to London the same day I am. I wonder if we will be on the same plane. They want all of us to get together. Then I called the Amblers and traced Smed Ambler all the way to Philadelphia of all places. So I called and he is here for the week.

That was all Sunday night in Ridgefield. We had a bit of wine and it led to one of our famous phone parties. Monday morning we were to leave for Philadelphia. Tom had to go to Atlantic City, but first to Philadelphia Airport, so we decided to have Kirsten go with me, and Tom will come to Philadelphia and stay overnight, and maybe go to the Holiday Inn to see Smed. Well Tom was to call us at 5 o'clock. In the morning when we woke up there had been a tremendous hail and rain storm and then frost. The schools were closed and the car completely encased in ice. We could not go, however by 10 o'clock there was a thaw and by working one hour we had the car cleared off and off we went. Kirsten and I stopped at Carol Baretz's and had lunch. I also gave her a sewing basket as a thank you. She was very touched. She wants us all to go out on the 18th. It's Roger's birthday. We will see.

Also the Thompsons from Pullman are going to be in Princeton and would like a visit. So much to do in such a short time. Kirsten and I had an uneventful trip to Philadelphia, drizzle and rain all the way - ugh. Got here at 3 o'clock and went to see Charlie. He is still cheerful and well cared for. I had 3 wonderful letters from my honey and several others. I'll send all in a large envelope. We waited all night for a call from Tom. Guess what - I had hit the phone system so it was off the hook. There was a huge Air Force station very frustrated, trying to get us - you know how hard it is to call out from a base. Well he got here sound and safe at midnight to two steamed up women. We thought he had forgotten about calling. Well all is well that ends well. We had a wonderful stew and apple cake your mother made, so we heated it for him. Your mother met Tom briefly. She liked him. The next morning we got up early to go junking on Market Street, way down, but it was noon before we knew it and they left.

I then called Smed and we arranged to meet in town. After your letter wondering about your place in society and life, I was very interested to see how one promising young man had done. Well let me tell you we aren't the only ones searching. Smed just got out of the Navy (Lt. Jg) and joined a publishing firm. He was with the first group to build the air strip at Chu Lai out of the sand before anyone was there. He goes around to different colleges to sell text books. He likes it but is quitting to go to the University of Pennsylvania for his masters in communications. Same program you were in. He only has 6 years of college already. His brother-in-law, Bruce Jackson, is with the Foreign Service, and is disillusioned about the system under Dean Rusk. His friend and mine, Ronnie, is a movie producer in Hollywood - and is fed up with the phony atmosphere there. It seems most young people like ourselves, if they have any minds, are searching for the right thing. We had a long lovely visit and I caught up on the news from my class. Most are doing well and should go far. Smed is a bit scared of involvement with life, and a bit on cloud 99. You will have to meet him. Someone a bit like Maury. He by the way is out of the Army. Jan Ficke's mother is coming to Philadelphia this week.

I was so happy to have your nice letter - it was the next best thing to having you here, but it won't be too long. Time somehow seems to fly. I feel very close to you today - and spent all afternoon bragging about my wonderful fellow - the greatest guy I've ever met, and you grow in my estimation every day too.

Much love and affection to my one and only. It too seems like I should be snuggling up to you tonight, but it won't be for a while.

Good night love,
Elin

Camp Zama, Japan
December 14, 1967

Dear Bill,

Received your letter a couple of days ago but have been a bit lazy in getting one back in the mail.

First off things here are showing a steady improvement with each day. I'm now eating only 4 times daily and still enjoying every bit of it. I do still have quite a bit of discomfort when the stomach muscles were cut but time will take care of this. My doctor told me today I would be here about 2 more weeks then I would be moved to main Camp Zama for physical rehabilitation. He also told me I would be profiled for approximately 6 months. In checking with other people I'm told that if I'm profiled for more than 90 days I will not return to VN. No confirmation of this. I was able to confirm that if I do return it will be in the replacement stream. Again I would like to return there if there is a challenging job for me.

I have been able to get out and around some these past two weeks so life here is a bit more bearable. Some of the nurses have some great parties planned for the holiday season. Hurry and get sick or something!!! They are a great bunch of gals.

I think it would be near impossible for you to wish I was there any more than I would like to be there. I'm so damn sick of hospitals it can't be explained. If this trip didn't do the job I'm afraid the job will never be complete!!

If there is anything I can get for you here please let me know and I will be most happy to comply. There are many good PX's near here.

Almost forgot, I received the efficiency reports 2 days ago and will have them back in the mail shortly.

My warmest regards to everyone and a happy holiday season.

Regards- Bob

P.S. Bill, I still haven't received my footlocker. Would you please check for me. Thanks.
"Screw Uncle Joe". Would like to have a couple of Americal patches if available.

Fröhliche Weihnacht !! ein glückliches neues Jahr !!!

Hamburg, Germany
December 14, 1967

Greetings! I see that the place where everyone is meeting is California - now that the Mole is in San Francisco.

I took a trip to Denmark & Norway in July and had a marvelous time. I hope to go back to see more of Denmark next year.

Happy holidays!
Jan

Note from Elin
I don't know if I dare tell her I'm in Denmark. I might get stuck with her for a vacation. I don't exactly owe it to her - so - I think I'll keep quiet. Sounds terrible but I really don't feel like having her mooch off me again. (Maybe she isn't so bad anymore.)   E.

Washington D.C.
December 15, 1967

Dear Elin,

My those good thoughts never appeared on paper did they? Have been thinking of you so much. Sent small gift to Bill. Know how lonely this time can be. Our house is as hectic as ever. Both Dee & Des are in the Xmas Program. We had guests from Colorado for 3 days last week. Jean has decided to take final comp. in April which let up some pressure as far as those yet un-started papers go.

Well you now are going to Denmark. Can't just imagine how slowly days are for you and weeks pass before I seem to realize.

Our Advent wreath has two hundred candles already. If you are staying on please come to D.C. for a couple more days.

We love you.
Mel, Jean & D's

Philadelphia, Pennsylvania
December 15, 1967

Dear Bill,

Today I had a card and a lovely letter from my love. It sounds as if your office is the envy of the Chu Lai camp. Who else has mahogany walls and wall to wall carpeting. Wow - joking aside I'm happy to hear that you are trying to make things home like. Always helps the spirit to be in pleasant surroundings. I'm glad you said everyone got boisterous. I read that to mean high, but as I read it to Mother and Uncle Charlie it sounded all right. The more impersonal letters I've shared - only the special ones I keep secret.

I paid our household insurance - $73.80 - for all the next year, and all the other bills. I'm showing about $500.00 (I'm not counting the mistaken $509.00) so I'm in grand shape. This year I'm giving from both you and me $50.00 to Mike and Kathy. That is their house warming, Christmas, and baby gift all in one. They need a new carpet and can put this toward one. I never want get into a gift trap with your family. Kirsten and I exchanged simple gifts, around $5.00 - but your mother sure puts a price tag on gifts. But I refuse to feel that I have to give certain things. Things don't make for happiness. Happiness comes from all the intangible things, like knowing you love me. I feel real good even with you gone just because of that knowledge. I also feel God's kind of love and that too makes me happy. I need not have it proven by material things, and I know we will always be happy. Only, honey, try to remember that pettiness exists at every level of human life, and utopia does not exist. Do try to be forgiving to some of those mundane people . Just think how poor they really are, and how rich you are. You can see real life. They might not ever know it. I always pity people that are spiritually deprived.

Hi, how about us both teaching someplace, then one can choose one's community at will and also serve mankind. For you to get out to go with a corporation with the purpose of making extra dollars would be pure folly and as empty an existence as that you now experience. At least there are real purposes in the military, and you are doing real things. I would be very happy teaching and I feel you could be too. I'm afraid a dream of private business would not work for you as that is even more petty and mundane. You do not have the make up it takes to make a hard, cold, but good businessman. Somehow you are not cunning enough, not screwed enough, and much too believing in people to ever guard for your interest in business. Of course I know not what you are dreaming of doing. Now to be a drop out completely from society at our age is also very unrealistic. The time for that has passed. I might be intrigued by the idea of an artist existence with no material cares, but I far too long been a social animal to be happy with that type of existence. That is my hang-up. I must be producing or doing something useful. I love to be creative, but truly creative people live in seclusion, and I love people around much to much for a hermit type life. In your one letter you only said you were getting out. Nothing about the practical side of it. When, how, where. What next.

I shall be saving not only my nickels but my pennies. I guess we will need a backlog to fall back on. I tried to get a check cashed at Girard today, from Spokane. Unbelievable. I've had an account there and they would not cash a $50.00 check. I shall never bank with Girard again. Ever, in fact I shall not even go into a Girard Bank again. Unbelievably rude employees. This city must have a lot of rats for them to get that way. Why in Ridgefield, Kirsten could get a $300.00 and a $200.00 check cashed right away, with a minimum of questions.

Then I went into town to get a reentry permit. Two pictures (one of them enclosed-horrible) - $2.00. Then $10.00 for the application. Those authorities have you paying coming and going. Also had to have a permit to leave from the tax people, and I'm restricted to travel to any country I didn't put down as intending visit. I put down a string of them. Hope I included enough. But now it all depends on what you are going to do next year. Please give some indications as I'm hanging in the air at present.

I have many cards written already and plan to finish them off tonight. This weekend will see Mike and Kathy and then I'm off to Connecticut on Monday and flying Thursday. If things get hectic there probably will be awhile before the mail gets to you, but I think of you always, you know that - don't you.

Say Merry Christmas to everyone from me, especially Beery. I'm glad he's still with you. He was such a nice boy. Happy New Year too, but I should get to you before that.

Your new acquisitions sound great. Remember Ilsa and Ib had one of those bells. The coins I don't think I've seen . I would be suspicious of anything really being old in that part of the world, but it might be. If it is pretty that's all that counts.

I bought a black wrought iron ashtray with red, for you for the bathroom. No more spilled pipe ashes all over. I'm leaving it at Kirsten's. Also a brass pot, and a salad fork and spoon. All very reasonable. I'm not buying much for myself and once this Christmas buying is over with won't have many expenses. For your Nanas I got nice black leather gloves. Jack, a box of goodies - Joan, Mike & Kathy money. Mother, the big porcelain platter and spice rack. I haven't got much for Denmark. Mailed an ice crusher to my father - wonder if he will use it. For my mother a $5.00 dress and some small shells. I might sew little things. Now I just need Charlie. For Mrs. Sternelle, because she is so sweet, I got some small lovely Italian made angels, gold and real sweet, $3.50. Her husband is in the hospital so I have been unable to reach her by phone.

I had an uneventful day downtown today, and only stayed long enough to get my business done. Then came home and bought some carnations for Charlie. He likes flowers. Elmer's grandson might come to play his harmonica, so he is excited about that. I truly hope he comes because Charlie has told everyone he is coming. Your card has proudly been shown to everyone. They must read it too, it means much to them in there. He wants to come home real bad, and he is better, but would need assistance for many chores.

Hope we both get through the holidays without too much melancholy. I'm holding out fine so you just do the same, hear now. I love you and we will be together in spirit.

Deeply felt- Elin

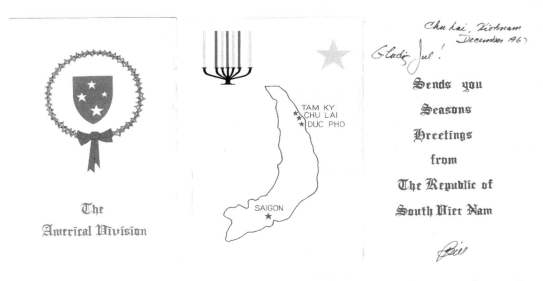

Hamburg, Germany
December 15, 1967

Gesegnete Weihnachten und ein Gutes Neues Jahr

To you, dear friends,

We are always thinking of you and hope that you are doing well.

Karl & Gaby Zushlog & Children

Elin's note to Bill:

Maybe I can see them when I go to Germany - or we both might visit them when you return.

I'm forever amazed at the amount of people you and I know. I often wonder if you get very frustrated at all my many scribbles. But using about $30 or $40 this month on mail, I have to use all the space available.

I wrote the bank for a statement. Still a mess there. It seems we disagree about $75.00. Did you write a check I don't know about? I still think they have made a mistake. Got the income tax form. Do you want it all forwarded to you? I got my refund on my ticket - $400.00, so I have loads of money - E.

Philadelphia, Pennsylvania
December 16, 1967

Dear Bill,

Just a short note. Uncle Elmer's grandson was at the home to play the harmonica, so the whole family was there - and they had a Polaroid and this is the result. His 9 year old grandson did real well and Charlie was very proud, you could tell. I bought Charlie a terry cloth robe and a clip-on tie today. Hope he likes it. Tomorrow we go to Kathy and Mike's. I'll give them a $50.00 check. The baby has dropped so it's due anytime now.

Your Mother is out with her bridge group this afternoon. Kirsten called and they couldn't come this weekend because of Tom's work but she is still fixing up the place.

I bought a cheap cocktail dress today - $15.00 - it's black and just plain, with a high collar. Nothing too daring but I needed something for evening.

I'm almost packed - what a mess it is to get everything organized. I'm only taking the two smaller suitcases. I'll just have to get along, that's all. I'm excited to see how long letters will take once I'm in Denmark. Probably will be pretty long, but I'll keep writing so once we get going we'll have continuity again.

The bank made an error with the $50.00 and it has been corrected. They gave no reason, only said posting error. I'm still struggling with my Christmas cards but hope to get most of them out. It seems I can never write you a short note. Too much to tell you.

Many thoughts go your way.

Love
Elin

Elin & Uncle Charlie at the nursing home

Philadelphia, Pennsylvania
December 16, 1967

Dearest Bill,

What a strange Christmas! You and Jack halfway 'round the world, my mother in Chicago, Nana Walker in Connecticut, and Mike about to become a father any day! That plus Elin going to Denmark Tuesday, makes everything topsy turvey. It isn't a good Christmas without family. I'll celebrate when you come home next year.

I do hope my package gets there but it could be delayed. Have the knowledge we are all thinking and praying for your safe return,

Love,
Mother

Norwalk, Connecticut
December 17, 1967

Dear Bill,

We were surprised and delighted when Elin & her sister stopped to see us when they came to find Kirsten an apartment.

We talked and talked, mostly about art forms. Sure wish we could have seen your place in Monterey, it must have been great. Aunt Ruth and Rube are coming up & Dave will be home for Christmas, now if only you & Jack were back everything would be great.

Take care of yourself, we are all thinking about you.

Love –
Aunt Helen, Joe, Jeff & Dave

Burlington, New Jersey
December 18, 1967

Dear Bill,

Just learned you address, otherwise would have written sooner. As I told Jack in his card I'd like to send you something but don't know what, so send some suggestions.

We worry about you and wonder how you are making out. I have a friend who used to work with me, now in Special Services. Named Terri Zuber. Her address is Service Club, HHC - 1st Brigade, 1st Infantry Division. Don't know just where she is but who knows you might run into her. She's a character with a terrific sense of humor.

We're going to Helen's for the holidays. All I wish for is for a safe return home and soon. Write if you can, we'd love to hear from you.

Love,
Uncle Rube and Aunt Ruth

*Front from left: Cousin Jeff, Aunt Helen,
Uncle Rube, cousin Jo, Nana Walker, Aunt Ruth*

*Rear from left: Uncle Joe, Aunt Rosabelle,
Uncle Charlie, Uncle Ed*

Seated front: Beth (Mother)

Chu Lai, Vietnam
December 19, 1967

Dear Elin,

I guess right about now you are flying over the Atlantic toward cozy Odense. I wish that I could be there too for Christmas.

We are going to have a party in the PSD on the 24th. Beer & punch. Also, the Bob Hope troupe will be here this week. The show will be in the amphitheater right behind the PSD & everyone is looking forward to it.

Things have settled down considerably & the shop is running pretty smoothly. LTC Chung is real fine to work for. There are no personality problems anywhere. I received a letter from Bob Dove. He expects to come back to Vietnam in January & I'm trying to get him assigned here. A major and a captain I knew in the 198th Brigade were killed in a helicopter crash last week with 3 other men. Apparently the rotor just came off.

They opened a new PX here last week. Quite nice & they have a lot of cameras, tape recorders, etc. However, there are so many people there constantly that I haven't been able to get to the counters. You can also get mail order.

20 Dec 67

Hi Honey -

Another day passed. Had to stop letter writing yesterday to get out a crash project for the colonel.

Today the Bob Hope show came. Was quite enjoyable, must have been at least 10,000 GI's there. We all got sun-burned since it was a beautiful - hot - day. Les Brown's Band, Raquel Welch (a real knock-out), Barbara McNair (singer), Phil Crosby and Miss World, a beauty from Peru. It was a treat to see some beautiful girls again, and you can imagine the reaction of 10,000 love starved GI's!! Hope was up to his usual flip remarks. Commenting on Lynda Bird's wedding, he said, "All the birds have flown from the White House now. The only ones left are Mama Bird and Cock-a-doodle do." That brought the house down.

Other than that it's been the same routine. The weather is getting nice again - the ocean was beautiful today.

I'm anxious to hear from you. I wonder how long it will take to get mail here from Denmark. Well love - I know you will have a nice Christmas with Mor & Far, and I'm glad that you can be with them. I love you & and give my love to them too.

Bill

Bob Hope Christmas Show – Chu Lai 1967

Bob Hope with Raquel Welch

Raquel Welch's autographed message to Bill

Ridgefield, Connecticut
December 19, 1967

Dear Darling,

This is positively the last letter from the States. I'm leaving in 5 hours, but we start driving to the airport in 2 hours. Last night we three, Kirsten, Tom and I went out for dinner with Carol and Roger. Her idea. It was Roger's birthday and my goodbye party. Bill you wouldn't believe it but in the end Roger suggested that he and Tom split the check. Tom just took it and paid the whole thing. And here I thought it was their treat. Some people are funny, and life keeps having surprises.

It is very mild today, almost spring - 53 degrees and sun, doesn't seem like December.

Saw your Nana Williams Sunday at Uncle Bob's. All send their love. Mother and I also had been at Mike and Kathy's. I gave them $50.00 and he almost fainted. They need it just now and it is well worth it. The baby is due any day now. We went and chose a tree in the field where it was grown and it was cut right there. Can't get any fresher. I took a spill on the stairs 3 days ago and my back was bad. Is all right now. I might have gotten a slight concussion though because my head has been funny ever since. That too is getting better. Leave it to me, if I have a big trip coming up something will happen. It's sure as day and night.

Your mother gave me a lovely silk blouse for casual wear and a pair of slippers, plus a book on American needlework. The latter I'm really excited about. I also like the blouse and slippers, but the book is one I've always wanted.

Just called the airlines and my flight is at least an hour delayed, bad weather in Copenhagen. Sure hope it's not too much delayed.

I'm in a fun state of excitement, not sorrow. Things are just happening and somehow I'm not too involved. Very unlike me, but so much is going on that one gets emotionally dull. If one constantly was excited one would burn out or that is how it seems right now anyway.

This might yet reach you around Christmas and just remember that I'm thinking of you and love you.

I can hardly wait for us to get together again, so many things to straighten out and solve. Happy New Year - the end of the year just might be happy anyway. Hope not too much sadness prevails for the fellows this holiday season. For every soldier over there is a mother and a sweetheart at home praying, so they are never alone. Next letter will be from Denmark.

Love Elin

San Francisco, California
December 19, 1967

Dear Elin and all,

So glad to hear from you "finally" - We've missed you both so much. Seems like this is home & you should be here. We just got a great letter from Bill & his address. We're so worried about him with so much going on over there & not knowing where he was. I have a "Fruit Cake" to send him even though it won't get there by Xmas but had no address before.

Sounds like Kirsten is doing fine and like you had a lot of fun. If they get to S.F. again be sure to tell them to give us a call. We're all fine here. Warren is very busy at work. Sue is fine. She's lost a lot of weight & feels & looks great. The family is coming here for Xmas Eve so it will be pretty active. Then Xmas day my brother's down from the Peninsula.

Well, dear friend - please do write more often & I'll try to do the same. We miss you. I hope you'll be back soon.

Love Marge

Warren, Sue & Marge Welter with Elin

Frankfurt, Germany
December 20, 1967

Hello,

   Where are you? Hope this reaches one of you for a very merry wish from us all.
   Come see us Elin, if you are back in Europe. We loved Denmark - and but oh, how expensive!! We're finding everything so much higher!!

Merry Christmas.

Jerry, Nancy, Tracy Buchanan

Glædelig Jul

Odense, Denmark
December 20, 1967

Dear Bill,

With best wishes for a Merry Christmas and a Happy New Year.

En riglig Gladelig Jul og et Godt Nytaar.

Far og Mor I Danmark

Spokane, Washington
December 21, 1967

Dear Bill,

Tonight I called Hazel to find out what was going on in your lives since it had been so long since had word from you.

Will get a note off to Elin now that I know her plans. This letter brings you up to date on us. If there is a chance you might get into Bangkok I'll send Gwyneth's address. Bill is at Korat - 100 miles north. Haydn will spend February in Tokyo, Osaka, Taiwan and Hong Kong. Don't know yet about Bangkok.

Congratulations on your Majority. They know a good man when they see one!!

Our best love to a great guy. H&E
(Hadyn and Evelyn Morgan)

Quantico, Virginia
December 21, 1967

Hi,

Hope this was forwarded. Scott would like to keep in touch so drop us your new address if you have a minute. We've also moved & Scott's had a promotion to Major.

4104 - B Lyman Park, Marine Corps School, Quantico, Virginia 22134

He goes to school until July but Vietnam isn't expected until '69. So guess we'll be here in some position or another.

Hope you are well,
Scott and Betty Weathers

San Francisco, California
December 22, 1967

Dear Bill and Elin,

I really don't know where you are - or which continent you're on - or even if you're on the same one, but anyway, tried calling you at Ft. Ord the other day - and I know you're still not there - that much for sure.

I'm happily out of the Army now and am happily situated in San Francisco. Isn't this city tremendous! I really love it! It's a wonderful combination of European, Western, and Oriental cultures all bound up in one swinging place.

Have a lot of real happy holidays, write sometime - about like where I can write you a more detailed letter - and best of luck in the New Year!

Maury

Note from Elin

Just wrote a note to Maury. Told him it hurt to hear someone so happy in our town - also told him to enjoy it for us - and that I haven't had any "Black Russians" lately. I gave him your address and told him that I was forwarding this to you.

Oh someday we surely will return to that town. I do love California. Always did – E.

Chu Lai, Vietnam
December 23, 1967

Dear Mother,

I enjoyed your letter and card received within last few days. I don't remember if I wrote that I received the box, and was delighted to get all of the Christmas associated goodies. I've been sharing everything so it's about all gone.

We have little artificial trees & other decorations up & tomorrow my section will have a Christmas Eve party - about 200 people. We are setting up a big tent outside the office (the "office" is a huge warehouse). We will have beer, soda, eggnog (we hope) and cold cuts and potato salad from the mess hall. Christmas music (and some nurses from the hospital have been invited).

The Bob Hope show was here in Chu Lai two days ago. It was quite enjoyable - about 10,000 men turned out for it. Hope, Raquel Welch (WOW), Elaine Dunn, Barbara McNair, Phil Crosby and Les Brown Band. About 2 hours long. The gals were all beautiful and of course the main attraction.

After a cold spell it was bright and hot that day, and we all got sun burned faces. The time is going pretty fast. Soon I'll have been here 3 months already. I think I'll go on R&R in February. I'm tossed between Australia, Japan and Hong Kong (I'll see Bangkok on the way home). I think I'll go to Sydney, then try to take another to Tokyo next summer. Anyway it's something to look forward to. I rarely ever get out of the Division Headquarters area (not too particularly interested in traveling in Vietnam). Everyone who has been to Sydney says that the Australians are great and very receptive to GI's on R&R & that it's a fascinating city.

Tell Uncle Charlie I send my best & I'm glad he's feeling better. Hope you have a cozy holiday with Mike & Kathy and Joan.

Much love-
Bill

Pebble Beach, California
December 23, 1967

Dear Major Walker,

Just received your card and was very glad to hear from you and have an address to send you a card. Congratulations on Major - we expected it.

Things are going fine, but there has been quite a change around the office - all rearranged again. Both Major Conway and Captain Madsen expect to be gone last of Feb; MAJ C to Vietnam and CPT M to school.

We have had a real cold spell for California and there is lots of snow on the mountain tops. Our office gets pretty windy around the corner.

Yesterday afternoon we had a little Christmas party down in the Com Center. Our new SGM did a good job of planning, decorating, playing Santa, and even had a tapper of beer and some spicy punch.

Sometime send Elin's address and I'll drop her a note. In the meantime, tell her hello for us and we miss you both and hope to see you back in California before too long.

Best wishes,
Doris & Joe and Frank, Mary & Audrey

Odense, Denmark
December 23, 1967

Dear Bill,

I'm home now since the 20th. I haven't stopped talking. I'm happy I came here. I'm still very tired from the time change and loss of one night's sleep. Also dragging 50 pounds of luggage by hand got my muscles sore.

Honey, we came into Copenhagen 5 hours late. It was a glorious day, all snow over the country and brilliant sun. Indeed rare for here. My plane for Odense was leaving at 4 o'clock. At 3:45 I looked out to see a small red truck pulling a small two propeller plane. It looked like a toy among the big jets. That was my plane. We had to bend our heads down to enter and there were huge things all down the aisle as separations. I wasn't nervous but did find the whole experience amusing. An older Danish-American woman across the aisle inside seat said it was much improved over 8 years ago when one could see the cockpit.

I bought a beautiful sweater for you, hand knitted. The store had it all Christmas wrapped. What a shame I can't give it to you now. Keep the spirit high. I'll send long letter soon.

Love Elin

ANSGARHUS *M*OTEL

ODENSE

ANSGARHUS *M*OTEL
KIRKEGÅRDS·ALLÉ 17-19
TLF. 66 12 88 00
5000 ODENSE C

Ansgarhus Motel was the home and business of Elin and Kirsten's parents, Bernhard and Ellen Rasmussen. It was where Elin and Kirsten grew up. The motel was actually a 20 room bed and breakfast with four parking spaces. It was given the name "Motel" by Bernhard Rasmussen when it was opened in 1955, because he wanted a modern name which no other hostellers in Odense had.

The Motel was created by combining three adjoining town houses in Kirkegards Alle. Elin's parents had purchased #21 when they were married in 1938. Elin's grandfather, Niels Jorgen Rasmussen, The Miller, bought #19 and #17, when he sold his Vissenberg Windmill and farm in 1941. When he passed away in 1947, Elin's mother began renting out rooms in the empty town houses. In the 1950s, work which took over a year, began to combine the three houses into the 20 room building which opened as Ansgarhus Motel in 1955.

Stiftstidende   **LOKALSTOF**

[Danish newspaper text, partially visible:]

nen saa fik pressen
og derfor naaede han

en forklarede videre,
e overhovedet ikke
revisorerne, og om
regnskab oplyste han,
blev underskrevet af
lemmerne, men blot
bestyrelsesmøde. Der
gt ikke foretaget bi-

ofte, naar folk kom-
situation, at man er
om regnskabet stem-
være smuttet penge,
er bilag for?

ikke tipspengene, der
kunne holde det hele

rod spurgte senere
aet resten af tipspen-

udbetalt til ungdoms-

den om regnskabet?

dt De da ikke paa?

altsaa med allerhøje-
e?

egærede anklagemyn-
ns Petersen fængslet.
ev afsagt faa minutter
                Skerbs.

Dødsfald i Odense

lderske Abigael Lund,
0, Aarhus, 67 aar. —
jer Niels Jeppesen,
ejhjem, 66 aar. — Fru
ederikke Madsen, Sct.
3, 82 aar. — Fhv. sned-
Christiansen, Aalyk-
3 aar. — Fhv. murer-
Knud Nielsen, Roer-
77 aar. — Fhv. Inkas-

ODENSES FØRSTE MOTEL. Saadan tager Odenses første motel sig ud. Det ligger som omtalt paa hjørnet af Ansgargade og Kirkegaards-allé, hvor man, som figura udviser, i gaar holdt rejsegilde. Nederst arkitekt Torben Andresen, fru Ellen Rasmussen, arkitekt Lorenz Andresen og Bernhard Rasmussen.

San Francisco, California
December 23, 1967

Hi Elin & Bill,

Felicitations of the season! I hope you're still at Fort Ord - would hate to lose track now - - - - -
How are you? Any little ones yet? None here - I'm still a social worker (supervising now). We went to Tahiti on a belated honeymoon this fall.
Do write - - - -

George & Ellen Brudvick

Elin's note to Bill:
Just wrote her a long note telling her all that has happened since California. My it's a lot and then I only say the outline. I sure hope she will be happy now. I told her to write me a long letter. We'll see if she does.

ke lo
eleletsa
botsalo ja
Morena

Gaberones, Botswana
Africa
December 24, 1967

Best Wishes for Christmas and the New Year.
We haven't a clue where you are for sure, except what
we can guess from a letter from Jackie a long time ago.
Hope this catches you, wherever you are. We'd love
to hear. We are all healthy & happy, & looking
forward to our September return to the States.

Curt, Sara, Gwyn & Chad Wolters

Seaside, California
December 26, 1967

Dear Elin,

How happy I was to hear from you!! Yes I had been wondering what had happened to you. Judge of my dismay when I went to your house and found out you did not buy it.

I did not enjoy my three months in Europe. I was too sad from Mitch's departure. I went to see him in Hawaii for Thanksgiving. It was like a dream - just 6 days! He has a stomach ulcer and cannot enjoy food anymore. His views on the war are very pessimistic. How is Bill and where is he?

Yes Elin I am at that Institute and they drive me crazy with 19 units each semester. My history class is very interesting. Spanish is OK but the rest I do not like because the professors are incompetent. I spent Christmas with my girlfriend from Paris. Her husband is assigned to Fort Ord since July.

I have only low days. I never thought the separation would be so hard for Mitch and I. We have six months to go now for he should be back by the end of June.

How lucky to be in Europe for the holidays! Hope I will see you again soon.

Warmest regards,
Monique

Elin's note to Bill:

I'm glad I'm not in California now. I bet I would be panicky all by myself. At least here I have my wonderful parents and I really feel I always have company and time goes better that way. We all get along so wonderfully. Not one argument yet (that is some record for me).

Odense, Denmark
December 27, 1967

Dear Bill,

I feel guilty for not having written my honey for such a long time. I still think of you constantly and talk of you constantly.

The Christmas was very quiet. No tree, no gifts and we only went to church and had a nice dinner. I went to bed at 8:30, a bit depressed. Today, my birthday, we still have no celebration planned. I'm not complaining, only explaining that we aren't interested in a huge Christmas holocaust. Seems unnecessary.

Also seems silly to exchange huge gifts. Our gift was $100 and I put in the bank. Our interest was another $100 so now there is well over $1,000.00. Nice.

Rita sent flowers for the day I arrived. I just had lunch with them at their parents. All are fine and very proud of a 10 month old son that's walking already. Only grandson on either side, what pride. I'm invited to their house this spring. I saw my friend Kaja. She is very ill, paranoid, unbelievable the things she says and thinks. Would make quite a book. Many of her thoughts are brilliant and many great people have had some of those thoughts, only they could draw consequences and conclusions from them. She is out of touch with reality. She claims I, her mother and her small world have used and abused her. We are the strong and she is the weak, and all of the strong are guilty in her mind. I'll explain more later. I never talked with anyone like it before. Very depressing for her mother, very, but she is beyond help. Or at least she needs lots and lots of help.

Things are not changed too much here, at least I haven't seen too much yet.

I'm going to take several courses next year. Doubt I'll work, too much tax to pay. I'm very anxious to hear from you now. It's been 8 days. Seems longer since my last letter. I imagine you will have the same long time span. Everyone is fine and sends their love.

Love you dearly
Elin

Chu Lai, Vietnam
December 29, 1967

Dear Elin,

Haven't written in several days. Didn't even get a birthday letter. The days slipped by so fast this past week. Right now it's pouring rain. Miserable weather after a beautiful day, hot yesterday. This weather is so unpredictable. I just got back from a briefing with the general, on a hot project that's been keeping me going. We worked all through Christmas, except on Christmas Eve the Officers and NCO's gave a party for all our men. Quite a blast. We had 50 cases of beer, eggnog (which I mixed so you know it was good - I even scrounged up a silver punch bowl that a mess sergeant had won as a trophy and brought over here). We set up long table & used sheets as tablecloths, and had a little Christmas tree on it, some artificial wreathes, and the eggnog punch bowl. One hundred pounds of salami and bologna, about 30 loaves of bread, cheese, pickles, etc. One of the NCO's made "Artillery Punch" which we had in the water cooler. The colonel came and spent 3 hours, singing Christmas carols. Some of the boys had to be escorted home (to the barracks) early. But everything was consumed. We got a lot of decorations from Special Services and made the office (warehouse) pretty festive. A lot of the men were "down in the dumps" the week before Christmas & the party helped take their minds off home & loved ones. It was a great success. We only had one casualty - one of my best men tripped and fell on a glass and had to have 18 stitches in his chin. Considering that there were over 150 men, nothing got out of hand and everyone appreciated it (I had been very dubious about what could have happened).

On Christmas day I had about 20% of my people at work. They had turkey and all the trimmings at the mess hall.

We (the officers) will all go to the club on New Years Eve. They will have a show or band there.

Honey, I know that you were glad that you were with Mor & Far for the holidays. I was really happy to get all of the cards and letters you sent. I had all the cards tacked on the walls. I got a nice letter from Hazel, the Morgan's & Carol Baretz because of her comments on "the bill" after what you wrote.

On Christmas night Ned Shivar, my XO & two Lieutenants who work for me went to Ned's hooch & spread out all the cheeses that you sent, with crackers, pickles and cold beer & had ourselves a real treat. One of the lieutenants, Jose Jaquez from Mexico played the guitar. I still have some of the delicatessen items left & will do it again. I received the little box the other day, with the Swedish figures. They are real cute and I have them in my office. I got a letter and card from Kirsten and will write them in the next few days. Also got letters from Joan and Mother & a playmate calendar from the DeNios, and a letter from the Reekies. So I have felt to everyone - especially my honey.

Much love,
Bill

Tell Far I managed to get a bottle of Hennessy Cognac. Wish I could share it with him & tell Mor I send my love. B.

Merry Christmas

Mừng Chúa Giáng Sinh

Odense, Denmark
December 29, 1967

Dear Bill,

It seems I'm not too busy writing you. The only reason is that I'm still not collected and have no organization. I only drift through the days. I have finally gotten used to the time change and now sleep the normal hours.

On my birthday Nina and Poul Erik came. They send many regards - we had a nice celebration, the only since I've returned.

My mother and I are planning to make a small trip next month either to Germany or to Rome or the Canary Islands. Will see what we decide.

I've heard "from trustworthy sources" that they have invented an injection for "love starved" GI's at war. Should make the whole thing more bearable. The source? My mother read it someplace. I had a good laugh.

Just checked in two fellows from Germany. It is strange to be with all the nationalities again. I have almost forgotten my German, but I hope it will come back. I can already tell my language will get very mixed up in the end.

I got one letter from you - only took 7 days. Not so bad as I feared.

Soon I'll send a box to you and also a nice fat envelope with more Christmas mail I received. I only want to answer it first.

Denmark is very small and quite cozy after the big world. Hope you are well my love. I have you in my thoughts.

Elin

Mor's sister Nina and Poul Erik in 1966

Spokane, Washington
December 30, 1967

Dear Elin & Bill,

Was your flight to Denmark good?

Thank you for the orange table runners, Elin. I have the downstairs bedroom & bath in Western white & orange & some brown so I put them on the white bedspread as runners. They look gay and cheerful.

Hope your Christmas was good there. I made an extra effort to do lots for shut-in cripples & hospital patients & children & then entertained lots. My Christmas season was just wonderful, not lonely. I was also entertained a lot. I'm exhausted now, but happy. I had several Christmas dinner invitations (even from the Morgans) but I decided they were all family dinners & I ate with Sood & the children. I had guests for dinner Xmas Eve, then went to midnight church services.

Talked to Evelyn Morgan yesterday. Did she send you one of their lovely Xmas News Letters?

Had a good letter from Bill. But he must know that in Civilian life he'll run into the same sort of obstacles & situations as in the military - believe me! Wherever there are people it is the same & you don't get to see the world as in the military nor have the fringe benefits always either. - So calm down, Bill!! Write. Kirsten sounds so happy!

Lots of love, Hazel
Greetings to all & a good 1968

Odense, Denmark
January 1, 1968

Hi Doll -

This is a bit mixed up letter. But then things are not always simple. I've been in a daze since I arrived. It all seems so long ago that we were in Europe and now all of a sudden all the memories swelled up - one again remembers all the sweet things, all the fun trips - my God how did we do it all, how did we have time for the whole of it.

All of a sudden the Army (to me, mind you - I know it's bad for you right now) seems like such a wonderful thing to be part of. Our life suddenly looks so very exciting and so much fun. Sitting here judging our past six years, they have been very, very rich in a way we never realized. Sitting in just one town like several people I've met have done, certainly makes one dull. Oh how dull, and I can't comprehend that we have really done all we have, and, that we have indeed seen all of those places. It seems like a dream, a sweet dream, but nevertheless a dream. I'm sure to you sitting over there, it is even more unreal. Even California now seems so unreal, like a show we once attended. I'm afraid we can never relive it all, but then there is so much more ahead to be lived.

I haven't started living here yet. Can't get going with anything, not even writing. I miss you but I'm surviving.

Love Elin

Chu Lai, Vietnam
January 1, 1968

Dear Elin,

Received your first letter from Denmark - only took 6 days which isn't bad. Glad it was a good trip and that everything is fine in Denmark. Well it's 1968 - and '67 was not mourned at all. '68 has a lot of hope in it, at any rate it means we'll be together again in another 9 months.

On New Year's Eve I spread out a lot of goodies in my hooch - herring, anchovies, cheese, the smoked Danish mussels you sent. Lt. Jose Jaquez got a can of dehydrated shrimp which we soaked in water and got about 5 pounds of shrimp. Plus crackers. Also I had two bottles of Chateauneuf-du-Pape which I opened. The whole crowd of AG officers plus some others came, & of course we had other drinks later. Everyone really enjoyed the spread, especially the Danish mussels. Later we went to the club where they had a bad floor show.

Last night at two a.m. the VC attacked the Chu Lai perimeter - about 4-5 miles from here. The return fire from our artillery units was heavy and lasted all night. It's the first time there's been anything that close since I've been here. This morning they found 37 VC dead on the barbed wire & know there were many more. There were only a few US casualties and none killed. The shelling lasted all night long. It was a violation of the New Years truce & apparently a long-planned attack.

The weather has been cold, wet and muddy for the past few weeks. Dismal.

I got a delicious fruitcake today from the Welters & shared it with PFC Beery, the Sergeant Major and Captain Ned Shivar (I think it was soaked in rum). I gained weight from all of the candy, cookies, etc. that everyone sent. Now I have to sit down and write a bunch of thank you letters, whether I'm in the mood or not.

Well love - that's all for now - take care,
Bill

Odense, Denmark
January 2, 1968

Dear Bill

I really must get in the old habit of writing almost every day. You must think I'm awful, but the slow days are over and we have started the new yard. Somehow it seems I can see the end now, at least I'll see you this year.

The day it was New Year's Eve all three of us went to my grandparents'. He was just 83 on the 28th, and, I must (tell you) "Mor-Mor" was very proud that on Christmas Eve she had received a card from you, from Vietnam. In her opinion I was married to the "best man in the whole world." Darling I was very touched that you remembered them. We all had tears in our eyes over it all.

We had New Year's Eve at Rasmussens - they own a bookstore and we always called them "Booktrader Rasmussen." It was very enjoyable with the traditional fish dinner - boiled cod fish, and then akvavit and Rhine wine. Mor found the almond hidden in the dessert and got the prize which was a book. Port wine with the dessert. Then whisky, beer, more snaps, more liquor. How those people could keep up is beyond me. At 3 in the morning they were still at it. By then we already had 12 midnight champagne. Herring, smoked eel, etc. on rye bread, and more beer. At 3 am we had coffee and cake (I gave up around midnight). We walked home and it was nice to feel safe walking. The streets were full of walking people. Very strict liquor laws prevent people from driving. No one does.

The next day we took everything easy. Today Mor and I started to collect Kirsten's things to send off. The man is coming to make an estimate tomorrow. It should be around $300 to ship her stuff. We really worked and it is quite dusty going through old papers, etc. I found many from my childhood that are interesting. Once we get her stuff out I'm going to sort through some of my remaining junk. Our sofa, the old one, is really magnificent. I only wish I knew if I should get it fixed or not. One wonders what the future will bring. If I get it fixed and we move to California as civilians we probably never would have it sent, so I guess I'll let it stand as it is. It would be more reasonable to have it fixed here anyway.

Prices have really risen in Europe since we left. It is no longer a shopper's paradise. I guess thank heavens for you, I am very glad for all we did buy when we did. The same articles today are close to 25% more today.

I have missed you terribly during the holidays, but I'm going to be fine now and will soon get myself involved in projects so I can make time go fast. I hope you are fine and that I'll see you soon - maybe the war will end. Who knows, something ought to give soon. My mind is very confused lately on most things about the war and about politics.

My deep affection and love
Elin

Philadelphia, Pennsylvania
January 2, 1968

Dear Bill,

Forgive me for not writing sooner, but I thought I would wait to get my pictures developed so I could send you some. My roommates and I were quite proud of our apartment when we finished decorating it. We made the fireplace out of a desk; and trimmed the tree with gingerbread Santas, homemade popcorn balls, candy canes, and chocolates covered with pretty foil. The red curtains are made with crepe paper. We had a lot of fun fixing the place up.

Mother and I spent Christmas with Mike and Kathy in their new little home. We all had a lovely Christmas; but of course it wasn't the same without the whole family home. New Year's Eve was the quietest one Mother and I ever experienced. I didn't have a date - since there is a male shortage on this side of the ocean. However some of my friends and I were going together. Unfortunately we had a snowstorm on December 31st so we didn't do anything. Mother and I stayed home and watched television.

Uncle Charlie came home twice since I've been here and I think he looks quite well. He has a good appetite and seems to be quite content.

Right now I'm beginning to get ready to go back to school –and real cold weather. It's below zero more than above zero in Minnesota.

Elin sent me a check for $50 as a Christmas present from the both of you. I was just flabbergasted when I received it. Thank you so much for being so thoughtful, as the gift was greatly appreciated - believe me! For a while there, I didn't think I would be able to make it home for Christmas.

I only have a little more than two months to go. I'll be glad to be making some money again.

I'll give you my Minneapolis address in case you don't have it:

2300 Nicollet Avenue Apt #38, Minneapolis, Minnesota

Write if you get a chance and I'll write again once I get back to the Midwest.

Love,
Joan

Joan at Humboldt Institute in Minneapolis

Killeen, Texas
January 2, 1968

Dear Bill,

Thank you very much for your Christmas card we received.

Congratulations on your promotion; it happened so fast, but I'm sure you deserve it. We hope that you had a nice Christmas even in Vietnam. Where are you stationed in Vietnam?

Well my sister-in-law's husband was sent back to the States. He is here at Darnell Hospital and is doing just fine. His orders for Vietnam are cancelled.

We received a card from Elin's parents saying that she was on her way to Denmark. We had a little birthday party for Jimmy on Christmas Eve that he was so happy about. Here is a picture of him. He sure is talking up a storm, every time I scold him he says "y'wanna fight" and he holds up his fists.

Well, we finally moved into a two bedroom house. It seems like a castle compared to our little trailer. Also it has a big yard in the back for King. New Year's Eve he became scared of the firecrackers and tore down the whole back screen door.

Mel DeNio wrote to me and sent some pictures of the kids. David is so big and fat, I can't believe they are all going to school already. That shows how time flies.

Well, I will close for now.

Best wishes and God bless you
Maria, Gus & Jimmy

P.S. Write when you have time.

Washington, D.C.
January 4, 1968

Dearest Elin

Thank you so much for the stainless. Absolutely lovely. We were so pleased. Maybe Mrs. Fulmer has written me, tried to wish you "bon voyage" but you move in too fast circles! Called Connecticut until our bed time! I know you made the best of the holiday and brought joy to your dear parents. I pray Bill isn't too unhappy and lets thing come as they may. "It" seems to get to the calm, easy-going types as well as the nervous.

Speaking of nervous J., we are on hi-C. Term papers are now due. Tests this week & next and then back to work. Ha! He decided against taking the last Comp. until completion of courses which means he won't receive degree until spring (providing he passes all!). We were in the middle of having house guests from Colorado when they were offered and he has just the one chance to make it without repeating the entire set. Our Christmas was jolly. Saw "Nutcracker Ballet" Christmas Eve. Had a Swedish dinner at the folks then they came home with us for the night. Our "big" present required 4 adults -- a 3 month old black female miniature poodle ! What a darling! We're in the middle of housebreaking now, but soon. Her name is Desse.

Be sure to let me know if Bill needs anything. I will write also. We miss you.

Love from all of us,
Mel, Jean, & D's

Philadelphia, Pennsylvania
January 5, 1968

Dear Bill -

It was so nice to hear from you, telling me that the package arrived O.K. I'm glad you enjoyed it. I sent a box to a boy out in California & he wrote back that they looked at the cookies & presto! They were all gone. Ha Ha - I have Mr. Sternelle at home convalescing from an operation since early December, and believe me these men can sure get in the way (sometimes). After he goes back to work - I'll try to get some more cookies off to you. You know I feel so proud to address your mail - Major. Isn't that wonderful?

I had a very pleasant surprise one morning a week before Christmas. I answered the doorbell and here was Mrs. Elin Walker. I was so glad to see her. She had tried several times before but I spent most of my day at the hospital so that is how I missed Elin. She brought me the dearest gift from she & you, darling little gold carol singers,. They are adorable & I want to thank you so much for your kind thought. I have them on the fireplace and everyone admires them. We think of you so many times when we listen to the news and see the maps of the war torn countries. I just pray this feeler about the countries meeting to talk peace will materialize. I'll even tuck a few prayers in to make it have more meaning.

I was talking to your Mother last evening and got a good briefing on all the family. So glad Mike is really preaching so well - and Joan graduates in March. I wrote to Jack at Christmas time. I didn't know where he was but Elin told me he was in Thailand. You boys sure do get around.

Be good & we sure are hoping the time goes fast for you and you'll be home.

Fondly
Mrs. Sternelle

Mr. & Mrs. Sternelle at home in Frankford, PA

Norwalk, Connecticut
January 5, 1968

Dear Elin

I'm sending a package to you. I hope you receive it. Did you have a nice flight home? I just received a nice letter from Bill, he said he entertained all his company at Christmas as some of them were homesick. I am sending a scarf to Kirsten, I hope she receives it. I am putting the code number on the package this time.

You have missed three snow storms, this is a large one. There is snow all over. Helen's husband Joe just came back from Jamaica. He was gone a week for the company. He came back all sun burned.

We enjoyed Christmas - Ruth and Rube were here 4 days. Remember me to your mother. I wish she was closer so I could meet her.

Love
Nana Walker

Odense, Denmark
January 6, 1968

Hi Love -

I was sure I would get a letter today, but none appeared. The last letter from you was dated December 18, so I'm really getting lonely for news. My mother and I went to a Danish film the other day. Quite fun to see one in Danish again. We are going to have elections here in Denmark this month and it's interesting to follow the debates. I've definitely outgrown the thinking of the Danes. My world is much bigger, and few of their problems have any relevance for me. We are also following the new peace feelers and something will surely happen soon. I only hope it won't end with more involvement in Indo-China. Time only shall tell. Do you get the daily news? - Papers, radio, TV or what? Please write about everyday things such as your wash, the food, reading? Do you want books or magazines? Right now I feel like you are so very, very far away. It's even worse than in the US, at least there I got the mail faster.

Are you really getting out of the Army? If so what are your plans? When do you plan to do it, wait till you get back or do it from there? I do hope you'll let me in on it, because since that one letter I've been up in the sky. I had just gotten used to the Army, and I feel you are far from ready to settle in some place - no more trips, no more the boss, just a small wheel in some corporation. I think you should come home and make a decision away from the war. I'm sure everyone wants to get out of Vietnam but that can't be helped.

I miss you terribly, and hope to get a good letter soon. I so miss talking to you. I guess I shall only wait. Wish I had someplace to look forward to, but that will come I guess. We are all fine here and talk of you daily. Hope you are fine.

All my love
Elin

Tempe, Arizona
January 6, 1968

Dear Elin,

Thank you for finally informing us of your whereabouts! I was wondering what you had been up to these past few years.

I thought you might like to see our "farm family".... which has now increased since the photograph with two rabbits, chickens and a big sheep named Molly (which I will shear this spring and use her wool for weaving). (Oh, Molly will have lambs in the spring...usually twins!)

This is all possible because we began buying a house this summer (note our address) with an acre of pasture etc. I hope you will come to visit us someday. Maybe on your way to California! Say, did you paint the pictures you hung in your show last year? 350 is quite a few! What have you been doing with your time lately, raising children or working or teaching? I would love to hear more from you.

We probably won't settle here forever. We really enjoyed living in New England and may return there some day...we also love the ocean too and would like to live near the mountains and ocean sometime. So keep in touch frequently.

I am presently working at the library on campus (Arizona State University where Doug teaches), but am getting a little tired of it and thinking of getting an M.A. in Art Education. I finished my B.F.A. finally last spring here at A.S.U. I'm not too anxious to start teaching but it would be nice to be able to if I ever had to or wanted to.

I thought you would like to see our card, even though the holidays have come and gone. (Yes, I'm a red head now, but soon am going back to blonde!) And this Arizona sun is really bright, even in the winter time... so we squint a lot and have dark shadows on our faces if we wear cowboy hats (like Doug). Perhaps we will get to see Denmark and the rest of Europe someday, too. There are so many interesting places to see in this world.

Our best to you both, and I hope this year goes quickly for you, until Bill gets back in October.

Love
Maralyn

I've been interrupted a hundred times during this letter. Hope it makes some kind of sense...without being too repetitious.

Odense, Denmark
January 8, 1968

My love

Spirits are high this morning. I got a letter dated December 29. I guess I have to get used to 10 days away. It seems very far and distant. I feel even more distant here than in Philadelphia. The news is not as much and not as good about Vietnam. Like yesterday I was nervous all day, the first since you left and then in the 10 o'clock news they say "16 killed and 46 wounded in attack on headquarters at Duc Pho"- no more, no less and nothing later. Today the paper had nothing but of course it's very upsetting. Did it affect the 198th Brigade or did I hear right. Maybe it was some other place that sounds like it. In the US they would have full news coverage. But I guess I'm better off not worrying my head off about it. Also seems nothing will come of the peace feelers. The world, as such, seems to be blaming the US for not trying this time. One wonders what is really going on. I suppose we shall never know.

I really love you my honey. Yesterday I read all of your letters from the start, and the feeling overall I get is one of resourcefulness and good spirits. Please keep it up, don't get too down on the Army or the war. All those people are human, and humans err more than not.

Today I'm going to enroll in all sorts of things: a trimming down exercise course (I really need it and haven't lost anything yet); lampshade making; sewing; porcelain painting; and maybe a few more things. Sewed an embroidery - real neat - almost finished.

Don't mind these Aerograms, but this way I don't have to go to the post office. It is snowing and blowing outside. The ears almost get stiff from frost and you feel like the whole face will freeze.

I finally am getting the pictures you sent developed and should have them today. Did you take any more?

I should do real well on $200. I don't spend much here. I got a new pair of gloves, not cheap - $30 (like the US). Everything has gone up terribly so won't be buying many things. Might take a short trip with Mor but doubt it. All of Europe is frozen in at the moment.

Take good care my love
Elin

Ridgefield, Connecticut
January 8, 1968

Dear Bill,

Happy New Year to you.
Tom and I had a Christmas dinner here in our apartment, and I cooked a traditional goose. It turned out pretty nice being my first one. I really like being back here in Connecticut. We had Tom's 12 year old brother stay with us for a week.

Mor - Far - Elin called up on New Year's day to say happy new year. It was fun talking to them. Tom is in Boston for the day, he really has to go far to work. He goes to Boston and Atlantic City, Washington D.C. It is a lot of time to spend on the road.

One of my girlfriends from Odense lives ½ hour from here, so I can go to see her. She is doing fine, I'm having the oil changed tomorrow and a new filter.

I think we will still be in this apartment next fall, so you can see it. We just got a fondue set, we haven't tried it yet. Tom has only had it at your house, he thought that was fun.

Best regards,
Kirsten

Philadelphia, Pennsylvania
January 9, 1968

Dear Uncle Bill,

Yes, the big event finally transpired and a son, Jonathan Isaac, has been born to Michael and Kathleen. He is healthy, looks like Mike, and weighs 6 lbs. 6 oz. Kathleen is well and did not have a difficult delivery. In fact she is supposed to go home today! The baby was born on the 6th so you see all is well.

How different from July 31, 1937! At that time, I was not allowed to leave my bed for 10 days! Then I could put my feet over the side of the bed and swing my legs - then get up on the 11th! I went home on the 14th day. But now, they get the mothers on their feet the first day if possible - to avoid an embolism (blood clot). They have saved more mothers in this manner.

Christmas and Joan came and went. What a dull time it all seemed! Except for our excursion to visit Mike, we did nothing - not even a movie. We kept saying that we will all celebrate next year. But on two different days, we brought Charlie home for a day. Then I prepared a big dinner and he watched his favorite T.V. shows. Even the theatre debuts were cancelled.

Why the stay at home? Mostly because of severe weather. I have been reminded of your letters from Germany several seasons ago when you described the bitter winds and severe cold. Those added to ice and snow keep people indoors. Today I was told by a "scientific" pupil that we are going to endure another ice age due to the inability of the sun to penetrate our polluted atmosphere. With the temperature at 9:00 A.M. at 8 degrees and the classroom at 52 degrees, I was inclined to accept his theory!

Your letters are cheerful but sometimes I feel you minimize the real situation. News reports and pictures of your area spell out big problems. I do think about you and pray for the safety of you and your men daily. Note the enclosed photo!

Joan flew back to school Sunday and has until March 19th there. Then she will try to get a position in the vicinity of Philadelphia if possible. If not, somewhere with one of the big airlines. I do hope she is wanted or again she will have a big disappointment.

Jack expects to leave Thailand at the end of February and I expect he will have 30 days leave. Am I correct? He says his assignment to New Hampshire is a lucky one.

Tom Williams, still in London, has joined a Little Theater group and has been in two plays so far. He is quite a "dandy" in contrast to his brother Herb. He is a fastidious dresser.

I had a letter from Elin which indicated that she was happy to be home. I guess there is plenty there to keep her busy as she plans to manage the motel while her parents take a vacation. Or do they plan to close and all go on a trip! I am confused but feel sure you know the answer.

Mr. Sternelle is not at all well. He is home from the hospital after a second prostate operation but feels his recovery is too slow. Mrs. Sternelle called me recently to say she had received a wonderful letter from Bill! Also Aunt Kay called to say they had a fine letter from you. How happy it makes people to get an appreciation note or a letter!

Mother flew in from Chicago last week, (two weeks was enough) and after visiting Rachel and me, went back to Trucksville Friday night - Aunt Rachel and I took her home. Now when she goes for a visit, she hurries to return to her cozy nest - as if she might not return.

Uncle Charlie looks so much better than when you last saw him - even Joan was surprised.

Do take care and if you hanker for any home made goodies, let me know.

My love always,
Mother

Jonathan Isaac Walker is born!
With parents Mike and Kathy

Spokane, Washington
January 10, 1968

Dear Elin and Bill,

I've been shut in for several days & taking antibiotics for a head & ear infection. Started with a sore throat. I've sent to Joan to get the name of the medicine that Dr. at Wiesbaden used to finally cure it this winter there so the Dr. here will not start a vicious circle again in treating it.

I seldom dream but yesterday sleeping off the antibiotics had a very vivid dream that I was visiting you Elin, and Bill came from Vietnam too. I've been wondering what it meant. Are you all OK? Do you help your parents with the motel, Elin & do you keep busy?

Surely been cold & lots of snow here. I've been shut in since Saturday p.m. & it is not good so I'm going to bundle up & go to the library soon. I just have to get this ear well in a hurry - can't go through what I did before. Have you shipped Kirsten's things to her yet? Hello to your parents and to all of your family we met there. Are things being undermined there by Communists there like they are in our country? Things are really going badly all over our country. I fear a complete Revolution!

I think about you & Bill often, Elin. Do write to me.

Much love,
Hazel

Chu Lai, Vietnam
January 11, 1968

Dear Elin,

Got a letter from you today telling about your New Years Eve. It sounded real Danish!

We've been very busy this week - lots of action in the Division. There are several North Vietnamese units in this area & the fighting has been very heavy. We've (Americal Division) lost about 80 men this week & over 400 wounded. One company was completely overrun. So we've (PSD) been extremely busy coming up with personnel statistics, and diverting replacements to the stricken units. We have another Brigade now - the 11th from Hawaii & their AG Section was integrated into the Americal Division headquarters. So now I have 11 officers and 220 men in my PSD, quite a huge operation. I finally got my efficiency report from Major Hurt & Colonel Trexler - couldn't have been better. Colonel Trexler has been reassigned as the Division G2. Payant is still with the Brigade & comes up and cries on my shoulder every day. It's getting annoying because he always comes at my busiest time of the day.

Got a letter from Joan. She sent some pictures - looked real glamorous.

Weather's been nice lately. Yesterday I went down to Replacement Detachment which is located on the beach where the 198th was when I first arrived - really beautiful. Next month will be swimming weather again, after the rough tides recede. I was thinking about going on R&R in February, but I may wait until the beginning of March. I still can't decide where to go - either Kuala Lampur in Malaysia, Australia, Singapore, or Tokyo (I've got it narrowed down to those). I just may go to Malaysia because not many GI's go there and I understand it's a tropical paradise & quite interesting, on the other hand the others might be more exciting. Hopefully I'll be able to take another one next fall before I leave. Ned Shivar is going to Sydney next week on his R&R & Lt. Jacquez is in Bangkok right now. Yates is going to Hawaii in February. Anyway, it's something to look forward to in the immediate future.

Well Honey, not much more to relate.

Miss you & love you very much
Bill

San Francisco, California
January 11, 1968

Dear Elin,

Juergen certainly appreciated the captain's bar you sent in your letter. With the new regulations he should make captain by July of this year. Thank you for your thoughtfulness.

I do hope that you had a joyful holiday season. I am sure it did lack something without Bill. Do give him our best when you write.

We left Maryland and made it back to the West Coast before the snow storms hit. With our snow tires even the icy roads were not bad. We made it in a record 4 days driving the northern route.

Christmas was really nice this year. We spent the holidays shopping for gifts and going to parties. For New Year's we stayed home. At midnight we opened a bottle of champagne which was the most exciting thing we did all evening.

Then came the chore of looking for an apartment. For two weeks we looked and looked. Property taxes were just increased so rents were running extremely high. For a one bedroom it was $150 to $190. Finally we decided to try studio apartments and in older buildings. Last week we found one which we took. It is out in the avenues close to the park and it is an equal distance from both parents. Neither one can complain now. Mom really wanted me to stay with them, but we put it clear that I would take an apartment. Everything is all right now.

I go for an interview with the Emporium next Tuesday. You should see Market Street now. They are tearing it up in order to build the new rapid transit system. The newspapers are on strike here in the city now so the T.V. has taken over its chores. On Sunday Herb Cahen reads the comics while the midnight news reads the obituaries.

My address is: 1501 Lincoln Way #202, San Francisco, Calif. 94122

Juergen is working on our car tonight. He is getting it in shape for my use this year. I am a little hard on the clutch.

How are you occupying your time? I remember your mentioning something about taking a job. I do hope that you will write soon and often, and keep me posted.

Juergen leaves from Travis A.F.B. on the 22nd around 7 am. I try to avoid thinking about it.

Fondly,
Mary Schleicher

Chu Lai, Vietnam
January 14, 1968

Hi Honey,

Received your letter yesterday where you wrote that the last letter you got from me was dated 18 December!! Hope you have gotten more by now. I'm getting yours in six days, but apparently it doesn't work so well the other way.

I've cooled down a bit since writing that I was going to get out of the Army. I agree that this isn't the place to make such a decision. I'm thinking of asking for Washington, D.C. This way you could go to school & I could take night courses, and it would be a stabilized tour (3 years if I get a DA assignment). I know I can get circuitous travel back - probably 45 days leave - & you could meet me in Bangkok - spend some time in Europe.

Starting this month I have $600 going into Soldiers Deposits, $200 to Spokane & $125 to me. Last month $600 went to Spokane (in case you didn't get a statement). I got $400 in cash last month (back money from the pay raise that was effective in October) - so I put $300 in Soldiers Deposits. I don't spend much and have about $100 extra in cash in my locker (will use on R&R). I don't eat breakfast - lunch costs 60 cents and dinner 45 cents. Drinks and snacks at the club & the PX items take the rest & I still have plenty left over. You asked about the food - actually it is quite good, but like any institutional feeding it gets boring. We have plenty of milk, ice cream, good fresh salads, cake, steak, spaghetti, meat loaf, casseroles, turkey and LIVER!!! (that's when I eat at the club).

Everyone looks at my pictures on my office wall & think I have a "stunning" wife - and a fantastic home (the one of you and me that Peggy took). I may get to go to Saigon to attend an executive course (about a week long) on data processing. We get our data processing equipment the end of this month. I wouldn't mind getting away from here for a few days.

We get the Stars & Stripes every day so keep up on everything. That is a good newspaper, without the trash that's in most US papers. Also have access to Time, Newsweek. Playboy, etc. Books are in short supply. They have some paperbacks at the PX, but few worth reading, so if you come across something interesting send it over (or "around"). Special Services is trying to get a crafts resale outlet here, where we could buy crafts material. This would be great.

They installed a hot water heater in our community shower, so now if timed right I can get a piping hot shower (about 150 people use the showers so normally you have to take one in the afternoon or late at night to get a hot one). I'm looking forward though to soak in a hot tub.

Haven't gotten any mail from Mother for a long time - or Jack. Say hello to Mor and Far -

Love you deeply- Bill

Odense, Denmark
January 14, 1968

Dear Bill

Received letter dated January 2 - I am glad that no one was killed in that New Year's attack. I must have heard wrong on the radio, but that is easy. I guess your supply of food or goodies is low now, so I'll get a box together next week. Probably be weeks before you get it. Do you realize it is about 20 days between questions and answers. That means only about 10 questions. I'm glad we have nothing pressing to discuss.

I miss you a lot and love you dearly. I've only had weird dreams twice, and only had real trouble sleeping three times so I'm not really doing too bad. But now I'm really busy. I'm making two hand sewed lampshades. Half finished with one. I'm using left over material from my wedding gown. Both are lined with satin and have a thin layer of fine material, one is in beige and the other in pale blue. Then I'm painting porcelain. Will make a lamp for the big shade for the bedroom. Haven't decided on a design yet. If you have any drawings or advice please submit same at this address. Then, most exciting, I'm making a porcelain tile table. I found an old one in one of the rooms - really my mother thought of it - and the tiles were most all broken. I'll have the legs shortened. I'm trying to get ideas for a design. So far I favor doing it as an aquarium.

Love from Far og Mor too –
Elin

Trucksville, Pennsylvania
January 14, 1968

Dear Bill -

Thank you so much for your Christmas letter. It was such a pleasure to hear from you and believe me we are proud of our men over in Vietnam. I can imagine that the weather is quite different than here today. We have a lot of snow and this morning my car was covered with ice so I did not go to church. I am not driving these days and intended to go with a neighbor.

Weren't you thrilled to get the news that Jonathan Isaac Walker had arrived. I will call your mother and find out if she has seen him. She went up yesterday, she and Janice Smith, and she declares he is adorable, small but perfect. Kathy got along just fine!

Christmas was wonderful out at Uncle Loren's. I went out by jet a week before so we would have the pleasure of preparation for the big day. Uncle Herb, as you know is convalescing from a heart attack so I saw quite a bit of the family and they had Christmas dinner with us. Their two boys are fine and a source of great joy to them. Randy the elder, helps to take care of dogs in a kennel on Saturdays and right now he thinks he would like to be a veterinarian. He is thirteen. Bill, twelve, is sold on aero planes and of course wants to become a pilot.

January 1, 1968 marked the end of my second term as Justice of Peace. I served fourteen years and your grandfather served twenty-two. As I reached eighty in August I thought it wise to give up police work. But I applied through my senator for a Notary Public commission and received it. I can transfer titles for cars, issue affidavits and so forth and do many things to keep in touch with people who I like.

Please thank Elin for me for the lovely gloves she sent me from you both for Christmas. I hope to get her address later. Your mother was making an applesauce cake when I called her. Doesn't that sound good!

All my love to you,
Nana Williams

VOTE
BEATRICE L. WILLIAMS
(Mrs. Herbert R. Williams)
For **JUSTICE-OF-THE-PEACE**
Kingston Township

FIRST ON REPUBLICAN TICKET
I Will Appreciate Your Support

Nana Williams' first run for Justice-of-the Peace – 1954

Bill with Nana Williams at her 90ᵗʰ birthday celebration
Irem Country Club, Dallas, Pennsylvania 1987

Odense, Denmark
January 15, 1968

Dear Mother

I have just been in the basement and cleaned out an old dresser - many of our old school books and work was down there. I thought as school teacher you might be interested in the work we did here in the 7th grade. One could read my writing then, and the drawing isn't so bad either considering the age - 13 years.

I was so happy to have a letter today and most happy about the sunshine news. So Mike and Kathy got their boy - what else, how certain that they were! I'm glad that there are rays of sunshine in this world. I'm going to make a small embroidery so please, what was the right date of the birth?

My mother was very excited over the Christmas ball - our only decoration. We didn't put a tree up or exchange gifts as we saw no purpose in it. Went to church, had a lovely dinner and by 9:30 I was in bed.

I made my embroidery Bell Pull, smaller than yours but quite sweet. Same material. I made it by my own design combined with a pattern. The Danish flag, map, name, a man, a woman, the US map, flag and "America" at the bottom. I'm pleased. Also am making hand sewn lampshades from left over material from my wedding dress. I'm attending classes to learn how to sew the shades. Also learning porcelain painting and will make a lamp base, so I have an all hand-done lamp. Going to embroider a name cloth. I did most when I was 14. I'll add too and put Bill's name and birthday on - mine - plus our wedding date. Never had the time before. I'll have it framed.

I am also going to exercise every day and hope to get a nice shape. My mother ordered a table runner for you before Christmas. She had the idea to have the design from the Royal porcelain put on the cloth. It has not yet returned so we will send it as soon as it arrives. It will then have to be embroidered and I'm sure you can figure a way to make it look nice. We also ordered one for Kirsten. Last week we shipped her things - it cost $300, and we insured it for $2,000, but by crossing the ocean it will double in value. She got the family dishes (like yours) and her beautiful oriental rug. Plus endless other things. We now hear that there was a terrible cyclone over on the Atlantic Ocean. I do hope it didn't ruin Kirsten's things, because they were on the boat then. She is missing one suitcase mailed on the 7th of November.

I'm enclosing two pictures Bill sent - only sent one of him and it's not too clear so I didn't think you would get anything out of it - he looks like he did before.

Aunt Rosabelle sent a long letter to me - very sweet.

About the mail. Regular takes over one month and any bills should be forwarded air mail. I will reimburse, I promise, regardless of the cost. I got the one bill in your letter, but should have some more coming. I know it's trouble but I don't know what else to do. Unfortunately they must be paid. I did not receive any envelopes yet.

The weather here has been around freezing with light snow. Today it thawed and we have a bad storm. The Country had fall storms that ruined half the forests, so we are not too happy about this one.

We are having elections next week and I hope with many others that the socialists will not get elected in again. The last 14 months they governed together with the communists - terrible. I do hope and pray the communists never get a hold in America, but I fear they are at work in the Negro communities and the underprivileged. Hazel fears a revolution. I won't go that far, but something will have to give.

We get terribly biased world news here, and I'm put out with it. Too long to give details but anyway we don't always get the whole picture as I know it exists from my friends.

Bill writes regularly and cheerfully. His letters take from 8 to 10 days - mine 6 to 8, so you see I'm doing fine. I too look forward to Jack coming out of the Far East.

Say hello to Uncle Charlie and all my love to the whole family -

Elin

Washington, D.C.
January 15, 1968

Dear Elin,

Thank you, thank you, thank you -- how we love your gift. It is just perfect and looks so lovely - when can you come see it!

We had a marvelous Christmas. Stayed here - which was good as the flu hit us on Christmas day. We're all back to normal now, but still tire easily. Tara and Gar were just adorable this year. They really appreciated this Christmas more than any before.

Take care and at least send post cards - I don't want to lose touch.

Once more thank you so much for your gift.

Karen

Chu Lai, Vietnam
January 17, 1968

Hi Love,

Got a nice letter from you yesterday & also the envelope with all of the cards and letters in it, which I was glad to receive.

Got a letter from Mother also - Kathy had a boy on 6 January - they named him Jonathan Isaac - I will write to them tonight or tomorrow.

The heavy action here has slowed down considerably. We are still involved in a lot of work in the PSD though as a result of it. One flap after another every day. Slowly things are shaping up, but it will be a long time before it's the way I like it. The machines will help a lot when they arrive in February.

(A rat just ran by my desk)

I think I'll wait until March to go on R&R. That will be the sixth month. The weeks seem to go by fast but there are still a lot of days left here.

This is just a quickie. I'm going to bed early tonight if the colonel doesn't call me before I get out of the office.

Best to Mor & Far -

I love you
Bill

Chu Lai, Vietnam
January 17, 1968

Dear Mother,

I was glad to get your letter yesterday and delighted to hear about the baby. I'll write to Mike & Kathy tonight.

The work grinds on here. As you may have read in the papers there has been a lot of action in the Chu Lai area during the past two weeks involving Americal Division units. Consequently my shop has really been under pressure to keep up with all of the resulting personnel actions - replacements, casualty reporting, awards, etc. We lost quite a few men & had many wounded in one of the brigades. The picture you sent of Chu Lai base, is right where I am. We are on the bluff & rocks etc. way down on the shore line.

We are getting our data processing equipment next month. I may get to go to a week long executive orientation course on data processing techniques in Saigon in February. I'd like to get away for a change. Then I think I'll wait until March to go on R&R. That will be in my 6th month here & split the tour. Still haven't decided where to go, too many choices.

I've gotten lots of letters from Joan & Kirsten, and Elin sends me all the letters she receives from friends. Joan sent me some pictures of herself - which I tacked up in the office - my men are all interested! And think my sister is a knock out.

I've been reading about the bad winter you're having back there. It's hard to realize - it never gets cold here, although the days in December and January are generally overcast & rainy. When the sun does come out it's like summer. The weather will start getting hot in February.

I'm glad to hear Uncle Charlie is doing so well - please tell him I was asking for him.

Well - I'm tired tonight so will try to get to bed early - unless the colonel comes up with a requirement.

Love
Bill

Odense, Denmark
January 18, 1968

Dear Bill

I had feared January would be slow but it is slipping by. Yesterday I made an embroidery for Ann's wedding gift. A bell pull done in green and purple from an old pattern, but very modern the way I did it. I bought rod iron for the ends. Will make several gifts. Only costs $5.00 to make and they would sell for at least $15.00 here, and more in the US. Also made a small embroidery for Mike and Kathy's new baby, only I need the time and other details.

Today I'll start a porcelain lamp. Think I'll make it all blue and then scratch a pattern out which will then be in white. It won't be a cheap lamp. I'm making a pale blue shade to go with it. Also the materials are around $10.00. So far I've used $100.00 this month but I've started so many things. I should save from my allowance. Haven't gotten the bills or the bank statements yet. Your mother sent it slow boat, (I had asked for everything to be air mailed , but she felt the cost was too high. I have offered to reimburse all the mailing costs – what else can one do).

I miss you very much but refuse to get down in the dumps & keep running all the time. Actually get quite a bit done.

Your Prudential Insurance was $8.50 this quarter instead of $27.50. We got a dividend – very nice.

We are deep in politics here. Election on Tuesday. Much unjust criticism of the US. Our press here is terribly biased and some borders on propaganda. I'm very mad about it, but what can one do? I fail to see why people can't see things the way they are. Europe is in an economic slump, and many fear unemployment.

I'm very healthy and doing exercises every day.

Love you deeply –
Elin

Bill's pencil drawing of Elin
(from some time in the 1960s)

Odense, Denmark
January 19, 1968

Dear Bill

Just returned from the travel bureau and there are many trips to Bangkok all around $500 to $700 with rooms. Tokyo, Malaysia, etc. are all too much more money. I could leave Zurich on February 10 - March 4; March 2 - March 25; March 23 - April 15 - cost: $600. One can get a double room when you are there. Or from Copenhagen March 9 - March 26, cost $700.

Very early in February would cause many problems as I won't hear from you till the end of January. You have to count two days for travel in either direction, but don't you think you and I could find time to get together?

Please give me a definite time and I'll make arrangements and send you the name of hotel, etc. It would be best if I arrive first as not to waste any of your short leave. Could you get two weeks? One can also go to the coast and stay at a beach hotel with swimming pool. One doesn't have to stay in Bangkok.

I really want an answer soon.

Love
Elin

Odense, Denmark
January 19, 1967

Dear Bill

I got your letter today - the one about your R&R. How about Bangkok? In March with yours truly? I can get on a trip (I haven't made reservations). It costs $650 - everything included - for 15 days in Thailand. I would arrive on the 10th of March and leave on the 25th of March. Please answer me real quick if you think we could have overlapping times together.

Love
Elin

Philadelphia, Pennsylvania
January 20, 1968

Dearest Bill,

Last week I watched the Bob Hope show alone and cried! It was so very touching to see 1/4 million young men from our nation across the Pacific and in our war effort. They showed Chu Lai and Takh Li. I looked for you and Jack with careful intensity but of course could not see either, but I felt I was closer to you somehow. It was very touching to us who have our loved ones "over there."

I have been reading disturbing news dispatches about Chu Lai area and know you have big problems. Do take care. It must be so dreadful to have these fellows you send out either wounded, killed, or captured. Young Bill Webster wrote to me Saturday from "Hill 861." He is with the 3rd Bn. 26th Marines and they live in fox holes and bunkers as you know, I really pray for him, too, as our news today was disturbing about that particular position.

Young Jonathan is a fine "braw of a boy." He is a good looking little fellow and is doing well. I saw him once and hope to go up again this coming weekend. Uncle Charlie is doing well. He made 35 cents playing Bingo on Friday! He seems content to be there and my problem is how to keep him there! I just called Aunt Rosabelle to tell her about the new baby. She had some unusual news. Ned is not marrying Brigette in February! She broke the engagement! He went to Germany in December and met her mother and family. All seemed well until she returned this month. She said she wasn't ready to get married just now. No other reason is known by Aunt Rosabelle but Brigette had chosen her silver, crystal, etc. and their wedding rings had been purchased. So_____. Elin will be surprised because she liked the girl and thought she and Ned would be very happy. As for Aunt R. and Uncle Ed, they hope it lasts because they didn't "take" to the girl, but were making the best of things.

Jack hopes you can meet him in Bangkok on February 25th but I guess that is a remote possibility. He has gained 20 pounds! The doctor said it is due to the excitement of coming home. His girl, Vivian, called on me again last Monday night. She is a lovely red head. Not a beautiful girl but vivacious and lovely. She is studying to be a teacher (Stroudsburg) and graduates next year. I hope they get serious!

I'm watching the Smothers Brothers and writing too! They are satirical! I saw the delightful "Hello Dolly" for the first time last week. It was so happy and a welcome change from the "message" type of theater. Ginger Rogers is not a young girl by any means but she really sparked the whole performance.

Do you want any U.S. food or supplies of any kind? If so, let me know. I so hope your R&R comes through as you have indicated. Australia is a place I, too, would like to visit.

My love always,
Mother

Odense, Denmark
January 21, 1968

Hi again -

I do hope you don't mind this kind of letter. Now I've really read about the different possibilities for the trip to Bangkok - I enclose pictures of the two hotels one can stay in - one trip is 18 days and one is 24. The 18 days costs $500 - the 24 - $575. They leave again as follows:

$500 from Zurich 18 days	$575 from Frankfurt 24 days
20 Feb - 8 March	10 Feb - 4 March
5 March - 22 March	2 March - 25 March
19 March - 5 April	23 March - 15 April
2 April - 19 April	13 April - 6 May

On this program you leave Frankfurt on a Saturday and arrive on Sunday in Bangkok's Don Mueang Airport at 11:20 local time, then by bus to Hotel Royal. Monday to Friday in Bangkok & all next week in Bangkok, then by bus to Pattaya, a 3 hour trip, and stay at the Nipa Lodge until following Saturday. Sunday by bus to Bangkok and fly to Frankfurt. I could make arrangements the other way, depending on you, I'm sure. I would also get a room ahead of time for us both in either Bangkok or at the shore.

Right now I have $400 coming from my ticket and also $250 in the bank. Haven't added the Jan 1 deposit, so I'm in fine shape. We can still save, also I can take the dates above and go economic for $400 that includes YMCA and a bungalow in Pattaya. Then we could find our own lodging and be real free.

So my love you tell me the dates and I'll be there. I have the money and the time so why not - who would have dreamed it would be so cheap?

Elin

Odense, Denmark
January 21, 1968

Dear Bill

Air mail from here is such that I must get mileage out of all the material I send - as you can see I get much nice mail which surely helps the spirit. I was glad that you also sent some of your mail to me to share. Somehow if we were together we would read it all. If you'd rather I didn't send everything I'll stop. But I figure you like to keep in touch. I can hardly sleep for excitement to my plan for the R&R. If we wait till October, you will be very anxious to leave and get to the west and we won't enjoy the place as much as we will now. You do want to see Bangkok don't you? It's the only practical place for me to go too, and I'll be safe with a tour, but not at all tied down - like Mallorca or Beirut. Oh my love I can hardly stand the thought of not going. Things can't go wrong.

Mor and Far send their love. Far misses you for a snaps now and then. He wants his two sons-in-law home for a good party. We talk of you every day.

Love Elin

Frankfurt, Germany
January 22, 1968

Dear Elin,

How wonderful it was that you received our card just a few hours before leaving for Europe! I'm so awfully glad you wrote, because we had talked about you and Bill so often and wondered if he had been sent to Vietnam. I hope that Christmas wasn't too terribly lonesome for him, and that the next nine months will go rapidly. I don't suppose that he'd be able to come to Europe when he leaves Vietnam, but I do wish that it were possible. It would seem so nice to be together again.

The best news in your letter was that you would come through Frankfurt on your way to Goppingen this spring. Please do come and spend a few days with us. Now that we are living "on the economy" we see fewer Americans than we used to, and we'd like very much to have a long visit with you. Did I tell you that we have rented the second floor of a large three-story house in Oberursel, twelve miles northwest of Frankfurt. The Taunus Mountains begin at the end of town and it takes only ten minutes to drive to Kronberg Castle. Bad Homberg is also just ten minutes away by car, so there will be a lot of places for you to see. We may take a quick, three week trip to the United States in May or June, but I'll stay in touch with you and let you know what weeks we'll be out of town. Right now it's so cold and miserable that I'm perfectly happy to stay home.

A niece of mine, who is on sabbatical leave from her teaching job in the United States, was at our house for a week over the Christmas holidays. Her brother evidently decided that if she could spend the winter touring Europe he could too, so he quit his job for three months and flew to Frankfurt on December 27th. He and his sister left for Italy the next day and are now in France, but we expect to see them again in February. Both of them brought too many clothes with them and we have two of their suitcases in our basement. Tom and I went to Amsterdam for four days over New Year's and we had a marvelous time. The people like Americans! And the food was so good we came back stuffed to our gills.

We were so interested in the news that your sister is married and living in the United States – only you didn't say whether her husband is American or if he was a European with a job in the States. Your parents must be especially happy to have you with them this winter because otherwise they might have been rather lonely. I had hoped that we would hear from Hanna Frank at Christmas, but nothing has come so far although Mary Hagele gave Hanna our address. According to Mary, Martin has a job again and things have gotten back to normal.

Would you say "hello" to Bill for us when you write, or perhaps you could even send this letter on to him. And do let us hear from you soon.

Love
from Emma

Emma and Thomas Haynes

Spokane, Washington
January 22, 1968

Dear Bill -

You are on my mind often. I even dreamed I was visiting Elin & you came home for a visit also, and I seldom dream - to remember the dream at any rate.

My good friend from Wiesbaden days, Emily Hughes' husband - Lt Col. James Hughes' address there is - 504th TAC Air Supply Group, Box 3572 APO 96221. Is that any place near you? He & Emily and I used to antique together. He's a very fine person!

What work are you doing? Don't get in a rush to get a civilian job - you will find the same problems there as in the military - believe me!

Had a Xmas letter from Col. and Eva Inman. He wrote the letters. Things have changed in Japan from his letter. I'm giving a talk tomorrow at a Methodist Church on Japan. It has been so long, I've had to really work & read up on a lot of things.

This being alone seems to get more so all the time. I don't know what the answer is for me. I love my home & enjoy it so much but there is too much aloneness, particularly in winter. In warm weather I'm outside most of the time & the walls don't seem to close in on me.

Wednesday night I'm having my church guild here & Friday night Suzi Jack & Kimball & I are having ten people here at my house to a Sukiyaki dinner. Wish you could have some of it. I've had people here often & cooked cheese fondue, salads, etc. Everyone enjoys it so much. During the Christmas holidays I entertained lots & tried to do things for cripples & shut-ins & older people. I worked at it hard and it made a wonderful Christmas season for me. I decorated my whole house, even the laundry and storage rooms!!

I have written to Elin recently but have not heard from her since the day before she left for Denmark. Take good care & write to me, Bill.

Much love,
Hazel

PS - I've sorted all of Strauss' papers - which I brought back - and there were so many beautiful poems & carbon copies of letters. He had a brilliant, beautiful mind & soul & very cultured. We were so rich without money!

Chu Lai, Vietnam
January 23, 1968

Dear Elin,

Got a long letter from you several days ago telling all about your projects - sounds interesting, and it's good to have a lot of things going on at once.

Things are about the same here except that there has been an upsurge of VC & North Vietnamese activity all over Vietnam since New Year's. We haven't had any major attacks in the Chu Lai area since the last I wrote about, but something happens every day.

I am going to Saigon about the 11th of February for a 5 day orientation course on Data Processing. It will be interesting to get away from here for a few days - you really start feeling confined and unaware of anything else when cooped up in one small area for so long. I'm anxious to see some of the people I know who are down in the USARV headquarters. Then I'll put in for R&R in March - to Penang - an island in Malaysia.

I haven't heard from anyone recently. I wrote to a whole bunch of people but never got answers (I did get a sweet letter from Mrs. Sternelle).

I liked the "Godt Nytar" card you sent & the Palace Guard post card (I have that on my wall). I put in my preference statement for assignments - 1st choice Washington D.C. (DA) - 2nd choice San Francisco & 3rd choice New York City.

Honey, I love you & miss you so much. With all of the discussions & arguments we (you) used to have on "direction" and "purpose" I know that we have much more purpose & compassion for life & love of life than most & this is a greater direction than anything. I see this more every day here & I'm really amazed at all we really do have.

Love you,
Bill

Palace Guard,
Amalienborg, Copenhagen

Bill at work (Elin's postcard on wall)

Ridgefield, Connecticut
January 23, 1968

Dear Bill,

It was real nice to hear from you. I know you are busy and don't have much time to write, so I appreciated it very much.

I'm waiting for our furniture and things that Elin shipped for me. I hope to be able to pick them up this week. That is going to make such a big difference in the room.

Today I took the driver's test, and I now have a Connecticut license. I'm very fortunate to have the car. Tom went to Boston this morning again, and he is gone 3-4-5 days like that, so I'm going to stay with my girlfriend in Darien till Tom comes back.

Today there are elections in Denmark. I'm anxious to know how it goes. Soon Jack will be heading home, all saw some of the slides he sent home. He is quite a photographer now.

Have you made up your mind where to go on your R&R? I do wish you a nice time for that week.

Take care of yourself,
Kirsten

Odense, Denmark
January 24, 1968

Dear Bill

I receive so much mail as I answer it. I send it on to you. Had a very good letter from you today, written on the 14th of January but not postmarked until the 16th of January, so there went two days. I've had no mail in less than 8 days.

I'm so glad you have started to save. From your letter I should have $850.00 in the bank at present. I do hope to get a statement soon. With the $400.00 coming from my ticket, I have more than enough for the tour to Bangkok. I'm trying not to be too excited 'till I hear from you, but it's very hard.

Yesterday the Danes got rid of the socialistic government. We sat up listening to election results until late at night and celebrated. We had many skals to you. Far was very happy that we now get a more liberal government.

Today I mailed 26 paperbacks to you. Agatha Christie murder mysteries, and many good, serious books. They were mostly some that Kirsten had read for her required reading in school. Also many that I've read. I hope you will enjoy them, some books were left by guests and are not of our choice. Please pass them out if you don't want to read them. A couple looked pretty trashy - maybe you can "forget them" someplace if you wouldn't like people to think you read such trash. Most are by the good authors - Somerset Maugham, Hemingway, etc.

If we go to D.C. we surely have to save for a house. One will need close to $40,000.00 as the prices are steep there but it might be worth it.

Well, that's all for today.

Much love
Elin

Takhli, Thailand
January 25, 1968

Dear Bill -

Would you believe that it has been busy around here! I have meant to have written sooner than this, the work schedule has once again been heavy. I have to think how funny it is that we are separated by only a few hundred miles, but we cannot see each other. We had a plane come in the other day for a cargo stop. His next destination was Chu Lai. I would have liked to have gone with him just for the ride.

Hi! I know that you've been kept fairly (Ha!) busy these past few weeks. Are you having your rainy season now? We are having good weather here, although it is getting increasingly hotter each day. The skies are clear, and I have been trying to get out in the sun in my little spare time. I have been made the project N.C.O., and when I'm not controlling air traffic I'm making a new chart of something for somewhere. It is too bad that I am not a private commercial artist! Oh well, it does make the time to go faster! I had a performance report written on me last month. I didn't recognize who they were writing about, until I saw my name! The person who wrote it was extremely good to me; I foresee a fourth stripe before I do get out in April of '69. I don't know if I am really worthy of the report that was written on me, but I will try to live up to it to the best of my ability.

My days in Southeast Asia are growing shorter now. If this Korean thing does not blow up to any major battle zone, I should leave Thailand on the 25th of February (possibly the 26th or 27th). I will get my port call on or about the third of February. There has been no way to let you know sooner, the Air Force gives us only one month's notification. Are there any possibilities that you can be in Bangkok then? Let me know if so, and I will send you the name of the hotel where I stay, and a map of the city, to help guide you from the airport. (A typical Asiatic city with European overtones). I'll send you the information even if you cannot make it over here at the end of February, so you will have a head start when you do come. I have really been hoping that you could come before I leave - we could really have a good time! Bangkok is a fine city.

I have been well, but extremely tired all the time. I gained over 20 pounds in the past month and a half. I am now well over 200 pounds. My speech has also become very erratic. I went to the Dr. last week and told my heavy tale of woe. He said that it was all a sub-conscience thing, that in the back of my mind I know I am going home soon, and I have become extremely excited inside. This causes the speech and weight problems. He assured me that everything would be back to normal when I did get home. WOW, I'll be even more excited! - Ha! One year is a long time to be away - really can't wait to see and be with Vivian again. I have missed her very much, I am hopeful for the two of us!

I received a letter from Elin yesterday from Odense. She sounds well, and very busy. I will be sad not being able to see her when I come home. I will write to her tonight also. She was very thoughtful and kind to me all through Christmas season. I will never forget her thoughtfulness, it meant so much to me. She is really great.

How does it feel to be an uncle! I was glad to hear that both Kathy and Jon are fine. I know that Mother must be very happy.

Well brother, I must sign off here and go to bed, the planes do take off early. Yawnnnnn! Let me know if it is possible for you to get over here or not, I sure hope you can.

So, take care-

Sawadee,
Jack

PS: I'm getting so short, I have to stand on my toes to tie my shoes!

Jack – on the job directing air traffic at Takhli AFB

Chu Lai, Vietnam
January 26, 1968

Dear Elin,

This will be a quick note. Got your letter today about Bangkok - Sounds great! I just called Special Services & they said they will guarantee getting me a quota for R&R to Bangkok during the 10 to 25 March period. The Colonel is not here right now but I know he'll go along with it.

I won't know for a week or so exactly what days but I think I'll try for about the 12th of March through the 16th of March. That way you will have had time to recuperate from the long trip (it's only 3 hours to Bangkok from here).

I am very excited to see Bangkok. I just wanted to save it until we could "do" it together.

Honey - this is very exciting, will write some more later.

Love you –
Bill

Odense, Denmark
January 26, 1968

Darling -

Yesterday got short letter from you - made me happy as I didn't expect it. I had one the day before too. I've figured my letters lose a day and yours gain one over the date line so both really take 7 days instead of 6 and 8. I was very happy that you are taking your R&R in March. I had feared you would decide something definitely before you got my letters with my ideas for an R&R. By now you should have my letter and by next week I should know your reaction.

We are anxiously following the big battle at Khe Sanh and the American ship in North Korea. So much going on. If the war expands to Thailand I might be barred from going there, but I surely hope not. I'm very positive about it working out - both the big picture and our own smaller world. I feel like I'm supposed to go in March and I'm sure we'll see each other soon.

I almost finished my lamps and I'm very happy with the result. I scratched the "Lonely Cyprus" on a blue background. It's very beautiful and I'll give it to you as a gift from our good times by the sea. Making all these things gives me much satisfaction and I'm very happy in my work.

Hope the rats get killed as there is a terrible danger for diseases from rats.

Much love and a thousand thoughts.

Yours,
Elin

THE BATTLE OF KHE SANH

The Battle of Khe Sanh began on January 21, 1968, when forces from the People's Army of North Vietnam (PAVN) carried out a massive artillery bombardment on the U.S. Marine garrison at Khe Sanh, located in northwest South Vietnam near the Laotian border. For the next 77 days, U.S. Marines and their South Vietnamese allies fought off an intense siege of the garrison, in one of the longest and bloodiest battles of the Vietnam War. Meanwhile, with U.S. and South Vietnamese attention focused on Khe Sanh, North Vietnamese and Viet Cong forces launched the Tet Offensive, a series of coordinated surprise attacks on cities and towns throughout South Vietnam.

Philadelphia, Pennsylvania
January 28, 1968

Dear Bill,

Today is one of those damp, soggy, and dreary Sundays - the kind that is nice to spend in bed with the covers pulled up over your head. Since Heather didn't take a nap, I couldn't either. She has really gotten bigger since you saw her last - she is 40" tall and weighs 33½ pounds; attends Nursery School two mornings a week. Of course, you would never recognize Tim!!! He was 2 years old on Jan 23rd and is quite a big lad 35" tall and weighs 28 lbs. Earlier this past fall I had a couple of traumatic experiences with him. He was riding a plastic "Tyke" bike and fell off and cracked his front tooth. Dr. Bates extracted it in Frankford Hospital, but before he could be treated as an out patient I had to get a urine specimen. What a panic trying to get 3 ounces of urine from an untrained 20 month old baby. I fed him water and he would "pee" on the floor instead of in the bottle. What an experience! Now he is toothless!?!

The second traumatic experience occurred while Derek was in Chicago for a couple of days. After an extremely hectic day when the kids were "dog tired" Tim fell and put a V shaped gash into his forehead which required 3 stitches at Frankford Hospital accident ward.

Carolyn was married on Nov. 3rd as is now Mrs. Herbert Harned. Herb & Carolyn live in an apartment near Rising Sun and Unruh Sts. Carolyn is working at Jeanne's Hospital. Nancy was married June 3, 1966 and is now Mrs. Max Cutshall. Max and Nancy live in a home in Morrisville and Nancy is working at West Trenton State Hospital. Mother is planning to be married on Feb. 9th (1968) to Kenneth Hahn. All four of us are very happy for her. Ken works at CBS-TV monitoring T.V. broadcasts. George is still foot loose and fancy free - although I don't know for how long as he is going with George Gibson's sister.

I have been sewing - in fact I made a mint green crepe cocktail dress. I was rather pleased with it. Now I'm working on a brown dress. An unexpected side result of my sewing are Timmy's and Heather's reactions. He now goes around the house saying "damn it." He has a keen knowledge of just when to use it. Whenever Heather sees someone else sewing, she says "My mommy sews too; but she has trouble getting it closed" (referring to the 5 times it took me to put the zipper in). Derek built a Heath Kit color TV set last year. He did a nice job on it. Recently we have been having some trouble with it and he's been trying to track it down but so far with little success. Tonight he has the tuner assembly spread all over the living room. He has some caustic remarks to make about it!

I've been sick on and off for the last month - acute sinus infection which had to be punctured and flushed (Ouch! rather painful) then the virus; and now a cold (I hope it doesn't go to the sinuses again). Heather had an ear infection; Tim, lung congestion and Derek missed a week of work with a head virus. We spent $90 in 10 days on doctors and medication, X-rays, etc. Spring can't come soon enough now! Do you know anything about classical guitar music? Derek got a Julian Bream record for Christmas. It is quite good, and different from the classical Spanish type guitar music.

I called your mother tonight for your address and she said that Mike and his wife and baby were visiting today and that Uncle Charlie was well enough to come home for the afternoon. It has just occurred to me that I could probably have sent a regular air mail letter. Is that true?

Take care,
Judy

Odense, Denmark
January 29, 1968

Dearest Darling

How I look at your picture almost hourly and how I talk about you. This weekend was quite eventful. Friday I visited a young couple - I went to school with her for 10 years and he is an engineer with Xerox. They have two darling children and a 3rd on the way. We had coffee and a very good discussion on life, politics, etc. They can take German TV and guess what? They showed the landing of the 198th Brigade at Chu Lai. My question? What was the Vietnamese girl doing with the wreath all over the place? Also saw part of a show at Chu Lai. I saw some officers' faces that looked familiar. Then they had the opening of Green Week in Berlin. There sat General Ferguson in full gala uniform. Later I saw a small Danish girl I know on German TV. Thought it weird I should see three people I knew.

We are anxiously following the Korean crises - oh how I hope it all will end soon and we can have peace again.

Saturday Mulvad had a 25 years anniversary jubilee for "Mulvad Mobler." Far and I went to congratulate him. They have expanded the old shop. He invited me to lunch in the new store. About 40 furniture people there - and he praised me in his speech. They also invited me to the store's Personnel Party at night in a very nice inn. We had the Danish "Cold Table" - two beers and two snaps, piano, music and many speeches (I gave one too) and it was quite fun. We all talked about you, and Mortensen had a "skal" for you. Their store has many new very exciting things. Everyone was glad to see me and Mrs. Mortensen invited me along on a Germany trip this spring.

Sunday Far, Mor and I took a small drive. Everything here seems so small, the roads, the houses, etc. I even miss American food, it's so bland here, but then I'm losing weight so shouldn't worry about the food anyway. I have a stubborn cold and I hope to shake by today or tomorrow.

I expect word from my love the end of this week. I do wonder if I'll get to Bangkok. I hope Johnson won't extend the war to Korea too. Then who knows what would happen.

I received two tax forms - one from the bank and one from Bergs. We made $29.30 in interest. I made $236.50 at Bergs. FICA $10.60, Federal income tax withheld $34.60. Do you want me to file a separate return? I'll wait till you inform me.

I haven't sent any food package yet - because if I go to Thailand I can bring it faster than mailing it, and I can then mail another after I return. I do hope you get all the books o.k.

We are all fine here. The weather is very mild just above freezing and I'm happy we had a pleasant January. It can be so dreary at times.

I still keep busy with all my handmade production.

Bought a gift for Ann Ahlstone and mailed it to Kalbfleisches. Also the same for Gyneth Browning, mailed to the Morgans. I bought a Royal Danish bowl and 6 plates, cost $5- in the U.S. it retails for $50.

Now we have 4 down 8 to go. I feel they too will pass, and with each day that passes I love you more. I'm sure I've got the only man I could ever share my life with or who could put up with me - oh how I miss our life, in our home. I belong where you are.

Hope you are fine -

Love Elin

Chu Lai, Vietnam
January 30, 1968

Hi Honey,

Sorry I haven't written for a few days - but we've been extremely busy. I'm tired tonight so this won't be a literary gem!

I got your next two letters & I hope that by today you got my letter saying that you should come! (You've probably been driving Mor & Far crazy - jumping around waiting for the mail! I could just picture it from your last two letters & I had to laugh). Honey, you can't take two weeks leave in Vietnam! I can take an R&R - 5 days in Bangkok with one day going and one coming back. It's actually 7 - or a 7 day leave. So it's the same, you can't take them together. Anyway we'll have a ball for 5 days. I think we should just go off on our own while I'm there & you can stick to the tour the rest of the time. Just take the plan that appeals to you most to you. Don't worry about the money, and when I get there we can either go to a different hotel for the 5 days or get a double room at the same. You'll have a couple of days before I get there to assess the situation. I think we should plan on staying in Bangkok. If we want to take a side trip on our own we can do it.

Everyone here who has been to Bangkok on R&R says it's the most fantastic place they have ever been. In fact quite a few have requested to be assigned there after Vietnam.

The weather here has been beautiful. I've been taking a sunbath during lunch hour every day, so will have a tan when you see me (also growing a mustache - so don't be surprised!).

The North Vietnamese are really acting up North of here in a big offensive, as you've probably read & there have been some mortar attacks on our units a few miles away - on and off.

I'm going to Saigon (USARV Headquarters in Long Binh) from 12 to 17 February to attend this Data Processing course. I'm looking forward to getting away & hope to see some of the people I know. Bob Gray - who was in the Career Class (the bachelor) stopped in here today (he didn't know I was here). He is stationed in Quanh Nai - about 40 km from Chu Lai as an advisor to the RVNs.

Well honey - I love you & am real excited about March. Say hello to Mor & Far

Love Bill

Chu Lai, Vietnam
February 1, 1968

Dear Elin,

Got your letter today - with the letters from Nana & Emma - it will be fun for you to visit Emma in Germany.

We've had considerable excitement here as you may have heard in the news. Day before yesterday the NVA and VC staged a well-coordinated attack on major U.S. and RVN installations all over South Vietnam.

They hit Chu Lai base for the first time in 8 or 9 months. The alert sounded about 3 A.M. We all got dressed. I came to the office. There a lot of firing and mortar rounds coming in about 1 to 2 miles away. Just as I got to the PSD building there was a large explosion (it took place 3 miles down the beach) that rocked the whole building. I ran outside to see a huge fire ball rise in the sky (we all thought it was a nuclear blast!). Then a terrific shock blast that knocked things over in the building & scared the "s h i t" out of all of us. The VC had fired a rocket into the ammunition dump that is located next to the area on the beach where I stayed with the 198th Brigade when I first got here (there may be some pictures on the slides you got developed). The ammo dump explosion and fire lasted 3 hours. Fortunately a lot of the big bombs were not hit.

They also got 4 jets on the air strip and several hangars - plus the little bridge going into the little village I wrote about. The next day (yesterday) I drove down to the area hit to see the damage. The Replacement Detachment is now located on the beach where the 198th once was & I have a team of my men down there in-processing replacements. Fortunately there is a big sand dune between the ammo dump & the beach where the Replacement Detachment is located, or it would have been worse. The shock blast damaged every building, knocked out screens & broke all support beams. It leveled the officers' club where we used to go. Amazingly only one man was hurt seriously - a piece of fragment in his shoulder (there were 500 replacements down there).

Last night they tried again but the situation never got out of hand (I spent most of the night in a bunker just in case).

Tonight is the last night of TET & we are expecting another attempt - but our Division units have been in the hills all day flushing out VC. Apparently, according to the radio, there is still plenty of fighting in the streets in Saigon around the American Embassy. The VC blasted a hole in it & were occupying it for a while. They landed U.S. Airborne troops on the roof to get them!

We're all sort of tired from being up most of the night - and the work continues in great quantities. This is really a good spot to watch the action from. From the billet area you can stand over the cove & watch the whole Chu Lai Base.

Well Honey - see you in Bangkok! Hope everything is going well back there.

Love
Bill

Odense, Denmark
February 1, 1968

Dear Bill

Oh how my heart goes out to all the boys involved in this war. The news we get these days is very disturbing and it's hard to make a clear picture of what is going on. One thing is sure - we know that the pressure is really on and the war looks larger than it has for years. I do pray not too many boys get killed - it all seems so useless, only hope the North Vietnamese would see it too and stop their fighting. It's very hard to live in this great society and act as if nothing is happening. I never thought it would be like this. I miss you terribly and if it is possible I'll go to Bangkok for sure if there is a trace of a chance I'll see you. I'm still waiting for your reply, but realize you may be too busy to write much these days. But just know I think of you constantly and I'm really very close in spirit.

Please eat enough and take as good care of yourself as possible - and don't let personal things get to you - they usually aren't worth the worry, not in the big picture. If I ever say something that you think is strange - remember my world is so different right now and one cannot always assess a mood 10,000 miles away.

I love you more than ever - and pray to see you soon.

Love
Elin

Odense, Denmark
February 1, 1968

Dear Mother

Thank you for the three large envelopes, all three came yesterday, January 31, and I've attended to all the business. My bank account is still not straight. We disagree over $100 now. Before it was $500. I sure hope it gets straightened out. It is the bank's fault.

These days are very hard with all the fighting in Vietnam. I hope it's not too hard on you all alone. I know one's imagination has more play when one is alone. I do pray it will be over - it's very hard on all the families and it doesn't seem right that our beautiful young boys shall die for dubious causes. I still believe in fighting for freedom, but this war is so muddled one doesn't see clearly what is really involved. Maybe these offensives are the last desperate attempts, but they say the North may yet stage a major attack on the Marines. I'm not satisfied with the news we receive here. It's not detailed enough for me, but of course I'm extra keen on getting information and I can't expect the papers to have as many details as an American paper would.

We are all fine, and send our regards. I think of you and Uncle Charlie daily. I am busy making hand work which is good therapy for making time pass.

With love- Elin

Limeport, Pennsylvania
February 1, 1968

Dear Bill,

Well, I'm certain you have heard the good news by now. Jonathan Isaac it is (or "he" is, I should say).

Kathy and are very pleased with him. Mother and child are very healthy and Father has survived the "long wait" apparently well enough. I'll give you and Jack belated cigars when you return to the States. Everyone has been very good to Kathy and me. They have really showered us with gifts. And your Christmas gift of $50 was quite generous and appreciated. We hope to put it toward a living room rug. Kathy, Jonathan and I just took a trip to Philadelphia to see Mother this past Sunday. She looks well, is working hard, as usual and is even stepping out a bit. She got home from the Booths the other night at 1:00 a.m. Uncle Charlie was at 1214 on Sunday and was delighted with Jonathan, although he seems to be the only vocal party who doesn't like the name we've given him. He held the baby and said it was the first time in his life he had ever done such a thing. I could believe it.

Work at the church has been continuing at a steady pace, although, confidentially, it is a bit frustrating at times. That is, frustrating because of non-involved, apathetic, "I don't care" members. You tell them that the Church is mission to others and they come to sit and be entertained. I guess that's the way it's always been except for those few great moments of concern and involvement through history.

Speaking of concern and involvement and relationships between persons, I just saw a T.V. adaptation of Steinbeck's Of Mice and Men. It was just as fine as the book. Steinbeck is just great, being one of my favorites.

You may be interested to know how the U.S. people have reacted to the Pueblo incident. From what I see, Johnson could make almost any move and the people would support him with it. He's gaining ground. The people are really concerned about the situation as I am sure you are. I feel that it will be settled diplomatically, without major confrontation, but there is still that possibility.

It's about 1:00 a.m. and I must get to bed - with Jonathan's odd hours and all. Hope this letter isn't too varied.

Take care– Mike

USS PUEBLO INCIDENT

On January 23, 1968, the USS Pueblo, a Navy intelligence vessel, is engaged in a routine surveillance of the North Korean Coast when it was intercepted by North Korean patrol boats. According to U.S. reports, the Pueblo was in international waters almost 16 miles from shore, but the North Koreans turned their guns on the lightly armed vessel and demanded its surrender. The Americans attempted to escape, and the North Koreans opened fire, wounding the commander and two others. With capture inevitable, the Americans stalled for time, destroying the classified information aboard while taking further fire. Several more crew members were wounded.

Finally, the Pueblo was boarded and taken to Wonson. There, the 83 man crew was bound and blindfolded and transported to Pyongyang, where they were charged with spying within North Korea's 12 mile territorial limit and imprisoned. It was the biggest crisis in two years of increased tension and minor skirmishes between the United States and North Korea.

Odense, Denmark
February 2, 1968

Dear Bill

Received letter dated 24 January today - made me happy - only now I'm very anxious for your letter about the R&R. You just give me a date and I'll give you a name and place I'll be. Then if something happens you'll have to telegraph as we no longer have time for long letters and answers.

I'm so glad you too think you and I have something very special. We surely do and I'm so happy we are married, and I feel so blessed to be your wife during these hard times - our love makes even that a bit easier.

Our news about the war is quite terrible at present. I refuse to believe but a 10th of the reports and I'm confident this spring will see negotiations, but until then it will be hard on our troops & I pray for them all every day. I do hope your base won't get hit (selfish) but I so hope no one I know will get hurt.

My spirits are good today. I have resolved my fears and I again look at positively at the whole outlook. Going for exercise now. Must get beautiful for the trip. It has helped some, but a long way to go. Love you more than ever -

Yours always
Elin

Philadelphia, Pennsylvania
February 2, 1968

Home, Evening, Raining

Dear Bill,

The news here is certainly far from optimistic concerning the war. I have been concerned for you and your men - and all the brave young Americans. Robert MacNamara gave a farewell yesterday and it too was pessimistic. I think it will be a fact, in time, that MacNamara has been the greatest Defense Secretary of the

U.S. But notwithstanding, how is this war going to be resolved? I am enclosing a clipping giving a Britisher's view.

Jack called me at 5:20 P.M. from Thailand. He is so anxious to come home and I surely hope the authorities do not extend him there. He said he is one of four controllers who bring the planes in after the raids. It was 5:20 A.M. when he called.

Joan will be finished March 19th and then hopes to get a position somewhere in the area of Philadelphia. Her grades were 6 As and 2 Bs. There is no question that she can learn what she wants to.

Michael and Kathleen brought their new baby to visit their "grandmother" last Sunday. He cried, slept and noticed no one! I think he will look like Mike but it is too soon to tell. At any rate, he is a strong little fellow and his features, etc. are normal. Lots of dark hair but that will go. I still have your baby hair!

While seated in the Griscom Street fish house last week, I noticed Mrs. Hanna and an elderly gentleman near me. She spoke and of course asked about you. She said she prayed for you every night. Then the gentleman, her father, twice asked me to tell you he wanted to be remembered to you. He is quite feeble. Mrs. Hanna informed me that she is remarrying next week - the widower of a nurse who was her friend since girlhood. The twins are married and George left Temple day school and returned to Willow Grove Air Base. She thinks he may reenlist.

I spent most of today at the Pedagogical Library in our Administration Bldg. choosing books for dear old Edmunds. I chose over 100 volumes which will come to us free. It was a different type of day.

Uncle Charlie came home last Sunday so that he could see Jonathan. He felt well but reminded us that it was time to go back at 7:00 P.M. I sat with him after school today and he is better than when you were home. But he still needs custodial and medical care 24 hours a day.

Bob Hamilton brightened Tuesday for me by taking me out for dinner. He earned 22 credits toward his doctorate and his marks were 3 A Excel. and 1 B. He explained the new tonal sound in music to me - 12 sounds instead of 8, in one range. I try to follow but get lost along the way. But I do like to learn some of it.

Nana Williams is doing well. She no longer is the justice but does notary business.

Aunt Rachel just called. She is a great comfort to me when I am lonely or discouraged. I laughed at something she said and she remarked that it was good to hear me laugh again. I guess I have been gloomy.

Next morning!

I stopped last night and watched Jack Lemmon on T.V. in "The Apartment." I am glad I never went to the movies but rarely because the majority of films are new to me. Jack is a fine actor, knowing how to combine humor and pathos in a subtle way.

Today I am lunching at the Bellevue with my sorority sisters. I am chairman of the by-laws committee and a duller job I've never had! They squabble over trifles. But this June will be the last for me and I won't get involved again in that area. My mother always liked parliamentary procedures, etc. but I can't get too interested.

Well, I'll go down and put the coffee pot on. Wish you were here to have breakfast with me. I'll drink one for you! Take care and always remember I love you dearly.

A hug and a kiss - Mother

Pound Ridge, New York
February 2, 1968

Dear Elin,

Barbara was very happy to receive your phone call and we had hoped very much to see you before you left for Denmark. Anyway, we always look forward to the time when we can see you & Bill again. Please send our best to him, & if you have an opportunity send me his address, because I would like to write to him.

I am writing to you for two reasons. First to say hello and second to ask if you would be interested in an idea that I have. I anticipate starting an import business, concerned with importing from Europe, antiques and other objects d'art. Of course to begin with I must develop sources of supply. You have always been interested in these things and you might wish to participate. There are many details to work out, but initially I would wish to know if you are interested in joining such a venture. If so, we can begin to organize and work out a distribution of any profits. I should say that at the outset I am not seeking any contributions of capital & that I am prepared to invest what is required to start the thing rolling. Please let me know what you think?

Kindest regards to your parents - please tell them we think of them often and we have fond memories of our trip to Denmark.

Sincerely,
Tom

Elin's remarks to Bill following Tom Roman's letter:

Dear Bill

Funny that Tom should write this as I have also always wanted to start something. I'm writing him that I'm interested and to expound more details. Maybe we can work something out, at least doing something with a lawyer one should have the legal advice. One can't lose by being interested. We will have to start now however, so I have the next half year to get supplies. Could turn out exciting. I'm not telling anyone, so please don't either as one likes to keep it quiet until it actually happens.

Mulvad has also offered a trip to Germany to sell, so I guess I'll go after Bangkok. So maybe I can make some spending money. Also hope to see Herr Maenner, and get some money there. Every little bit helps.

I finally got a statement from the bank and our account is all straightened out. At present I have $800 and I need $300 more for the trip so that leaves $500, plus $200 next month, so I should have plenty of spending money.

I am so busy (still exercise every day) that hardly have time to get real excited about going.

The war development is impossible to judge from here. We run from the T.V. news to the radio news - the German news on the radio in my room - the 7 o'clock news - the 10 o'clock news and by night's end it's total confusion because the information is never the same. They never repeat the same information, so it's a puzzle to know what is happening.

I pray for you all and surely it doesn't look too good, or let me say, it looks like our men are fighting heavier forces than before. This will surely end the war.

All my love – I miss you much and look forward to March.

Elin

Odense, Denmark
February 3, 1968

Dear Bill

Just got this sweet letter today - Maria surely is a sweet person, and I'll write to her again soon. Also will try to visit all the other people, seems like I have mail every day. These days with all the "bad" news from Vietnam it is extremely hard to get through, it's like a powder keg. I'm sure you will also push back this attempt, but they promise more to come. It seems like the "real" war is just starting. I hear they have attacked Da Nang with rockets - sounds terrible, no one is really safe.

I sent my blue lamp to get burned in the oven. I'm very pleased with it, and I hope it comes out nice. I'm half finished with the shade for it.

I've lost 3 or 4 pounds, but with all this news I've started to eat again. On Monday I will diet again - boy, how hard it is to lose. I enjoy my daily exercises and the sauna - makes one feel so much better. Maybe we can have one built into a future home. I also enjoy sitting in one, and I don't think they cost too much.

The joke for the day - one weary soldier wrote his wife - "Stop nagging me in your letters and let me enjoy this war in peace."

I too think we have something very precious and we do have direction and purpose. I love you more and more and your happy face is always in front of my inner eye.

Much love
Elin

Chu Lai, Vietnam
February 6, 1968

Dear Elin,

Before I went to bed last night I finished a letter to you saying "everything has quieted down since I wrote last about the attack on the ammo dump and maybe 'Charlie' is going back in the hills." That was at 10:30 P.M. when I turned out the light.

Was just drifting off to sleep at 11:00 P.M. when there was a terrific explosion about 30 feet from my hooch. I pulled some clothes on, got my steel helmet and armored vest on in 3 seconds and ran for the bunker. There were explosions occurring all over & we could hear the "swoosh - bang." There were about 40 officers already in the bunker I dove into, in various stage of dress. All of us scared to death (believe me!). It was a rocket attack by the VC on the Division Headquarters - the first since it has been here. The attack was apparently over in five minutes, but we stayed in the bunker over an hour, then ventured out to inspect the big crater in the road by my hooch made by the rocket. That wasn't so bad but there was a lot of damage elsewhere. About 1:30 A.M. we got an "all clear." I went to check on the people in my section - the hooch in which Captain Ned Shivar (my assistant whom I wrote about), Lt. Jaquez, two warrant officers and Lt. Ozvath - all from the PSD live, had gotten a direct hit by a rocket. Ned and Jaquez, and the warrant officers and the Special Services officer were all in bed and had just gotten up (a rocket had just hit near the officers' club first) when it hit. It tore the hooch completely apart. Beds, lockers, pin-ups, all in a pile. Ned got some shrapnel wounds - not serious - and is in the hospital now. The Special Services Officer, they think, had punctured ear drums & Joe Jaquez a banged up shoulder. Mr. Buxton lost his false teeth. Miraculously none were more seriously injured or killed.

Another rocket fell a few feet from the General's house, another a few feet from the Chief of Staff's trailer, another crashed into the Officers' Mess & tore off half of it, and another landed on the doorstep of the Division Tactical Operation Center - but it was a dud and didn't explode. Two fell into the 23rd Admin Company troop billets area and burned three billets to the ground. They housed 72 of my men from the PSD. Again miraculously they all got out & except for scratches and some minor wounds no one was hurt. They lost everything they owned except what they were wearing - but no one is bemoaning that, they're so glad to be alive. There were some others too - several officers had to be hospitalized, but no one was killed or seriously injured, which is hard to believe. It's the most frightening thing I've gone through & and we're all sort of pinching ourselves today. So the war really became personal for the first time! "Peaceful Chu Lai!" and "safe and sound" AGs!

Apparently it was another coordinated attack in key areas like last week. Da Nang and some other places were also hit last night - although our news is about two days late & we don't often find out what happened 40 miles away until two days later.

Ned Shivar had just returned from R&R in Australia last night & Captain Uplinger (Special Services) just got back last night after being stuck in Saigon for a week during the fighting there. Lt. Yates and "Judge" Springer were in the same bunker that I was. Well that's the excitement for the day. We're all ready to dive for cover tonight if it reoccurs.

Got four letters from you today dated from the 26th of January. Can't understand why you hadn't gotten my letter about Bangkok yet, although the mail has been held up (incoming and outgoing) in Da Nang because of the heavy attacks there on the air strips & no planes came in or went out foe a while. In fact the APO there was hit last week.

I hope you are still planning on March. The only thing that could prevent or delay me would be some big attack. However even during all this we are sending people out on R&R every day (some have had to wait a day to get out) - and others at R&R sites couldn't get back to Vietnam (because the air fields were closed) and had to stay in Hong Cong or Sydney for two or three more days!

Anyway - I'm flying to USARV Headquarters on the 12th for a week (it can't be anymore dangerous there than it is here!) & I will be glad to get a change of scenery. Soon it will be March & we can forget the mess the world is in for a few days.

Honey - I love you & think about you all the time. Don't worry about me - somebody was sure looking out for all of us last night here at Americal Headquarters!

Much love
Bill

Captain Shivar's hooch

Bill in bunker

Odense, Denmark
February 6, 1968

Dear Love

We are now over 4 months. The last week was the longest with all the trouble in VN, it makes it worse to have you gone.

Yesterday I got the wonderful news that you like my R&R plan. I'm waiting to make a reservation till your next letter. I think I might take the 9th to 26th program. I think I will be too lonely if I come for 3 weeks - in those countries one can't go out at night unescorted and I think I'll have enough to do in 17 days. That trip leaves from Copenhagen too. I got the refund for the other ticket and I only have to add $200 to make the trip so it will be a cinch. I'm so excited I can hardly contain myself. It sure will help break up the year.

Please honey, still put some money in Soldiers Deposits. If we don't start we won't have anything saved.

I want to be free to buy a house, if we want to some day.

I'm really starting a diet now. Now there is a real purpose and I have something to look forward to. I only pray that something won't prevent you from getting off. In war so much can happen & I realize that maybe all leaves will be cancelled. But it cannot happen to us - it seems so right that I shall go see you next month.

I still keep very busy and am as happy as circumstances allow. I know you all are very busy and we miss you and love you.

Yours Elkesede
Elin

Odense, Denmark
February 6, 1968

Dear Mother,

I have thought often of you during these past weeks. I hope being alone isn't too hard on you, and with all the added war activity I fear you would get extra upset. I did a bit, but I'm sure it will all be resolved and we will once again have peace and have our wonderful boys home. I just can't believe how long we have to live with this war as the norm of the day. I pray that our leaders be given the wisdom enough to do what is right (I have given up trying to know what that is, it all seems so involved).

I so enjoy my silver thimble. I sew with it daily and think of all those who sewed with it before. I also have received compliments on my beautiful blouse. I almost finished one lampshade and started a second one. Also finished several small embroideries. I painted one porcelain lamp and started second. Will also start a tile table - all very satisfying work.

How is Uncle Charlie? And how are you? I hope Jack soon comes home, so at least one of your boys is back. It's so hard to have them so far away. This last week has been the worst yet to take & I get bombarded with many unkind remarks from ignorant people. I feel that of all things to fear, the worst is ignorance and stupidity. But my spirit is intact and will remain so. I'm still glad to be home as I have a chance to know my wonderful parents again. We have many good discussions. We talk of everyone and we think of you always.

Give my love to all the dear friends in Philadelphia.

With love
Elin

Bill writes cheerful letters.

Chu Lai, Vietnam
February 9, 1968

Dear Mother,

I don't remember when I wrote last. How is everything going in Philadelphia? Well, I hope.

Things have been pretty hot here in the past few weeks with the big push by the Viet Cong and the North Vietnamese all over the country. They hit the airfield and the ammunition dump two weeks ago (the ammo dump is located right next to the beach area where I first stayed with the 198th - now our Replacement Detachment is located there). Some 500 pound bombs went off creating a tremendous explosion & fire ball (we all though it was a nuclear explosion). It did a lot of damage to the Replacement Detachment but few men were hurt. Then on Monday there was a rocket attack on the Division Headquarters. Quite frightening! Miraculously no one was killed & there were few injuries. We have bunkers all over & after the first one hit everyone ran for the bunkers & stayed there until it was over. Right now the big action here in the north is at Da Nang & Hue. They're apparently making a big effort to take over a significant city - however the enemy casualty rate is fantastic & we don't see how they can keep it up much longer.

I'm going to USARV Headquarters outside of Saigon on Sunday to attend a data processing course a week long. Will be nice to get away from here - but Saigon's not much better these days.

Elin is coming to Bangkok in March & I'm going to meet her there on R&R. Will be real exciting. She can get a real inexpensive trip with a European travel agency. She will be there two weeks.

I've asked to be stationed in Washington D.C. after this - hope it comes through. Will return to the U.S. via Europe & pick Elin up for a vacation in Spain or some place. Just passed the 4 month mark - nine to go.

Got a letter from Jack today - he is counting hours now! How are Kathy and Mike & the baby? Am real anxious to see Jonathan.

How is Uncle Charlie doing? Tell him I said hello. Got a nice long letter from Nana Williams (can't remember if I wrote to her) recently.

Take care

Love
Bill

Odense, Denmark
February 9, 1968

Dearest Bill

Yesterday I had my reservation confirmed for Bangkok. I leave here the 9th of March, arrive Sunday the 10th. Leave Monday the 25th, arrive Copenhagen the 26th.

I am supposed to stay at "Asia Hotel" which still has to be confirmed. When you arrive we will get a double room. I'm not arranging that ahead of time. My bank balance is $850 (I just paid the motor registration) and I have to add $300 to pay for the whole ticket. That will give me $500 left plus the $200 for March. How much money do you want me to bring? I still want to save the $500 for February and March. You do that, OK? We must start or we won't save a dime.

I'm very excited about my trip and I realize the whole thing will be around $1,000, but it's worth it. I hope you feel the same way. I decided not to come for too long. Somehow what will a lady do alone in the east after dark - one would have to stay indoors or hope to find a group, but I feel 16 days is sufficient. This probably will be cheaper in the long run, and it's much easier to leave from Copenhagen than to leave from Germany.

I love you dearly and I'm praying for all our dear boys up north. It's very sad news we get.

Love you –
Elin

Going to Rita's and Jorgen's this afternoon to spend the weekend. Should be fun. I really keep busy.

Chu Lai, Vietnam
February 10, 1968

Dear Elin,

Still haven't gotten a letter from you saying that you received my letter (written over 18 days ago) about your coming to Bangkok. The mail has been all screwed up because of the heavy fighting in Da Nang &

Saigon. Anyway I'm still shooting for my R&R for around 12 March. If for some reason your trip is later, don't worry. I'll just take 7 days leave instead of an R&R. The colonel will go along with it. It's maddening though to have to wait so long for the answers to each others questions & I know you are going through the same thing.

Well, we haven't had any more rocket attacks, but believe me there are some jumpy people here, too much so in fact. I'm very apprehensive about some of the officers, really scared to death, sleeping in the bunkers every night since the attack (from 6:30 p.m. on) - looking like moles, not sleeping, etc. You have to take it all philosophically. If the first rocket has your name on it - sayonara - if it doesn't you have time to get in a bunker. Even if the first one hits you, there's a good chance to get out (as my officers found out on Monday). They are all back from the hospital now except Ned. He was evacuated to the hospital in Qui Nhon and from there today to Cameron Bay. Seems that the blast punctured an ear drum and they are going to keep him 2 or 3 weeks. One Lt. Colonel was writing a letter to his wife in a hooch not far from mine. A piece of fragment came through the roof and hit him in the shoulder. They evacuated him to Walter Reed Hospital in Washington D.C.

There were some humorous episodes during the rocket attack. One Lt. Colonel was taking a shower when the first rocket hit. He ran to the nearest bunker in the nude and dove in & was confronted by two Red Cross girls. He ran out and went to his hooch & got dressed - then came back (all during the attack!).

Lt. Yates has been busy for the last few days directing the building of a bunker right outside our hooch. I let him take 3 days off to do it. It will be a masterpiece and will be finished tomorrow. The nearest bunker to us was about 150 feet away. Now we'll have one outside our door.

I'm flying to Saigon tomorrow. Will go directly from Chu Lai to Tan Son Hut air base & from there to Long Binh. The course starts on Tuesday, so I'll have a day to do some business at USARV Headquarters, and hopefully look up some friends - John Getchell, Dan Tasotta, Gerry Kelly and others. Colonel James is quite ill and will be returning to the States. After he recovers he is scheduled to be U.S. Army Europe AG in Heidelberg! If he is still here I'll try to see him.

Got a letter from Jack yesterday (took 15 days to get from Thailand to here). He is leaving on the 25th & hoped I could meet him before he left but that would be impossible. He is real happy to be leaving, which I can understand.

Da Nang is really getting a whacking. We (Americal Division) have sent some units to help out and casualties have been very heavy yesterday and today. This whole thing is very frustrating & there are too many "holds" on the military. "Permission" has to be granted in many cases before the artillery can fire rounds on an enemy position & by the time it's granted the rockets or mortars have been fired & the enemy gone. Da Nang area is, I'm afraid, building up to be another Dien Bien Phu, especially in the Khe Sahn valley. Although so many Viet Cong and North Vietnamese have been slaughtered since TET (22,000!) that it's bound to slow down their effort soon.

I can't honestly judge anything right now - little comprehensive news & what does come in is late and sporadic. It's frustrating, especially when you are right in the middle of it!

Honey, hope I'll get a letter before I leave tomorrow - about Bangkok, otherwise it will be 8 or 9 days until I get my mail when I return.

Much love, miss you very much & wish you were curled up with me on my bed right now! (That's where I'm writing this letter & thinking about making love to you!).

Goodnight sweetheart,
Bill

Lt. Yates' bunker

Chu Lai, Vietnam
February 10, 1968

Dear Uncle Charlie,

How are you? Mother writes that you are feeling real good & looking great. I'm glad to hear that.

The weeks are flying here for me, but not fast enough! Lots of work to do, but recently a bit too much excitement. We've had a few rocket & mortar attacks on the base, but things have quieted down for the past few days. Tomorrow I'm flying to Saigon to attend a course on Data Processing for a week.

Elin is flying to Bangkok in March and I'm going to meet her there for a few days. Will be great to leave here for a short time & especially nice to be able to be together in Bangkok.

The weather here has been overcast for the past week, it was warm & sunny during most of January - but now it's a bit chilly - in the 60s. Still warm for February! Anyway the monsoons are over with and we might as well enjoy these "cool" days because in another month the warm weather starts. I understand that in July and August it gets very hot.

Take care of yourself & know that I am thinking about you.

Will write again soon

Best regards,
Bill

Arhus, Denmark
February 10, 1968

Dear Bill

Had a long letter written and then I left for Arhus and forgot to mail it so here is a quick note to tell you my reservation for the place is confirmed. I leave here the 9th of March home on the 26th of March. I decided on 16 days as longer would be too much when one is alone.

The hotel is the Asia Hotel, yet to be confirmed. I only made reservations for me. We can make arrangements when you arrive. I'm sure they will give me a double anyway even when I'm alone.

I am visiting Rita and Jorgen and enjoy catching up on all the news. I hope you are fine and I'll tell you, here is one that is excited about seeing my love. Can't believe I might really see you in a month.

All my love
Elin

Minneapolis, Minnesota
February 10, 1968

Dear Bill,

Thought I'd write and give you the latest happenings in Minneapolis. On Wednesday I had an interview for Irish International Airlines. I never thought I had any chance of getting hired because 93 girls applied for jobs. On Thursday they called me back for a test, and that afternoon I had a second interview. The representative returned to New York that same afternoon and called the school on Friday stating the airline wanted to hire me. I will be working in New York City on Fifth Avenue as a junior secretary for Irish International Airlines. My starting salary is $415.00 a month, including all the benefits of the airlines. They fly to Ireland, England and Europe. Sound great? I am so happy! My 9 months of training really paid off. The school gave me this week off, so Mother wants me to come home. Then I must fly back to Minneapolis for a week of special classes. Then on February 25th Irish will fly me free of charge to New York and will put me up in a hotel for 7 days. About 9 other girls, but they are working as reservationists and space controllers, and all are on night shifts without weekends off. My job is a 9 to 5 one with weekends off. I can hardly believe it.

Our only problem will be finding an apartment. The rent is so high in New York. I may have to start off living with 3 or 4 girls, until I can swing rent better.

Here I am writing 2 pages about myself without even asking you how you are. It's just that I'm so excited! I will write to Elin and tell her about my good fortune. I understand how terribly busy you must be, so I do not expect you to write. I will write again as soon as I get situated in New York.

Take care -
Love Joan

Minneapolis, Minnesota
February 10, 1968

Dear Elin,

Sorry I haven't written to you but so much has been happening out here in Minneapolis. Between tests and term papers I have really been keeping busy. I am very anxious to tell you my good news. I have been hired as a junior secretary for Irish International Airlines. I will be working in New York City on Fifth Avenue (a very good location). My starting salary is $415.00 a month and I will have all the benefits of the airlines. They fly to Ireland, Britain, and from there to Europe. The school gave me this week off from classes, so Mother wants me to come home. Then I will fly back to Minneapolis for another week of special classes. Irish will fly me free from Minneapolis to New York, and put me up in a hotel for 7 days. I am happy! I can hardly believe it all happened in only 3 days. I never really expected to get hired, because 93 girls applied for jobs with them. They did hire 9 other girls, but they will be working as reservationists on night shifts. I will have a 9 to 5 job with weekends off. I hope we don't have too much trouble finding an apartment. Five of us may have to live together at first, so that we can swing the rent. We'll just have to wait and see what happens,

I will be able to see Kirsten often now. It's not too far from New York. I will call her when I get home. I'll write you again once I get settled. Please give your parents my fondest regards.

Take care - love,
Joan

Long Binh, Vietnam
February 14, 1968

Dear Elin,

What a sprawling, dreary place this is. Been here 3 days and now I'm anxious to get back to Chu Lai. USARV Headquarters is huge & Long Binh post - which houses 45,000 troops covers 24 square miles outside of Saigon. You have to take a bus to get to the mess hall, billets, work - everywhere. Very impersonal & another parody of the war. The headquarters is in modern, air conditioned buildings - like those at Fort Benjamin Harrison.

I flew from Chu Lai to Tan Son Nhut late Monday afternoon. Things are still hot in Saigon & to get to Long Binh (18 miles) you have to go through part of Saigon. I had to wait and come with an armed convoy, with machine gunners ready. Quite dramatic, we sped though the city. There were tanks, bunkers in the streets, and lots of ARVN military. The streets were filthy, garbage piled up, lots of squalor. Looked like parts of Beirut.

Saw John Getchell (4th AD) who works here and hates it, and Jerry Kelly (Fort Ord), and Lt. Colonel Ganley (Fort Hood) and Jim Tracy (career class - Indianapolis) during the last few days.

This class lasts through Saturday then I've got to try to get back to Chu Lai. May take several days. This is too big here. Just like an analogy to living in a big city, or a cozy place like Monterey.

Honey - I hope you're all set to come to Bangkok & that there will be some more letters when I get back. The mail has been all screwed up because of the action in Da Nang.

I'm really looking forward to Bangkok (then don't know how I'll last out the following 6 months - but it will all be down hill then).

Say hello to Mor and Far.

I love you– Bill

Philadelphia, Pennsylvania
February 14, 1968

Dear Bill,

Happy Valentines Day!

Bad news today from Jack. He has been extended and he doesn't know how long it will be. His port call had been 2/24th.

News from Joan - a job in New York City as junior secretary with Irish Airlines on Fifth Avenue. She is coming home on Monday to give me more information.

Our news here is rank! I have stopped listening to T.V. coverage. The newspapers are bad enough. This war is either right or wrong - depending on one's viewpoint,. For the sake of you fellows - I hope it is right.

My love,
Mother

Odense, Denmark
February 15, 1968

Dear Bill

Just got your letters about the two attacks - ammo dump and the Headquarters. I too agree that it's a miracle no one was killed.. I'm so glad you could look forward to Bangkok, during all this mess. Somehow, when one has something ahead it makes the present not so bad. Of course the attack itself must have been a nightmare. All during those days I felt very uneasy and upset, but now I'm fine too.

I'm still coming in March of course that's what I think about all the time now, and I'm so glad we will be together. Even the money part seems like nothing now. It's really only money and I only wish I had the thought earlier so we could have planned more. But there is so little to plan. Now we will just need a place to meet. But I guess you can tell me what day you expect to arrive and you know I will be at the Hotel Asia. So we'll get together.

Jack's tour has been extended a month so I'm writing him where I'll be in Bangkok. Maybe we all can see each other, or maybe I can see him when he comes through Bangkok. It's all very exciting and I only pray nothing will keep you away, like they stop all R&Rs or something. Oh they couldn't do that to me and you.

I do love you and think of you constantly. Please take good care, you hear now!

Love
Elin

Odense, Denmark
February 16, 1968

Dear Mother

All of a sudden I have two letters to answer. I'm sorry to hear Jack is delayed a month, but maybe that means we can see him next month. Bill and I are planning to meet in Bangkok next month. I just found out we could do it. Mail takes 10 days so it's been 20 days since I had the idea. I'll leave on the 9th of March and return on the 26th. Bill will come for 6 days. Please pray that the Army doesn't decide to cancel all leaves. We so look forward to this.

Bill and all around him have had several days of attacks. He said it was a miracle that no one was killed or seriously injured. 72 of his men lost all their belongings in a fire in their billets. Bill's billets were not touched. He really is looking forward to next month.

Every girl dreams of working in New York and I think it sounds real exciting. Joan can take care of herself. I wish her all the best. I'm writing her telling her that if she gets a vacation and cheap passage she can spend a couple of weeks with me here. We would all love to have her, and one can't see all of Europe in one trip. One place is enough at a time.

I'm writing Jack and telling him the name of the hotel where I'll be staying. I agree with you about the dysentery. Once you have had it, the germs stay dormant and can flair back again at any time when the conditions deteriorate and when one is weak. That is the unfortunate thing about having once contracted it. In the States he should always be fine though. I hope we don't get it while there.

Your letters sound like you keep very busy. I'm so glad, I also hope the situation with Uncle Charlie is not getting you down. It doesn't sound like it.

Much love
Elin

Odense, Denmark
February 17, 1968

Dear Bill

Christmas is still with us. It is so hard to get all cards and letters organized and answered. I write about 3 letters a day. Today I wrote about 10 and might write more. Three Christmas cards enclosed.

I congratulated Joan on her job, wrote your Mother and Uncle Charlie, and to Jack telling him where I'll be in Bangkok. Also wrote to Hazel, haven't heard from her in a month. Told the Morgans in a letter that if Gwyneth is in Bangkok, I'll love to see her.

It's like Christmas here today - beautiful snow, but mild, so it's pleasant.

Later -

I have never seen so much mail as we really get. It's so hard to keep up with, do many people write to you directly? Has Mike written yet? I haven't gotten one from him.

I'm to say hello from Mr. Mulvad and Mr. Mortensen. Also my Aunt Nina and Uncle Poul Erik. My grandmother calls you "the world's best man" - she so loved your Christmas card. Rita and Jorgen send their regards, as do many more, don't even know how many. – E.

Philadelphia, Pennsylvania
February 18, 1968

Dear Bill,

We thought that you might enjoy some news from Frankford and North Torresdale (as we are called) - the elite of Torresdale who live in Crestmont Farms and along the river deny that Parkwood Manor exists in "their Torresdale" and to be asked by one of them "Where exactly do you live?" makes us unable to tell them without laughing or smiling.

Mother and Ken were married and the affair had only minor problems, which at the time seemed major to me as I had to solve them. She is now Mrs. Kenneth Hahn. The new life seems to agree with her as she has never looked better (the lines and circles have seemed to disappear) and her mental and emotional state is much calmer. For the first time in 25 years she is just a housewife with no responsibilities of a 24 hour office nurse. At the last minute my brother-in-law Max slipped his disc for the 2nd time in 3 months, so Mother had to ask Derek to usher. Although nothing was said it was a great emotional strain for her as neither she nor Father came to our wedding. We found it slightly amusing since I was her Matron of Honor.

My best friend Dora Michael Rush babysat for us. You might know her as she is a 1957 graduate of Temple and was one of the "Ten Young Women" (I'm not sure that is the exact title of the organization). She dated Buzz Johnson during '53 & '54; and majored in psychology. We have much in common and enjoy each other's companionship. Cary, Dodi's husband, and Derek are good friends and so are the children Karin 5½ years and Kristin 3½ years. We're contemplating a week's vacation in Ocean City if vacation dates can coincide.

The Horn & Hardart's of Frankford has been "rejuvenated." Mother and Ken received a special invitation along with 145 others to the grand reopening of the restaurant and store. Mother was quite impressed as there were carpeted floors, new tables, attractive lighting, etc. This is part of the operation uplift of Frankford Avenue.

I've been confined to the home for 2½ weeks in an effort to rid myself of the acute sinusitis. During this time I have shortened 11 skirts (all of which you would probably recognize). Now that I have gotten in style again I'm sure the hemlines will make another drastic change. Heather thought it was funny because I had to take out some zippers due to gaining some weight.

Friday Heather and Buster (Tim) and I made some birthday party invitations for Heather's first birthday party on March 5th. She is so excited about this party. It took us 4 hours to make 5 invitations - all different. Enclosed is one she made all by herself. The only thing I did was the house. I was rather pleased with her creativity. It seems almost impossible that she'll be 4 years old. Tim's big birthday treat was a trip to the 5 & 10 cents store where he got a turtle, a soda, and 2 miniature matchbox cars. He was 2 years old on January 23rd. He also got a clown chenille bedspread (white with a clown on it). He thinks it's great!!

As you can see the kids love to fingerpaint. The secret is to get the painting away from them before all the different colors become one. Tim's always turns out better than Heather's because he loses interest before she does!

Enclosed also is an article from last Sunday's Bulletin. We thought you might be interested - we were, because so much of the news reporting is slanted towards the American Conscience that it gets to the point where we read only the weekly news from the National Observer as it seems to have the most objective and unbiased reporting we have found.

Yesterday was the first day I ventured outside in a long time. We made a trip to Frankford Avenue and Woolworths. The only thing Tim is really interested in is balls so he got his 2900th ball!!!! You should see Buster's face light up when he sees a ball - he just loves to play with them, and heaven help anyone who touches one of his balls!

I wear a skier's face mask, red head hat, a scarf wrapped around my head (boy! Do I look sexy!! Ha!). People's thoughts are written all over their faces - thoughts which say "Is this a stick-up" to "Poor girl, such a badly scarred face." They can't stop staring. I wind up laughing at the situation. Spring can't come too soon this year. Will write some more news later.

Take care- Judy

Odense, Denmark
February 19, 1968

Hi love

Only 19 days till I leave. Time does go, but not as fast as before. I'm very upset about the war news. Seems there are constant attacks on places that before were "safe." I do hope you are not in the midst of it, but love I'm praying for you and you are constantly thought of - if that helps. I'm drained of things to say or tell you. We are doing the same old things. That seems so banal next to all your trials.

Saturday night a female guest had a purse I had long been hunting for - so she let me buy it. It's orange, like my old black one, and I wanted it for the trip.

Now losing weight is slower. When I hear bad news I eat. So I haven't lost any new pounds, haven't gained either.

I'm helping my mother every morning. Our help is in the hospital, but this is the slow season so we really don't have too much work.

I have gotten some very sweet letters from your mother. The tone is quite different from what it used to be, and she sounds like she is doing fine. I sure hope so. I also think she likes me now, at least her letters are very confiding, so I'm glad.

Bill I'll close, you know I love you. This, if anything, has strengthened my love for you, and I have not dreamed of next month. When I do I fall to pieces. But I'll just wait.

Many thousands of kisses, huge hugs -

Love always- Elin

Da Nang, Vietnam
February 20, 1968

Dear Elin,

I'm on the last leg of an exasperating trip back from Saigon to Chu Lai that began 4 days ago! I feel like a "pioneer" crossing the prairies to reach the West! On Saturday I got a helicopter ride from Long Binh to Tan Son Nhut Air Base in Saigon. We flew right over the city & could see smoking ruins in some sections. Saigon is a sprawling sight from the air. That was in the afternoon. I got to Tan Son Nhut & found that there were no planes going to Chu Lai, or Da Nang that day, so I stayed at the Tan Son Nhut Replacement Center. About 3 a.m. there was that familiar "swish - boom" nearby & we - I was in a barracks with double bunk beds, holding about 50 men - scrambled to the floor & put our mattresses on top of us. The attack continued for about ½ hour, all around. When it stopped we looked out & saw huge fires over on the runways and a few blocks from where we were staying. They got the chapel, which was completely destroyed., four or five planes & many other buildings throughout the area. I don't know how many people were injured. After that unnerving night I went back to the terminal, which is a dank, smelly, crowded hole with no facilities & got booked on a flight to Da Nang that afternoon. After waiting all day they told us at 7 p.m. that the flight was canceled. So that night I stayed in the Air Force Transient Billets right on the base. At 1:30 a.m. - "swish - boom" - they did it again. This time a rocket hit one of the terminals where over 100 GI's were waiting for planes. 30 were injured - most of them were waiting to go to the States after a year in Vietnam.

February 21 *Chu Lai - 7:00 p.m.*

- continuing - After that night I decided I would go anywhere on the first available plane. Since they did not replace the cancelled flight, everything to Da Nang was booked up, so a Marine lieutenant I met who was also trying to get to Da Nang & I caught a plane to Cam Rahn Bay. We stayed there last night in a peaceful atmosphere & got to Da Nang this morning. We are expecting more trouble all this week.

Well - I had a pile of letters waiting for me & about 5 from you, one from Mother, Joan, Mike, Uncle Loren & Aunt Kay. So I spent about an hour reading them.

GREAT about your reservation for 9 March (copy of orders enclosed for 11 through 15 March). I will leave here on the 10th to Da Nang and leave from there. I am really excited about it & know you are too. Let me know the name of the hotel as soon as possible so I'll know where to go. I don't know when the plane gets to Bangkok. I think it best for me to meet you at the hotel. Don't panic if I don't show up on the 11th. The planes have been held up a day, but not too often. I'm sure it will all work out.

Joan wrote that she has a job with Irish International Airlines in New York City. Sounds great for Joan & I'm happy for her.

Even though my recent journey was frustrating, it served to show a panoramic of the war - or some results of it - that I hadn't seen before. The hundreds of faces in the terminals waiting for flights. Vietnamese soldiers with their families & all worldly possessions being shifted to other locations; the press correspondents going to the action spots and covering from them on BBC, CBS, ABC, NBC and the papers. Then the GI's, troopers right out of the field - muddy, fatigued, unshaven, sleeping on benches, the floor, anyplace. And the brand new replacements just arriving from the States - clean new fatigues - suitcases - wide eyed, perhaps not realizing, or maybe fully realizing that in a few or months they will be veterans like their comrades, dirty and tired curled up in a corner in the terminal catching some needed sleep.

Ned Shivar is still in the hospital. I got a letter from him today & he said he'll be back in 10 or 15 days.

Much love honey… love you dearly. Say hello to Mor & Far- Bill

P.S. A lot of the guys here won't write and tell their wives anything about these rocket attacks since it's upsetting. But you should know what's going on & I'll share all the "news" with you!

Odense, Denmark
February 20, 1968

Darling

Got your letter - 10 Feb - the day before you were to leave. Now I wonder where you are, maybe stuck in Saigon with all the mess there. I hope not. I'm coming - coming on the 9th of March I leave. I must have written 10 times about Bangkok. Tomorrow I get my second shot. Seriously I don't like them. Your date of March 12 is perfect.

I bought a new swimsuit and a purse, otherwise I'll bring old things. Do you want me to get anything for you? Too late even to tell me I guess as letters and answers take 20 days, and I only have 18 days left here. I wrote and told Jack that I'll be at the Hotel Asia. He was extended one month so maybe we'll see him.

I'm glad you have a good attitude to the attacks. One could not live for weeks in constant fear & know nothing will happen to you anyway. The war news is depressing. Looks like more war and bigger and more force, and to think you are in the thick of it. I miss you and knowing I'll see you soon has made the month much more bearable. I only wish you knew too that I am coming. Then we can really talk and talk and talk. And oh I dare not think or I can't wait.

Love
Elin

Chu Lai, Vietnam
February 22, 1968

Dear Elin,

This won't be a long letter - late - not much to tell today. Back in the fray of personnel work up to my neck, and other than work only thinking of Bangkok in 16 more days!

Received three letters from you today & all the Christmas cards, etc. The venture Tom writes about should be explored & I know you will. We'll discuss it in Bangkok.

It was good to get all of the cards and letters you sent to me since Christmas from all over the world. I agree that it's fantastic - these marvelous relationships we have, some of them covering a number of years. There will be many more. Maybe we'll see Jack in Bangkok. At least you should if he leaves exactly a month later. I wonder if it is an individual extension or an Air Force overall policy. I haven't read anything about it.

I talked to some friends who have been to Bangkok and they said that The Asia is a nice hotel.

The R&R flight is supposed to leave Da Nang at 0930 & arrive in Bangkok at 1130, but is often delayed two or three hours.

Well good night Honey. Say hello to Mor and Far.

Much love - Bill

Chu Lai, Vietnam
February 25, 1968

Hi Honey,

Don't know how many more letters I can write that will reach you before you leave. Enclosed is a letter I got today from Jack. I wrote to him and said as far as I knew he could contact you at "Hotel Asia" - that will be exciting if we can get to see him in Bangkok.

Only 15 days now.

Activity around Chu Lai has been quiet. Although Tan Son Nhut is still getting rocketed. Also Da Nang got hit again last night. It's drippy, rainy and a bit chilly - has been all week. Work is one flap after another. Never get caught up.

Got a letter from you today. I enjoy getting the cards from friends that you send. Take care love - see you soon.

Love
Bill

Odense, Denmark
February 25, 1968

Dear Bill

By now I surely hope to get a final letter from you that you have heard from me that I'm coming. So long between questions and answers. No one's fault but frustrating anyway. Life goes on here. I'm still very busy, our help is ill so I'm also the maid. We will have to get new help as Mrs. Larsen can't work for the next 3 months.

As soon as your letter comes I'll pay the rest of the ticket. I only have one more shot to get. I'm very pessimistic now that the war is being intensified. I had a vague hope it might end soon, but now it doesn't look like it from our end. I'm also upset that Da Nang is getting so much VC attention.

Mor says to say "hello to our dear Bill." Once again I'm coming the 10th of March to the 25th. I'll be at the Asia Hotel, and please send any messages there so I'm a bit informed as to your arrival, etc. I can't wait but must. I've even started to have sweet dreams about it. It's only two weeks and I'll see my Honey.

Much love
Elin

Chu Lai, Vietnam
February 25, 1968

Dear Jack,

Glad to get your letter. Too bad that your departure was extended, but at the same time happy that we may get to see you.

Elin arrives in Bangkok on 10 March. My R&R is from the 11th to the 15th, so I'll be arriving some time on the 11th. Elin will be there until the 23rd of March. She is coming with a tour and supposed to be staying at the Hotel Asia (?) Depending on what it's like we may stay there or go someplace else. Anyway, unless I let you know differently that's where we can be reached.

I received letters from Joan and Mike recently. Joan's job sounds great. Should be exciting for her. Mike, Kathy and the baby are fine.

Hope we can get to see you in Bangkok. At least you'll probably get to see Elin.

Bill

Odense, Denmark
February 26, 1968

Dear Bill

Monday and no letter. My ticket is all ready to be picked up and I need only pay $300 more and it will be all paid. So as soon as I get the next letter from you I'll pay the rest, and then in two weeks I should see my love.

I'm drained for things to say. It seems useless so close to seeing you to write long letters. I hope you have it quiet from the VC. We hear that they are getting more arms from the Soviets, not pleasant news, that is. That war just has to end soon.

I think of you constantly and love you deeply.
Elin

Philadelphia, Pennsylvania
February 26, 1968

Dear Bill,

I meant to sit right down and answer your most welcome letter when it came last week but somehow I became involved with lesson plans, correcting papers, etc. and delayed doing it. Sometimes I think I'll keep a diary or log and write what I do each hour of the day but I never have the time.

One sad happening that drove everything out of my mind happened two weeks ago. Mr. Hauber, my principal had four fine sons. They are all grown and last August, Bill the third and the best looking, married. He joined the National Guard. While at the camp two weeks ago he and some fellows engaged in horseplay with a small truck. He was thrown from the running board and fractured his skull. He died in a few hours. How strange it is that he went into the Guard to avoid Vietnam but how much better if he had given his life in a more heroic way. As you told me last September, more young fellows die on the highways. But is that true now? Our news media is far from pleasant.

I watched a broadcast from Vietnam yesterday where CBS interviewed the president. Things became a little clearer when I noted the philosophy of the Asian in contrast to our way of thinking. They see things in a different way. Right?

Did you go to Saigon? I wondered.

So you, Elin, and Jack will rendezvous in Bangkok! How exciting! Jack wrote that he can't believe he will actually meet you there. I will pray that it all works out the way you want it.

Charlie is the same. He complains one day and feels well the next. The doctors tell me to keep him there as long as I must or have day and night care at home. I probably will have to mortgage this house soon as I don't want to sell it yet. Perhaps Jack and Joan will want to live here for a while before they settle down. In addition, I teach nearby and it is convenient to work and to the convalescent home.

Did you know Joan started work today on Fifth Avenue, New York? She is employed by the Irish Airlines starting as a secretary and hopefully working up to a better position. She will call me on Wednesday night with more details. She is going to send me some money each month when she gets started but I know how expensive it is to live there. I had hoped she would have lived here for a year but she was most unhappy and bored the last year at home. I knew this and I can't blame her for trying her wings. Don't you agree?

I haven't seen your nephew for several weeks as I have had a strep infection in my throat. It is highly contagious and many students and teachers have been sick. I missed two weeks of school. Maybe it isn't a mess to be very sick and be alone in a house with no one to make a cup of tea or a hot toddy! But I am better now and back at work again.

Aunt Gladys wrote a long letter to me recently. She said Jane is married to a doctor who is finishing his internship and going into the service. She also said Dee had been in the Peace Corps but was disenchanted with the Figi Island assignment. He quit, came home, and is teaching mentally disturbed children in New York. She thinks he will be drafted.

Mrs. Webster wrote again about Bill. He is in the Khe Sanh area and you know what that is like now. She is very upset as all the parents who have young Marine sons there.

Nothing else interesting to tell you except that I saw a crocus on the lawn today! Also a cardinal welcomed me as I stepped outside this morning! Perhaps the long cold winter is on the wane and better days are coming. I hope they are for you and all the Army.

My love always,
Mother

Ridgefield, Connecticut
February 26, 1968

Dear Bill,

I expect you must be looking forward now to your R&R. We just had a letter from Elin today, saying she has her vaccines and everything ready for her trip. I'm very excited that you are going to meet like this now, so unexpected. Any chance of seeing Jack there? Talked to your mother, she said Joan may be working in New York.

The car is running fine. Tom's Porsche keeps breaking down. Twice I had to pick him up one hour from here, so I think he has had enough of sports cars for a while.

I wondered if maybe your letters to Elin would go faster through the U.S. if you put special delivery stamps on. Try it, some are enclosed. I'm waiting to hear news from Elin after your trip.

Love from
Kirsten and Tom

Hamburg, Germany
March 1, 1968

Dear Elin,

Many thanks for your letter of 18th. It is nice to hear from you again. We hoped to see you already in January or so before going to Bangkok. We are happy that you are all well and that you could meet Bill in Bangkok. By the way, in the meantime I saw Bangkok too, on my last year's visit to a dozen of countries when traveling to Singapore. Bangkok I enjoyed in November. It is a nice place. I too had a stay of 5 days, but my business did not leave me too much time for sightseeing. But the trip to the floating market I managed too.

Gaby and I hope to see you again in Hamburg soon. It would be good to contact us beforehand, so please note our phone number.

I think we shall have much to talk about when meeting you again. You are heartily welcome.

Kind regards
Karl Zushlog

Elin's note –
I don't know if I told you, but when I called them, Gaby sounded just like me in her dissatisfaction with life in the suburbs. There is little differences between the outskirts of any big city anyplace. It's pretty monotonous for the women. I told her this year I kind of envied the tranquil life of house and garden in a suburb, but that wouldn't last either!

New York, New York
March 7, 1968

Dear Elin,

I received your letter last week - my first letter in New York City. Do you believe this is the first chance to sit down and relax since I've been here? Almost 2 weeks! We have all been on the go. Finding an apartment was our most difficult problem. We finally found one outside of Manhattan for $300 a month. Five of us have to live together, since it is the only way we can handle the rent. The place is sparsely furnished, but there is a lot we can do with it once we get some money.

I simply love my job so far. Everyone at Irish is wonderful - they are all so helpful. I would say about 75% of the employees were born in Ireland and have delightful Irish brogues. Right now I am working as a reservationist, but in a few weeks we will be moving into a brand new building right up the street. Then I will get the secretarial position which they hired me for.

By now I guess you are back from Bangkok. I hope you had a pleasant trip. I imagined how wonderful it was for you to have seen Bill once more. Does he look well? I hope so. Did Jack come down to meet you both in Bangkok? He mentioned something about it in a letter to Mother.

As regard to coming to Denmark this summer - I'd love to come of course. But I don't have any airline passes as of yet. I won't get them until at least a year from now. Irish does fly into Copenhagen, so I'll definitely have to get there.

Well, Elin, I must close now as I am quite tired and morning comes too fast. Please write when you can, and take care. Give my best regards to your parents.

Love
Joan

Odense, Denmark
March 9, 1968

Dear Mother

I leave in 10 minutes. It's 8 o'clock in the morning. At 3 p.m. I fly from Copenhagen and at 9 o' clock Sunday morning I should be in Bangkok. Bill starts out at 7:30 tomorrow from Chu Lai to Da Nang. He said he would leave Da Nang at 0930 on the R&R flight on Monday the 11th and arrive in Bangkok at 1130.

I'm traveling in the blouse you gave me for Christmas. I have an orange purse, shoes and everything matches beautifully.

Jack wrote that he too plans to meet us in Bangkok.

I hope you are over your throat illness. I too have been very ill from all the shots I had to get, but I am fine now. With the war the mess it is, it's been very hard to take lately, but this reunion should cheer us all. I think of you daily and hope you are not too lonely. My parents send their regards.

Love
Elin

From Odense to Bangkok

Elin's long anticipated journey to Bangkok was not without incident. She later recalled:

The day to travel to meet my sweet husband arrived. I took a taxi alone to the train station (in my many trips to and from Odense, my father only took me once, much later in my life). The train trip to Copenhagen took over four hours. In 1968 there was no bridge, and one had to cross the great channel from Fyn to Zealand by ferry. The train stopped at Copenhagen's main station, and then it was by bus to the airport. I was booked on an SAS flight to Bangkok which was scheduled to make a brief stop in Tashkent for refueling.

I was seated in economy class, up front in the row with the door to exit. There was only economy and first class seating. After flying awhile over Russia, the plane was buzzed by Russian jet fighter planes. Our pilot announced that the plane had been ordered to land in Moscow. We circled the airport for over an hour to get rid of fuel in order to make a safe landing. After landing, we were escorted to a dark room and required to relinquish our passports. No reason was given. After about an hour, we were given back our passports and escorted back on the plane. Needless to say, I was a nervous wreck during the whole time, since this was at the height of the Cold War.

We landed again, as scheduled, in Tashkent. We were met by blaring loud speakers announcing, in English, that we were entering "The Worker's Paradise." The announcer's message was interspersed with traditional Russian music. Each of the plane's windows was guarded by hefty Russian women carrying machine guns across their chests. I commented to a fellow passenger that I guess they were there to prevent us from fleeing into their Worker's Paradise!

My seatmate was the wife of the plane's copilot. Her husband told her that the Russians never explained why we were brought down in Moscow. My guess was that they were looking for someone.

The rest of the trip was uneventful. At the Hotel Asia I was given a suite when the travel agency learned that I was meeting my husband who was coming from Vietnam on an R&R. It was super deluxe. I went next door to a flower shop and ordered $50 worth of flowers delivered to the suite. I have never before or afterwards ever seen so many orchids and exotic flowers in one place. $50 bought more flowers in Thailand than I could have ever imagined. My only regret was that we did not take pictures. Bill arrived, and we had the best five days ever!

R&R – Bangkok

Elin & Bill reunite in Bangkok – March 1968

Bill and Elin meet up with Jack

Bangkok Market

Floating Market – Bangkok

Looking for a bargain

Having a swim at Hotel Asia

Ventura, California
March 16, 1968

Dear Elin,

I've been thinking of you so often. This weekend I came out to Dad's to take care of the dog & cat as they have gone out of town and Art is on a trip to France and Spain. Your package came yesterday and of course I am thrilled with your lovely gifts - can't wait to show Art. The plates and bowl arrived in perfect condition. I was holding my breath! Elin, you have exquisite taste. Nearly all of my favorite things are from you. This set is very special to me. Will be perfect for desserts, salads, so many things. Of course I'll save it for special occasions. I just can't thank you and Bill enough for such a lovely, lovely gift. We appreciate this more than I can say. I know Art will love it as much as I do. We thank you and Bill from the bottom of our hearts, Elin.

Do write all the news! Time is going fast - I've been married over 3 months already. We are so happy and have so much fun together. We are renting in Ventura but this summer we will either build or buy our own home. I'm really looking forward to this. I hope you can meet Art - I know you will approve; when I get my wedding pictures back I'll try to send you some.

How is Bill? When you write me next time please send his current address - OK. Hope time is going fast for you both. When are you planning to meet him? Believe me, I can really understand how you feel - but I guess you are like me - when you're with him somehow you forget the time you were apart.

Are you working or what? Guess it was a good idea to return to Denmark & be with your family and friends. I am working 11-4 (just 5 hours) at the Broadway in Ventura while someone is on leave. Probably in August I'll quit again. Did I tell you Art gave me (& himself) a bike for Christmas. Sometimes we go riding 10-15 miles & have a ball. Think I mentioned his parents are from Sweden. I'm learning to cook some Swedish dishes - his Mom has been a big help.

Peg and John are looking for a house too. Peg works part time & John does things for Newsweek. They are very involved with photography - develop all their own prints. The last time Art went away (to Japan) I went to San Francisco. We had a great time.

Next week – I somehow got delayed writing! Since I started this Art has come home. Also I've had a luncheon for 6 and used your beautiful plates. I served Swedish food! Everything turned out & the people really admired your dishes. Thank you, thank you!

I wish you lived closer so you could help me on some art projects. We're thinking of getting started on mosaics or using broken colored glass, etc. I visited a hobby shop and they are great about helping you get started. Will keep you posted.

Elin - do pop me a line soon. I love hearing from you. How is your sister! Hope your parents are well too. Thank you from both of us for the wonderful gift.

Much love to you both – Ann

Photograph by Peggy Burks

Camp Zama, Japan
March 18, 1968

Hi

Enjoyed your note, but don't send me any more work… I'm a patient, didn't ya know??
Enclosed are OERs.
Doing well… hope to be in the US by the time you receive this.
Sounds that Americal AG has beau coup AG types on board. So I guess twas good riddance in my case. Seriously, I've heard that Major Batts' replacement was already in???
So "Bii-lllll you wouldn't even have a <u>critical</u> need for my assistance on a requirement."
Arf!
Hearing is improving - right ear is dragging. It doesn't seem to want to square away. Legs are OK. Left a little sore yet-mixed up nerves/muscles (?), and a little bit of metal seeps out once in a while.
I shall always be available for contact in North Carolina.
So please keep in contact and let me hear from you. You aren't that darn busy.
Sure hope that Bangkok went on schedule and you found the lovely wife in A+ condition.

My best - NS

Regards to all those types

Pound Ridge, New York
March 19, 1968

Dear Bill,

I just want to send along a brief note to let you know we are thinking of you and pray that you are safe & well. Had one letter from Elin & I hope to hear from her again, soon.

I have only heard bad reports from Vietnam and I can imagine what you must be going through a terrible experience. As you know, the war has torn this nation asunder, and the unrest here grows every day. What this has on your morale, I don't know, but I can't believe it helps. Nevertheless, we hope you come through it all safely and that we have a chance to see you in the near future. Have you made a firm decision about an Army career, or is it still under consideration? In any event, I would like to learn about your present assignment and how Army life is treating you. I believe I told Elin, but I shall repeat that we are not exactly overjoyed with "fun city" and we are always considering a new home away from here. For the time being, I'm staying with the work I have, i.e. an associate with a large firm which specializes in admiralty law. I have several cases where our clients are suing the Government for damages to vessels in Vietnam harbors - everyone profits except our soldiers and the Vietnamese people, I wish it would end very soon.

Please look out for Pete White (CPT) - 507 Replacement Company, an old friend of mine & Gerry Lynsley, also a CPT from good old Goppingen.

Best wishes & please write a brief note to let us know how you are.

Tom

Return to Vietnam

Chu Lai, Vietnam
March 20, 1968

Dear Elin,

Back entrenched in Chu Lai after six of the most beautiful days ----------wasn't it fabulous? A little gem in the middle of a volcano. You really looked svelt and beautiful! Nice memories for the next six months. Well right now you should be at Pattaya. I'll be anxious to hear how the second week was & you meeting Jack again.

I'm enjoying the two pipes. Tell Mor thank you (Tusind Tak!) for the one she sent. Also all the other delicatessen items, which I'm saving for a special occasion. My trip back was uneventful. Got back to Da Nang about 5 p.m. I stayed there that night & got to Chu Lai the next day.

Everything is as turbulent as usual here. Everyone jumping through their ass! Weather considerably warmer - will be from now on.

Mrs. Sternelle sent me the clipping about Joan. Got the box of books the day I got back. Will enjoy reading them. Thanks Honey.

Did you do anymore shopping in Bangkok?

I'm on staff duty tonight. Long night. Will be anxious to get your letter when you get back. Give my love to Mor & Far –

Much love-
Bill

How about your Sister [handwritten]

NEWS CLEAN

Joins Airlines

MISS JOAN N. WALKER

Miss Joan N. Walker, daughter of Mr. and Mrs. Charles B. Fulmer, of Harrison street, Frankford, Philadelphia, has been placed with Irish International Airlines, New York City.

Miss Walker, a graduate of Frankford High, has also attended Humboldt Institute, at 2201 Blaisdell avenue, Minneapolis, Minnesota, a business school specializing in travel and traffic careers.

Chu Lai, Vietnam
March 20, 1968

Dear Mother,

Back in Vietnam after six glorious days with Elin in Bangkok. Everything worked out perfectly and it was a delightful respite from here. Elin arrived the day before I did. From Copenhagen (SAS) over the U.S.S.R. (her plane was forced down in Moscow for unexplained reasons!). I flew from Da Nang to Bangkok (1 hour flight). We stayed in a luxurious hotel. Jack came to Bangkok the second day & we spent a fun day seeing the Temples, etc. He'll tell you about it.

Elin is still there, she leaves on the 25th & Jack will meet her on the 24th before he leaves. Bangkok is delightful (we found many similarities to Beruit). - and the Thais are perfectly charming and ingratiating people. We can easily understand Jack being enamored with them.

Well I'm back in the rat race - almost to the half way mark. It's a long year!

What do you think of the Primaries? We are watching with real interest - R.F.K.'s move last week was somewhat of a surprise.

Say hello to Uncle Charlie, also to Kathy and Mike.

Will write again soon -

With love
Bill

Nipa Lodge
Pattaya Beach, Thailand
March 20, 1968

Dearest Darling

Nothing can express the happiness I've felt the week we were together. It took me two days to have my body settle down. I shall always be glad we had that week. Oh honey we do have a beautiful marriage and a very special "thing" that few are blessed enough to have. I'm so happy you are my one and only.

After you left I went back to the jewelry store to pick up the rings. I shed a small tear, and the topaz ring I wear now as if it were my wedding ring. It stands for a reaffirming of our love in Bangkok. I think I'll wear it every day until you return. I then had my hair done next door. The girls in the jewelry store arranged it. One girl had a bracelet made with U.S. dimes. I gave her a quarter and she was grateful. I'm sure she will add it to her bracelet.

Having one's hair done involved getting your ears cleaned out and having a face massage. They did a lovely job all for $1.00. By 4:30 I returned to Hotel Asia. Went swimming and Colonel Phillips, the pilot, joined us and bought a beer. He was going out that night with his reporter chick. I changed and went down for dinner. A 40 person Danish trade delegation was there and I had a nice chat with them. All were for the war and understood the reasons. It was so good to get other views than the one from our crummy paper. I went up at 8:30 to sleep and cry.

Sunday morning at 10 I called Gwyneth and I went over there at 11. She was in her PJs. We went to the Sunday market in the afternoon. Bought many small trinkets and had a ball. Very colorful and kind of like Beirut. I bought a small bone carving for 50 cents, and two bracelets for a dollar. Also bought some old fashioned brass kitchen utensils, all very cheap. Guess what? They sold new irons for coals, like our antique one. Amazing. We went home all loaded down. Got a watermelon, etc.

At night I had invited Gwyneth at Hotel Asia. First we went to the officers' club. Not my idea. We had a drink, and some pilots that knew Gwyneth's husband, Bill, joined us, and they all insisted we go out for dinner. I told Gwyneth I'd rather not. Anyway we spent the evening listening to their bragging big loud mouths. I was bored. Gwyneth is very naive, and doesn't understand too much about men and sex. I was furious to have to be dragged along. We got home at midnight. No incidents but still - she is crazy to run around with all of Bill's buddies.

On Monday we went shopping. Got a neat wood carving, gold for $15.00, just gorgeous. That day and the next we mostly shopped. Had lunch with her friend Sissy at Erwan. Both disagreed with me on everything. I went to buy my father a bottle. Gwyneth had to say she couldn't spare her ration. I got one anyway. That girl is a bit mixed up but she is basically a good egg.

Yesterday we came down to the coast. It's very hot and nothing to do. The coast is beautiful but already from ½ hour I've already gotten enough sun. The Danes here get very sunburned. The ocean breeze does it to you. I think I'll only stay one day. Too much of a bore for someone like me who doesn't like sun worshipping. Well I think I have rattled enough. I have to change rooms. They put me in a suite. This place is not half as nice as the Asia. There one really got smiles and good service. Here they are different to the guests.

Hope you got back all right. Take care,

Your love
Elin

Elin with Gwyneth on Pattaya Beach, Thailand

Asia Hotel
Bangkok, Thailand
March 24, 1968

Dear Bill

As you can surmise from the heading I'm back at the Asia. We really had a beautiful room before. This time I'm in a normal double, normal size room and bathroom. Nice, but not as luxurious as our "Love Nest." Almost cried today. There was a couple in the lobby downstairs. He tan, she pale. They were exchanging letters from friends and obviously catching up on 6 months separation. I'm so glad I came to catch up just a little bit. So much living to do, and it's only fun with you.

I left the beach after two days. I really got bored. One night I talked and talked to Mike Cassidy, Colonel Cassidy's son from Goppingen. The Colonel is now post commander at Fort Hamilton, and Mike is a 2nd lieutenant in the Air Force stationed at Korat. Also talked to two very interesting NBC guys that have spent two years in Vietnam. One has taken several now famous pictures. Like the Newsweek cover of the MP at the Embassy. They are most intelligent and very objective on the war. Gave me tremendous insight into the mind of the Vietnamese.

Jack just called. He and "buddies" will be over in a little while. Wonder how many "buddies?" His port call was changed to Thursday, and he doesn't get per diem so it's out of his own pocket for 4 days. Poor guy. Here he had so looked forward to a real blast.

I have $80.00 left of my $300.00. That money sure went fast. I bought a very beautiful pin for my mother today for $20.00. Got my dad the Cognac, and bought many small gift type things. Gwyneth is mailing a box for me.

I hope you are all fine. I read about the Americal Division daily. Seems like they are really involved in things lately.

Love you and miss you, but at least it is downhill now.

Love,
Elin

Bangkok, Thailand
March 25, 1968

Dear Mother,

I just spent the most beautiful week of my life with Bill – he looks great – suntan and healthy. Jack came down – he too looks great. He is taking me out for dinner next Sunday – just before we both fly home.

Love, Elin

Ridgefield, Connecticut
March 25, 1968

Dear Bill,

We had a postcard from Elin from Thailand so you really did meet and you saw Jack. I'm very excited, did you take any pictures?

I called up your mother and she told me that Joan is working for Irish Airlines in New York, and Jack is coming back to the states. I hope to see him on his way to New Hampshire.

Tom's brother-in-law Ed, finally decided to get out of the Marines after 12 years in.

So they are not going to pass the bill about control of dollars spent by tourists abroad. I didn't really think they would, but people got all excited and talked about as if it was a fact already.

I hope to get some first hand information from Jack about you, and the time the three of you spent together. Half of the year is gone already. I'm glad.

We are waiting for spring to break through, this was our first week without snow on the ground. After all the snow had melted there was a sea of mud outside, and we had to wear boots to get to the car.

It is quite different for both of us to live in a place like this. We are so close to trees and hills and lakes, it is already starting to look quite pretty. The closest lake we can see from our window, so we will only have 2 minutes walk to go swimming this summer.

We are listening to the war reports on Radio Pacific. Did you listen to that when you were in California? There is one in San Francisco.

Two more weeks and we'll have our anniversary, can you imagine.

Tom's mother asks about you every time I see her. There are lots of people who think of you Bill, even if all don't write too often.

Best wishes to you Bill

from Tom and I - Kirsten

Killeen, Texas
March 25, 1968

Dear Elin,

Thank you for your letter I received yesterday. We have had quite a few colds. Right now I have sinus trouble which affected my teeth and ears. My face is so swollen I look ugly. I have to get a penicillin shot every day. My arm is sore already. Jimmy is the only one who hasn't had a cold yet. This morning he got a hold of Gus's razor and cut himself beneath the chin. He's always getting into some trouble.

I hope I will finish this letter today. By now Jimmy is sick, Gus had to take him to the doctor. The reason I haven't finished this letter yet is because we have been working in the hospitals & old age homes. This week is National Beauty Salon week. So we donated our services to the public. We gave permanents, haircuts and shampoos & sets to the older people. You should have seen how happy they were. It really made us feel good. We had our own affiliate election. Here is a picture.

We are renting a two bedroom house, which is real nice and in a nice location. I have three German neighbors.

Well, about my brothers-in-law. One of them got wounded on a mission; he's been back for 3 months. He was here at the hospital. But is doing great. He has to have exercises every day to get his leg in shape. My other brother-in-law is still in Vietnam.

Have you heard from Bill? I hope that he is doing all right.

Well this is all for today. Give our love to your parents.

Love –
Maria, Gus & Jimmy

Chu Lai, Vietnam
March 26, 1968

Dear Elin,

Well you must be home today - providing you didn't get to visit Moscow again! I'll be anxious to hear how the rest of the trip went. It all seems like so long ago - already for me - although it's just a little over a week. The pace has been hectic here.

I've been swimming in the ocean twice this week. The beaches are open now & the water is great. Managed to slip away for an hour's dip while on some other business.

Well in a few more days I'll be at the halfway point - 6 months and then it will be down hill. One of my men took these photos this week - in my office.

This is a dull letter! I'm tired & can't get inventive tonight.

Love you very, very much Honey -

Take care & give my love to Mor and Far -
Bill

Odense, Denmark
March 27, 1968

Dearest Darling

I'm back home safe - a bit tired but so filled with happy memories that I can live on them for months to come.

Jack came Sunday night with a friend, Tom, from Frankford. Jack was so bubbling and so happy. The end was in sight. I was talking with to two Finnish TV people who were about to go shoot a piece for TV about the American GI on leave in Bangkok. They were under the impression that the GI's preferred to have their leaves there (the fun) rather than in the USA. I quickly told them that it was not so, but that there were only a few places they were allowed to go, and the US was too far away to be allowed. They abandoned their plans to shoot the TV report. I was happy about it as it easily could have been propaganda against the US, based on the wrong assumptions. Jack talked and talked to the Finnish people. He didn't understand that I had suggested to them that they go out with Jack and Tom later to interview them, and in his burst of talk he blew the chance. So we had a nice dinner, Kobe steaks at the Asia, solo dining. Then we went to the President Hotel for a drink in the neatest bar in Bangkok right across from where we had ice cream sodas. I was sad we had not discovered the place while you were there.

I bought a pin for my mother and a small princess ring for your mother. I came home with $80. Had to pay $20 for my extra days at the beach.

I called your mother this morning and talked. She was very, very happy to hear that you were fine. I had to tell her that Jack will be a day later than planned. She said Mike and Kathy are coming down, and that the baby is cute. Your mother sounds like she's in very good spirits which is nice. Her letters are cheerful too.

My parents send their love. We have talked and talked. I unpacked all my goodies. Now I only wish I had used up all my money. Away from there, they are lovely. I have many, many letters to write today. So much to tell everyone.

Soon I'll start counting weeks. Should only be around 26. I feel closer to you than I ever have.

Love
Elin

Odense, Denmark
March 28, 1968

Dear Joan

I guess being all surrounded by Irish you should really like Kirsten's husband Tom. He is the only Irish I know – but if he is any sample they are great. Mother wrote you are now a secretary and will work soon in plush offices right by Rockefeller Center. If I didn't have a rich happy life myself I could easily become jealous of such a life as you must live – every girl should be on her own for some time and feel the world without the shield of a house or husband. You will find that this experience will really mature you – and it won't all be roses either. We live in a strange world with many types of people and I always have been sad when some people get their "culture" shock late in life. Then it can upset the cart – when one is going it all helps to make for a fuller person and you will know what other people are all about. The best of luck in the whole venture.

About Bangkok – Jack no doubt has told you how we all met (he is great) and the whole thing was like a dream. Bill looked better than ever – suntan – slim – but not thin – calm and so happy to see me. I was likewise happy to be with him – and it all seems like a dream now.

The country was fascinating – but since Jack no doubt will show pictures and explain I shall leave the travelogue part to him.

What are the girls like that you room with? What is the apartment like? How much fun you'll have getting it fixed up.

I'm mailing you a Thai rice rubbing for the wall - might take a while to get there.

The weather is lovely here now.

Just got a box from Kirsten with goodies, like cake mixes and nuts – a bottle of Calif. wine – my favorite and some books – in all her letters she sounds very happy.

Thank you for writing to Bill and me – we really appreciate it during these hard months.

Love
Elin

Odense, Denmark
March 28, 1968

Dear Bill

As you can see by the two letters I sent from Joan waiting for me when I came home, she really is writing now. I'm really happy about it and wrote and thanked her. Also told her I was so glad she had this fabulous job, and if I didn't have such a rich life I could get jealous of hers. It's every girl's dream to do what she is doing, and I'm glad she has a period where she is not shielded by a home or a husband - some people get their "culture shock" too late in life and then it might upset the cart. When one is young it only matures you.

I am so busy writing letters to everyone. Wrote a long one to your mother, and to Kirsten. She is so good about writing and they just sent a box to us with San Martin Wine, cake mixes, books - one called "More in Anger" by an American woman. It's from Tom and he had told me before it was like I had written it. I'll read it and see. Also got several magazines and the embroidery book your mother had given me.

Haven't heard from you yet. Do hope you made it back with no trouble or delays. When you get this it will have been two weeks since I waved good bye.

The sun is shining so nice today and we are all smiling.

Love
Elin

Odense, Denmark
March 28, 1968

Dear Mother and Uncle Charlie

I'm sitting here with your letter, and how right you are that this is a strange century - and I certainly never dreamed that I should find myself - even in my wildest dreams - that I would find myself in California - in Europe - in Thailand, all in the span of one year.

Nothing can describe the happiness of being with Bill again, the whole trip went perfect and I'm sure was meant to be. Being the thrifty housewife I really had qualms about spending the money, but we both agreed that it was worth that and more. Bill and I really have an unusual marriage - maybe everyone feels that - but ours is special. This year has brought us much closer than ever, and we thought it was great before.

Your four children certainly are all outstanding and I'm so proud to be related to you all. Jack is such an outstanding young man, Mike such a fine minister, and Joan an up and coming "private" New York secretary, and of course Bill is Bill (Jack says he's a real leader - I agree).

I was so glad to talk to you, and happy the call didn't wake you up. I had tried 5 times to call but with the 6 hours time difference I would be asleep when you were home, and vice versa.

Spring is arriving and summer and fall can't be far away. In October we should be back in the States. If Bill can't go home via Europe I'll return in September. Maybe it all depends on Bill's new duty station. He has asked for the East Coast, but no one knows what the Army decides.

Hope you are all fine. My parents send their regards.

The embroidery is a runner for a table on top of a white tablecloth. If you want I'll send the blue yarn but you have the same at Wanamaker's and I felt it was silly to waste the postage on yarn. I figure I owe you $15 for postage by now. Do you want it in the form of hand work or in cash.

Much love,
Elin

Thank you for forwarding my mail

Odense, Denmark
April 1, 1968

Dear Bill

Just woke up to the news that Johnson is going to order a stop to the bombing. I hope and pray that Hanoi will understand reason, but I have not got optimistic until we see what they will do. The next couple of weeks should be very interesting. I had planned to have a letter from you this morning, but no luck. I guess you have been very busy after having been gone for 6 days.

I keep busy as the "maid" and writing letters. Also going to exercise every day again, having my hair done, and my mother and I are going to a tea-bazaar tonight. Tomorrow night I have the final evening for lampshades. We will have a "smorebrod" with beer and snaps, and everyone is dying to know about my trip.

I ordered the Indian rug, it's $200 and very beautiful. The material for the sofa is $20 a yard so I'll try to see in Germany if I can get it cheaper. I saw a very neat white old restored Danish phone. It's $85, but I might get it for your birthday (up to my gift giving tricks again).

Yesterday I sat home while Mor and Far went out. I told them they only have me 4 more months. One I'll spend in Germany and unless you come home via Europe, I'm going back to the U.S. a month early to look at the new post where it will be. Life is really exciting when one thinks about it.

I guess I better get myself to a dentist. How I dread the thought. Ugh. My tan is fading but yesterday I stayed in the sun for 2 hours. I hate to lose it. I feel so healthy looking tan. You looked just great. I really can't get over how great you looked.

Hope you are not too busy and that you can find time for a few relaxing moments.

Much love
Elin

Chu Lai, Vietnam
April 2, 1968

Dear Elin,

Well I received your letter from Bangkok (Asia Hotel) yesterday (takes as long from Bangkok as Denmark). Am anxious to get a letter from Denmark telling me about the trip back, etc.

A little excitement here - found out last night that I'm getting a new job - Deputy G1 of the Division. I'm glad to be leaving the Personnel Services Division in one respect (6 months under these conditions on top of 198th Brigade experience is enough) - on the other hand I don't like to leave all of my men. Anyway it should be a good job & I'm looking forward to the change. Will let you know more after I move in on the 5th.

What did you think of Johnson's announcement? We've been doing all kinds of speculating but haven't gotten any newspapers yet, so only know what we heard in his speech on the radio. Not getting the news for a week or so after it happens is very frustrating.

I've gone swimming almost every noon this past week & getting black. The water is great & it's real refreshing to get out & limber up. Right now it's very windy - blowing sand and dirt over everything.

I'm sending this letter from Joan & Mother.

Miss you very much (188 days left). We (the "old crowd" from the 198th AG and Finance sections) are having a "going over the hump" party Saturday night. Six months left in Vietnam.

Give my love to Mor and Far -

Much love Elsking –
Bill

Spokane, Washington
April 2, 1968

Dear Bill,

You are on my mind & in my prayers always. I do want you to be safe & return safely at the end of your year. Evelyn Morgan has read me letters from Gwyneth & she and Elin are having a wonderful time together. How nice for them. I think Gwyneth is lovely & most mature. Did you like Thailand & did you see a lot there?

We were all shocked by President Johnson's announcement on Sunday P.M. We can only hope that this will make some changes in Vietnam & America too but we are living through a "Dark Age" in our country & I fear for our outcome.

I've kept busy studying tonight classes, now working outdoors again & am selling Avon products a few house calls sometime each evening. It makes good income easily but I'm sure I can't do it when I have to start watering the lawn and garden. Increased cost of living has me frightened.

Had the Haydn Morgans here to a Chinese dinner Sunday night with 3 other couples. They are a grand & down to earth couple. Holy week & Easter are nearly here. No need to say have a nice Easter & a meaningful one, when you are in such an environment, but at any rate I'll be thinking of you, dear Bill.

Remember John & O'Rosia McHugo - you went to dinner at their home the night you got your orders to Europe with us. Mr. McHugo's 32 year old son, Don, an Air Force Major was killed last week in Vietnam. He was a very fine person & had a Masters degree, a wife and 10 year old daughter who were in Manila.

Bye now & God keep you Safe!

Much love,
Hazel

Norwalk, Connecticut
April 4, 1968

Dear Bill

I was so glad to receive your letter. I don't write many letters anymore. Your picture looks fine. You put on a little weight didn't you. I think Jack looked fine when we saw him at your Mother's. He said he will stop up and see us. It is nice here now. The water from Long Island Sound passes right by our back yard when the tide comes in. The ducks and swans come around to be fed. Helen feeds all the birds.

I went to the dentist to get my false teeth repaired & have 7 teeth to be put on and they said they will line the upper plate for $150.00 dollars. Isn't that something. Everything is expensive here. I am glad you are getting out in 4 months, that will be a long time. I am glad Joan has such a good position. She looks fine. Your Mother hasn't been able to visit us yet. Aunt Helen painted every room in this house. Mine is blue.

The Dr. said I was good for my age. Jeff bought a second hand boat. He is remodeling it.

I just spent one week with Aunt Ruth, and one week with Edward and Aunt Rosabelle. Your Mother said Mike's baby is wonderful. I haven't been able to see him.

Love
from Nana Walker

Odense, Denmark
April 5, 1968

Dear Bill

When it is night here it is day in the US. Every morning I tune into the news, and this week I have not been able to believe what I hear, it's a shock treatment at 7 o'clock. First Johnson's speech, then Hanoi's answer, then more bombing, then Honolulu - then the death of Martin Luther King. By now I'm numb to more shock from news. Things happen so fast one wonders what the outcome of it all will be. These times sure are troubled.

I was so happy to receive your letter yesterday. No wonder it takes forever if you wait 4 days to mail it. This is not to criticize but could you write me every other day, just for a while. I really get encouraged by letters, even short ones. I know you can't write long dissertations but just Hello is enough to make the make the day ten times better.

I got the pictures back, all great except not enough of my handsome honey. I wonder why we took so few, do you have a roll? I'm getting a couple made into pictures to send to your mother. She promised to send a bill to me when we talked. Haven't heard from anyone in the family about the homecoming, or gotten the bill. Every day I help Mor. We are usually through it by 12 o'clock and them I'm off for my exercises. I really get stiff again so this week is a drag. I have to force myself.

On Tuesday I went to the party for the finish of the course in lampshade sewing. I had too much beer and snaps, so the next day I was so tired. Just can't take drinking anymore.

Next week is Easter. We will have the house full, but have no plans to do anything.

I miss my love a lot, but am so looking forward to a beautiful reunion and years of bliss.

Love
Elin

Philadelphia, Pennsylvania
April 8, 1968

Dear Bill,

Jack is home as you know and "how sweet it is!" Sweet, too, was your radio conversation last week and (my first). Uncle Charlie feels better, my mother looks well, and perhaps this year will be better.

Jack looks fine to all of us - lively and happy. He brought unusually tasteful gifts to the family and close friends revealing innate feelings for the best!

Yesterday Nana Williams sold him her Ford (1955-56 vintage - 36,000 miles). Jack is pleased and can afford the $300 it cost. Of course the insurance is nearly the same amount for a year but he says he can swing it.

How surprised we were to hear you via radio! I was nearly asleep and of course could not readily make intelligent statements! But for many days I remembered how you sounded, "over."

Evidently you and Elin had a marvelous reunion in Bangkok. How fantastic! My friends think my children are having experiences that few families of our social standing achieve. "When Bill was in Moscow," or "Remember Elin being put off the train at the French border?" So goes our conversation.

Uncle Charlie complains about being eighty (he isn't until Dec 9th) and headaches, etc. but he looks quite well in the face - better than when you saw him. Jack took him for several rides.

Your new nephew is a doll and will be able to sit up by the time you get home, maybe even creep. He turned over last week alone. Mike is a thoughtful parent and helps Kathleen in many ways. I like the way he holds Jonathan and plays with him. To tell the truth, Joan and I think he is a more loving person since the advent of the baby! He was sequestered with theological people for many years. He is coming back into the world. His sermons are good! Pithy and yet tender. I did not think the area he preaches in was the right place to begin but he is getting practice. The people are what we used to call stiff necked!

Martin Luther King's assassination has made everyone pause since last Friday and re-estimate his feelings toward black people. The T.V. was dedicated to his burial from 9:30 A.M. today until 5:00 P.M. Everything was sublimated to it. Kennedy, Rockefeller, Nixon, Lindsay (I like him), Romney, Humphries, Javitts, and others attended. Harry Bellefonte stayed with Mrs. King and family all day and was visibly shaken during services. All great Negro leaders were there. It was something to see. 150,000 people marching!

This news put the great Johnson news and Hanoi's acceptance for a truce talk in the shadows but the meeting will take place I am sure and perhaps the war will end soon. I hope!

Are you taking care? I baked you a nut cake which I will mail tomorrow. Because of our trip to Nana Williams ' home I didn't get it off sooner.

Have a prayer for peace with us Easter morn. We all prayed together in church last Sunday. Joan came home. She is happy too.

Much love,
Mother

Chu Lai, Vietnam
April 8,1968

Dear Elin,

Received two letters from you today - you said you hadn't gotten any letters from me since you returned. There is often a big delay in mail getting out of Da Nang. Hopefully you've gotten them by now (today).

I haven't written for about 6-7 days. Involved in moving to my new job. I've been here now 3 days & I think I'll really enjoy it. Involved in PX operations, clubs, funds, etc. and out of the nit-picking stuff I've been living with for 10 months. The G1, LTC Quarles, is outstanding & a pleasure to work for. It's a change of pace and will help the last 6 months go faster.

Well, the developments over the past week or so have been shocking. We all pray to God that something will come of the possible negotiations. I'm still not sure of LBJ's motives in this move regarding the nomination. Still skeptic in view of prior politicking - but on the surface it looks like a great gesture. Then, Dr. King's assassination & the resultant rioting!! America is a sea of unrest & the surface is very thin and any scratch unleashes the turmoil & unrest within. Again, our news is so delayed that I'm not really up on what's happening right now.

I enjoyed Ann's letter that you sent, she sounds very happy. When are you going to Germany? That should be exciting to visit those familiar places & see some old friends. It's hard to tell whether I'll be able to come thru Europe or not. The Army is trying to get exceptions to LBJ's travel bans & things might well change in 6 months time. I hope so.

It's starting to get hot - the sun is a huge bright red ball at night - quite spectacular. We (at my hooch) barbequed chicken tonight. Last night I marinated it in Vermouth & Pernod - interesting taste however without any spices, etc. can't really do it right.

Well love - time will fly now - love you immensely.
Bill

Note new address

Barbeque in back of hooch

Odense, Denmark
April 9, 1968

Dear Bill

After I wrote you yesterday Mor and I went for a long city walk and I found and bought (prodded on by Mor) a lovely dress and coat. It's a white dress and a matching tweed looking coat. Very timeless and high style. It was about $70. I also sent $50 off for the insurance. Haven't gotten the bill yet. Your mother either forgot or sent it slow boat. But I figured out that we usually pay $25 for four months so I hope this will do, and that I'll get a statement from them.

My mother is so excited by our bedroom rug that she wants one too so now we are working on Far. We would put it in the dining room, but he thinks it's foolish. My bet is that we get one. Ours is really lovely.

This half year just has to fly because I'm getting impatient . As soon as you have an assignment and as soon as you know how you can come home, over Europe or not, I'll start packing. Would you believe I arrived with two suitcases, and it's a truck load by now. How do other people contain themselves from shopping. I've often wondered.

I haven't heard about Jack's coming home yet. But I guess I will in a month or so. Also am anxious to hear some comments on the late developments from someone in the States.

This week I'll start writing to Germany to plan my trip. It should be fun, but it will be sad too without you. It seems like oceans of time since we were there, and yet it's only been 2½ years. I wonder how it will seem going back.

We will be very busy over Easter. The house is full, and I'm the maid so you know we will be busy.

Love you
Elin

Chu Lai, Vietnam
April 10, 1968

Dear Elin,

Well - another day on the new job & so far I like it. Flew by chopper today to Duc Pho for the morning & had lunch there in the 11th Brigade's CO's mess.

A few things I forgot to tell you in my last letter - I cashed one check for $10.00 at the end of last month - ran out of money. Also, I talked to Mother and Jack last week. The MARS Station, which is right behind our hooch, had an open patch to the States during one noon hour. One of the operators ran out & said "Anyone want to talk to the States" - I was taking a sun bath & ran in my bathing suit and got right through. Jack had just gotten there the day before. Mother sounded good and said she felt wonderful.

Got a nice letter from Kirsten today. Do you realize that they'll celebrate their first anniversary this month!

The time, days are going fast again. I've got plenty to do, but it's a nice atmosphere.

The chicken I wrote about didn't turn out too well! The refrigerator stinks now!

Well Honey, nothing exciting to write about. Hope you are all in good spirits.

Love you terribly much –
Bill

Bill sitting with G1 Sergeant Major

Odense, Denmark
April 10, 1968

Darling

Just felt like sending a spring greeting to you who are in the middle of the summer.   But Easter is at our door and spring is lovely. New hope is born in the spring.

Someone once said "Separation is to love - what the wind is to fire - small fires it blows out - big fires it makes bigger."   My love for you has never been greater.

I'm making a small picture embroidery for a lovely oval frame I found, and the rug still gives me joy every day.

We have the house full of guests today and much activity. The sun is shining and life looks promising.

I saw Martin Luther King's funeral yesterday, and cried and cried that the spirit of love cannot enter people's hearts. If only they could realize that only love and trust creates happiness. The world needs Jesus' words as much today as they did 2,000 years ago. His teachings are so simple yet so hard for some to understand.

Love Elin

Chu Lai, Vietnam
April 12, 1968

Dear Elin,

Received a letter today - the one with Maria's letter. I'm enjoying my job - lots of new areas & all interesting. We have a Vietnamese Captain in the office who is liaison officer to the Division. Today I went through the huge PX operation - which is under G1 - over $2 million a month in gross business. Also getting involved in the clubs operation. 66 Army clubs in the Chu Lai installation. We're going to consolidate. So many projects & all interesting. Will make the remaining months zip by.

I don't wait 4 days to mail letters! The problem apparently is at the APO here. I talked to the Postal Officer once before about it when you wrote that the postmarks on my letters were 3-4 days after date written. I don't know what the problem is but anything is possible here.

I bought a new watch today for $6.00, my old one stopped running the other day. As soon as I get a chance I'll put in an order for some things from the PX catalogue. Don't forget to send a picture of the china you want to get for Mor.

I haven't heard from anyone except you for a long time. Get little mail except from my Honey. Of course I rarely write to anyone else. Did get a letter from Kirsten, though, the other day.

Well Honey - that's all for now - back to work. Things are looking favorable in the news for some settlement of the war - let's hope.

Much love –
Bill

Odense, Denmark
April 12, 1968

Dear Bill

I'm still trying to sort my thoughts after yesterdays new developments in the war and Johnson's not running for president. There is so much speculation all over, but what really matters is what Hanoi will do. One can only pray that they have enough intelligence to come to their senses - but who knows what goes on in the minds of the Asiatic. I do think they are different and quite stubborn.

It has been 18 days since I waved good bye and still no letters. I so hope I get one tomorrow. I hope you are all right.

I am sore today from starting the exercises, but at least I had not gained this past month.

They promise snow and frost so it was too early to be happy about spring.

Write soon my love
Elin

Odense, Denmark
April 13, 1968

Dearest Bill

Just received these pictures today, sent two to your family and two to Kirsten. Gave my parents some, so please keep these as they are the last. I kept two just of you. They are very good pictures of my honey. Boy am I glad we met.

Today is sunshine and lovely. We are all booked up for Easter so every morning Mor and I are busy. I'm finishing a flower picture embroidery for a lovely mahogany frame I found. Also today a little man in my favorite antique shop gave me the most beautiful table, white marble top and gilded wood. Just perfect for the bedroom that's going to be. I also bought an old red spice arrangement for the kitchen. By now I just can't wait to become domestic again.

I just hope that with all these race riots, if you get sent to the Pentagon, it might be like going from the frying pan into the fire. It sure doesn't sound too good sitting here, but I guess the press blows it up a bit out of dimension. It's very depressing anyway and I have cried over it a lot lately. Really saps your energy to think that people cannot live in peace with each other.

I hear through Kirsten that you talked to your mother over the radio. How did that come about? When you get this we only have 5 months again, and I don't count the last because I'll be packing, and I don't count the one in Germany because I'll be too involved to be depressed, so I really only have three months again, and they are during the lovely summer months. So really, I guess we'll meet tomorrow. Time will fly. I hope it will fly for you too.

I haven't any more news for today, except the usual.

I miss you and I love you.
Elin

Odense, Denmark
April 13, 1968

Dear All,

I just got these pictures back and thought you would enjoy having them. As you can see Bill looked wonderful and healthy.

I am still anxiously waiting to hear how Jack's homecoming went. I hear from Kirsten that you talked to Bill over the radio - how did that happen? Did he sound all right or was the connection bad?

I'm very depressed by the news that reaches about all the demonstrations & I link all of the troubles to Communism. They are stirring the young up wherever they can. Now the unrest has spread to Europe too. We must all keep our faith in God and law and order, but the world is infected with a tumor, and one has to cut it back wherever it advances. I'm confident that the good citizens of the U.S. and the world will succeed in the end, but one had hoped that we all had learned from the past war that Hitler too used the young. But, I guess the young haven't lived so they haven't learned. The young Negroes surely are being stirred up for no good ends, and it's a sad day when law and order breaks down.

Now at Easter time one can't help but think that the world needs Jesus' words as much now as it ever did. I pray that all mankind will see the light.

We are very busy here - all booked up for Easter, and the weather is lovely, sun, a bit warmer and the first signs of spring are here. It makes me joyous - means summer is not far off, and at the end of summer the reunion with my love.

I'm making a small embroidery for a lovely old oval mahogany frame I found. I have an idea - could you please send the pictures of the farm to me. I have one but it is not clear. I'll return them all. I hate to tell you why, because it may not work out, but if I could only borrow a clear picture - I mean the upstate Williams farm.

I got Joan's picture from the paper through Mrs. Sternelle. She is so nice to write to Bill.

I hope everyone is fine in Philadelphia, and I send all my best thoughts to everyone.

Love- Elin

Chu Lai, Vietnam
April 15, 1968

Dear Mother,

I received your long newsy letter today - with Easter card & was real glad to hear from you. It was fun to talk via radio. Am glad Jack made it home as scheduled.

Did I write to you about my new job? Don't remember - if this a repeat, ignore. I was reassigned as the Americal Division Deputy G1 ten days ago - on the General's staff. A real good assignment & one that I am thoroughly enjoying. My boss Lt. Colonel Quarles is terrific & I'm involved in a lot of areas I haven't been before, such as PX operations (our PX does $2 million a month gross business), safety, chaplain activities, of course personnel. The G1 has overall responsibility for personnel, morale & welfare & all related activities for the Division Commander. I was ready for a change & was delighted to get this job.

We are all full of optimism for a change in light of the impending negotiations - but the fighting is still keen & there's little indication of any respite on this end. Just hoping that the time continues to zip along - I'm ready to leave!

You sounded real chipper on the radio! Elin wrote too that you sounded real happy when she called you. Glad everything is going well. Say hello to everyone for me.

Love Bill

Frankfurt, Germany
April 15, 1968

My dear Elin,

I've thought of you and Bill so often these last four months and keep hoping that the war in Vietnam will end soon and that Bill will get home safe and sound. When you write to him, will you please tell him that we send our very best wishes and that we hope to see him in Germany before many more months go by.

Is the weather as beautiful in Denmark as it is in Germany? Unfortunately, it's just another work day for us Americans and I feel a little envious of all the Germans dressed up in their Easter finery. But I really shouldn't complain because we just got back from a two-week holiday in Greece. We flew to Athens on March 29th with the Scharnow Travel Agency. It was one of their package deals and we were given a hotel room and breakfast without any extra cost. Tom and I joined a six-day bus tour to Delphi, Olympia, Mycenae, Sparta, Nauplia. etc. and then a two day island cruise to Delos and Mykonos, but it was nice to have a hotel room in which to keep extra clothing. The weather was just perfect, except for the last morning, and at that point it didn't matter. Our fellow tourists were more interesting than the people one is likely to meet during the summer months, and we came back to Frankfurt feeling that we had a new lease on life.

And now comes my main reason for writing: when can we expect to see you in Frankfurt? In your Christmas letter you wrote that you would be coming to southern Germany in the spring, and now that spring is finally here, we are getting very impatient to see you. Our second bedroom (complete with bed and wardrobe) is waiting for you, and we do hope you will come for a few days. Tom has asked for state side leave starting on May 29th, so don't put it off too long. We still don't have a telephone, but as long as you give us a few days' notice, I'll meet your train in Frankfurt. It's very easy to get to Oberursel, because there are local trains every thirty minutes.

We were so pleased to get a letter from Hanna Frank last month. Their new address is Wilhelmstr. 13 in Offenburg. Hanna has opened a store of her own and Martin is an independent agent for four British firms. (You probably know all of this already). I'll try to write to her this week too.

Both Tom and I do hope that you are well and happy, and that the winter hasn't seemed too terribly long. We'll be waiting to hear from you, and we do hope to see you soon.

Much love from,
Emma

Oberursel, Germany

Odense, Denmark
April 17, 1968

Dear Bill

Thanks a million for your sweet letter (8 April) today. Took a lot off my mind. It was two weeks and no news from my precious husband.

We are all fine here and very busy. I'm having three girl friends over for slides tonight. There are some I took two of and they're not very interesting.

Please tell me more about your new job, sounds nice and good to have a change.

Mel and Jean bought a house.

I'm going shopping with Mor so must make this quick to get it in the mail. Will write long letter tomorrow.

Love Elin

3 of Elin's neighborhood friends

Chu Lai, Vietnam
April 18, 1968

Dear Elin,

Just a short note in the middle of the day. Got a sweet card & note from you yesterday.

----it's no longer the middle of the day - 100 phone calls & visitors ago I started this. Things really jumping here today. Some VIP visitors coming.

Next morning! 19 April

Quite a day yesterday. Worked until 11:00 P.M. Now will try to finish this morning. I'm sitting here eating Danish chocolate wafers with my coffee - still have lots of goodies left that you brought. I mailed a picture which one of my former PSD boys took & developed yesterday. In my new job at G1.

It's starting to get hot - was 97 F yesterday. You can feel the heat already at 7:30 in the morning.

I'm very disappointed with the haggling over the site for negotiations with Hanoi. At first was real optimistic that something good would come of it, but it looks like just so much more propaganda.

Now I've been reading about all of the demonstrations in Berlin & other places in Europe. There is revolt everywhere it seems & the world needs a basic adjustment of beliefs.

Well Honey, must get to work. Say hello to Mor and Far.

Much love –
Bill

Odense, Denmark
April 18, 1968

Darling

I got a sweet note from you today with the neat picture of my love. Thank you, helped the mood which has been down lately due to the new troubles in the U.S. Where is it all going to end.

Today I walked out to Mulvad's to look at new furniture. They had many lovely things but not too many to tempt me. We have lovely things. They will send a man out to look at the sofa so I can get it fixed. It will be lovely. Also today they brought the Indian rug down from the store. I paid $166 for it and it's lovely, luxurious and you will love it to run your bare feet through when you get out of bed in the morning. It was marked down from $300, and even that was a good buy. It looks like an oriental only in very pale colors. White, light green and light blue. A powder tone all over.

I finished my purse, the embroidery, and will try to find a handle today. Should be nice too. I'm having a couple of pictures developed and will send you one when I get it in 10 days.

I found a lovely copper coffee urn for $11. It's old and I will try and have it tinned inside so I can use for parties. I'm doing great still on money & I really feel like I swim in it. All $200 of it.

I'm still losing a bit of weight and hope to keep in this shape forever. Never fat again, never.

Last week I had so much emotion about the news. I sure hope the news slows down, it's really hard to always be wondering what is next. Just today, I'm beginning to long for our home again. The first time really. I always miss you but today I also miss our home - funny - maybe it's getting things for it. That does it.

Love you – Elin
Love from Mor og Far

Bill in G1 Office

Odense, Denmark
April 18, 1968

Dear Bill -

Last night Rita, Kirsten, Hanne and I had much fun reminiscing about old school days. We remembered how we pulled each other's pig tails and other things. I showed the slides from Bangkok - we sure didn't take many - I only have around 40. We had a cheese plate with red wine, and a fruit salad with Kijafa wine after. Very nice and the first time I entertained since I had the DeNios at your mother's house. As you can tell from the letter from Emma, I have an invitation for Frankfurt. I guess I'll go in May. Mor still doesn't have help so I guess I'll have to wait until Harriet is well again. She should be back on 15 May. I'm kind of looking forward to seeing everyone, only sad that you can't be there too.

I paid $50 car insurance and $27 Prudential insurance. That leaves $100 in my check book, so I guess I'll have just the $200 next month to travel, so I won't be doing any drastic shopping. I hope to buy the material for the couch in Germany. If you want snail plates how about sending $10 in a letter. I really don't need money, but I had forgotten about those two insurance bills. I guess the car will be another $50 at least. I haven't received a bill yet, just a renewal questionnaire which I mailed in. Kirsten writes that it runs smoothly. They just had it in for a 35,000 miles check-up.

I'm taking a sun bath on the balcony. Very lovely weather we are having. I hope that the heat is not too bad for you. Oh how I'm looking forward to settling down with you again. We have so much of a beautiful life ahead of us. I get all happy just thinking about it. I'm so glad you were persistent 8 years ago - or is it only 7.

I love you more now.
Elin

Odense, Denmark
April 19, 1968

Dear Bill

How uneven things are, now today I get two letters, and one yesterday after two weeks of no mail. The two letters today were from 2 April and 12 April. I'm very happy to hear about your job. Sounds like fun for a change, couldn't you keep Beery, or do you have a secretary any more.

My tan is just fading so I guess I'll look pale next to you when we meet again. I'm so glad you can find time for a swim. Did you have any of my goodies for the "over the hump" party? Did you drink the snaps and liquor yet? Have you read or are you reading the books I mailed? I wonder if they are enjoyable or only bearable. I was glad to get the two letters from Mother and Joan. Sounds like everything is going smoothly. What a change - your mother fixing a night-cap! Maybe she is more loose and free now, sounds so.

The weather is changing today, clouds are rolling in. I'm writing everyone that I'll be in Germany the first week in May, so I guess I'll be on the train almost when get this. Still send your letters here, and I'll have them forwarded to wherever I am.

The chestnut tree is starting to get the very first leaves, a green tint is over them. When you get this there will be about 150 days left. When exactly is your rotation date? I forgot. Also, don't you think you will get orders soon. I really hope you can come home through Europe. We can vacation so much cheaper here than in the U.S. 2 weeks in Rome with flight and hotel with breakfast sells for $85. A week on the Canary Islands is $50, Rhodes, Greece is about $75 - $100 for two weeks. We could use Denmark as a home base and take several jaunts. It's only a couple of hours by plane and so cheap, you wonder how it can be done. 3 weeks with flight and a good hotel in New York is $300.

You know all of a sudden the remainder of the time doesn't seem so bad. I feel it will fly for me and I hope it will fly for you. I pray that they start to negotiate soon, but I'm afraid the Communists have to stir all the west up real good first. The demonstrations in Germany sure don't lend aid to the west, and I'm convinced they are done by remote control. Also feel the Negroes are being used in the U.S. Sure, they have a real legitimate gripe, but I feel their situation is being manipulated. Seems strange that everything happens at the same time we are trying for peace.

I still go and do exercises every day, I haven't lost anymore, but I guess I'll take a week now and try to lose 5 pounds more. Then I don't want to lose anymore. But I've got to be thin so I can eat some good wiener schnitzel and have a beer or two.

I'm trying to fix a box up. It will include some spices. If you won't have many weeks to use it, maybe you can give it to some chef who can enjoy using it. They are our old spices and my mother would never use them. She doesn't cook like I do. I haven't cooked much here. We mostly eat cold stuff or easy frozen things that only need heating. I don't think I'll cook so much next year. One only gains so much. I feel so much better now I'm not so fat.

I really have nothing more to tell except endless chatter. I'll write soon again.

All my best to my dear love
Elin

P.S. Wasn't Joan's letter neatly written? She will do real well I'm sure.

Chu Lai, Vietnam
April 20, 1968

Dear Elin,

Just had a big ceremony here with General Westmoreland & a lot of VIP's. My boss took the picture with his new Polaroid camera.. I think I'm going to get one, they're a lot of fun & you don't have to wait forever to get the picture.

I saw Colonel Hutter from a distance - couldn't get to talk to him - he was over on the reviewing stand with the VIP's. He is with the 2nd RVN Division as an advisor. Bob Gray (career class) works for him.

Well - just a quick note - to send the picture of rough and ready combat troops.

Much love
Bill

*Chief of Staff directed that white picket fences
be built in front of headquarters buildings*

Chu Lai, Vietnam
April 24, 1968

Dear Elin,

Well I finally got two letters from you today - after 8 days. The mail has been held up again & it's very frustrating to go days without a letter from anyone - but everyone else is in the same boat. I enjoyed the pictures too & have them under the glass on my desk.

Did you get the large photo I sent? The fellow who took it, took some more today & I'll send one to Mor & Far & one to my mother. Incidentally I got a nut cake from Mother today that she baked - so it was a good mail day.

We had a tremendous rain today - everything was a sea of water & the underground bunkers filled up the top with water. We needed the rain though - it's been very dry. No rain for three months, and the water supply has been very low.

We had a rocket attack on the air field the other night, first since February. No one was hurt & damage was light, but it's an indication that Charlie is getting ready to kick up his heels again. Rumors are that there is a big enemy build up around Saigon again. The "negotiations" don't appear to be going anywhere & it's very frustrating, especially since Hanoi is using the bombing lull to resupply & build up.

My job is very interesting & I'm becoming more involved in civilian hires, clubs, PX - etc. Lots of projects to keep me busy for the next 5 months. Also involved in field grade officers assignments & a lot of other actions "close to the flag pole," which makes things more interesting.

You don't say when you are going to Germany, I assume in May.

Well Honey - love you very much & I miss you as usual. Time is zipping by fast now.

Much love
Bill

Odense, Denmark
April 26, 1968

Dear Bill

I'm on the balcony writing in the sun, and you seem so far away. Also seems like ages since your last letter even though it's only a week. I have such an uneasy feeling about you. You aren't sick or anything or depressed. I pray for you every night.

Mor had an advertisement in the paper for help, so now we are anxiously waiting for a couple to come for an interview. I do hope Mor gets help again as it's too much for her to do it alone. I help now but won't be here forever.

I plan to leave for Germany on Friday the 3rd. I'll spend the afternoon and evening in Hamburg. Karl Zushlog was just in Bangkok on business. Then the night train to Frankfurt and spend some time with Emma and Tom, and see who else I might see while there. Then on to Goppingen and over to Offenburg to Hanna and Martin's home.

Since I feel very depressed today, I'm treating myself to the hairdresser. Might do the trick. I feel most uneasy about the world situation, so much unrest all over the place. It kind of gets to one after a while.

This month we have had the most glorious weather. I never remembered as beautiful Danish spring like this. They advertise with many small thatched roof houses for sale and some days my hands just itch to buy one to fix up for a summer house. But, when would we use it? I can just see you and me in the country setting, you smoking a pipe and painting and I tending the garden, cooking and handy-crafting. Dreams, dreams - only 5 more months to go. I do miss you and Mor and Far and I talk about you every day. They send their love and thoughts.

Love you deeply
Elin

Odense, Denmark
April 27, 1968

Bill

This month has been the worst yet to take. I've had 4 - I spell four letters from you. If I - wife - only rates 4 time 10 minutes each it takes to write, it isn't much. I cried again this morning when there was no mail. But I guess you aren't a Walker for nothing. No one has written. No thank you from the Reverend, nothing from Jack or Joan. Your family surely doesn't include me in sorrows or joys. Very selfish really. Makes one sour on many things.

How is your new job going. Have you met any nice people?

On Monday our help starts . A nice woman, so now I hope we will have more spare time.

When do you all get orders, has anyone started to receive theirs yet? I'm very excited to know where we are going. But you never mention the future. So what do I know if you can even imagine civilian living again in normal surroundings.

Bill I need you. I need your strong shoulder to cry on. I'm so disillusioned with the events in the world and without you to talk to, it all gets out of proportion. Please have more time to write.

Today is Saturday, next Saturday I should be in Frankfurt. I'm not looking forward that, but will be once I'm involved in the trip. Had a sweet note from Emma , and a short card from Margarete, She is very busy in May so I guess I'll stay in the BOQ or a hotel in Goppingen. I am invited to see Hanna and Martin in Offenburg. I'm really sorry that we aren't doing this together. So unnatural to be just one. Are you taking that other trip, and when will that be? I really enjoyed that trip out. Seems like a dream now, an unreal and unbelievable. I love you more than ever and almost can't stand being alone.

Hurry on home –
Elin

Odense, Denmark
April 28, 1968

Dear Bill

Our beautiful spring weather is keeping up - in the 70s. Berlin had 85 degrees or almost 90 yesterday, the highest ever registered in Berlin in April. We have summer weather here, and all the trees are all of a sudden green. Very lovely.

Right now Mor and I are on our way to choose a painting from someone who lived here once. Also, last night we had a ceramist staying here. An American married to a Dane and living in a converted farm house. He makes pottery. We have the creamer and sugar in orange. Their place makes them and they are part of Den Permanente in Copenhagen. They do well here in Denmark. Interesting to talk to someone who has done something like that.

Mor and I just took a walk. The painters here sure get good prices for stuff I consider junk.

The war news is not too encouraging. Oh I so do hope it will all slow down. This week I've started dieting again. I hope to lose 8 pounds before Germany, then I'll buy a bikini, not before, but I have 2 weeks yet so maybe will send picture of new me.

Love you and miss you terribly –
Elin

Chu Lai, Vietnam
April 29, 1968

Hi Honey,

Enjoyed getting another letter yesterday. Your trip to Germany is going to be fun. I wonder what it will seem like now.

We've had some tremendous rains here this week. In fact it just started up again. In between it gets real hot. I just saw Colonel Hutter. He wanted to know how you were. Said Mrs. Hutter is living in Sacramento, California. He looks real good, has been here only a month, about 30 miles from here where is he a senior advisor to an ARVN unit.

I continue to like my job. Have been getting involved in the club system (which is rather primitive here as you can imagine). We are trying to improve & make things more attractive. We are going to make all 24 Army Officer Clubs in Chu Lai into annexes of the main club. They make all kinds of money because they provide the only form of recreation at all here.

Lt. Colonel Clarke always asks how my "beautiful, vivacious wife" is, and then proceeds to tell anyone around how great you are! He is quite an admirer (makes me feel good!).

(Later)

Went back & cleaned my hooch after dinner - was really filthy. Now back at work (9:30 P.M.) & tired. Good night for now Honey. I love you - say hello to Mor & Far.

Bill

Odense, Denmark
April 29, 1968

Dear Bill

You always said to tell you if I had troubles, well I do. I have been so depressed over not hearing from you. Yesterday I cried most of the time and now today again no letter. Before Bangkok I always got them, now all of a sudden nothing. Are you ill, depressed or have any problems. Please tell me. If I don't hear I'll cancel my trip to Germany. I'm in no frame of mind to even think of a trip. It was planned that I should leave on Friday but I haven't even bought a ticket or inquired as I don't feel like doing anything. I'm so worried something is wrong. Maybe you have found something there to be interested in - but then you would tell me first so it isn't that. Maybe you are in a slump. But please share it with me. Honey I love you so much and it's so hard to be so far away, and without letters I feel like I have no contact. You surely must have something you want to tell me, enough for a letter now and then. If it's the Post Office, tell them it is putting stress on the family. I shall tell you I shall not go through 5 more months like this one. I've been so depressed and cried so much. Have I said something in a letter that made you mad? Sometimes things sound different than one intended them to sound.

Did you have a disagreement with someone at work? If you are sick please tell me. I would want to know.

Honey let us at least help each other through these trying times by communicating. I realize that it is hardest on you, much worse than on me, but how can I help if I don't know how you are doing.

I do love you and miss you, and I wouldn't want to hurt you, so please don't be disapproving of this letter. Only I need you to talk to, but when I get letters I'm all right.

I just had a letter from Nancy Buchanan. She said to say hello to Bill when I write.

We still had lovely spring weather and maybe I'm just sad I can't share it all with my beloved darling.

Well enough of my moaning and complaining you know that you have never complained in one letter to me - so if that's necessary now you have a long credit here - got mad - get sad - do anything just react.

All my love
Elin

P.S. Feel better now - but I hope I never have my monthly troubles again while I get no mail. So hurry on to that paper and pen - some letters!

Odense, Denmark
April 30, 1968

Dear Bill

Yesterday when Mor and I returned, I had a letter from you dated the 10th of April - only took 19 days, and this morning I had the short note dated 20 April. So now I'm better. At least you are not sick. I loved the picture you sent. Oh how I love that big hunk of man. I feel like hugging you and squeezing you. Only 5 more months. Today I think I shall last. My only sure thing in life is our love - such turmoil and I get my strength by thinking of you my love.

Yesterday I bought a lovely lavender trench coat for $20 and a dress for $5. Today Mor gave me a purse to match a new hat I bought a while back - a tweedy look. I deducted the $10 you wrote about. I bought my ticket for Germany and I have $238 left in the checking account. I'll take $100 out for expenses. That should do me. I really feel I'm doing well with my money. Never felt richer. Taking the grill (small) for Margarete. I also have 3 plates in Royal Porcelain for gifts and several other small things I've accumulated since January. I called Gabby and I'll see them Friday afternoon, then take a 23:50 train on to Frankfurt and spend the weekend with Emma and Tom. Then on to Goppingen and over to Offenburg and home. I don't plan to be gone more than one week, maybe two. I'll see how I feel and how my money lasts.

I think it's exciting you talked with Jack and your mother - really amazing.

Now that I've heard from you I think it's all right if I go on my small trip, only I know I'll miss you terribly when I see "all of those familiar places and faces." And you can be sure I'll talk about you.

I think it would be fun if you got a Polaroid - really fun - also get anything for yourself. Spoil yourself a little bit. I sure would if I were there. Funny - love is great.

How many more days 'till love days -
Elin

Odense, Denmark
May 1, 1968

Darling -

The sun is shining again, now three days in a row I've had letters from my sweetheart. The one today was dated 18 April - only 12 days - an improvement over 19 days. I'm sorry it's getting so hot there. I agree with you that the immediate chances for peace are not very optimistic. Our papers say Chinese troops are in Laos and North Vietnam, ready to invade South Vietnam. Do I pray we get peace!

Today I joined a course that will start on 10 June in sewing. We go all day from 8:00 to 15:00, for three weeks. I'll learn to make plain dresses and suits. Should be much fun. I'll sew from the material I bought in Thailand (not the silk - I'll pay to have that done). This sure has been the year for me to do handicrafts. In a way it is very satisfactory to produce things with your own hands. Much more than buying things.

I'm packing my suitcase today, going to the hairdresser, and picking up my ticket tomorrow. I leave early Friday morning. Only sad you and I won't be on that train together.

Sure sounds like you enjoy your new job, and that it's keeping you busy. Would this be considered a step up from the last? Were you picked for the job? I would think it's challenging to get new tasks all the time. No one can say you are in a humdrum job with never any changes. Wonder how you'd do tied to one desk for 20 years. You would probably go batty.

You know the poem we have about chaos and love. It's more true now than ever. I really feel the only solid ground, the only sanctuary for me, is your love. Without it I would see all the world as hopeless but with you it's very hopeful and I'm very excited to experience life with you. We do have a belief and sound foundation. I'm smiling now just thinking of next year - "When the lights go on all over the world" - "When the boys come home again."

Well enough today. Keep your chin high, and your spirits - and do take care and think of your love before dozing off. I always do.

Love
Elin

                                            Odense, Denmark
                                            May 1, 1968

Dear Mother

Thank you so much for your letter. Sounds like life got hectic there for a while with Jack home. How long did he have leave? We had a lovely April, the weather was unusually good, sun every day. They say that we will probably pay for it later with rainy weather.

I got a good letter from Bill. He is happy about his new job, likes the atmosphere and feels time will fly. Most of the time it flies for me too, but I get very lonely for Bill some days, and with all the unrest in the world I can get very discouraged, but that only lasts a short time and then my spirits are restored. It sure looks like the people of the world need to have new faith in life and humanity. It's not all as bad as one would believe listening to the demonstrators. I have as much faith as ever in the U.S. and the West and in our kind of culture. I have yet to see a better one. It's fine to hope for utopia but one must be realistic. Some of the demonstrators, both here and there, are misguided souls. I pray that we shall not have to contend with any fanatic like Hitler and Mussolini again.

On Friday I'm going on a short trip to Germany. I will be interested to see how things have developed down there, and I'll be sorry Bill won't be there to "do" all the old haunts with. We had such fun during our first married years there. But still, we both miss California the most. That year on the beach is the most perfect year in our memory.

Now we only have 5 more months and Bill will be home. Seems far but that too will go. Soon we should know where he will be stationed. He has been asking for the East Coast, but the Army often has other plans so we will just have to wait and see.

How is Uncle Charlie doing? I hope you haven't had any more colds. I've started a mild one today but hope it leaves in a day or so. We are all well here and busy. In June I'll attend a 3 week, all day, sewing course. I should learn how to make plain things, and lose my fear of the sewing machine. I always shy away because I've done so little.

This has been the year for hand crafts, but it's good to produce things. It gives you a better sense of accomplishment than just buying things.

My mother has gotten help again, so now we don't have quite as much work. Doing it all was getting very hard for her, as it was 7 days a week and from early morning until late at night.

Say hello to Joan, Jack, Mike, Kathy and Uncle Charlie.

Love Elin

Chu Lai, Vietnam
May 2, 1968

Dear Elin,

Got a letter from you today. The mail is so sporadic it's very frustrating. Sometimes your letters get here in 5 days, others 10-12 days. Some days I get 2, 3 4 at once! You are probably getting ready for Germany right now. It will be a fun trip.

The Colonel was in Saigon for two days so I had to attend all of daily briefings with the Generals & Staff. Very interesting - really get a birds eye view of the whole operation. You've probably read about the big U.S. operations going on up here.

The weather is muggy, rainy & generally miserable. I am fine & in good spirits & enjoying my work. The time flies in a new job & now it's only 5 months! I'm getting anxious now to find out what my next assignment will be.

I bought a new Seiko (Japanese) watch for $30. The $6 watch I bought a few weeks ago went kaput right away. The new one is really nice - self-winding, waterproof, calendar, date.

Well, no other news tonight.

Much love to you
Bill

I don't think about anything else but being together again.

Chu Lai, Vietnam
May 3, 1968

Dear Mother,

Haven't heard from you in a while. Hope everything is ok. I did receive the cake - delicious! & much appreciated. I shared it with the people in my office & everyone enjoyed it.

I'm enjoying my new job. Quite interesting to be on a General Staff, especially in this situation. Our (Americal Division) are engaged in heavy fighting again right now. Don't know what to think about the war anymore. It keeps going on & on despite the brief ray of optimism after Johnson's speech. But that has died away here. Same terrible numbers of men being killed or seriously wounded every day.

We had a lot of heavy rain last week - almost monsoon proportion - but today it's bright and hot again. Well - I'm starting on my 8th month here - the rest of the time should fly - I hope! Anxious to get back to civilization.

How is Jack doing in his new assignment & Joan in N.Y.? & Mike, Kathy & Jonathan? Say hello to everyone for me please - also Uncle Charlie - hope he's still in good spirits.

This isn't a very interesting letter! Sort of in a vacuum here & it's an effort to be imaginative!

Thanks again for the cake-

Much love-
Bill

Spokane, Washington
May 3, 1968

Dear Elin & Bill,

Spring is here & I'm working out 'till late every night - also doing spring house cleaning every spare hour. Tim has his orders. They are for SAC Headquarters at Omaha. We are so relieved that they were not for Vietnam or Washington, D.C.

Is Bill OK and what are you doing Elin & how is Kirsten? The political campaigns are of interest here. I think Rockefeller will win easily now. I do not know if that is good or bad!

Everything is still a turmoil in our country. Unless we have some strong leadership soon - we could easily have a civil war before things are settled. I don't leave my place alone so unless I find someone to stay here, I won't even be going to Omaha. They will have to come here.

My best regards to your parents & families. How is Charlie now? Write.

Much love
Hazel

Elin's note to Bill:
I'm going to write to Hazel that one just can't sit home in fear the rest of one's life. But it's a shame that good citizens feel such a fear in their own towns. But you know I have long been disturbed about the crimes, guns and unrest in the U.S. I guess now most people have become aware of it. I do think the country will work it out, and order will be restored. The balance just has to be found. I also have much faith in God and in the goodness of people.

Chu Lai, Vietnam
May 4, 1968

Dear Elin,

Got a very disturbing letter from you today saying that you only got 4 letters and that I don't write. I don't know what in the hell happens to the mail - I write every two or three days. Have written at least 10 letters in April & also sent an 8 X 10 picture. Honey you have to realize that the mail gets hung up in Da Nang a week at a time often - it just doesn't have the priority that ammunition & food have. I go 10 days sometime without a letter, and the only person I ever get mail from is you. My mother writes once a month. I guess nobody really cares & I'll be damned if I'm going to write to solicit letters. I have to sit in this hell-hole for a year & they could take the initiative for a change.

This place, atmosphere - is a real vacuum. I don't know what I believe in anymore as far as the war - U.S. etc. is concerned anymore. All these young guys blown apart - legs, arms blown off - thousands of them. It's not worth it. The U.S. society is sick and I feel like running away from it sometimes.

I got with the Education Advisor & he is getting me all the information on the Army graduate programs. I'll let you know what I find out. I am very anxious to get my assignment but probably won't for several more months.

Don't despair my love - life is a churn for many people these days & most don't have the strong foundation that we have to fall back on. I love you very deeply.

Bill

Chu Lai, Vietnam
May 5, 1968

Dear Elin,

A hot Sunday - things rather slow - lay out in the sun 1½ hours at lunch time. Yesterday I bought a Polaroid camera - $60.00. It's a lot of fun. I've always wanted one & I went to the PX to order some things from the catalogue - but they didn't have any order blanks. The PX officer is getting me some & I'll order some things next month.

Last night the base got rocketed again - none came into our area but they did about ½ mile away. 3 people were killed & some wounded. Everywhere got hit last night in another coordinated attack on U.S. & RVN bases.

We got word of the Paris selection & beginning of talks on 10 May. Not openly optimistic but miracles can happen.

I guess you're in Germany now. I'd mail this there but it would probably miss you. It's hard to get Polaroid film here. Colonel Quarles gave me one pack (8 pictures) of which these are two. This camera also takes color pictures, has electric eye etc.

Well Honey wish this was a cozy Sunday afternoon at "home' or a picnic on Carmel Beach.

Much love - anxious to hear about Germany reunions.

Bill

Vietnamese day laborers - fascinated by Polaroid camera

Vietnamese grave on base

Odense, Denmark
May 5, 1968

Dear Bill!

I think Elin is in Goppingen now - we remember the time we visited you and Elin there. She is going by train Friday morning past week to Hamburg, Frankfurt and Goppingen. I think she will come back on 10 or 14 days perhaps.

The time goes so fast for all of us. Hope it is the same for you.

We are in springtime in Denmark. The trees are green and the flowers are beautiful.

Every springtimes are as a start of a new life, but this springtime we hope it will be peace over the world. It is horrible things we read about in the newspapers and hear on the radio and on the T.V.

Dear Bill! We are looking forward to see you soon. Maybe this year.

Karlig Hilsen. Far and Mor in Danmark

Excuse my English, is not good but I have no time to learn it.

bye now
Mor

                                              Oberursel, Germany
                                              May 6, 1968

Dear Bill

It's Monday morning and Emma is fixing coffee and cake. On Friday I started at 7:45 in the morning by train and arrived in Hamburg at 1:00. Took the S train out to Wellingsbuettel (remember when we did it - we laughed so). Gabby was there to greet me, and she looked like herself. Karl was home recovering from having his tonsils out. We had dinner, and then sat and talked and talked all afternoon and evening. I left at 22:30. They gave me a most beautiful shawl from India. Karl had made a 7 week trip in November and December to Egypt, Iran, Pakistan, India, Bangkok, Singapore - so we talked about our trips. Poor Gabby is suffering from suburban boredom, so we talked about what women like us can do. They really are nice people. They wanted me to stay a week, but I couldn't quite see that.

Then I got a midnight train out of Hamburg. Got a seat with only one other woman so we pulled the seats together and we could rest. The schlafwagen was sold out. I arrived in Frankfurt in a dreary, grey, rainy mess just like I remembered Germany, but by the time I got to Emma and Tom's in Oberursel the sun was out.

Tom took us on a trip to see the Taunus Mountains. Very interesting, beautiful old ruins and beer on an open air terrace. A lovely dinner with spaetzle and sauerbraten. I really enjoyed it. I'm only real sad you are not here. I can't enjoy it the same without you.

Yesterday, Sunday, we went to a rebuilt Roman fort. Very interesting and had a long walk in the Forest. The chestnut trees all have white clusters of flowers, and the birch is a pale green. Again we had lovely weather. We came home and had a very good turkey dinner. I really enjoy German and American food again, and I'm guilty about having it while you are suffering in the heat.

This morning I hear where they have launched a second wave of attacks. I pray your installation wasn't hit, and I pray that they won't do too much damage anyplace.

Today Emma and I are going to Frankfurt to shop. I'll call Joan and Tim and the Buchanans. Tomorrow I'm going to a luncheon with Emma and then I don't know what we'll be doing. Everyone asks about you and sends their regards.

Closing for now - love and miss you -
Sawadee - Elin

Hello Bill - How we wish that you were here in Oberursel too.

Much love
Emma (& Tom)

Tom and Emma Haynes, Taunus Mountains

Elin, Taunus Mountains

Elin in front of Roman fort

Frankfurt, Germany
May 7, 1968

Darling

I hope these letters going through the APO get to you faster than lately.

Yesterday Emma and I went shopping, mostly in the PX & commissary. It's so nice to be back with the Army (I would have sworn I would never have said that 5 years ago!). I did some shopping for cosmetics etc. then I tried to call Nancy Buchanan. She was at the hairdresser, and I called there only to find out we were talking from either side of the same wall - so I went over to talk to her. I'm going to their place on Wednesday for the afternoon and dinner. She said Jerry is very busy and seldom home for dinner, but he should be that day. I'll stay two blocks away. They have two buildings for enlisted and company grade officers, and then a VIP hotel. I'll be staying there because you are now a Major. It was strange to be shown the nicer facility because of rank. Poor dear, you have never gotten that and here I am getting special treatment, haven't even earned it, but it is a nice hotel - $3.50. Then on Thursday I'll go to see Joan and Tim in Wiesbaden. He is in the States but will be back. His sister was ill. Then on Monday they go to Italy so I guess I'll go to Goppingen then. Now the weather is "cloudy turning mostly cloudy" as AFN reports.

Frankfurt is all torn up - shades of how I remember Germany - it's the perennial road work.

If I have any left over money from this trip I might get a transistor radio. Ours is broke - did you buy one over there? If you want a stereo do not hesitate to get it. Also anything else. When you get orders we can then decide if we will need two cars. In D.C. one does. Everything is far apart. By now I'm very excited to know where we will go next.

Oh Bill I have so prayed that no one gets killed now during this new terrible offensive. It sounds from here like the Americans have light casualties, but with any fighting one knows people get killed.

I love you, miss you and am optimistic that the next 5 months will go fast. I'm out of my slump. I had a terrible week at the end of April. The first real bad one, and now I'm cheerful again.

Deep love –
Elin

Chu Lai, Vietnam
May 8, 1968

Dear Elin,

Yesterday I got a sweet letter from you (30 April) and was glad to hear that you are getting some of my mail - but 19 days is ridiculous. I don't know what happens to it.

We were on alert for the last three nights - slept in the bunkers (or tried to sleep - hot - humid & mosquitos precluded sleep). So everyone's been dragging their tails. There is still some fierce fighting going on not far from here.

It's really getting hot - sweating all the time - but sometimes we get a nice breeze off the ocean at night.

Just got a letter from you (29 April) - about no mail. Honey I write all the time, the mail is all screwed up & there is nothing you or I can do about it. Considering everything, it's amazing that everything gets through that does.

I don't know whether I'll take a leave or not. I'd rather not & save the time for a long leave in October - but it depends on whether or not I really need to get away. I'll at least wait until August. Actually I wouldn't mind taking leave right here & spending it on the beach. But that would be hard to do.

Later —Evening

Well - we had an alert at 6:50 pm tonight. Charlie lobbed a couple of rockets into the air strip. Unusual for day time. They are at it in Saigon again. Although this thrust doesn't appear to have the punch that the TET Offensive did.

I'm tired of it all, don't feel creative or inspired to do anything but exist from day to day & that's bad.

Hope your Germany trip is proving to be fun. Anxious to hear about it & our old friends.

Well Honey - that's all for tonight - love you very much -

Bill

Oberursel, Germany
May 8, 1968

Dear Bill

Went to a big "Buy American" luncheon where Consular G. Johnston spoke. It was with the 3rd Armored Division in Frankfurt. Did not see one person I knew.

We got orchids (my first) from Pan American and many small favors, one of which was this packet of Kool Aid. Thought maybe you could use it. The weather is still dismal. I'm leaving Emma's house, going to visit the Buchanans. Will stay at the VIP Hotel that I told you about. I am really cheered by this trip. I had hit a real low point and this has put my mind back in order again. I so hope you are not too uncomfortable in the heat.

I'm real excited to see Major Buchanan and Nancy. Also looking forward to talking to Tim and Joan. Everyone asks about you and I tell them about our great times in Bangkok. I'm still living high on that trip. How I love you, let me count the ways, I will run out of fingers and toes.

Stay cheerful lover, I am (it's easier for me).

Love
Elin

Frankfurt, Germany
May 9, 1968

Dear Bill

I'm at the Buchanans now. Nancy is driving me to Wiesbaden this afternoon. She is at the dentist so I have an hour to catch up with some letter writing.

Last night we had the best time talking 'till about midnight. Seems the Buchanans have been in the middle of things since Fort Ord. Major Buchanan is due to make Lieutenant Colonel in June - July. He is now the commander of Armed Forces Radio Frankfurt. He arrived when there was a big scandal going on, and I guess had 8 unpleasant months before he left. They moved once already and are not sure they will stay. He does get to travel a lot, been to Berlin, Holland, Denmark, two weeks in Greece, and once to the U.S., on official business. Going to England next month, and will take his family. Sounds not too bad.

We had wonderful barbequed steaks. I'm really enjoying all this good American food. Not helping my diet any. Gained two pounds at Emma's.

The VIP BOQ only had a nice lobby. The rooms were like a thousand other BOQs in Europe. One shared the bathroom with two rooms, in between an unknown next door neighbor. With the noise from street workers and garbage cans I got very little sleep. The Buchanans only have two bedrooms so it was still better than to inconveniencing them. They live in State Department housing, very large living and dining rooms and generally superior to any European military quarters I've seen.

Jerry says to come to Europe. I don't know that I would enjoy it so soon. Also say that this Infantry school he went to runs three times a year - only passing on information.

They had a long letter from Mrs. Ryan from Fort Ord. Did you know that General Ferguson's only son and child died from battle wounds received in Vietnam? I was shocked. She had a long spiel about who is where, and I guess the office has been rearranged. Sergeant Price stopped in and will be getting an advanced degree in September. Joe Ryan has started a partnership to operate a resort complex at Big Sur.

I'm very concerned about all this fighting going on now again in Vietnam. I'll call home this week to see if I have a letter from you and have it forwarded to Goppingen.

Everyone is very concerned about you, and send their regards and thoughts. And of course you know mine are with you every minute -

Oceans of love
Elin

Frankfurt, Germany
May 9, 1968

Dear Uncle Charlie,

I'm on a trip to Germany right now, visiting Bill's former boss from Fort Ord. Then I'm going down to where we used to be stationed with the 4th Armored Division in Goppingen.

I miss Bill, but am enjoying being with friends.

Hope you are fine.

Love
Elin

New York, New York
May 9, 1968

Dear Elin,

Please forgive the long delay in writing to you, but I've hardly had any time to myself lately. I was very happy to receive your last letter, and so glad that you had such a wonderful visit with Bill in Bangkok. Jack told me how great it was to see you both again - and how wonderful you looked!

I'm still enjoying my job with Irish Airlines so much as ever. I get to meet all the big bosses - was even secretary to the top man in North America for 3 days while his secretary was out sick. He even sent me a thank you note. Pretty nice, huh?

As far as our apartment goes, all the girls I've been living with have moved out. There were too many of us living together. I also am moving out tomorrow night. A girl from work (went to school in Minneapolis also) is getting an apartment with me. She was born in Germany, but has been living in this country since she was 12 years old. She's really a lovely girl... and closer to my own age than the other girls. She'll be 21 in a month or so, whereas the other girls were only 18 years old.

Our new apartment is really cute, and much cozier than the one I'm in now. Once we get it all fixed up I'll send you some pictures of it so you can see what it looks like.

Jack brought me back some beautiful jade earrings. They were for pierced ears but I had them changed to screw-backs. I just love them!

I'm quite anxious to receive the Thai rubbing. It will be great for our apartment. Right now our walls are barren of any type of art. Thank you so much for thinking of me during your visit to Thailand.

I received a letter from Kirsten today. She said she may be coming down to New York City for a day next week. If so I will meet her for lunch. It will be wonderful to see her once more. I'd love to go up to Connecticut to visit her, but it will have to wait a while until I get settled.

Well, write when you can and remember to send future mail to my new address, as all mail coming to this address will be forwarded to home.

Take care and give my best regards to your parents.

Love,
Joan

Chu Lai, Vietnam
May 10, 1968

Dear Elin,

148 DAYS

A nice, quiet afternoon for a change - real hot out but the office hooch is fairly comfortable with two fans blasting.

The sun is very hot now during the day. I haven't gotten to the beach since coming to my new job but still get out for 40 minutes or so of sun each lunch hour & am getting black with just that much exposure.

Joe Jaquez - a Captain who used to work for me in AG just got approval for circuitous travel to Europe when he leaves here next month. His wife is Dutch. So I guess I'll be able to still do it despite the conflicting stories in the papers and in official messages we've gotten. The messages do say "approval will be granted for compassionate cases" - that worked once before! Anyway I'm going to plan on it, things usually work out for the best. It's too early to apply now - 60 days before. But I'll try for a 45 day leave. We can spend a couple of weeks in Spain, Italy or Greece, then some time in Denmark & in Philadelphia - depending on where we go - if it's the East Coast we'll just spend a day or two in Philadelphia & go to the new area to find a house.

Some people are starting to get assignments to Europe from here whether they asked for it or not. So anything could happen. Most officers aren't getting orders until 60 days before departure.

I wonder if the peace talks started today? The North tried - attempted - a second TET Offensive last week. As you've undoubtedly read, but it wasn't too successful, however Saigon is in trouble right now. One of our Captains from G1 & an enlisted man are there right now (in the city) & can't get out.

Anxious to hear from you & about Germany.

Much love –
Bill

Lunch hour sunbathing

Wiesbaden, Germany
May 10, 1968

Dearest Bill

This morning I'm in Wiesbaden at the Buchers. Joan is at the hairdresser so I have an hour to write.   I called Margarete and will stay with her next week in Eislingen. Yesterday I bought 8 yards of white brocade with gold for the couch. It was $35.00 and I like it. I hope you will too. I shopped in Denmark and here for velvet, but in Denmark it is $25.00 a yard. Down here where it is made it's $10.00 a yard, which was all right but the colors were real dull and too drab. So I got carried away and was impractical and got the brocade. Also yesterday I bought cake mixes and other every day things so I'm making up a box to mail to Denmark.

Nancy drove me to Wiesbaden. I had checked my suitcase through. My luggage weighs 60 pounds so by now I really have to mail some.

Joan was home alone. Tim's sister (33 years old) was given 50 days to live, so at first they were all going back permanently. They are scheduled to leave Germany end of June, but they had already made long plans for a trip to Italy, so he went home Monday. Will return tonight. We will go to the airport and eat, and meet him. Then on Monday they start their trip to Italy. Three days after their trip they get packed. I said I didn't think they needed company, but oh no Joan insisted that I come - so here I am. The kids are real nice and behave beautifully. Barbara made the "book" for you and asked why you didn't come, also asked why Kirsten wasn't along. I guess I'm kind of a disappointment.

I'm very upset about all the fighting still going on. I'm glad I'm too busy right now or I would go to pieces. I really had that one bad week, and this trip is good for me - not for the waistline though. I hadn't had one beer or drinks for 8 months - except for Bangkok - so this is a big change. You remember how freely the liquor flows in Europe.

Wish you were here too - oh we have such good times.   I love you and you are constantly being talked about.

Elin

Chu Lai, Vietnam
May 11, 1968

Dear Elin,

Good day today - got a letter from you from Frankfurt - one from Mor & one from Mother.
I sent off two rolls of film to you today - one has been sitting here for months - the other the camera

jammed on the 18th picture. But get it developed anyway the rest should be good.

Things are quiet here in Chu Lai at the moment. Elsewhere - in Saigon and other places things are hot. Captain Amaker from my office just got back from Saigon yesterday. He was trapped for 3 days in a hotel in Saigon with heavy firing going on all around. Almost got gunned down in the street (I'll stay right here if I can help it).

I flew in the Staff Chopper to a company fire base on top of a hill about 15 miles yesterday to pick up a Captain. Really desolate up there - they had lost a few men the night before on a patrol. As we flew over the area the Captain pointed out a village where VC controlled one half & his men the other. Amazing.

Well Honey that's all for today - love you

Bill

Chu Lai, Vietnam
May 11, 1968

Dear Mor,

Thank you very much for your letter - I was very happy to hear from you. I am glad that Elin has a trip to Tyskland. I wish that I could be in Europe now also. Maybe in October. I can come from Vietnam to Europe for a month. It is not certain yet but I am very hopeful to see you and Far in October.

Kirsten writes to me regularly and I guess she and Tom are very happy.

We are all very anxious to see what comes of the peace talks in Paris and hope that this war will end soon. Right now there is a lot of fighting in Saigon and other places.

I still have the snaps and "goldwater" you sent with Elin and I will have a Danish cold table some night - Tusind Tak!

My best regards to Far and you - and thank you for having Elin in Odense this year. I know she is happier there this year than any other place -

Love Bill

Wiesbaden, Germany
May 12, 1968

Dear Bill

Sunday, today - Tim came back yesterday. One Army Major arrived from Vietnam at the airport - his wife was there. I sat and shed a couple of tears. I really wished it was me there at the airport meeting you.

The weather is still not too good. Tim's sister is 33 and dying. Liver troubles from too much drinking. Her husband is also sick and just got off the critical list. One of his kidneys went out, also due to drinking. Sad when young bright people ruin themselves that way. Tim was real shocked at the dirt in New York, the slums, the crime etc. It really hits one in the face after Europe which is still clean and neat in appearance anyway.

I called home yesterday and I have a couple of letters from you, which Mor will forward to Margarete's house. By now I'm really looking forward to finding out where we go from now on. I'm ready to set up house again - and to be your loving wife again. So take real good care that nothing happens to you.

I bought a real sweet Royal Doulton figurine for your mother's birthday, so you only have to send a card. I'll send your box as soon as I get to Denmark.

Tomorrow I go to Goppingen. This trip has really lifted my spirits - and I can go home and live on this for a while. By the time you get this only 4 more months. When are you scheduled to rotate? Oh we are really going to have fun.

I'm sorry I have only my $100 to spend here. Really are so many good bargains. Only wish I could buy stuff for you too. What size sandals do you use? I'll go to Flensburg one day or so and get the kind you had before and really liked. They still all wear them here and I thought of yours.

Well I'm real fine except for missing you so. Seems like you should be here with me - all the places we used to go.

I love you deeply and think of you always.
Elin

Chu Lai, Vietnam
May 13, 1968

Dear Elin,

Here are some more pictures - I thought you could give the big one to Mor & Far so they can get rid of that crew cut college boy on the bookcase for a more up-to-date realistic version.

Also enclosed is a letter from mother (she is undoubtedly the world's greatest sentimentalist!).

Our units have been going through some hell this week in separate operations. The NVA's have really stepped up things in the wake of the negotiations. We get a few rockets in on the air field every other night but nothing much right here at Chu Lai. No mail today - planes couldn't get in.

Went to the beach today for a swim during lunch hour. First time in over a month. The water was fabulous. We went to a different beach, little inlets surrounded by coral rock (like Pacific Grove). Some pools in the rock were filled with fantastic tropical fish & crabs, all colors and varieties. Wish I had a whole day just to wander around the rocks, like we used to do in Monterey.

Well love, that's all for today. Oh, I may have to cash a $10.00 check near the end of the month. The Polaroid cleaned me out. If so I'll send you a $10.00 money order after pay day (I have to wear a clean, starched pair of fatigues every day in my new job so laundry bill is way up too).

Much love–
Bill

Chu Lai, Vietnam
May 13, 1968

Dear Mother,

Sure enjoyed getting your letter the other day & glad to know everything going well in Philadelphia.

I'm fine & with 4 months + some left - begin to see the end of this tour in sight. Elin is in Germany right now visiting some old haunts & friends - wish I were there too. Depending on my new assignment, I plan to return to the U.S. via Europe & spend some leave there in October.

The weather is hot - hot here, but I get down for a swim once in a while & don't mind the heat anymore.

The NVA's & VC have been stirring up increased activity all over in the wake of the Peace talks. Probably will continue through the negotiations as in Korea.

One of the men who used to work for me took this picture.

G1 is a section of the Commanding General's Staff. The G1 is a Lieutenant Colonel and I am his deputy. We are responsible for policy making in the broad area of personnel morale, welfare & put out policy for the CG. Before I was in the nuts & bolts of personnel work. This is much broader & an entirely different role.

Very interesting because we are in on all of the overall Division operations & attend conferences and briefings with the Commander etc. - all the time.

Say hello to Uncle Charlie.

Much love-
Bill

Philadelphia, Pennsylvania
May 13, 1968

Dear Elin,

Your welcome letter came last week but until now I have had no time to answer it. I am happy you are well, as are your parents, and that time is ticking away as fast as it is for you.

Jack's homecoming has been exciting and happy for me. He is manly but still needs encouragement and love as do we all. He went to base a week ago but returned unexpectedly Thursday evening (with a big bundle of laundry - 8 shirts, etc.). He does not begin work until this morning, Monday, and last week was used for physical check-ups. He is having extensive dental work including caps on his top four front teeth. But he is feeling well and has become quite involved with his romance with Vivian. I have cautioned him about involving himself too much at this time. She is still in school and he has nearly a year of service to go.

Why am I home today on a Monday morning? Because I have another sore throat, my fourth attack since you left. I will go to the doctor when he opens his office. How I wish my tonsils had been removed when I was a child! The doctors say it is too late now - that the damage has been done.

Joan came home also this week end to wish me a happy Mother's Day. She has moved into another apartment with a German girl, Angela, and hopes this arrangement will be more congenial than the first. Kirsten wrote to her and expects to be in New York this week to shop. Joan is very happy with her work.

Aunt Rosabelle, Uncle Edward, Nana Walker, and Josephine were our dinner guests two weeks ago. They all looked great and dined well (I had an elegant dinner with my beautiful Danish china). They all asked about you and send their best wishes. How surprised they were to hear about your Bangkok reunion!

Bill's letters are terse, lonely, and sad. It must be dreadful for him to see how many fine young men fail to return from combat. Thank you for the pictures. I have them in the living room for all to see. You both look great.

Mrs. Sternelle called last week to say she was shipping another box of cookies and goodies to him. She certainly has been faithful. I have always thought she imagines Bill to be the son she never had.

My mother is quite well for her, but problems arose when her housekeeper quit. Now my Aunt Alice, Mother's youngest sister has arrived for a visit so the present time has been taken care of. As for the future we shall try to get another housekeeper.

Uncle Charlie is in good spirits these days. Baseball season is in full swing and he sits in front of his television (I took him the portable) by the hour. They say he refuses to turn it off at bedtime and watches until nearly midnight! I know all about his stubbornness when he wants his way. So - they give in to him - just as I did. Somehow it is easier.

I have secured a summer job teaching English in a junior high school for July, but guess I'll have to bring him home for August as there are no job opportunities for me then. The only difficulty is the problem of getting him back on a waiting list to re-enter.

Mike has been very busy for several months filling other church engagements. Right now he is at a conference at Pocono Manor and Kathleen is in Lancaster with her parents. I have not seen them since Easter. The baby has had casts on his legs to straighten his feet. They turned in at the toes. Jack said he is adorable and so good. I will try to drive up when my cold is better.

The political picture is exciting and I hope Rockefeller gets the nomination. But events shape the future and only time can tell what will happen. Bob Kennedy and wife will have their "eleventh" child next

January. Instead of "There will always be an England," it will be, "There will always be a Kennedy."

My love,
Mother

Eislingen/Fils, Germany
May 14, 1968

Dear Bill

Today I'm at Margarete's. She looks real good, has lost weight after her surgery, and is now better. Sure works hard with her job and has kept the yard and house spotless.

The sun came out for me yesterday. I arrived at 2 o'clock, and the day was very nostalgic. I took a taxi out to the 4th Armored Division officers' club. Still closed on Monday! And nothing has been changed since we left. Went to meet Margarete at the AG office. One girl I remembered, Frau Franks, still works there, said it isn't what it used to be. The Hoots left last month, and I guess I wouldn't know any Americans then. I got the keys to the apartment and went out to Eislingen. I took a walk and believe me it was a nice day. I talked to the Wahls., our former landlords. Erich Wahl has gotten very fat, a real beer stomach. They said to say hello to you when I write. Their farm looks just like it always did. I stopped by the Moltes (she had the little cosmetic store in Goppingen). Her mother was home babysitting their year old daughter. Rosmarie was out. I'll go there to visit after I have my hair done at the Burgs. Sylvia Mause has been married and has a child. She isn't 20 yet, the Wahls told me. I'll try to see Mause today too.

Margarete works a lot for the Generals now and they call her their "female aid." She loves her job and keeps very busy - also does voluntary hospital work 2 days a month.

Both Colonels Allen and Hawkins are on the list for full bird. Margarete doesn't know when they will make it.

Today is a glorious sunshine day, so I'll walk all over Eislingen and get real homesick for you here. The place has so many memories, we sure did a lot here.

Well this is all for now. It's 7 in the morning and I want to get this letter to the APO. I do hope you get these letters a little faster.

Love you deeply.
Elin

Hairdressers at Burgs in Eislingen

Philadelphia, Pennsylvania
May 14, 1968

Dear Bill,

This is a rare day - to be home in the morning on a school day! But I am "grounded" with another chest cold (bronchitis) and I have several days away from school to get over it. Although I do not feel real sick, I cough, and cough, and cough! Exasperating. A vacation in the Virgin Islands or better yet, in California where you were stationed is what I need!

Joan and Jack came home last weekend to share Mother's Day with me. They both look well and of course both were broke. Weren't you, also at twenty-two? But Joan has moved into a new apartment with a beautiful blonde German girl and had to put down two months rent in advance ($215). The apartment is that amount each month. So she took a few dishes, silverware, curtains, food, etc. to make it more livable. I hope to go over some weekend soon. My last trip to New York ended in disaster. (I am excepting our dash with Michael in February to take Joan over).

Jack took back the much used and by this time the treasured green curtains you chose for the third floor long ago. They are still in good condition - never faded nor worn! Also, his easel, canvases, paints, and a few pictures for the bare walls. He is getting major dentistry - 4 front teeth capped.

On Monday afternoon he telephoned from base to tell me that he might be able to come to McGuire Field and come home nights if I get certain letters from certain peoples to him quickly. I suppose you know all about this procedure as I remember you telling about mothers trying to get their sons home, etc. I do not want him out of the service but I surely wish he would be close enough to help with Uncle Charlie when I bring him home this summer.

So - I wrote to Dr. Shore, Rev. Sharp, Michael, Mr. Hauber, and Mrs. Sundgard asking if each would write "To Whom it May Concern." Jack didn't give me any name of any commander. Do you think it would help if you wrote? Jack didn't say.

His romance is proceeding slowly for him but this is the type of girl that one can't rush. She has another half year of college and I am guessing she won't make any promises! Remember, I am only surmising this because of your brother's impatience.

Nana Williams had a happy day last Sunday. I called her in late afternoon fearing she had been alone all day. Aunt Ethel had come Saturday for a long visit and on Sunday morning (early) Uncle Lacey and Uncle Loren and their wives came for a surprise visit. The uncles took Mother to church, Uncle Loren sporting a moustache, and the aunts cooked the Sunday dinner. Mother "bubbled" as she related the day's events. She had been alone for three weeks.

This is your nephew Jonathan, and although Michael sent it to me I must send it on to you. I'll get another one. He is the best baby; rarely cries and smiles a crooked smile. He is not afraid of strangers, you and Joan were to my embarrassment, and looks like a real boy. His hair and eyebrows are reddish! Don't you think he has the Williams "jib," (his upper lip to nose)? By the time you come home he will be trying to walk or at least be crawling. Mike plays with him a lot and this is good, both for the baby and Mike. (If Mike sent you a picture like this please send mine back).

Elin sent Charlie a pretty card from Germany that he shows everyone. Yesterday he asked me to bring him some writing paper. He is going to try to write some letters. This is a hopeful sign as he has great difficulty in signing his name. There is no change in his condition, but his days are happier now that baseball season is here. The Zenith television I bought last summer when he and Mother conflicted over the shows they wanted to watch, has been a great source of comfort to him.

Is there anything I can send you? I have the new sexy book "Couples" by John Updike which I thought disgusting although I concede a message might be there. I can send it but hate to, even though I know all your men would want to read it. I never knew people he describes a "typical" group of Americans.

The political picture is getting more and more confused. My man, Rockefeller, is moving too slowly to suit me and I fear Nixon has the edge. Really, if it becomes Nixon and Kennedy next, I will vote for Kennedy. At least at this moment I will. Who knows? Maybe the Democratic convention will find LBJ taking over.

Roses are in bud in our yard. The tulips, daffodils, and hyacinth have gone and now pansies, sweet William, and the lilies are flowering. There is only a tiny "posy patch" but I do enjoy keeping something in bloom so that I can have little bouquets in the house. They are fragrant and add to the joy of a home.

I was happy to find that Elin likes growing things and especially flowers. You were always clever arranging flowers, from the time you would get up early in the morning on Mother's Day and decorate my breakfast plate. That is a warm memory of mine.

Your picture doesn't look very much like I remember you - the features are the same but "tiredness" and "sadness" are evident also a great awareness of our tragic life or lives. I hope the time flies for the next few months and that we can all put some sunshine back in your face! Now I know you will smile at the baby's picture. Right?

My love always,
Mother

Eislingen/Fils, Germany
May 15, 1968

Dear Bill,

Yesterday I got two letters from you, forwarded here from Denmark. One written 24 April and one 4 May. I'm so sorry you too are having mail delays. I haven't received the large photograph. I did receive one small pocket size photo. I wonder if you will have big rains again, is that usual or do they normally come every day. How is the heat? Does it bother you? I'm so glad that your job is interesting and engaging. Bill, I'm sorry about having written a disturbing letter. I realize you have it so bad, only I was so worried something had happened to you. From now on I'll realize that the mail gets hung up. Please forgive me. I'm sure it's hard to be there where you see these young fellows. I remember how sick I was when I went to the hospital in Texas and saw the amputees there, I pray every day that the war will end. I hope you get something out of talking to the education adviser. I too am anxious about your next duty station. Now back to what I'm up to.

I got up early and had coffee with Margarete. She leaves the house at 7 o'clock. Then I weeded the garden for one hour, real nice weather. She just keeps this place spotless. Then I walked over to the area where we used to live. I had my hair done at Burgs by Marie Louise. They were all surprised and happy to see me. I was to say hello to you from them. Then by noon, I went to see the Maas'. The house at Birkenstrasse 17 looks the same. The garage had been torn down and young Erich Wahl is building an identical house next to the old. The yard is all grown in now and the trees are getting large, in fact huge. They have a new dog, the old one died. Sylvia is married and has a year old boy. The house was real dirty. The grandmother was there and I guess she is still the one who works most, and she is getting old. We had coffee and large cakes with loads of whipped cream. So typical. At two I left. Birkenstrasse is still a dirt street. Half has been asphalted but they are waiting until the house is finished to do the other half.

Then I went over and saw Rosemarie Molte. She had the store in Goppingen, and she sold it when her daughter, Melanie, was born, a cute girl now one year old. Their house is as darling as ever and has a larger living room and a darling girl's room. That woman has so many original ideas one should take notes to remember them all. We had coffee and a cheese cake. I thought of you and shed a tear because you weren't here, you so liked that. We planned to meet Thursday noon. Heinz will be home for dinner and that afternoon Rosemarie will drive me to Dettingen to Herr Breyer's place.

I bought the food for dinner and Margarete made wiener schnitzel, salad with oil, and we had the first strawberries of the season. This is pure torture to tell you all this. I really enjoy walking here. The farm carts, the cows across the street, the mountains - oh, it's just so nice and all so fantastic. I so hope you will still get to come this way, you would enjoy it so. More than I realized, this means as much or more to me than Odense. I guess because I have so many beautiful memories from our happy times here.

Today I go to Goppingen. I will try to see Herr Maener. I don't expect to get anything out of it, but will go anyway.

The weather is real nice today. Honey my love, hope the last months won't be too bad for you. I so love you and pray for your safety every day. Just remember I always think of you, talk about you. We will have such a beautiful life. No man could be better than my own honey. You always are good to me, I really appreciate it. As I've said before, I feel guilty that you are there in misery while I live so well. But I'll try to make it all up when you return - cook for you, spoil you, love you - just can't wait to have you back to do things for you.

Enough for now or I will go off in a dream world.

Ten thousand tons of love (so hard to get original every day)

Elin

Herr and Frau Maas

Rosemarie Molte

Eislingen/Fils, Germany
May 16, 1968

Dear Bill

Well I had another full day in Eislingen. Got up early yesterday. Had coffee with Margarete at 7 o'clock, washed, then missed the bus to Goppingen. So I started walking. Went by where the Baretz's used to live, Tante Otto and the Schmids were there. He died, remember he had taken all those good pictures? They all send regards to you, and want me to come by for coffee and cake (my steady diet these days).

On Friday I then got the bus, went straight to the lawyer Ernst Maenner's office. He moved to a new nice and big office. At first he said "Are you still alive." I guess he never expected to see us. He had a long song and dance, ending in that the case had slept in his drawer. I asked how much we would owe him if we took the case from him. It came to 300 DM ($75.00) so I let him keep it, just didn't have the 300 DM. Then he took a letter he is writing to the insurance people. The case came back that we had no guilt, and we should get anywhere between $500 - $1,000 still. My claim is $750 and yours is still not all paid. We'll see if we get anything. I told him I really wanted something done.

Then I walked through the street. Much progress, many new buildings. Met Herr Hegeler on the street. He was real surprised to see me. I was to give you his best regards - also from Herr Maenner, by the way. Then I bought your snail plates - every home has just got to have them. (My mother had just sent a letter with an extra 50 DM, so I guess they are really from her). Then I went to Herr Lichtmann's - the junk store. He was glad to see me, also sends many greetings. I must say the Germans are really for you guys over there. It seems they all had the war, and been in the war so they sympathize an awfully lot. He had two beautiful grandmother clocks for $12 each. I might go back to get them on Monday and mail them to the U.S. We could keep one and sell the other. Remember they were $150 in California.

Then I walked up to see Frau Bitzer. She looks like herself, had tears in her eyes. I had to assure her that I would send many regards to you. We had coffee and cake. Then I walked down to where Herr Martinique works. He was real glad to see me. I'll go on Monday to visit Frau Martinique. He drove me to the Flugplatz. I went to the PX, all brand new and beautiful. I had wanted starter fluid and charcoal. They had none. The big blond behind the cosmetics counter recognized me, I didn't buy anything.

Then I tried to mail a letter to you at the APO. The post office has the same colors that you had it painted. Not one sign or one thing had been changed. The damn lieutenant wouldn't let me mail the letter. I was so mad, so I guess it will take longer now. Margarete had an SP4 in her office put it in another envelope and mail it in his name. Crazy Army, with all that's going on, they refuse one silly little letter. I do hope you got all the ones I mailed from Frankfurt and Wiesbaden.

I had wanted to buy steaks for Margarete and I, but the commissary was closed, so I went to sit in the AG's office to wait for Margarete. Lieutenant Colonel Brock is the AG now and going to Vietnam soon. Major Browning came the month we left, right from Vietnam. Your office looked just the same, moved the desk around a little bit and that's all.

Margarete and I walked down the road we used to go up and down twice a day. All the little gardens are so sweet still, and the smell of hay was marvelous. We took the bus, and bought hamburger meat, coals, starter fluid, wine, vegetables, in about 6 different stores. Well, I started the coals, too few, and finally about one hour later we did have a nice barbequed dinner. Margarete will really enjoy the small grill I brought, by the way of Indiana, California, Denmark, and now here. And now, you can buy them in the German stores!

Today I'm going to Rosemarie Molte's. She is driving me to Dettingen, and I just called Lilo Burkhardt and will see them on Sunday. They were very surprised to hear me.

Darling Bill, everyone remembers you with many fond thoughts and I really miss you even more here where we had such good times. Oh, you just have to get home via Europe, but I dare not hope for it. I'll be too disappointed then if you don't come. I hope the days aren't too long for you - my sweets, and I hope life isn't too grueling. I still feel so guilty having it so nice while all these young fellows suffer.

Well honey that is all for today so until tomorrow remember I love you - Elin

P.S. I wouldn't want you to go to all trouble of ordering anything like Jean did. Just seems like too much and it wouldn't be worth it. I just want you to buy things for you, if you can get it. Remember, you don't have a nice stereo. That is about all we really need.

Love again- Elin

Eislingen/Fils, Germany – Sketch by William Walker

Eislingen/Fils, Germany
May 17, 1968

Dear Bill

Today on the news they said there are attacks on Da Nang and fighting in I Corps. I sure hope your base was not hit. I feel silly rattling on about my small doings when things are so tense where you are. I pray for your safety.

Today is a drippy day and cold. Yesterday Rosemarie and I drove to Dettingen. Breyer was closed and we went on to Welzheim. Totsauer wasn't there, his wife was. They have a little girl, 8 months old. She makes four. There were very few things for sale. I bought some cow bells (every house is not complete without some). Then we went by one more junk store and I found a small shelf (gold) for $2.00, and a beer mug for my honey, with a pointed top. We drove on to Schwabisch Gmund. Only Mullers was open. He is in the hospital so we didn't get into the "good" room. That house is 300 years old, and they live in it like they did 300 years ago, fantastic. I got a small porcelain doll for $1.50, and a few small things. We drove over the Hohenstaufen and it was lovely, the sun was out. I had forgotten how lovely it is here.

We went back to Rosemarie's house and I stayed until 10 o'clock at night. They are really a sweet couple, so much on the ball. Their daughter is the most darling girl.

We really had a good time. Rosemarie had never been to most of the places. Now I'm going to mail my package home.

Oh honey I miss you so - and at times I get panicky that something will happen to you, but it won't. Bill I love you, I adore you, I worship you. Keep your spirit up. Four more months - at times it seems short and at times it feels like ages.

Well enough of my small matter for today.

Oceans of love –
Elin

Chu Lai, Vietnam
May 18, 1968

Dear Elin,

I'm wondering if you are still in Germany now - & how the visit to Goppingen went.

I got a nice letter from Kirsten yesterday - also a picture of her in her little kitchen - she looks very svelt.

It's getting hotter every day. I'm going to try to go for a swim during lunch today. Need to exercise. Since in new job don't move around as much, and not as much the same kind of daily pressure so I've put on a few pounds around the middle.

Colonel Quarles was in Saigon for 4 days so I had to fill in at all of the general's briefings this week. He's back now.

They have some Hong Kong tailors here in the PX so I may order a suit & see how it turns out. They start at $35.00 for a tailor-made suit - nice material.

As of now I've got $2,600.00 saved in Soldiers Deposits. Will have $5,350.00 saved when I leave. This, with the other money in the banks will put us in pretty good shape. Also we're scheduled to get another pay raise in July.

Nothing much now - (141 days left)

Miss you - much love
Bill

Eislingen, Germany
May 19, 1968

Dear Bill

Today is Sunday and I just listened to a beautiful sermon on AFN radio. Now they have a jazz mass, real different. It's 9 o'clock. At 11 o'clock Gunther Burkhardt will come to pick me up. Margarete left at 6 o'clock to work in the hospital in Geislingen.

Yesterday Margarete and I spent the day in Stuttgart. We took the train in and went shopping. It all brought so many memories back. Margarete had to have her contact lenses checked. I made arrangements to try once more to see if I can wear contacts. On Wednesday morning I go to Offenburg and then on back to Frankfurt and home.

I didn't realize how much I've missed Europe 'till I'm back. There really are so many nice things here. Oh Bill how I pray you can return this way. You really would enjoy it so much. Anyway, if you don't we'll take next year's vacation over here. It gets cheaper all the time to fly, pretty soon you won't be gone any longer than a Grafenwoehr trip of 3 months. Oh Bill I love you so dearly and deeply. You are my rock in life. I really don't think you have done anything I couldn't admire you for. Yesterday Margarete and I discussed being ladies and gentlemen. I said you were what I think is a gentleman should be. I by the way, don't consider myself a true lady, but I'll get there yet.

I think I'll come on down in July or August again. It depends on what orders you get but then there is so much to do and things to buy, so when I get financially re-couped, I can take one more short trip.

Bill I hope your spirit is high and I hope it's not all too hard for you over there. My heart is with you and with all the soldiers.

Will close for now -

With love –
Elin

Gunther Burkhardt and Elin - Donzdorf, Germany

Elin with Lilo Burkhardt and children

Chu Lai, Vietnam
May 20, 1968

Dear Elin,

I got two letters from you yesterday and one today from Wiesbaden. It must be fun to be seeing all those old friends again. I enjoyed the card too.

I got a long letter from Mother yesterday. Said Jack and Joan had been there for the weekend.

Got to the beach yesterday during lunch hour for a swim. The sea is as placid as a lake now - no surf at all so you can see the tropical fish. I picked up some little "sand pennies" & may try to make something with them.

- later -

Back in the office. After dinner I spent two hours cleaning my hooch area. It was filthy. Cleaned everything out of my wall locker. It's amazing how much junk you accumulate - even here. I'm going to give away, or throw out everything except pictures, papers, & one set of khakis to wear on the plane. Will buy a new wardrobe in Italy from socks on up!

Today was unbearably hot - took 3 cold showers. Tomorrow it's supposed to be 102 F. I drank at least 12 sodas & many glasses of water today. Also am now taking salt tablets. You get very groggy if you don't.

Well I'm going to get an ice cold beer at the club & go to bed.

Love you very much
Bill - 139 days

Mildenhall, England
May 20, 1968

Dear Elin,

For so long I've been meaning to write to you, but alas, I am terrible about "putting off for just one more day."

We arrived in England on Christmas Eve Day after being quarantined Stateside for a week when Erich got the chicken pox. Housing is a problem here so we lived in a hotel until the 8th of February when we finally were assigned quarters.

Merle is on a joint staff assignment so we are at an air base. This base was formerly R.A.F. and is now being leased to the U.S. for Silk Purse Group that Merle is with. His schedule is like nothing we've ever experienced because he's on flight status in this tour. England is not my cup of tea, but it's not all undesirable. And now that the Fungs have orders for Germany, I'm feeling happier.

We hope that you will be able to see your way clear to visiting us. We are at Mildenhall which is not so far from Cambridge, where I could meet you. London is a problem because we have a big car and it's a headache in the traffic over here.

I think of you often, hoping your year is going as quickly as possible for both you and Bill. Please remember us to Bill next time you write, okay? Meantime, give some thought about visiting us before you return to the States. Merle has the first 10 days in August off, and except for a trip to Scotland, perhaps, we're home.

Let us hear from you, Elin.

Love,
Barbara
Major and Mrs. Merle Prinz

Eislingen/Fils, Germany
May 21, 1968

Dear Bill

As I'm writing this I have contact lenses in. I spent all day yesterday in Stuttgart. Had the same man that Kirsten had, fit me with the lenses, and so far they feel real fine. I don't foresee any troubles.   They only cost $56.00, so this was the time to get them if I ever did. They had my old record so it wasn't very hard to do. I ate in the butcher shop where we also had wurst once. Everywhere I go there are so many memories.

I took the slow train back to Goppingen. I remembered how you almost missed getting off the first time you came here. Then I took the bus out to see Frau Martinique. She was real happy to see me, so were the boys. I had brought them coffee and cake. I think that by now I've gained 5 pounds. This diet is heavy.

Well I have to tell you, there is a popular song right now - "When you're all alone and blue, No one to tell your troubles to - Remember me, I'm the one who loves you."   I always think of you when something happens that isn't quite pleasant.

Well tomorrow I go to see Hanna and Martin. Wonder how that will go.

My very deepest kind of love
Elin

Eislingen/Fils, Germany
May 21, 1968

Dear Mother

A quick hello from Germany - I have had an interesting two weeks, and it was very good to see old friends again. This week I go home again and this month is gone. Soon we'll be counting the days. I hope everyone is fine - my best to everyone.

Elin

Eislingen/Fils, Germany
May 22, 1968

Darling -

7:30 in the morning and I'm leaving Goppingen today. Taking the train to Stuttgart and quickly have my eyes checked - I have the contacts in and I'm doing real fine - then on to Offenburg. Hanna sounded real excited on the phone about my coming.

In the news this morning they said they foresee more heavy fighting in I Corps. I get so upset when I hear the news. It doesn't make sense now when peace might come, but I guess each side wants new victories to have a better bargaining position. It looks like the Communists are real busy all around the world. I'm convinced they are behind many of the troubles on college campuses and in big cities.

I pray that nothing will happen to you, please take good care of yourself.

I'll stop quickly in Frankfurt on Thursday the 23rd, and then on home. I'm getting so I'm missing my letters from my honey, but I told Mor not to forward any more. I got several but I hate to have any lost in the mail.

I'll give you a report on the Franks. Herr Haber sends his regards. I stopped at the gas station yesterday on my way walking to the Flugplatz, Then I walked to Eislingen. The old couple with the dogs and small hand wagon still walk that same road, as does the shepherd and his sheep, and the forester dressed in green with his dogs. It was all so familiar.

Margarete says hello.

Much love - I must run.
Elin

Washington, D.C.
May 22, 1968

Dearest Elin & "Sweet Bill!"

It is sometime shocking how quickly time goes when you are involved and busy. I've found this definitely is my best therapy. I'm in my 5th week of my course and still amazed at how little I really do know. I have a part time job lined up in a Nursing Home close to the new house. I may not be as happy there as in the hospital but feel better about being only 5 minutes away from home, than 30 minutes. This will be case through the summer, however, as I intend to start June 1st or 15th. It seems Jean has had more free time (week days - never weekends) since I've become so busy, but he spends it recuperating from his drastic hours and shifts. School work still at a stand still with no hopes of returning in near future. Darn.

He bought a second hand Volvo so we can do all this commuting waiting on license and insurance and we will have reached next "status" level "Two car - Home owner." Ha!

Since we are so committed here, now, I pray for you two to join us. We have such good times together. You must let us know the minute you hear. Now know also the welcome mat will be out in September. As for "tips" - really it's both facts and concession that "money dictates!" Hand on dreams if you know what I mean, I've come to think of it as an investment. It's such a long waiting period before we move that enthusiasm is low right now. But we did save by shopping early as houses went up $2,500 since March.

I'm enclosing $35.09 but wonder if that's adequate for rug and silver. Be sure to keep track so we will be square. I haven't sent Bill a "Deli" box. Does his mother do this? Let me know if he would like it. Our friend doesn't want any food so Yvonne sends him nude pictures. Everyone to their own tastes I always say! She is to go to Hawaii on R&R in June.

I hope Margarete was happy to see you and trip was a success. Did you see Lawyer about accident insurance? (Jean could not buy a V.W. as a second car!!)

Jean wants to know if "Iceland" goat skins - like you bought before are still available. As you know using ours on the purple chair will need a replacement. Let me know and I'll send money.

Love to dear friends,
Mel, Jean & D's

Chu Lai, Vietnam
May 24 1968

Dear Elin,

Received two letters yesterday & one today from Eislingen. I can imagine the nostalgia of going back there with all of the memories & seeing the German friends again. I hope I'll be able to stop there in October. Right now there doesn't seem to be any problem in my returning via Europe. I'll ask for 45 days leave. That will depend on my new assignment (whether it will be 30 or 45 days).

Ned Shivar wrote to me from Naples & they are looking forward to having us stay with them for a few days - which I would like to do. I can get a confirmed flight from Saigon to Karachi Pakistan. From there it is space available & I could end up anywhere but we'll have a pre-arranged meeting place (Spain or Italy) & I'll fly to it wherever I land. So, start thinking about it. I think we should meet in Rome - romantic & I can get a new Italian wardrobe. We may even want to go to Greece.

A lot of the men who worked for me in AG are leaving this month & next. So is my present boss, Lieutenant Colonel Quarles & the CG, so we'll have a lot of new faces & I keep getting shorter. We had a rocket attack the other night . None hit right in our area but a few went right over. A Marine PX down the road got a direct hit & everything was destroyed.

"Charlie" is really stepping up harassment these days - & the talks in Paris don't look at all optimistic.

Did I tell you that I talked to Dan Schneider on the phone every other day? He works in officer assignments in USARV & I have to deal with him all the time.

Colonel Waldie leaves the 198th Brigade for USARV next week. Lieutenant Colonel Trexler left 2 weeks ago. Lots of other rearranging of personnel whom I came over with. I told you Colonel Clarke is in Hawaii right now meeting his wife.

Well honey - miss you terribly - 135 days.

Much love-
Bill

Offenburg, Germany
May 24, 1968

Dear Bill

Writing this from the Franks house. Martin is in England. Hanna and I went to Strasbourg yesterday. It was very nostalgic to be back Rue de la Rapr. Hotel Swisse, the river - the whole experience of being there in 1965 all came back.

I sleep downstairs in the antique shop. This is a wild place, wilder than ever, but one must say there is life here! Opa, saying that the antique business is a funny business; Steffan arriving from his out of forever job - all broke; Danny looking like a Mod teenager and defiant; Raffy - sweet big and quite fresh; the house help; Martin's secretary; and four of Danny's friends. All coming and going.

Yesterday I helped sell antiques. Sold quite a bit. A rich family from Munich here for a funeral, all 12 of them wanted to buy something. Hanna still has nice things and not too expensive. But by now I'm all out of money until 1 June. I guess I'll come back to Germany in August to try to get the money from Maenner, and then I could shop for more old stuff.

It really has done me good to take this trip. Only it seems so short. I didn't realize how much I missed this place until I came back. It really is so lovely and interesting, always something new to look at and I have eaten here like I had never seen food before. The bread is better than I remembered, and the wurst and the rolls and Opa's cakes are divine. He still bakes - he fixes it in his own room.

Well I'll leave here tomorrow or the next day. A short stop in Frankfurt first, and then home. By now

I'm really excited to get news from my love.

Honey if you don't get a decent U.S. assignment such as D.C., NY, SF - or another half way decent neighborhood, please turn anything in the South down.

Also honey, please see if you can buy yourself some nice stereo equipment. We really need that. Gunther has Japanese equipment and it was real nice. I am sure you would be happy with it. It is so high in the States. If you want to tell me how much money you might need, but please don't write checks now as the contact lenses brought the balance way down and next month I have to pay the rest of the car insurance, about $75.00.

Bill I miss you something horribly and pray your life is not too miserable.

I love you dear.
Elin

Frankfurt, Germany
May 26, 1968

Dearest Bill

Today I'm back at Emma and Tom's in Frankfurt. Tomorrow I'll take the 8:11 train and be in Odense by 21:00. I'm ready to go back. I only brought 3 winter things and due to the weather I never got to wear any summer clothes. Needless to say I'm tired of my 3 outfits.

Friday night Hanna and I went to a German movie by a new director. Quite funny and to my surprise I understood most of it. On Thursday Hanna had shown me several gold watches she had on commission. We had a crowd there of 12 people from Munich , all well dressed and all bought a lot. Then Thursday night Steffan came home. Hanna had her purse by her all the time - she said just in case. By Friday morning the most valuable watch had disappeared. Very unpleasant. She questioned all the kids and called Steffan. He had gone back to the town where he works. He said he didn't take it. I wonder & feel he still has his old tendencies.

I left early Saturday and got off in Heidelberg at 9:30 and called Mrs. Dort. She came to get me and I had lunch with her and had a long talk. How she talked. Else said to send you many regards. She too met her husband in Hong Kong and Bangkok when he was in Vietnam. They live on the economy and have no closets, small sink. Had to buy curtain rods, curtains - oh it all brought back memories. She too had problems with the fuses. Remember how I used to blow the fuse if I had the electric frying pan and the hot plate on at the same time (I'm sure you really could care less about all this in your present circumstances - but I'll go on chatting anyway). They see the Polks and Fergusons often. The Ferguson's only son died recently. He had been wounded once in Vietnam, recovered, and was wounded again. He was recovering in Japan and Mrs. Ferguson went to Washington to wait for his arrival at Walter Reed Hospital when all of a sudden he died from pneumonia. I guess it was a big shock to Mrs. Ferguson and they waited to tell her until the General could come from Berlin. So many tragedies in this war.

Colonel James is not scheduled to come to Heidelberg, at least according to Else. A Colonel Robinson is coming in. Colonels Hawkins and Allen are on the full colonel's list. General Shedd is on his way back to Vietnam. I guess working for his second star.

Honey I have gained weight again. I'm afraid I have been wined and dined so on this trip and my old habits are all back. I've eaten this German bread like there is no tomorrow, really.

Then at 3 o'clock on to Frankfurt just to arrive here at 5 o'clock.

Honey I miss you terribly and I love you more than ever. Please take good care of yourself. I have so many dreams about you it seems now that your return is closer, the separation seems harder. I guess I've started to let myself think of when we do this and that. In the beginning that part of my brain I just blocked out. But now, with being down here, you are present in everything and so I dream about all the nice things we will do when you return (quite some dreams some of them - the censors would never allow them really -

but they are interesting movies nonetheless - with the hero being quite a "dream boat"). Love keeps your spirits high - only 4 more months and it will be our 7th wedding anniversary. I have set that as your return date. I don't know if that's right but that is my date for our reunion. I do hope you don't have to spend all of October there. Do you have any idea what your date for rotation is?

I just heard of someone returning to Europe from Vietnam, so maybe you can still come this way. So much to wait for so many things to look forward to.

Love you more and more
Elin

New York, New York
May 27, 1968

Dear Bill,

Sorry I haven't written for a while, but I've been in the midst of moving from my apartment with 5 other girls to a smaller one with just one roommate. What a job! I didn't realize I had accumulated so many things just since I've been in New York. My new roommate is from Kentucky - originally from Germany (somewhere near Stuttgart). We get along just fine. Angela is closer to my own age than the other girls. She will be 21 next month, whereas the other girls were all 18 and 19. Our apartment is really cute, much nicer than the last one. When we get it all fixed up I'll send you some pictures. I want to make some curtains for the living room yet.

I'm doing just fine in my job at Irish. My boss is quitting, however, and is going to work for Piedmont Airlines. He feels he can advance more rapidly with them. He even offered me a job with them at a request from the Station Manager. I would be secretary to the Station Manager at La Guardia Airport, do a little ground hostess work, ticketing, some public relations. It sounds quite interesting. I'd have more prestige than I have now. I really don't know what to do yet. I enjoy working for Irish, but don't know if I'll get much of an opportunity to advance. All the girls in Irish with high positions are Irish. I feel honored that I was asked by my boss anyway. He must think I'm a fairly good secretary.

This coming Saturday I'm going to an art exhibition in Greenwich Village. It will be going on all week long. I'm hoping that I'll find an inexpensive painting for our apartment. Something wild!

Well, I must close now as I'm expecting some girl friends any minute now. Take care and keep well. Write when you get a chance.

All my love,
Joan

Frankfurt, Germany
May 28, 1968

Dear Elin,

Our bed is covered with open suitcases, but before I start packing, I do want to tell you once more how very happy it made Tom and me to have you come and see us. We both felt very flattered that you took the time to stop over in Frankfurt, and we hope that you will do it again in case you come through Frankfurt next August.

It was also so very nice of you to bring along from Denmark that lovely plate of Royal Copenhagen. It's much too pretty to keep inside a china cabinet, and I'd like to figure out some way of hanging it on the wall. This is my only piece of Danish china, and I do appreciate your bringing it very, very much.

Please stay well; give Bill our love, and let us hear from you after June 24th when we expect to be back in Oberursel again.

Much love,
Emma

Odense, Denmark
May 29, 1968

Dear Bill

I have in front of me 8 letters - so let me read each one again and comment as I go. When I returned Monday night at 9 o' clock what a home coming with all this mail. Really hit the jackpot.

April 29:   You said Colonel Clarke admires me, I hope you return the compliments by admiring Mrs. Clarke. She is surely is one of the nicest women I have met in the Army. The work you do sounds interesting. If you see Colonel Hutter again give him my best regards.

May 2: Getting to sit in with the General - Huh - moving up in the world or something? You said I had probably read about the operation there. On the contrary, since the Paris talks started we hear little or no news anymore. Weather sounds terrible. I guess you will appreciate decent cold weather when you get it. You are anxious about your new assignment, so is this "baby" - can't wait. I'm glad you got a new watch - does it look nice? $30, isn't that cheap?

May 5: The camera should be much fun. I surely enjoyed the pictures, especially the one of you and the one of your room. Now I have a better mental picture of your everyday life. Are the circles under you eyes from lack of sleep, over work or from the sun?

May 8: I'm sorry about complaining about the mail. I really do get a lot. It only was held up. I have only good days since. I don't blame you for not feeling creative and uninspired, everyone would get that way under the circumstances. But, you will be back in civilization before too long. Four months or less by the time you get this. Cheer up, I love you.

May 10: Getting the sun every day, I'm sure you must be black. I'm so encouraged to think they are letting some people go home via Europe. We have our fingers crossed that you to get permission, it would mean so much to Mor and Far, they love you so and really miss not seeing us as often anymore stationed even in Europe, I will enjoy that too. In fact more than someplace in the South or some place like Hood.

May 11: The rolls of film arrived and I will turn them in today to have developed, plus my Germany film. Yes, I think you better stay put in Chu Lai too. Saigon sure is not the place to be.

May 18: I can't believe anyone could gain weight in that heat. Could it be the beer? I don't think you will gain too much, but then I gained 8 pounds back during my Germany trip. All the cakes, beer, drinks, good food. And, we exercised to go with it. Also went wild over the bread. Will have to suffer now for the next two months until it's off - darn. Yes darling, do get a suit please. Please get stuff for you. I have gotten so much. You said 141 days left ten days ago. Today it's down to 130. I loved the earrings, look very sophisticated. I would not think of giving them away. Love you dear. I put your picture up - the large one. You only have such circles under your eyes, but it's a good picture. Thank you love.

I will run this to the post office now. More news tomorrow. I too only think of when we will be together again.

Love
Elin

Ridgefield, Connecticut
May 29, 1968

Dear Bill,

How are you. We still haven't seen Jack here. Well it is still far from here to New Hampshire, 4-5 hours.

We almost had a storm here yesterday and today, the little brook in back of our house, has gone way over it's banks 5-6 yards. It looks like the trees grow out of the water.

My mother wrote me that she was very happy to hear that maybe you would go through Europe from Vietnam in the fall? You know she dreams to have the four of us there together, but now Tom has already asked for his vacation in December, January, so we can't come together this time.

A new computer is going in a laboratory that Columbia University has chosen in Irvington, one hour south of here, the company wants Tom to be taking care of it, so we will have to move closer, probably in September. We are looking forward to that, as we will be closer to Manhattan that way, but of course this company changes its mind from one minute to the next, so we will see what happens.

Elin wrote that she is going to take a quick course in sewing at my old school. I think that is a good idea, she is so creative I'm sure she can make some real original outfits.

I wonder how Mike and Kathy are, the baby is almost ½ year, I don't even know the name yet.

Tom is only working in the afternoon these days, it is quite a job he has, sometimes it is almost too good to be real.

We took a ride up the Hudson River last Sunday, it is as beautiful as the Rhine, it really is, I never knew that and it is so close to us here.

Take good care Bill,

Love
Kirsten

Chu Lai, Vietnam
May 30, 1968

Dear Elin.

This week flew - the Colonel got back last night & we were really busy while he was gone. I've been up to my ears in club projects - which is really interesting. We are remodeling our officers' club here & coming up with new drinks named for units in the Division, putting in a new bar & rearranging everything . Will really be a fantastic improvement. Also we are annexing all of the clubs (60 or 70) in Chu Lai into a big open mess system. Quite an undertaking. I'm really enjoying it - good experience for when we get a place.

I had to cash checks for $20.00 to get through the month. Didn't like to do it but they won't clear in the States until this month's $200.00 goes in. I'll send you a money order for the $20.00 after pay day. I bought the Polaroid and the watch out of this month's pay ($90.00) & didn't keep enough to get by on (my laundry bill is now $25.00 - $30.00 a month (clean set of starched fatigues every day. Got to when you are in all these briefings with the generals and Chief of Staff, plus all the commanders come in here to talk. The enlisted men do the same.

I'll probably be going down to Long Binh pretty soon for a liaison visit.

Well, going to get a cold beer & a shower. I guess you're back in Denmark by now. The Franks sound the same as ever - fantastic existence!

Love you very much Honey –
Bill

Odense, Denmark
May 30, 1968

Dear Bill

Sorry about this paper, but since I'm so verbose the thick kind gets to be so expensive to mail. Today it was 50 cents and when it's every day I have decided to start using thin paper.

I'm home watching the house, Far and Mor are at Nina and Poul Erik's for dinner. Next week my parents have been married 30 years on 5 June. On Sunday we have "Pinse" a European holiday.

The weather here was so beautiful as it can only be in Denmark. I arranged my room. It looks not too different from your space. I have a bed and a wall locker. I put your pictures all over the cloth door, but I have a carpet, the sink with hot water and a desk. Also no rats paying visits, and it stays clean. Just think, in a few months you will have me to pick up after you. I hung all the lovely things on the wall that I have been acquiring. Did I tell you I bought a beautiful inlaid wood picture from Heidelberg. It is of flowers, real amazing work. Also today I bought a small copper plate for a wall like my grandparents have. The room is much more livable now that it is painted.

Just wrote Hanna and Margarete, plus paid off the rest of the car insurance, $44.50, the whole bill was only $94.00. We got a $17.00 dividend, so that leave me $164.00 for this month. I really did dry out the old account last month, but I took the trip, got material for the couch, contact lenses, and I feel I did really well. This month I have $70.00 in known expenses, so I'll be just grand. I'll get the couch fixed next month, and my teeth. A man is supposed to come and give me an estimate on fixing up the couch. I hope it is worth it. If it is too much, I won't have it done.

May 31, 1968

Got a letter from you today - sounds dreadfully hot. Yes, do take those salt tablets. Swimming in the sea and looking at tropical fish does sound nice, even if there is a war on. After living two years on the coast, I guess I'll never get you away from the sea, not that I would want to - by now the sea is part of your blood.

I am watching the house again today. It is such lovely weather, I want Mor and Far to take a small trip out in the country.

I hope that you and I will meet in Italy but I hardly dare to dream about it for fear it will flop. Don't tell people about it too much. Remember if one talks a lot about something and it flops, then it is doubly hard to take. The weather here is glorious. Hope you keep your spirits during the heat.

I feel for you my love.
Elin

Nina Wonge Andreason, Mor's Sister
Army Reserve Signal Officer

Odense, Denmark
June 1, 1968

Dear Bill,

My spirit is so lifted since you keep writing that you may return via Europe. I would favor a Rome meeting. I can get there real cheap. Would you want to buy a new car, maybe a small Fiat sports car? They are about $1,545.00, quite snazzy looking. Of course that would depend on the new assignment. If you get Europe again, I have enough furniture here to make a place real cozy. We would only need your wardrobe shipped and the Texas shipment. I'm so excited just thinking about seeing you again, it's unbelievable.

Yesterday I did something that made me very homesick for you. I stripped a chest of drawers (Ha - Ha - had you worried there for a second!), and painted it blue. Also did a chair. I remember the small gold chest in Indianapolis, and the huge monster in California that you did. It just seemed to be something that "we" do. The result is very nice and my "hole" of a room is getting very livable. Today I painted a lamp and an old chair.

Anyway if you get Europe, I have a living room rug, the couch, enough pictures for the walls, this chest I painted, several chairs, and many things from the basement. It would not be the end of the world, even though I would enjoy the U.S. too. It is only so you don't get upset over a Europe tour. You would love it anyway.

An old girl friend of mine, Vibeke, called yesterday. She is home on vacation from the U.S., she lives in L.A. and had lived in Indianapolis at the same time we were there. It really made us mad that we did not know it at the time. She was a good school friend. She is a chiropractor and is now on her second husband. In fact many of my earlier acquaintances are on their second.

Today is a glorious day and I'll miss you as I strip and fix the chair in the back yard.

Hope you are fine and that none of the rockets come in any more – they do worry me.

Bill I love you so, and I'm so happy I'm still on my first.

Love
Elin

Chu Lai, Vietnam
June 4, 1968

Dear Elin,

Haven't written for a few days - things have been pretty hectic since we were all caught up in preparation for the CG's departure (he left yesterday), plus a number of other activities.

On Saturday night I went to the 198th Brigade to attend a cocktail party and dinner for Colonel Waldie, who left yesterday. It was nice to see some of the people again but it's still a lot of the same old bunch. Maybe the new commander will change things. Colonel Waldie asked about you.

On Sunday afternoon we had a reception for the CG in the newly renovated (partly) officers' club. That kept us hopping to get ready in time. It was just the Staff officers and everything went off fine.

I'm going to USARV Headquarters tomorrow for one or two days. Will be dealing primarily with Dan Schneider's section. It will be nice to see him, plus a few others down there who I know.

Yesterday at noon Lieutenant Porta (the club officer) & I went "snorkeling" down at the beach. He bought two sets of fins & snorkels when he was in Manila last week. It was really great, you see a completely different world on the ocean floor. It is especially interesting here because there are a lot of coral rocks with growth on them & all kinds of tropical fish, brightly colored crabs, and shell animals. Just like a huge aquarium. We are going again soon to another location. We'll have to get some snorkels the next time we're near the water.

Later -

What a day, 10 million things going on. I leave for Saigon at noon tomorrow for 3 or 4 days.

Got your letter this afternoon, the first one from Odense. Also got a letter from Kirsten and Nana Williams. Good day.

Honey - love you so much - 124 days left here then we'll start life up again.

Bill

Odense, Denmark
June 4, 1968

Dear Bill

We are now down in the 120th days. When we reach 100 it sure will be down hill.

Today I put the final touches to my room. It is real cute. I painted the walls blue too. Two chairs and my desk, chest of drawers, rearranged the bed and hung the pictures. I feel much better now that it's all fixed up. I spent the last two holidays doing it and was glad for the chance to have work to do. The holidays are the worst to take as everybody is out with their husbands enjoying the good weather.

I also moved the sewing machine to my room, so I'm set to start next week on my sewing course which will last 3 weeks.

Tonight my girlfriend Vibeke comes over. She is married to a Scotch man and lives in L.A. - home on vacation. The weather is glorious and Mor and I are going for a walk. I hope you are fine and not too hot. If you need anything please tell me - OK?

Love you dearly-
Elin

Odense, Denmark
June 6, 1968

Dear Bill

We cried yesterday at the news that Robert Kennedy had been shot. It just seems that the lunatics of this world are getting the better of us. If America doesn't pass an anti-gun law now, I don't know what it will take.

Yesterday also was my parent's 30th wedding anniversary, but we were in no mood for celebrating. We talked about 5 years ago when we were all together at the family party in Ringe. It also rained and thundered, so my parents stayed home. They had planned to take a small trip, but decided against it.

I found two small oval frames -one for an embroidery I made for my parents for a gift. I painted and retouched them in gold. One I'll keep for a small mirror.

Just heard that Kennedy died, we get news constantly and much direct from satellites. One wonders why. We certainly live in violent times, not just in the U.S., all over violence is becoming commonplace rather than the unusual.

I got the films developed. You got some terrific shots of people's backs and others at a parade. If your surroundings are as monotonous as they look, I think I would go stale. Three small pictures of Emma, Tom, and me in the Taunus Mountains, right by where they live, and a shot from here when I had my girlfriends over. Half of my shots from Germany were dark.

Life must go on. Oh my love, how I long to be in your strong arms.

Elin

P.S. No mail came this week, I guess it is held up again.

"Hey, Shorttimer, you're safer over here!"

Cartoon appeared in Southern Cross, Americal Division newspaper

Amsterdam, Holland
June 7, 1968

Dear Major Walker,

Here is a letter as (you know) I promised. After hearing the adventure I went through you probably want to go through CONUS to Europe.

I arrived in Amsterdam on 5 June and still have not gone out. Could be that I'm still a little bit nervous from the last rocket attack I went through in Saigon on 29 May.

I left Saigon on 30 May by a C-141 jet "Embassy Flight." We stopped in Bangkok for two hours. From there we continued flying to New Delhi, India where we spent two nights due to aircraft troubles. From India we flew to Karachi, Pakistan. In Karachi the space required status terminated and the chances of being bumped were great. The temperature there is 120 F. "An undesirable" place. This is the place where my leave started (2 June). As soon as we went out of the aircraft, we rushed into the air terminal to see the Military Airlift Command representative to get manifested on the same flight to Spain. Before Spain we had to stop in Saudi Arabia for refueling. That place was hot too. Due to the trouble in France no transportation could be obtained to Holland nor Germany, but by commercial air or a "Hop." I waited for a "Hop" because commercial air was too expensive with all my bags.

The temperature in New Delhi was 117 F, in Pakistan was 120 F, in Saudi Arabia. I didn't check but it wasn't different from India. Here it is 17 degrees centigrade - Beautiful!

If you can avoid carrying radios, cameras, or very expensive items, do it. You'll be better off if you ship all valuables to your next unit of assignment. Also they check your money when you enter New Delhi and when you leave. You must have receipts if they ask you for them to show in what you spent a great amount.

Right now I can't tell you how easy it will be getting out of Germany to CONUS with dependents, but passing through Rhine Main AFB, I noticed a tremendous number of dependents awaiting transportation for

CONUS. I might have to pay my wife & kid's way to CONUS. I'll let you know how I'll get out of this place when I arrive in CONUS.

Here in Amsterdam, the time goes by fast. But I'm enjoying every minute of it. I'll be here for 10 more days. I'll go to Mexico if possible for a little vacation by my relatives before I report in for duty at Santa Fe, New Mexico.

Well, I can't tell too much more, for I still have much to experience. (I'm surely keeping my wife busy!)

Please give my regards to Mr. Middleton, Sneaky Yates, LTCs Chung and Callahan. Also to Pappy Batts and Capt. Damato. I wish I could mention everybody's name, but please say hello to all the "Good Gang." If you can, please send Capt. Shivar a "Field Can Opener." Something he always wanted and I never got a chance to send him.

My address will be:

> US Army Advisor Group
> (NGUS) New Mexico
> P.O. Box 4277
> Sante Fe, New Mexico

Please drop a line and keep the "old Irishman" posted. Sleep tight and lay low.

Sincerely,
Joe

> Chu Lai, Vietnam
> June 8, 1968

Dear Elin,

Got back from Saigon last night - two wonderful letters waiting for me - love you.

Had a good trip this time. When I arrived at Tan Son Nhut Air Base in Saigon, Dan Schneider had arranged for a jeep to be at the plane to take me to Long Binh. We raced through the city streets - mobs of people, refugees. I was a little uneasy driving through in just a jeep but it was fascinating. I have never seen traffic like it, thousands of people on bicycles & motor bikes, pedicabs, etc. just pouring from all over - people bathing in fountains.

Dan had everything arranged for me at Long Binh - I got lot of coordinating accomplished and it was fun seeing him again. We went to a floor show at the officers' club the first night & the second night went to another club & just reminisced.

Got a flight back in a small plush plane that the generals ride in, terrific ride - plush seats etc.

Things fairly quiet here, except that several of our units have been getting into some bad fights, lost a lot of officers recently.

The news of Bobby Kennedy's death is so shocking. The general comments here are "I don't even want to go back to the U.S. after Vietnam." A lot of men are - I think seriously - looking at Australia.

I got a letter from Captain Amiri, Iran. He wants us to visit him in Tehran. Says he will help us buy a rug. I'd love to - maybe we can meet there in October!?

Give Mor and Far a big hello from me & I send you all of my love and more.

Bill

Odense, Denmark
June 8, 1968

Dear Bill

Got a nice long letter dated 28 May, it had been over a week with no letters so I was real cheered. I'm glad your spirit is all right - soon it will only be 100 days.

I've cried the last few days. I feel as deeply about Kennedy as I would a close personal friend. If I believed in the devil this sure is the devil's work, and now Johnson has appointed a committee to study what is wrong. Committees and study groups lack common sense. All it takes to know what is wrong is human compassion and common sense. If a housewife like me can see what is wrong, how come the biggest men in the country can't. I feel very sad for the whole world that we lost Kennedy. Maybe it was a mad man, but also there are groups in this world out to destroy it. Some are all the way to the left and some to the right. One could disagree with Kennedy, but in a Democracy there has to be room for different viewpoints. The funeral will be on TV today.

I made a rustic blue lamp yesterday. It has a rope shade - never thought I'd get through the tangle.

Kirsten is fine, she is real good about writing. Tom gets a lot of overtime pay so they are doing real fine. They are going to Europe in December for a vacation. I'm sure they are looking forward to that. They also may move in September to Irvington, where Columbia University has bought a computer that will be Tom's responsibility.

Time goes on - life goes on and soon the two greatest lovers will be reunited. I miss you.

Elin

Offenburg, Germany
June 9, 1968

Dear Elin -

Thank you for your letter - and I must apologize for not answering sooner, but life is such that I am simply too knocked out in the evening to think straight.

It did finally get warmer here, which means for me, work down in the storage space. At the moment there is so darn much work - and such which unfortunately does not bring much money. Oh well. I shall be glad when I get the chairs finished.

As far as the items you mention. The pail and dipper is clear but I am a bit confused about the wig box. Do you mean the bottom piece which stood on top of the closet down in the store? You know it has no top. Let me know as soon as possible.

The prices are as follows - the pail   66.   For you 65.
                              the dipper   29.50   25.
                              the hat box 38.   <u>35</u>
                                                      125. DM

As far as the garnets are concerned, I have still reserved them for you. I don't see why they could not be sent together with the other things. There are two other customers seriously interested in them. So please let me know. The price as you know is 60. DM.

Martin was disappointed in not being able to see you and I do hope you manage to be able to come in the summer. I will go to England again for a week on the 1st of July. It is stupid that I have to close the store but I do not know of another way of doing it.

When you write to Bill send him my very best regards and of course give my regards to your parents.

Fondly,
Hanna

Odense, Denmark
June 10, 1968

Dear Bill

Today I got a wonderful letter from you dated 13 May. Unbelievably slow mail, and it had two beautiful pictures of you. They are the best yet, really terrific. I now have your picture on every wall so no matter where I look in the room your smiling face is before me. This last one got framed in a small oval mahogany frame at least 100 years old - real sweet. I found it for 50 cents. Also picked up my small oval gold mirror today - $2, and had my embroidery framed in an old gold frame for my mother. They forgot to put glass on it so now I have to bring it back. I will also have the three horses temple rubbing we bought in Bangkok framed in a double gold job with orange in between. The guys at the shop think I'm crazy, but I know just what I want.

Today was the first day of sewing. We drew patterns. It should be real nice - only 5 in the class. After it is over at 3 o'clock I go to my gym, and am home about 5:30. This month surely will fly.

I called an old girl friend of mine, she was a year ahead of me in the "Studenter Kursus" and guess what - on Saturday they are having their 10th anniversary reunion, and yesterday they called and invited me. It was not my class but I was real well liked among all of them. So needless to say I am excited to see everyone again and find out what they all have done and are up to. The class is only 14 so I knew everyone real well. Did you meet Gunhild? She is married to a teacher, has 3 kids now, and is herself a teacher, and they just bought a farm. The reunion is going to be at their place. How I wish I could show you off. I guess I'll just have to bring pictures.

Enclosed is a letter from your mother. Dear, none of your letters to me have been sad, as she says yours to her are - only one, and I had expected more but instead they are very cheering. I always feel lifted after hearing from you. I know you suffer, many do, and I know you feel for all the men there - I too feel - my heart is often crying for them. Your mother sounds fine, however, which is good. I have yet to hear from Jack, the rascal. The end of your mother's letter, where she mentions that Robert and Ethel Kennedy are expecting their 11th child, is so sad now in view of what happened. I'm trying not to think about it, as I have cried a lot over it. It looks like a plot to Europeans. I talk to so many every day and they all feel it is extremist Americans that do not want progress in integration and erasing poverty. Unless the U.S. solves those two problems they are really in for bigger ones. As I have often said a house divided will fall, and all the talk about the good the U.S. has done, is undone by extremists. The U.S. is not sick, only a small part that does not have enough love to help its own. We are helping all over the world, in God's name, let's help at home first. I feel stronger about this than ever.

In a strange way I'm happy you are in the military. There we are mixed - and I believe many people are learning to live with one another through the military. I hope our generation will show more love and compassion for their fellow mankind than previously. But in light of history these times are peaceful, only through communications does it seem so bad. In the thirties what followed was much worse than these times. It is a good sign that people are so outraged, maybe that reaction will hold the groups back that believe in violence. I still hope we do not bury common sense, it gets pushed in the back so often that people forget to use it.

Only 120 days, it is beginning to be bearable at least for me. I can slowly see the end to our separation. So much good lies ahead of us two - so much good life. I'll be the best wife you ever had, a whole new wife because I do believe I've learned by this year, and I think small things shall not upset me as easily again, but then again I'll still be just as human.

Much love
Elin

Chu Lai, Vietnam
June 11, 1968

Dear Elin,

Got a letter today - the one with Carol's letter enclosed. They really are vagabonds!
Days zip along here. Hot weather continues & getting worse, too hot even to lie out in the sun more than 15-20 minutes. Went to the beach again the other day with snorkels & fins and investigated another area. Very fascinating - lobsters living in shelves in the rocks underwater, all kinds of colorful fish - wish I had an underwater camera.
LTC Quarles had some clothes made through the Hong Kong tailor here - really nice. I think I'll get some made, including some uniforms. They really do a beautiful job, and cheap.
I got a nice letter from Joan. She apparently is doing well in New York City.
Only 118 days — so will go under 100 this month. Anxious for it to be over with.

Love you & miss you. Say hello to Mor and Far.

Bill

Chu Lai, Vietnam
June 12, 1968

Dear Elin,

Another hot day. The heat really takes everything out of you. Yesterday I felt so tired I went to bed at 8:00 P.M. Today I started taking more salt tablets & feel a surge of energy back again. I tried to get an international money order today, but you have to send an application to Washington D.C., etc., etc. (I thought they sold them here) & it would take a couple of months. I'll get a Treasury check to send you the $20.00 I promised. I decided to cut down the amount of money I'm putting in Soldiers Deposits to $450.00 for the last three months & buy $300.00 of clothes (tailor made) from Hong Kong. For that I can get 3 suits, one green uniform, one dress mess uniform (with the short waist jacket with braid) and about 3 or 4 sports outfits (will get a blazer). All beautifully made. Then I'll be ready for civilization again.

If I do go anywhere on leave it will be to Hong Kong to buy things. It all depends if you want some things because I'll get the clothes by mail. LTC Quarles bought $500.00 of things in 3 days, including two wigs for his wife and all kinds of jewelry, handmade shoes to order for $15.00 & $12.00 (the $15 pair were in patent leather for him to wear with formal attire).

After wearing these same green fatigues for 12 months I'm going to come on like a peacock when I get back! At first I was going to get new clothes in Europe but I doubt if I could get prices like in Hong Kong. (Yates is in Hong Kong right now, met his parents there).

The base continues to get rocketed one or two times a week, but none have hit the Division headquarters area since the February attack. B52's bombed the mountain range that rings the base the other day (that's where the VC rocket battalion has been for 5 months). It's 16 miles from here but when the 1,000 pound bombs hit, it was like an earthquake. All buildings rattled, no wonder the North was anxious for us to stop the bombing. The situation in Saigon is not good. The VC are rocketing the city every day with lots of carnage and death. Something's got to give soon. The peace talks appear to be going nowhere. We don't even read about them anymore in the Stars & Stripes.

Thanks for the pictures. I'm sorry mine were all of people's backs! OK - I flunk as a photographer!

Love - miss you - should get my assignment next month, then we can start some plans -

Love –Bill

Odense, Denmark
June 13, 1968

Dear Bill

Back to writing on people's old letters. I feel it does keep you a little better in contact - the bad times referred to in the enclosed letter were when they had to borrow from everyone to make it through. Their friends in England loaned them $1,000 as so did a distant cousin. Please tear this up as there is no need for it to get all over. They seem to be straightened out now, but I did get a long tale about how much they had paid back, etc. I feel that I can help out by buying some antiques, which I will, but I would never lend money.

Today I finished my first dress and wore it to a coffee at Mrs. Rasmussen's. We have weather in the 90s - real nice - everyone complains it's too hot. They don't know what heat is.

I'm minding the Motel. Far and Mor are at Nina and Poul Erik's. Nina bought a $1,000.00 grass mower for her yard. She is a nut. Now she sits and mows the lawn. We have a house full of many interesting visitors from all over Europe. It really is interesting.

Much love and thoughts,
Elin

Enclosed letter:

Offenburg, Germany
April 15, 1968

Dear Elin,

A quickie - your letter was here when we arrived from our trip to England. I was glad to hear from you and about Bill. I can now admit very honestly that I simply did not know how to write two, three months ago when things were really bad, although I wanted to.

I am looking forward to seeing you in May. Not only will we be here in May but I am glued to the joint. Our telephone is up above. We can put you up but unfortunately not in very grand style but I hope that will not deter you.

Love to your parents and sister.
Hanna

Odense, Denmark
June 13, 1968

Dear Mother

Such a long time now since I last wrote. Last week I was simply too depressed by Kennedy's murder to write anybody. I feel there are small groups out to undermine our Democracy - when one looks at the whole world one can get to fear that there is a "master plan" to undermine the whole West. I only hope common sense won't be a casualty too. I do not feel the murders are an outgrowth of life in America. I'm sure it's only an outgrowth of certain "sick" groups. I hope they find out "if" there is anything behind it and "if" there is a connection between the different murders.

The weather here is glorious. Denmark can be so lovely when the sun shines. I keep very busy this month - get up at 6:30 to help with serving breakfast until about 8:30. Then attend sewing school until about 3:00. Then two hours of exercise to get rid of those darn extra pounds. Now that I am sewing, there really is an incentive. I usually sit in the office in the evenings so my parents can get away a little. I feel that keeping busy is the best therapy against loneliness and worries.

We have many interesting people in the house every day - professors, doctors, journalists from Britain, Germany, Holland, America - workers and educated all in one big group. I find it fascinating to talk to them all. Everyone was sad about Kennedy and all feel it is a plot, and all our papers think so too.

By the way, I enjoyed the clipping from the paper about the Americanizaion of the masses in Europe and the intellectuals in the U.S. going European. Quite an acute and correct analysis. I'm sorry I can't mail you clippings from here, as I'm sure you would enjoy to read the comments about the U.S., made in Europe.

I hope you haven't forgotten about the picture of the farm. It has to do with porcelain painting. I can only do it here. I'm not sure I could do anything real nice, but I'd like to try. I made a lamp with the windmill that my grandfather used to have, I painted on it after an old photo. So would like to try something from the other side of the family.

I finished a cotton shirt today and cut out a linen dress. I bought several nice pieces in Thailand. Material was so cheap there and now it really comes in handy.

I often wonder how you are doing all by yourself but I'm confident you lead an active life, maybe even more active now. I hope so, I'm convinced that inactivity is bad for people. My parents look so young and I'm sure it's because they lead an active life. Parents of many of my friends look much older, even though they aren't much older.

This Saturday I'm invited to a ten year reunion of my school, should be interesting to see how everyone has changed. I don't think "life" will have marked anyone yet. We are all still so young. I wrote Bill and said I was only sorry I couldn't "show" him off. I'm sure I have the nicest husband, they just don't come any better.

Give my regards to Uncle Charlie, Mrs. Sternelle, and all the other people I know in Philadelphia. Soon we'll know where Bill gets sent to next. I hope it's one of the coasts of the U.S. Somehow I favor them.

Love Elin

P.S. I have some friends 45 years old who just had their tonsils out. She had it done last year, and he this year. They said it wasn't bad at all. I sometimes think I should have mine out.

Ansgarhus Motel office

Chu Lai, Vietnam
June 15, 1968

Dear Elin,

How's my love this morning? It's 0830 and already about 90 F. Yesterday it was 122 F about 15 miles in from the coast. We're fortunate here by the sea because the sea breeze keeps the temperature down in the low hundreds.

We had a sad accident the other day. A small fixed-wing plane flew into a helicopter carrying one of our battalion commanders (a lieutenant colonel) here in Chu Lai. Also killed were one captain, one lieutenant, two pilots & two enlisted men, and the pilot of the other plane. The battalion commander was a real fine person. I had talked with him several times.

The intensity of the fighting is sporadic but comes on real hot when it does. Saigon is getting rocketed every day, the talks are going nowhere and we seem to be back where we were a long time ago. Very depressing and frustrating.

These last three months are going to be the slowest of the year! I'm ready to pack up now!

Honey - I love you
Bill

Odense, Denmark
June 15, 1968

Dear Bill

Got two letters today, one before and one after your Saigon trip. I would not have liked to drive in an open jeep, I can guarantee you (thanks for the letters, they were very good).

Going snorkeling sounds very fascinating and I'm sure it's good recreation, even if you just get away one hour. It must be nice to get in the water and experience a "new world."

Tonight I go to the ten year party in the country. I'm going to stay the weekend. I'll let you in on my reaction to "youth revisited." The weather is glorious so it should be nice to get to the country.

How did Dan look? Well, I hope. It was nice of Amiri to invite us to Tehran, if I can go there. I'm sure you could. It might just be too expensive to go there. I would rather have some extra money for you to get equipped. Shall I have your mother mail your suit to me? Please answer now, OK. You have very few domestic problems but please attend to this one. Tell me, and I'll ask your mother, or ask her yourself. Anyway, tell me.

I too am looking forward to a normal life again. This year has taught me I have the greatest husband, and we have everything going for us. I also feel we have a sense of what is important in life.

Love you darling-
Elin

Wiesbaden, Germany
June 16, 1968

Dear Elin,

A note only -
First, we want you to know how glad we were to have you here. We really enjoyed you very much. You came at a good time.

Second, thank you for the beautiful plate. I think we've used it every day for something. I just hope it gets back in one piece.

We had a wonderful time in Italy. Rained most of the time, but we were sightseeing anyway. Rome is our favorite city in all of Europe, I think. We saw all of Italy in 2 weeks. Feel like typical American tourists - see Europe in 6 days.

Tim's sister at her last letter was improving, and they seem to think she'll be O.K. - or make it I should say. Her liver is ruined, and she should live for quite a full life if she can stay away from drink.

We fly from Rhein Main the 3rd of July at 2:00. Hold baggage gets packed 25 June (day Bob has a physical at 8:25). Others packed 27 & 28 (day Barbie & I have dentist appointments). Clear quarters on 1 July. There is so much red tape, forms, papers, go to Wiesbaden Air Base, go to Headquarters - run, run; and then all these silly German holidays when everything closes up. This move is not pleasant!

Give our love to Bill, and we say prayers for him each day. Let us know where you're going to be sent - when.

New address: Hqs. SAC, Offut AFB, Nebraska

Come see us if near there.

Love always,
The "5" Buchers

P.S. Give our best to your parents. Guess we won't make Denmark again this tour - next time. Our one car left here Friday, and other one next week. Too much happening too fast. Also our best to your sister & husband when you write. Tell them if they ever want to see the midwest (heaven forbid) come see us.

Chu Lai, Vietnam
June 17, 1968

Dear Elin,

I got a good long letter today - the one with the letters from Joan and mother in it.

18 June –

Never finished this yesterday - got tied up in a project. I'm enclosing a letter from Captain Jaquez who used to work for me. He just returned to Europe through India & and I had asked him to let me know how the trip went. It took him 6 days, as you can read.

I'm getting impatient to get my assignment instructions. A few people who are leaving in October are starting to get theirs.

I have been working a lot on our club annexation - we now have taken in 10 annexes for the NCO/EM clubs (with 25 more to go). Only three so far for the officers' club, but will eventually be 15. It's turning into a big operation.

We've got some new attractions at our club here at the Headquarters. Every Sunday at 6:00 P.M. broil your own steaks, a small buffet (rustic) - and a combo (from the Division band - very good). Mobs of people are coming to it - something different. It's very pleasant to look at the view out over the water & listen to live music. People are looking forward to it. We're also going to get up a bar menu (printed in Tokyo) where we'll name drinks for each unit in the Division - some real exotic (my idea). It's a lot of fun & I'm learning a lot from Sergeant First Class Bagby (the NCO Club Custodian who's been in the club business for 14 years) and Lieutenant Porta.

At the end of this month I'll hit 99 days and will be - as Garni our driver says "a two digit midget!"

I love you love - wish you could see the fabulous evening skies here south of the equator over the South China Sea - could be so romantic.

Love
Bill

Chu Lai, Vietnam
June 17, 1968

Dear Mother,

'Tis a long time (I think) since I've written - can't remember. Had a trip to Saigon since. Flew into Tan Son Nhut and drove through the teeming streets to Long Binh (USARV Headquarters) in a jeep. A little unnerving - lots of refugees & whole blocks where police were flushing out Viet Cong. Saigon's not for me! Got a flight back in a small plane that they use to fly the generals in. Very plush & a delightful flight back along the beautiful Vietnam coast.

The fighting incidents have intensified as the talks drag on. It's all frustrating. The weather is hot. It gets up to 102-103 F every day now here on the coast & inland it's 120-125 F. We are fortunate for a breeze off the ocean, so sleeping is pretty good at night. Also I've been getting a swim in during lunch hour once or twice a week.

I got a nice letter from Joan last week - sounds like New York & her job are very agreeable to her.

I'm going to order some tailor-made clothes from Hong Kong this month. We have a Hong Kong tailor representative here in Chu Lai. My boss just got some and they are beautifully made & extraordinarily inexpensive for the quality.

Well, the weeks are ticking off - soon I'll only have 3 months left. Very anxious to start packing!

Please say hello to everyone for me.

Much love
Bill

Odense, Denmark
June 19, 1968

Dear Bill

Haven't written for several days so I guess it's time to start. I am very involved with my sewing. Finished a suit yesterday. The material was from an old skirt. Today I will finish a plain summer dress, and I'm altering an old thing. I think I'll sew the month of August, too.

We had lovely hot weather yesterday, with thunder. I'm a little sad that I'm not at a lovely Danish beach. But alone, it wouldn't be fun anyway.

The party on Saturday was interesting. The farmhouse that my good friend lives in is out of this world. So much lovely room, and in such a lovely spot. We would love a place like that. The party was rather boring. They have all become too staid in my opinion. Thank heavens we still have a spark. Several certainly let their self importance be known, which I despise.

Must run - I'm in the middle of serving 20 for breakfast.

Love you and miss you.
Elin

Chu Lai, Vietnam
June 20, 1968

Dear Elin,

Got two letters today - I'm getting your letters now in 6-7 days, very good. Going the other way though is still a problem - don't know what route they take. These are some old pictures that my hooch mates took a long time ago.

No orders yet, although some people are getting them. Bob Dove is going to the Presidio of San Francisco! He is going to bring his wife & children there from Italy (after 5 years of carousing). Many people going to D.C. I'm getting itchy feet thinking about it, as I know you are. I'm also excited about the new wardrobe I'm going to order from Hong Kong. Will do that on pay day.

Oh - we get a pay raise starting next month. I get $56.00 more a month. This means back in the States I'll be getting over $11,000.00 a year. Of course here, there's been the extra $100.00 per month. Right now I have $3,150.00 in Soldiers Deposits. Will have $5,000.00 when I leave.

Your sewing course sounds like fun. Another good creative outlet for you.

Say hello to Mor and Far for me.

I love you very much, honey, just waiting to get back to reality again -

Bill

Odense, Denmark
June 20, 1968

Dear Bill

Really hit the jackpot yesterday - got two letters (June 12 & 13) and I was happy to hear that you have started to think about civilian life again, about clothes anyway. I think that it is grand that you are getting new clothes. As far as things for me, I don't need anything. I have half a wig that I never wear. I have loads of clothes, enough jewelry, and shoes I have to try on. So worry about yourself only - OK? I would also like to have little bit of money when we are together. I kind of feel like I have enough things - they aren't that important anyway, so enjoy getting stuff for you, I will enjoy that too.

Mor gave me $20. Is also giving you some money for your birthday, for new clothes, so please don't mail that check - OK?

They say in the papers that July might be bloodier than ever in Vietnam. I pray it won't be too bad. I don't know how you still have energy to keep going, but I admire you tremendously. I love and adore you - and do come on as a peacock - I'll love it!

Elin

Philadelphia, Pennsylvania
June 20, 1968

Dear Bill,

Remember me? I'm sure it has been ages since I last wrote to you but May and June are my hectic school months. In addition, I have been getting involved in my summer school work which began last Thursday. We are doing team teaching throughout the city this summer and I am in a team with five young men - all dynamic and revolutionary in their teaching methods. When I asked when we would schedule basic English review, I was practically laughed out of the room! They think it is old fashioned. If they can prove differently to me, I'll go along! Tomorrow we begin with a movie, "Afro-Negro Culture in Urban areas." Then we separate into small discussion groups. Any written work will be incidental and rise out of the movie. The policy seems to be one of, "Keep the kids cool this summer and off the streets to avoid violence!" If that is what they want, I'll go along with it.

I often wonder if you get all of my letters (Jack didn't) because you do not mention various subjects where I may have asked for your advice or opinion. One such request was Jack's transfer to a nearby base. We went through with all the letters, etc. but it was turned down. At present a colonel became interested and is trying to effect a transfer. The first board suggested a "hardship" discharge but first, I am reluctant to have Jack terminate his tour of duty, and secondly I'm in no mood to file a detailed financial report of the family. If Jack could come home nights, and it becomes necessary to bring Charlie home, I could work things out. He is going to call me tomorrow night to say whether or not his transfer has finally been approved.

Last weekend I went to New York to visit Joan. She has a comfortable apartment and is working in a most delightful area of the city. But what a hectic place to live and how difficult to meet desirable young men! I guess she will stay there at least a year. We had dinner in a delightful French restaurant. There are really hundreds of wonderful places to eat.

Joan came home this weekend but I have not seen much of her. Yesterday she went to the Kutztown Fair with Janice Smith and today she is in Doylestown with a classmate who shared her room in Minneapolis.

As for me, I am doing very little in 94 degree heat. Do you remember how I always perspire on my face in hot weather? Aunt Lillian, my mother, and Michael all had the same affliction. Therefore, when the weather is like this, I do little work. I wondered how you can stand the 100 degree heat you have in Chu Lai.

We read about Saigon and also see very graphic news on the television. How can there be very much left? It seems as though the war is endless. From the latest Paris report, the negotiations are moving very, very slowly and promise to be very lengthy.

Uncle Loren and Uncle Lacey are on their annual fishing trip to Canada. They have promised to bring me fresh pike and bass. Last year they brought me enough for about six dinners! It is so very delicious, and as their wives refuse to clean and prepare fish, Nana Williams and I are the beneficiaries.

Michael must go to W. Virginia for two weeks and Kathleen is coming here for a week with the baby. He is a good baby so I do hope the weather is not too hot in the usual July style. I can remember you with measles in a miserable July and I kept an electric fan under your bed. I gave you and Mike cool sponge baths every hour. You both ran fevers and looked mighty sick. Do you know that you brought home the childhood diseases to Mike from school?

Barbara Carpenter is getting married on July 20th and will move to Kansas City where her husband will be employed. She is very, very thin. Janet has a new boyfriend.

Bob Hamilton invited me to a bachelor dinner last week. He can cook! When his mother comes to visit in mid-July, he wants me to go with them to New York for a day to have dinner and go to Lincoln Center. We shall see.

Well, I must do my lessons and get ready for the morrow.

How many months have you left? Three? I do hope the time goes quietly.

My love always,
Mother

Odense, Denmark
June 21, 1968

Dear Bill

Friday already - this week flew. I am still sewing. I get frustrated at times when things don't come out right, but most of the time I'm very contented with my work.

The weather continues to be nice and I'm only a little bit sorry that I'm not at a beach with my honey, enjoying it. But now we can see the end, can't we.

They say July will be bad in Vietnam. I hope not. Don't go to Saigon unless you really have to. That city is really getting barraged according to the papers.

I have not much to report today. What I do is rather monotonous and when I try to write as often as I do, the pen does dry up in between. Sorry love, but you know I think of you and love you much, even though I can't always write poetic letters.

Love
Elin

Spokane, Washington
June 21, 1968

Dear Elin & Bill,

I simply don't write letters as I'm either too tired from my "farm" work or too depressed from the state of affairs in our country & the world. But I do think about you often & I'm very concerned over your safety, Bill.

This A.M. I got up early. I am dressed and waiting for Evelyn Morgan to come for me. She has asked me to go to their lake home with her for today and tomorrow. I do not like to leave my home for over night with all the break-ins etc. now, but I am going to take this chance & just worry. I need to get away and relax & also just be a lady again. I feel like a farm hand! But my garden, flowers & yard are beautiful & my house too & patio.

It was two years on Friday June 2 since Straus died. I sat all day and watched the Robert Kennedy TV tragedy & got myself in a sorry & self-pity state. At least I've made it for 2 years.

I'm glad you found Joan at home Elin. She said she enjoyed having you there. They finally did get out to Italy & were delighted with all they saw.

How is Kirsten?

Bill, I wish I could talk to you in person about all you've seen & learned over there. Is there any answer or is it too late to stop a Communist takeover all over the world? I for one am willing to work against it all, but oh how many people here are brain-washed & confused & some are dangerous to our country's welfare. It is all shocking.

Do write soon. Bless you both & may you be reunited safely soon.

Much love,
Hazel

                                                        Chu Lai, Vietnam
                                                        June 23, 1968

Dear Elin,

Another Sunday - hot & humid. By the time you get this I'll be down to 99 days. We just had a change of command ceremony. The new commanding general is Major General Gettys, a very large man who is said to have a great propensity for scotch & is an outstanding soldier. He must be, to be given command of the Americal.

Action was a little slower in I Corps this past week, however the North used helicopters the first time near the DMZ as gun ships - also some MIGs. Also I read today that we bombed some military targets above the DMZ for the first time since the Peace Talks began.

Captain Woodard who works in our office, just got back from Saigon this afternoon. He stayed in the city & says the people are in a panic because of the continued rocket attacks. Also, that he saw a lot of the damage, and it wasn't on military targets, but civilian homes, etc.

My boss LTC Quarles, leaves in about 20 days; General Young, who was Assistant Division Commander & has acted as the commander since General Koster left, goes to command the I Corps Support Command, and he is taking Colonel Clarke with him to be his chief of staff. A feather in the cap for Colonel Clarke. Lots of changes. Beery, who went to work in the Casualty Branch when I left the PSD is now a Staff Sergeant E6. He was only a chubby Private First Class one year ago when we started out at Fort Hood.

A lot of things have happened since then. I won't try to assess anything until I can look back in retrospective from another environment.

Honey - I love you. Won't be long now.

Bill

Odense, Denmark
June 23, 1968

Dear Bill

Just read an article about what one's handwriting tells about a person. It's fantastic. You have a good handwriting and only flattering things - well adjusted, imaginative, outgoing, artistic, active, happy, easy to connect with other people, etc. Only good things in your writing. Mine I can't decipher - I'm a bit emotional, but also have some of the good characteristics - outgoing, assertive, imaginative, vital. By the way, you are vital too. Anyway it's quite interesting, wonder if it's always right.

Yesterday I spent $22.00 on cloth for 5 dresses. Now I only hope I'll have time to get them sewn. I must say, sewing each day makes time fly. I just cut a suit out from the Thai material, not the silk. I'll save the silk for when I am a little better. If you have a chance at all to buy nice pieces of material I would like some. For a dress I need 2.50 meters; for a dress with sleeves 4 meters, but don't worry about it. It's only if you suddenly find yourself in Hong Kong. As for other things, I can send for them. The only other things I could think of is perhaps two tablecloths for wedding gifts for Jack and Joan. I have a feeling that both will get married the next year. They are getting to that age. Remember how nice ours are? Not the very expensive - they are too impractical to be real useful, but the white and brown is lovely. If you are getting suits over there, I won't bother about the one in Philly.

I'm sitting watching the Motel, my parents are gone all day to the beach. It is Sct Hans - the mid summer festival when we have big bonfires and burn off the witches. I told this to an English gentleman, who was a guest, and he pointed at his lovely wife and said "We keep ours." He is with Reuters news. Very nice people. I'll be here 10 hours by myself, and I helped do up the rooms today, so Mor gave me a new pair of shoes for the "trouble." They are lightweight and nice. About shoes from Hong Kong - none for me, please. I like to try them on and don't care for expensive shoes. Italy is just as cheap for women's shoes, and more stylish. But you get some for yourself if you want. Remember how they are in the States. Italy is nice for men's shoes also.

I have given up on the Peace Talks. We get so little information. One minute there is talk of a break, the next a stalemate, so now I'll believe something when it is official. All the rumors published in the papers are too flimsy to pin one's hope to. These Sunday afternoons are nice for getting some correspondence out of the way. Now that I am so busy, I find no time for correspondence other than to you during the week. I hope the heat is not too bad. I transferred the Fahrenheit degrees into Celsius and Far wouldn't believe me. He had to check for himself, and they were duly impressed. What brought it up was we had 80 degree heat yesterday, and their was much complaining about the "heat." I told them it was nothing compared to you with 100-130. They thought people died in that kind of heat. That's Vikings for you! (How hot DOES it get there before I stick my neck out too far in this argument?).

This letter just rattles on and on. I miss my honey, but you know that. I only repeat it about 5 times a week.

Love
Elin

SiNCe I MeT YOU I've BeeN LYiNG awaKe NiGHTS WONDER-iNG WHaTs WRONG wiTH Me.

...aND I've FiNaLLY FiGUReD iT OUT!!

Odense, Denmark
June 24, 1968

Dear Bill

Found this card yesterday - and chuckled. What I figured out must be that you are not here. It belongs in the "air mattress times," when I was in Denmark shopping for furniture. It all seems so long ago - with me on the air mattress that always lost air! Our lives have been many things, but never monotonous. When I think back to the things we have done (this year I do think back quite a bit). On the radio, they said yesterday was real bad in Vietnam. Oh how I pray that this war will find its end.

Hurry on home so I can hug you - so I can spoil you real good - and if you don't get enough sleep it will be because we will be too busy!

Love Elin

New York, New York
June 24, 1968

Dear Bill,

Was glad to receive your letter. I received one from Elin about 2 days after yours came. It was great to get both, as no one else has written to me for about 2 months. For one thing, some of my mail has been lost; since I moved the post office mixed up my forwarding address with someone else.

I phoned Kirsten this evening and she may come down to the city this week sometime as Tom is away. If not I will go to Connecticut in a week, if nothing comes up.

Mother spent this past weekend with me in New York. She came up by train and I met her at Penn Station. We went for lunch on Saturday at a downtown small hotel and then came to my apartment to relax for the afternoon. Saturday evening we went downtown with one of my roommates - ate dinner at an exclusive French restaurant (with all the trimmings!) And then went to the movies to see "Prudence and the Pill" ....quite funny! The next day we just sat around being nice and lazy. I took her to Penn Station this morning before going to work. It was great having her here.

I must go home next weekend as my very dear friend whom I met in Minneapolis is coming. She is working in St. Louis for Frontier Airlines as a reservationist. I plan on going out to St. Louis in the fall sometime to visit her. That's one place I haven't seen in the midwest.

I don't know if you remember my friend Judy Knies. She was married 2 weeks ago. It was a shame, as her groom struggled down the aisle on crutches –sprained his ankle playing basketball. What a way to begin their marriage. They didn't even kiss at the altar!

Well Bill, I hope all is going well with you. We're all praying you will get your post in Washington, D.C.

Take care, and keep well

Love,
Joan

Joan in her New York apartment

Philadelphia, Pennsylvania
June 25, 1968

Dear Elin,

As you probably know, this is the busiest time of my school year. From May 1st until the end of June is always hectic. Now I am into the summer program and things are settling down a bit.

Did I tell you that I have been trying to get Jack transferred nearer home? Many letters, phone calls, anxious moments, etc. but so far he is still stationed in New Hampshire. However, it looks as though he may be transferred in the near future.

Last weekend I went to New York by train and spent two days with Joan. We enjoyed a day of sight-seeing and being together. Her new apartment is much better than the other and I trust that her roommate will be better, too. New York is a fabulous city but the rushing of people sort of gets me confused.

Uncle Charlie asked that I bring him paper and a pen. He wanted to write to you, but when I went the next time, he admitted that he couldn't do it. He appreciates your cards and letters. I wish I could take some of those exercise courses with you. I am seriously thinking of going to the Y.W.C.A. this month and take swimming as an exercise. The pounds creep on and then are miserable to get off.

Also, you mention that you are having sewing instruction. That you will never regret and when Bill comes home, he can buy you one of these new beautiful sewing machines that do incredible stitchery, button-holes, etc.

This is the only photo I have of the farm at present. I sent one to Bill when you were in Monterey, if I remember correctly, that was a little better. However this is about the way it looks. It will be wonderful if you can do anything with it. You surely are making beautiful things. I like the gift you sent the baby very much. Michael hung it in their living room.

Speaking of Michael, their home has a problem which has been a headache. The rain (very heavy this year) comes down the hillside carrying soil with it and it goes into their basement. Last week six inches of mud covered the floor! In July, Michael is being sent by his ministerium to West Virginia for two weeks. Kathleen is coming here part of the time with the baby. It will be good to have someone home with me.

Uncle Loren and Uncle Lacey are going to Canada next week to fish. They told me they are going to bring me fresh water fish again and I am delighted. It tastes so good. The strange thing is that their wives refuse to prepare the fish for eating so my brothers divide it between my mother, Rachel, and me!

When I finish this letter, I will visit Charlie, do some shopping for food, and prepare to go out this evening. I do keep busy and have not had many lonely nights. It may be necessary to bring Uncle Charlie home for several months while I do not work, but I'm waiting to see if Jack will be near enough to sleep at home. I worry about the night time when Charlie wanders about and I am asleep. That is when he falls.

Well off I go. I am counting the days until Bill gets home. It seems like such a long time ago that he left.

Love, Mother

P.S. Joan called Kirsten and they plan to meet soon.

                                                                    Odense, Denmark
                                                                    June 26, 1968

Dear Bill

Bingo - today I hit the jackpot - went to get the mail and came home. I had 3 letters from you. Two only took 5 days, unbelievable.   I got the three pictures. I like the one in the mini-bikini. If you roll that down any further you could spare yourself of putting it on! I really think you look sexy, I couldn't look that sexy if I tried. I really like that, but didn't you gain a "tummy?" You look like you have a spare tire. I too am excited about your new wardrobe - please promise not to suck in your stomach when you get measured.

Mor just gave me a measuring tape. On Monday I start cutting off inch by inch of the tape measure - one inch for each day left. 100, 99, 78 etc. I do hope those days will fly.

I'm almost finished with an orange suit in cotton that I've been making. Also making pants to match. Then in August I'll sew again. I really enjoy it. The days fly when one is occupied. This year has really been a productive one for hand work.

I have no plans for July yet. There is no school or exercises due to vacations. Sewing starts up again on August 6, and I may go at least a month, and maybe more, depending on your new assignment. Boy, am I looking forward to that, then we can start making plans.

I have to finish this so I can make it to the post office. I love you and miss you, etc., etc.

Bill, I bought a gift for your birthday, but I'll give it to you in person. It takes too long to mail it to Vietnam. Also it's silly to mail food from here - it would spoil, but will gladly do it if you want something.

Love Elin

Cooling off

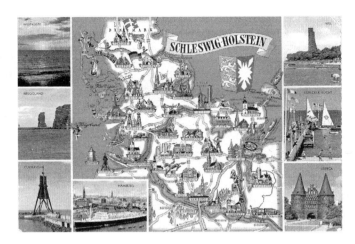

Kiel, Germany
June 26, 1968

Dear Elin!

Best regards from my vacation in Schleswig-Holstein. I enjoy every day of being here. Time is almost too short to get around to see everybody. Arrived in Kiel on 22 June, leave for Goppingen on 29 June. How are you? Do you have good news from Bill? Thank you very much for your long letter of 31 May. I was so busy at home and at the office that I could not answer it. Also many thanks for the nice card and the DM 10. you left upon your departure. You should not have done that. Does Bill know about his new assignment yet?

All the best,
Margarete

Odense, Denmark
June 27, 1968

A drippy day it is - today I finished a pair of yellow, cotton pants, very tight, one can hardly sit in them. I anticipate a further loss of weight. It's been slow since I returned from Bangkok, in fact I weigh exactly what I did then. I hope for 10 pounds off before we meet again. It's kind of good to have a deadline to work towards.

This is strawberry season and our diet consists almost entirely of strawberries. They are not better anywhere as they are here in Denmark. Tomorrow we finish the sewing course with coffee in the afternoon, and at night we have a finish from the exercise course, so will be a busy day.

Disturbing news - the 2nd Viet Cong Division moving down from the North, and the South is being moved. Sounds like too much activity and I'm sure it comes with trouble.

Hope it's not too hot these days my love. Miss you. I have the tape on the wall.

Love
Elin

Ridgefield, Connecticut
June 27, 1968

Dear Bill,

How are you. Joan called me up the other day. She hadn't had a phone before so I hadn't been able to call her, so now maybe she is coming up here next weekend.

We have had so much rain lately, and only a couple of hot days so far, but this attic apartment gets unbearably hot. We have put an air conditioner in the living room so now I feel better about facing the summer. What am I complaining about with the kind of heat you must be having.

We almost had a small party the other day outside on the terrace. We used the grill and had a nice time.

I just finished making a dress out of some material your mother gave to me last November. It is a darling dress and I'll wear it Saturday for the theater. Isn't that nice of your mother. I must write and tell her how it turned out. Tom is in Boston for 5 days. I hope he makes it back for our lesson on Saturday. We are taking our first lesson in horseback riding. There are all these English riding schools around us, so we finally decided to give it a try.

Bill if you can't understand my handwriting it does not matter. What I really want to tell you is that we think about you and miss you.

Kendig helsen
Kirsten and Tom

Tom & Kirsten at home in Connecticut showing off Tom's red Porsche

Chu Lai, Vietnam
June 28, 1968

Dear Elin,

100 Day's Left! That's getting short! We're saying good bye every day now to people we've worked with these 9 months & there is a whole new crew evolving. Still no assignment instructions, but a lot for October are starting to come in, so maybe in July I'll get them. I hope so, so we can start planning.

Tomorrow we're having an awards ceremony with General Twan, Commanding General of the 2nd ARVN Division presenting Vietnamese awards to my boss, LTC Quarles & 5 other departing colonels. So, I have to take his place with the staff on the parade field. We had a rehearsal this afternoon. The heat is miserable when you have to be out moving around. We're all getting heat rash. I've got it in one armpit but I put some salve on it and it's going away.

Nothing much new. Action is a bit lighter this week. Say hello to Mor and Far & thank Mor for the $20.00 (I won't send check).

Love you elskling
Bill

Odense, Denmark
July 1, 1968

Dear Bill

We are over the mark now - all of us are counting days. We had a toast to your 100 days yesterday. Nina & Poul Erik, plus their 3 sons, two daughters-in-law, and 2 grandsons were here to celebrate Far's 55th birthday, which was yesterday. We had a beautiful Danish Cold Table and had an enjoyable evening. Everyone asked me to send many regards to you.

The weather has turned nice again after several rainy days. I just received the enclosed letter from your mother today. It sounds like a good solution to get Jack closer to civilian life again after 4 years of barracks living. He has not written since Bangkok, so I don't know what he thinks about it all. Also enclosed is the only correspondence I've received from the Reverend and Mrs. but I'm sure they are fine. Your mother sounds like she is doing well, the letter seems cheerful enough.

Today I go to the bank and pay a couple of bills and make a budget for the month. I wonder what I'll be up to this month - no schools or anything.

I hope you are fine, not too hot, not too bothered, and I have a feeling the days are creeping. I'm not sure that the last won't be the longest.

Miss you my love.
Elin

Chu Lai, Vietnam
July 3, 1968

Dear Elin,

Got letters yesterday & today. The mail seems to have improved - time wise - lately. We've been real busy - lots of turnover as many people leave in July & we're programming majors and lieutenant colonels into slots, along with working on the clubs annexation - which gets bigger all the time, & a few other projects. It's been fairly quiet recently but things are building up in I Corps & we expect some action.

I ordered some clothes from Hong Kong and I'll get them in 6 weeks. I ordered a set of greens and a mess dress blue uniform. Also two suits - one in green silk & worsted (Continental), the other is an orange & brown weave. Real beautiful material. Then I got a blazer in a black and white weave, with black slacks. The whole bit cost $260.00. All tailor made & good material (the mess dress uniform alone in the States is about $150.00). I may order some more, but may just go with these & pick some things up in Rome.

I have $3,700.00 in Soldiers Deposits now, so we'll be in good shape by October. Still no assignment. Should be soon though. Will be anxious to see your clothes that you are sewing. Sound great!

Well Honey - not much news & too tired to philosophize.

Much love to you.
Bill

Chu Lai, Vietnam
July 5, 1968

Dear Elin,

Another hot, sticky day. I've not really gotten used to the heat, one thing that aggravates me is that when you sweat, your clothes which are washed in the stinky rice paddies, begin to emit odors.

The enclosed picture was taken last night at the opening of our officers' club annex at the Combat Center - a real cozy little club. We had the CG officially open it yesterday afternoon. We have a Filipino sergeant running it & he mixed exotic drinks served in pineapples, etc. Really went over big. Anything different here is really appreciated. Our club system is really building up & the profits are great.

My new boss came in yesterday - he's going on R&R tomorrow. When he gets back LTC Quarles will be departing for the Pentagon.

Haven't heard from anyone recently except from Joan. She said Mother visited her in New York for a weekend, and that either Kirsten was going to visit her in New York or vice versa.

Say hello to Mor and Far -

I love you and can't wait to leave.
Bill

Opening of new officers' club - annex at Combat Center on the beach

Odense, Denmark
July 5, 1968

Dear Bill

I feel so good and tired, I just finished refinishing a seaman's chest for you. I got it yesterday at an auction for $5.00, and I spent 3 hours yesterday and all day today sanding it down and painting the handles. It's very small and solid oak wood. It looks nice. I took all the old screws out and am putting in brass ones. Far says he has to do it right, in fact it almost turned into his project. I remembered the clock that became your project, and since it makes him happy, I'll let him put the new brass in. But it looks nice. They had so many cheap things at the auction - old chairs for $1.00, marble top vanity $5.00. I was absolutely itching to buy more but restrained myself do to the cost of shipping. Until we know where we are going I'll keep quiet.

I would love to pick up an elegant old dining room to replace the table and 4 chairs, but again if you are going to Georgia or something horrible like that, it would just stay here. So hurry and get those orders.

Bill I don't even dare think house - home anymore. I get so homesick for you that I just keep busy each day with no further planning. I'm sure it's worse for you, in fact I know you must just try to think of each day as it comes, but it won't be too much longer now. I keep saying that but — Honey, not too much news from here. Kirsten and Tom are starting to take riding lessons, and she is busy sewing. He is gone a lot, but she keeps busy and they sound happy.

I hope to have a letter from you tomorrow. Keep the spirit up. I love you, love you, love you.

Elin

Odense, Denmark
July 7, 1968

Dear Bill

On Saturday (today is Sunday) I got a letter with the paper. I really enjoyed that, since I get to read so little news from Vietnam. Tonight I'm watching the Motel. Mor & Far are out for dinner with friends. I'm going to start a new embroidery for a guestbook cover. It should be nice. I also bought a small embroidery for your mother, and tomorrow I'll mail that together with a small Royal Doulton figurine I bought in the PX. It's for her birthday in August. I guess I better start wishing you happy 31! Gosh, are we getting on in years dear. I would mail something if I thought it would be there for you to enjoy, but 5 weeks, plus the heat would make most things awful, and if you want some deli items please tell me. You never say that you want anything.

Tomorrow I will also mail a wall rug for the DeNio's. It is really nice, I hope they will like it. It's always difficult to shop for other people. I'm painting a cover for a giant beer bottle guaranteed to be the largest you have ever seen. It has a flip top, and Far got it for me. It holds a gallon and a half. I painted the metal on the case black and I think I'll paint the wood red to match our kitchen. I'm also painting a small coffee grinder. In two weeks I'll attend the auction again. It's really fun and I hope by then to know where we are going. Boy it's getting high time I can hardly wait. Today it is 3 months until our wedding anniversary. Are we going to celebrate it together by then do you think? What is the date you go by?

Bill, I miss you so, and I have little to write about. The real issues of the world are too complex for discussion through letters, but the real important things you know what I think about. In a way, I have learned a lot this year.

Just know a couple walked in from Eislingen. They know all of the people we knew - really fun. The world is small.

Will finish now my love
Elin

Odense, Denmark
July 9, 1968

Dear Bill

Another day almost half done. My tape says 91 to go. Boy these last days might easily become the hardest to take. Took a walk today with the girl from Eislingen and her boy. He is 4 years old and fun. She is 28 and real nice. We will make it to the beach, and different places while she is here.

I have tried to finish this letter for about 5 hours. We have so many reservations and they all haven't shown up yet. Then we have so many others who come to the door looking for rooms and we have to turn them away, quite frustrating.

The weather is fresh and cool, about 60 degrees but really quite nice. I hope it's not too hot for you. Kirsten is suffering in the heat and Tom tells her that you have it worse. They have started horseback riding and love it.

We really are busy today. I wondered if I could ever finish this. I have no other news to report so I finish with my usual

Love you and miss you my sweetheart.
Elin

Odense, Denmark
July 11, 1968

Dear Bill

No letters in a week so I know I'll get one tomorrow. I told the postman that he was a jerk for not having any mail. He laughed.

Yesterday I went to the beach for the first time. Really lovely, too cold for swimming but we got some color. Mrs. Hirt from Eislingen got too much sun. She thinks she is going to die, it was their first trip to the beach and you can't tell people to be careful until they have had too much sun just once.

I really enjoyed the beach and I missed you terribly. I remembered all of our Sundays at Carmel's beach. The weather was such yesterday that I bundled up most of the time. You would have loved it. My tape reads 89 days. Ten days down already from 100.

Today it is raining. We were going to go to the beach but no doing. So will take a walk with Mor instead.

Hope you are all right. Take good care of yourself. Love you dearly, deeply, and at times hurtfully because I miss you so.

Love Elin

Odense, Denmark
July 12, 1968

Dear Bill

Today I went to the Funen Village with the German couple. We saw a fairytale play and had lunch. Very enjoyable. We then drove to Kerteminde to the beach for a short walk. Tonight I'm watching the house. Mor and Far are on a short drive. We have all rooms full and it's now 10 o'clock and everyone is in.

The weather is cool, but nice. Maybe we will go to the beach again tomorrow, it would be fun.

By now I'm going out of my good skin for news about the future assignment. People ask me where we will live since leaving Fort Ord, and are astonished that I don't know. I guess the ways of the military are hard for civilians to understand. Most find it impossible that I can have you in Vietnam, my stuff in California, be in Denmark, and not going all to pieces. But I'm doing fine, thank you, only I must admit I'll be glad when this is all over. I wonder if you know yet. Maybe as I'm writing this your letter is on its way here to me.

Hope all is well, also hope the heat is not getting to you too much. My regards to all there who I know.

Love from Mor & Far, and most importantly, love from little old me.
Elin

Chu Lai, Vietnam
July 13, 1968

Dear Elin,

We had a going away party for Lieutenant Colonel Quarles last night with the whole office, held in a warehouse. Real nice, had lobster tails, fried chicken, charcoal broiled steaks & potato salad. We got some long tables and put some sheets on them, so we all sat down to eat. He enjoyed it, and the men really enjoyed the "luxury" meal.

The new boss comes in tomorrow so we'll be jumping through our tails until he gets oriented, I'm sure.

Nothing very exciting going on here action in the field is fairly light too.

Got a nice letter from Kirsten today - she is very thoughtful.

We have a Korean floor show at the club tonight, so will draw a large crowd. (This is a real skimpy letter, nothing much happening).

Honey I love you, you know. Say hello to Mor and Far.

Bill

Odense, Denmark
July 14, 1968

Dear Darling

Today, Sunday. I went to the beach for 5 hours with a picnic, with the Hirts from Eislingen. It was nice, I went in the water but didn't get all wet, only the legs. I fixed the picnic and coffee and they enjoyed it. Tonight I have invited a guest here for coffee. She is a widow with a 5 year old boy. She lived 15 years in San Francisco. Her husband died 1½ years ago and she just moved back to Denmark. She likes it here and I guess a bit lonely considering that she has been away so long. We should have a nice chat.

I have almost finished embroidering a cover for a guest book. I really enjoy all of my hand work. It makes the evenings go faster. Right now it stays light until 10 o'clock at night, so it doesn't appear as a long evening.

If I want, I'm sure I could go back down to Eislingen in two weeks. We'll see if I do. Boy, am I waiting for mail tomorrow, it's now been 10 days so I should get a whole bunch all at once. I wish you were here to enjoy the Danish summer with me. I love you sweetheart.

Elin

Odense, Denmark
July 15, 1968

Dear Bill

Well at least we have less than three months to go. I still had no mail so I'm a bit worried about you. I realize that it's probably a delay in the mail at Da Nang, but when I don't hear my imagination gets into free play. I'm to say hello and love from Mor and Far.

I am starting a new embroidery, a wall hanging in white wool. I also found a neat brass desk lamp today. Mor liked it so well I just had to let her buy it. She is very excited about some of my finds. I also found an old copper fire bucket, she is now using as an umbrella stand.

A lovely widow, Mrs. Huber who stayed here, lived in San Francisco for 15 years in the neighborhood of the Welters. She invited me to stay with her in Copenhagen, and I'm going to take her up on it, as I know no one else to stay with there. Will probably go sometime next week. It depends on the mail. Also by now you should know where you are going. The waiting is hard, especially when one is named Elin. Bill, I think of you constantly and I love you so. I pray it's not too hard on you but please think of me when you are depressed… I'm with you all the time in my thoughts.

I am enjoying Denmark tremendously. It's so peaceful here and so nice and neat. I do hope you can come for a couple of days, keep cheerful.

Love Elin

Odense, Denmark
July 17, 1968

Dear Bill

Another day with no mail. It's now over 2 weeks. Your last letter was dated 28 June. I'm beside myself for fear you are sick or something. When I get mail I am all right, but this waiting is very hard on the nerves. Pray that it's only a delay in the mail delivery.

The weather is fine again and we are all doing fine here. The house is constantly full of guests so that keeps us jumping. I'm grateful for the work so I don't get moody.

Bill, I miss you so - you are in my thoughts day and night. I hope you didn't have a sunstroke at that parade. It seems strange to have parades in such heat. If I don't have a letter by next Monday, I'll call Jean at DA to see if he can find out if you are all right. This whole thing is silly. By the time you get this I will have had 10 letters, and then you get upset that I complain. I'm not complaining, only very concerned.

I've started a new embroidery and it's a good way to pass the time. Each new stitch brings joy as flowers begin to appear on the cloth where before there was nothing. While doing it, one is too involved to have nice thoughts wander too far off.

This letter should arrive a bit before your birthday. We will have to celebrate it along with our other celebrations, but despite the circumstances I hope you manage to have a happy birthday. Think of how soon your year will be up and that will cheer you. Boy, I wish I could skip over and be with you.

I'm doing gloriously as far as money is concerned. I'll try to save up for my ticket home, but I doubt I can save much. On $200.00 a month not too much is left over at the end of the month. I don't think I have any more bills (insurance, etc.) so I only have to keep my wishes in bound. An old saying goes that to make a man happy don't give him more - things and money take away his wishes and will give him less desires. It really makes sense when one thinks about it.

Bill dear, please try to get the mail through (I know you can't do a thing).

I love you
Elin

Chu Lai, Vietnam
July 18, 1968

Dear Elin,

It's been a few days since I've written - mucho busy here with new boss in. Lieutenant Colonel Beers is a real fine person & will be fun to work for. He has a good sense of humor, which is important over here.

Still no assignment & I am getting frustrated (I know you are too). I put in for my circuitous travel, it has to go to Saigon for approval. Also I am getting visa applications ready for India, Pakistan & Iran (if I can get a hop to Tehran on the way - I will see Captain Amiri & buy a rug). The prospects are exciting. I hope it goes through. I am going to ask for 45 days leave.

Things have been fairly quiet this month, but according to Secretary of Defense Clifford, who spoke in Da Nang today, the North is poising for another big offensive this month or next, with a major attack on Saigon in an effort to gain control of the city. Very frustrating, and there doesn't appear to be any relief in sight at all.

I got a birthday card from Kirsten & Tom & a nice letter. Also got a letter from you yesterday and today. Wish I were enjoying summer in Denmark with you.

Haven't been swimming for at least 3 weeks. Hard to get away now.

Only 80 more days – but the time does go slow now!

Keep the spirits up & know that I love you
Bill

> Odense, Denmark
> July 18, 1968

Darling

A rose for my sweetheart for his birthday. Happy "31"!
We will make a toast to you on that day. By then our days of separation will be down to 70.

Much love you forever
Elin

> Odense, Denmark
> July 18, 1968

Dear Bill

What a day of joy got three letters dated 3, 5, 9 July. Boy am I relieved, now I can go on in my daily jobs. I was beginning to stop wanting to do anything. Love the pictures, and, here you are having gin and tonics, lobster tails, steak and I was worried sick. Last night I had a beautiful dream about you so I knew this morning today I'll get a good letter, and sure enough. Everyone is happy again. Even our regular guests are happy. Everyone was asking "has the mail come yet?" Boy, I just can't wait for those orders. Then I'll get busy with 1000 plans. I'm sure life will pick up from one day to the next. I really look forward to normal married life again. I'll appreciate even your foul moods in the morning, the socks on the floor maybe, and all the ashtray duty perhaps.

I might go to the police station to have my license marked so I can drive myself. Hope this finds you all right. I am so happy to have heard from you and to get the pictures.

Much love
Elin

Chu Lai, Vietnam
20 July 1968

Dear Mother,

About time for a letter – I don't know when I last wrote to you. The days and weeks just roll into one. I enjoyed your letter a week or two ago. Did Uncle Charlie go home? And what about Jack?

Things have slowed down a bit here in I Corps the past few weeks – but everyone is bracing for the expected offensive. There doesn't appear to be any end in sight.

I still haven't gotten my assignment yet. A friend of mine at USARV Headquarters in Saigon called the Pentagon yesterday to see if it had been made yet and it hadn't. So -- I just have to wait. Only 78 days left now.

I am having some clothes made in Hong Kong (we have several Hong Kong tailor representatives in the PX here) – 2 suits, a blazer and two uniforms (one green and one formal). They are comparatively inexpensive and beautifully made. I wasn't planning to take a leave here (we are authorized to take one 7 day leave in addition to R&R), but may change my mind. If I do, I'll probably go to Hong Kong to buy some more clothes in August or September – will see.

Are you going to get any vacation this summer? Joan wrote that she really enjoyed your visit to NYC. She sounds quite happy with her job. I'm sure it's exciting for her to be a "career girl" in the big city.

I have a new boss as of last week – LTC Quarles left for the States and now LTC Beers is the new GI – he had commanded a rifle battalion in Duc Pho – a very fine person and I'm enjoying working with him. Lots of new faces here. Those of us who came over with the 198th Brigade are the "old timers."

Hope you are in good health and spirits. Say hello to U. Charlie, Kathy and Mike – Jack, Joan etc.

Much love,
Bill

Odense, Denmark
July 20, 1968

Dear Bill

I have had some busy days. Yesterday I got Far to drive me out on a wild goose chase to look at an old farmhouse priced at $4,000.00. It was an absolutely adorable thatched roof farmhouse with not one improvement made to it during the last 100 years. All complete with a barn with rats and a yard with a gorgeous old trees. Also an old kitchen with a wood stove. My Far only thought such places were in the Funen Village Museum. He talked and talked against it - all the upkeep etc., etc. I'm sure I could get it for $2,000.00, one acre and all. It sits high on a hilltop in beautiful Danish farm land - a summer retreat. Of course I won't buy, but I sure would love such a country idyll with my honey. But someday my dream will come true.

Then I had tea with Thorkild and his wife Annette. We went to the USA together as American Field Service exchange students. Plus, we sat next to each other in school here. He is getting a Master's in Bio Chemistry this year. She is real nice - kind of looks like Barbara Romans. They invited us to visit them in Copenhagen in October. I really enjoyed talking to them.

Tonight I am going to the circus with the Hirts from Eislingen. We are all fine here. Kirsten writes that she has trouble getting her horse to ride straight - she is a riot!

Love
Elin

Alexandria, Virginia
July 20, 1968
(David's birthday)

Dear Elin,

Rya rug arrived in fine shape, so nice we all love it. There was not another package with the stainless pieces, however it appeared to be shipped from the company so you may have changed your mind about including it.

Working 3 days a week now. Jean still working crazy shifts but hopes to change jobs & return to normal on August 1st. Settle on house and move in August 15th.

Any word from Bill on orders??? Have fingers crossed. Also have package ready to send to him. All D's are fine - a busy summer learning to swim!

Thanks and love,
Mel & Jean

Odense, Denmark
July 21, 1968

Dear Bill

Happy Birthday 31/7

You are not spoiled with letters from me, it is not however a sign of no interest in you but Mor's letters are also my impressions. Yes Bill we think about you every day this year. We understand the seriousness of the risk and are looking forward very much to see you again here. Now most of the time has passed but the last two months can be as unbearable in that climate and under those uncivilized conditions you have to exist under. But as I said before, we are looking forward very much to have you here and for you to have some civil recreation on top of that cursed year.

We often talk about those wonderful trips down to visit you in Goppingen it really was an experience every time we visited you then. Everything here is fine. We have the house almost full every night, so we are all busy. Elin is good about helping (I think she enjoys it) and we are very happy to have her. It is almost like 10 years ago. I get a quiet talk with my big girl now and then. We also have much more free time often take a drive in the evenings and Sunday outings. It is nice to have someone from family look after the shop and Elin is very well qualified with good common sense and very good language ability, so it runs smoothly. I hope you will get this for your 31st birthday. Hjertelig Tillyke, only wish we could "Skale" with you here. I have saved a couple of bottles of the many you have given me previously and they will be saved until you arrive. We are very excited about wishing you welcome again here after October.

Dear Bill thanks for all your kind regards, Christmas gifts as well as all the other gifts you have given us through the year. Best of all though will be to have you come personally here to be with Elin.

Elin will translate this and typewrite this. Receive my and Mor's loving regards with the hope to see you soon. Happy birthday my dear boy.

Your Mother and Father in Denmark.

Bern. Rasmussen

Chu Lai, Vietnam
July 22, 1968

Dear Elin,

Still no assignment, and me with only 76 days left! I thought for sure that I would have it by this time. Just have to wait and see. Nothing new here recently. Job continues to be interesting & I really like my new boss. I never hear from anyone except Kirsten, Joan and my mother occasionally.

Weather still hot & muggy but occasionally we get a cool night breeze. It's all bearable. I got a new PX catalogue. Will order some things right before I leave. Right now I've got to pay off $300.00 in clothes from Hong Kong. I'll order some smaller things to use as gifts.

Next day 23 Jul 68

Never finished this yesterday. Saw an excellent movie (for a change) last night "The President's Analyst' wish you could have watched it with me. A beautiful satire on the American society. I howled.

I talked to Lieutenant Brown (Special Services) today - he said he could get me out on an R&R flight if I wanted to go on leave. If I do it will be August or September. He said if I went to Kuala Lumpur in Malaysia that I could also go to Singapore & Penang - all in the same area. Janie is meeting him in Hong Kong next month.

Later that day

Boy, I just can't get this letter written. Real busy day today now 6:30 P.M. and just leveling off. Today was a welcome relief cloudy & a cool breeze, still is. Good sleeping tonight.

Looks like Charlie is starting to act up again after a long lull. Da Nang got hit last night & Saigon had a terrorist bomb kill & injured a number of Vietnamese.

I'm anxious to see all of your crafts projects. They all sound terrific.

Tell Mor & Far hello.

Love you dearly
Bill

Odense, Denmark
July 23, 1968

Dear Bill

Today the Hirts from Eislingen left, so no more trips to the beach. We spent Sunday on the beach. I have a lovely tan by now. I really love Denmark more than I had realized. I wonder if I will adjust back to some huge American city after this quiet country type living. By now, you really must get those orders - the wait is getting too long.

Yesterday at the auction, I bought an English ceramic table. It weighs a ton and cost $15.00, and an old English pewter teapot for $8.00.

Have you heard what Jack is doing? I haven't heard from him at all, so I often wonder how he is. We still have the house almost full every night so we are really busy. I am beginning to wonder how I'll get all of my junk to the next duty station. If it is not at a harbor town it will be almost impossible, unless we are allowed to have a pick up in Philadelphia, and then ship it from there.

Bill, I so long to talk to my best friend - you. Besides missing a lover I miss my good "buddy." With so many things going on in my head, there are not too many people to really talk to about. If I put them in a letter, you could easily get the wrong idea. So, I'll save all of the things I want to discuss, until I have you "au naturel."

My calendar reads 76 days left, so now we are under 3 months. When I think back at how fast a summer vacation used to go in college, I'm sure these 3 months will go too. By the time you get this it will be 2 months anyway.

I'll finish this letter. Little news anyway. We just live quietly, day by day. I'm trying to save up a bit of money for the trip back but it's not as easy as I thought. Next month I'll have to pay for fixing up the couch.

Love you, miss you.
Elin

Alexandria, Virginia
July 23, 1968

Dear Bill,

It's unbelievable how time flies on this side of the coin. I just hope it's going by half that fast for you.

We have been very busy this summer. Our house is a motel for passing tourists. I'm working part time. Jean still trying to squeeze in a few winks in his 12 hour work days. David has been in summer school still trying to keep up with all our moving about. Des and Dee are taking swim lessons and doing well. "Desse" the dog has grown almost out of the miniature class but still not too big to handle,

We will be moving into our house in about 3 weeks. Or I should say we will start decorating and cleaning and painting, etc.

As I wrote to Elin we have our fingers crossed that you will gain us in the fall. It's not a bad place to live once you make up your mind. You and Elin haven't been spoiled with "past living" either which makes it so hard for most to accept the high cost of living.

Another day gone by. Biggest complaint here is weather. After last year's long winter must complain about summer this year. Blow was for air conditioning to break down in the middle of a "hot spell." Repairs are slow, so should be moved before it's fixed. A good excuse for doing nothing and spending time at the pool.

Love from all the D's.
Mel & Jean

Philadelphia, Pennsylvania
July 23, 1968

Dear Bill,

It seems that I write very infrequently but there hasn't been much of anything to interest you. However, there has been a happening or two so I'll relate them to you. Also, happy birthday! Whether this reaches you on time or whenever it does, I'm sure you know I can never forget

July 31st. That brings up pleasant memories. Next year perhaps we celebrate it together. I'll start wishing.

First happening. Jack is stationed at McGuire Air Base as of last Thursday and will be able to commute from here. He is happy about it and I am certainly happy to have him here most every night. I know that when his time is up he will probably go off again but this year will help me get a perspective of what I can do in the future. He had to sign on for three extra months to get to McGuire.

Second happening. Aunt Rachel is moving to an apartment at Castor and Dyre streets under the former apartment of Bob Hamilton. She must vacate the place she rents in New Jersey within the month and found it most difficult to get anything within her price range. We are all going to help her fix it up as the former tenants left it rather shabby.

Third happening. Joan has been notified that she may not have a job after September 14th with Irish Air Lines. If they don't place her she might come home and get a position with an airline here.

We are hoping you will be stationed somewhere in the Northeast U.S. For the past nine years, you have always been far, far away. Joan and I were talking about it recently and we both wished and wished it would come true.

Do you remember my friend Ina Trethaway who lived in Detroit? She and her husband Charlie were your Dad's and mine closest friends before Aunt Gladys and Uncle Paul. She wrote last week to say she was marrying again (Charlie died three years ago) to a minister, Rev. Leslie Williams, who is taking her to Europe for a honeymoon. Her son, Bill, is a college teacher (art). He was named for your Dad.

We are having intense heat this summer. The thermometer was 95 degrees again today and this is the second week of heat 90 or more. The high humidity in this area compounds the discomfort. Every time I'm hot I try to remember that it is hotter in Vietnam and then I can stand it a little better.

Charlie is the same. His room is air conditioned as is the whole building so that he hasn't felt the heat. Right now he is interested in the baseball games and spends many hours viewing and listening to the men play. The Phillies are in 5th place much to his sorrow.

Do you want me to continue with National Geographic for your birthday? Do you get it there? I told them to send it to you. We are mailing you some salt water taffy. Hope it doesn't take too long to get to you.

My love always,
Mother

P.S. How many days? Did you ever get to meet Maj. Gen. Worely who was killed last week?

Philadelphia, Pennsylvania
July 23, 1968

Dear Elin,

Kirsten telephoned and said she had recently received a letter from you and you were counting 89 days until Bill returns. Of course it is less now. This really has been difficult for both of you and I know you will be overjoyed to have it over.

Jack is home evenings as of last Thursday. He is now stationed at McGuire Air Base, and sad to say, had to extend three months to get there. But he did it without telling me first so I guess he wanted to come nearer to home. Of course I know he wanted to be near Vivian but as of now, they are just good friends. Whether or not, he goes to see her, as it might be something someday anyway. I am keeping quiet about it.

Joan has been given notice that her services may be terminated as of September 14th. She does not seem to be very upset about it and thinks she can easily get another position with another airline. I hope so because she really enjoys this job.

Uncle Charlie is the same. The home is fully air conditioned as it has been 90 degrees or more for two weeks, he has been more comfortable than we have been. Today it was 95 again!

Please give my regards to your parents.

My love,
Mother

Chu Lai, Vietnam
July 24, 1968

Hi Honey,

Just a note - thought you might like to read latest issue of the Division paper. General Gettys is quite a character & really well liked. Big drinker too, really gets with the troops and junior officers. Quite a change from the last commander.

It's raining today all day and cool, a nice relief, first rain in a month. Can't understand why my mail takes so long. Hope you've gotten some by now.

Much love,
Bill

MG Gettys Takes Division Helm

SOUTHERN CROSS
AMERICAL DIVISION

Vol. 1, No.3   CHU LAI, VIETNAM   July, 17 1968

Arrives Here From Pentagon

CHU LAI—MG Charles M. Gettys assumed command of the Americal Div. in June 23 ceremonies at division headquarters here.

The division's fourth commander since it arrived in southern I Corps on April 20, 1967, as Task Force Oregon, MG Gettys formerly held the position of deputy special assistant for strategic mobility in the office of the Joint Chiefs of Staff in Washington.

He replaced BG George H. Young, Jr., who has been named commander of the Da Nang Support Command.

With 82nd Abn.

A holder of the Master Parachutist Badge, MG Gettys has served as a battalion commander, regimental executvie officer, regimental commander and battle group commander within the 82nd Abn. Div. during various stages of his 32-year Army career.

From 1959-1963, he served successively as assistant chief of the Special Warfare Division and assistant chief and chief of the War Plans Division, in the office of the Deputy Chief of Staff for Military Operations in Washington. During this time he was the Army Planner and was active on matters for the Joint Chiefs in conjunction with other service planners.

VIEW CEREMONY—MG Richard G. Stillwell (left), deputy III MAF commander, MG Charles M. Gettys, new Americal commander, and BG George H. Young, Jr. (right), outgoing division commander, watch the activities during the change of command held June 23. (Photo by PFC Michael P. Balwin, 523rd Sig. Bn.)

Limeport, Pennsylvania
July 24, 1968

Dear Bill,

I imagine you are counting the days by now. Would you say that we don't truly realize what war is like over here in the States? I just heard on yesterday's news that the Americal Division was under fire. Does that happen often or just once in a while?

This is really some political year over here. Reviewers say that there is a good chance for the election of a minority candidate who would have the support of only one segment of the country and a minority of the Legislature. Then I'm sure we'd get a lot done in the cities and in the war!

I've just had an exciting two weeks in Morgantown, West Virginia at a Leadership Training School for Clergy. It was held in the West Virginia University. It was also just like seminary in courses. I took a course in Communications, on Instituting Change in the Church, on Rapid Reading Choice, and on Science and Moral Decisions. The latter was really excellent, taught partially by Dr. Lidon Augunstein, a physicist from University of Michigan. He forced us to make various decisions - like he'd give us names of four or five persons with a brief background of each and say which one would you vote for to get the use of a kidney machine - the rest will die. And we would vote; then he would give more information about each! Anyway this type of thing is going on today and will continue especially in light of the genetic revolution. It is really difficult to make these kinds of decisions, yet science is forcing men to make them by their discoveries.

Besides these morning classes the school had many evening sessions, learning a bit about Appalachia - it's poverty and culture. And we got a little "culture" ourselves - saw a production of "The Boyfriend" a funny little musical, and went to the banks of the river in Morgantown to hear the Pittsburgh Wind Symphony perform on a barge. Both of these events were produced by college students and well done.

Church work is going well. I guess. Right now I'm trying to channel some strong feelings that are being expressed by my members about the Union (U.C.C. Luthern) into effective action to dissolve it - either to merge or ban. But that is difficult to do where there are so many personalities involved, and a heritage, and an apparent natural resistance to change.

Kathleen, Jonathan, and I are all doing well. After I returned from West Virginia I couldn't believe how Jonathan had grown - he didn't know me the first day! Kathleen had her first tooth pulled the other day and her first shot of Novocain - she's gotten over it now. (Local Color!)

We all give our love and are anxious to see you again.
Mike

Mike, Kathy and Jonathan Isaac

Odense, Denmark
July 25, 1968

Dear Bill

Everything fine here - lots of guests and still warm. Excited to hear about your orders. The days are slow, but surely moving off my tape. I'm going to an auction today. Bought shoes on sale yesterday for $4.00 - usually $15.

So many nice buys for men too. Suede jackets for under $50, like the one you tried on in Carmel for $100. Would love to buy one for you, but hesitate because of not knowing right size. Save a bit for here, too.

Love you more than ever and have your pictures in each direction in my room.

Write with those orders soon, you hear now. Did I tell you I got a pewter coffee pot and a ceramic table? I have junk to fill a whole container.

Love
Elin

Oberursel/Taunus, Germany
July 25, 1968

Dear Elin,

I just wanted to let you know that we are back in Oberursel safe and sound. Actually, we've already been here a month, but between buying a new car, looking at living room rugs, and doing lots of dull household jobs such as washing blankets, every day has been rather busy. Nothing in life seems to go as smoothly as one would like. We were so sure that by this time we would be riding around in our new Fiat 124, but the factory in Heilbronn is busy right now making changes in their latest model, in order for it to pass American safety standards. As a result, we will have to wait for another six or seven weeks until the car is delivered. We're so happy that the old car still purrs along without giving us too much trouble, so it really doesn't matter too much.

The new rug is proving to be an even bigger headache. I thought we ought to get either a bright red or green, but when we bought samples home and tried to visualize what the room would look like, I began to get cold feet. We finally ended up with two bright Jugoslav runners for the hallway. They are predominately red and look quite pretty, but we may end up with something light (but not bright) for the living room. I've been trying to find the kind of rug you bought in Denmark, but haven't been able to find anything similar to what you described. Perhaps you'd be good enough to tell me again just where it was made.

We keep watching the news reports from Paris, and as always think of Bill when we hear anything about Vietnam, but so far nothing has been very encouraging. And still, it just can't go on forever. People back in the States seem more concerned about racial problems than they do about the war. I was rather shocked by the intensity of the anti Negro feeling that has developed among most of my middle-aged relatives. But it was also noticeable that young people were a great deal more tolerant. There really was a definite cleavage based on the age of the person to whom I was talking.

Tom and I had hoped to spend our last days in New York, but our time was so limited that we decided to stay in Philadelphia. Tom had never been there in his whole life, and I hadn't seen the city since 1940. The weather was just perfect and we had a very good time doing all the touristy things like visiting the Betsy Ross House, Christ Church and Independence Hall. We were especially interested in the Urban Renewal Program and hope it will be completed some day.

Do you remember the discussion we had, Elin, about the fact that only rodents and men "kill their own kind?" I was so sure that similar animals do kill each other sometimes when fighting for the same mate or over food. The other day I found the enclosed article in an old copy of Time, and I wonder if the explanation lies in the word "habitually." In that case both of us were right.

You had so many projects going while you were here, and were planning to do so many more things after you got back to Denmark, that I hope the last two months have gone rather quickly for you. We were so very pleased to hear that Bill just might be able to return via Europe. If he does, you really must stop at our house even if it is just for a few hours. After all the worrying we've done about Bill, I want to give him a big hug and kiss to help welcome him back. So please don't forget us. And do send Bill our love and very best wishes.

Much love to you too,
from Emma & Tom

Elin's note to Bill

I think Emma is so sweet - she really does worry about you Bill. I hope we get to see all of our friends in Germany and here before we go to wherever we are going.

By the way, Kirsten sounds very happy in all her letters. They go horseback riding, and sound like they're having a ball. She sounds well adjusted.

Chu Lai, Vietnam
July 26, 1968

Dear Elin,

Last night we had a little gem of an evening. I got out all of my Danish goodies (akvavit, shrimp. liver paste, herring, red and black caviar, goldwater liquor, etc. Another officer had some Danish & German things.. cheese, etc. & we invited two other officers for a smorebrod. We set a table up in the little barbershop at the club (only private area). Used a sheet for a tablecloth, glasses, etc. I made open faced sandwiches (shrimp & mayonnaise, liver paste & cod roe), then we had the other things as extras on the table, garnished with lettuce. Had the schnaps in the freezer all day - what a treat! The one officer had been in Europe - the other two had never had akvavit before and it was quite an experience for them. We did everything the "right" Danish way including "skoals" (we toasted the King of Denmark and you). We had a very cozy dinner and good conversation and for a moment it was like being back in the world just a moment.

I got your letter today telling about the little farmhouse. Sounded great, why don't you buy it?

We had three days of rain. Today it looks like it's going to clear up & get hot again. Humidity today was 100%.

Love you Honey, only 72 days left.
Bill

Odense, Denmark
July 26, 1968

Dear Bill

Had a wonderful letter from you today - no news except that you are fine. How about writing a letter with news about where we are going - joking of course, I know you are more anxious than me. But boy, they are dragging that out something ridiculous. I'm glad your new boss seems ok and has a good sense of humor. I'm sure that's hard to keep in Vietnam. Hope you still have one left.

I have 72 days left on my tape, but I guess I should count 6 or 7 more until I see you. Everyone told me the last months would go fast. For me they seem slower than ever.

Enclosed is picture of Mrs. Molgard from Iowa. She and her husband had been here every year for the last 12 years. Now he is dead and she traveled alone. She is 72 and drives a small VW - brave, would say. The first time they were here it was 1956 just before I went to California. We have a standing invitation to visit her in Atlantic City. The other old lady in the picture is 93 and from here. Very bright and alert, - amazing, hears and sees well. My dress is my own production.

I had a two hour chat with Thorkild yesterday. He is about to finish his PhD in Bio Chemistry. We had some interesting discussions about the world. The problem of food, for example. The West and other developed countries in more protein from underdeveloped countries than we give back.

In my mind I have a penthouse in San Francisco all decorated and my stuff shipped from here.

Now, if you get orders to Fort Hood I'm ready for either a divorce or a fit. I guess I'd stick with a fit, but honestly you'd honestly better not get someplace like that. If you get Florida, I have outfitted a dream boat. Even New York would not stump me. I would start a shop there.

Enough of my rattling. I won't close this in the traditional "I love you" manner. One should be able to be more original so how about "I adore you."

Life goes on in its usual rhythm - no ups, no downs, and we continue to be full every night - the Motel, that is.

See you soon "my buddy"
Elin

Chu Lai, Vietnam
July 30, 1968

Dear Elin,

Thank you for the card & letter - also Far for his very wonderful letter which I really appreciated getting. A very wonderful family I have in Denmark. We've been real busy this week, still no orders yet - very frustrating. Hopefully I'll hear something soon.

It's miserably humid this week - clothes stink, etc. Well, we got a pay raise this month $47.00. I am now making, in Vietnam, $1,028.00 a month. In the States it will be $933.00.

Am enclosing letters from Mother and Margarete. First word on Jack in a long time. I should be getting my suits from Hong Kong in two weeks. I'm anxious to see how they turn out.

Well Darling - not much news except that I'm anxious as hell to wrap up these last two months.

Much love
Bill

Odense, Denmark
July 30, 1968

Darling

Had a good letter from you today & was sure it would have "news" in it as to our next station, but alas our patience is being tested once more. I'm still glad that you have your job and that you have a nice boss. Somehow that does make things easier. I pray there won' be any terrible attacks anymore. I get panicky at the thought. If I were you I think I would get away for a short R&R, but only you know if you could afford it. I got a $27.00 insurance bill, my $30.00 school fee, $100.00 for the couch refinishing, so August is pretty tight bankwise. But if you go I'll leave a small amount balance so you could get $10.00 or $20.00 at the end of the month when you return. I would do anything for you, but please tell me right away, as I work on a small balance. I'm afraid I won't have enough saved for October, but I do conserve as much as possible. Money, at least, is no problem at all.

We had glorious days. I went to the beach yesterday. Drove with two American kids newly married and traveling through Europe since January. We had a good day until we got back into town and the gears locked up on me in a crossing. Boy how embarrassing. Had to call for a mechanic, but got them unlocked before he got there. But anyway that happened the very first time I borrowed the car. It must have been fate. I doubt I'll borrow it again.

We have many interesting guests. Some from Sydney, Australia, English, Germans, three from Egypt (they have wares to sell), but not bargains. I guess one has to bargain typical.

I hesitated to go to Copenhagen, because I kept wanting to hear about those orders. I guess I'll just go and get that over with. I'm down to 69 days, so time does move along. Mor said to tell you that tomorrow we will celebrate your birthday, and intently think of you. So if you feel pulled toward a strange planet it's just us from here, my dear.

Love
Elin

Ridgefield, Connecticut
July 31, 1968

Dear Bill,

A quick note to tell you that we meant for you to have this package today on your birthday, and it looks like it will be a little late, but we hope you will enjoy it the same. We tried to pick things that wouldn't go bad in the heat,

Elin is keeping us posted on how many days are left before she and you are back, almost two months now.

Hope you get this package all right.

Kirsten & Tom

Odense, Denmark
July 31, 1968

Dear Bill

Happy Birthday to you - Happy Birthday to you, so sorry we can't celebrate together.

Today I went to sales in town. Got a black corduroy suit for $10.00, one dress for $10.00, a black dinner dress for $5.00, and one in between for $12.00. Tomorrow I might get a real neat cocktail suit for $15.00. There goes my trip to Copenhagen. I would rather go with you anyway.

Tonight I'm going to Odense's Tivoli with two grad students from Cambridge, Massachusetts. I haven't been there yet and waited for a chance to go. The weather is absolutely glorious these days. The Motel is full so I am busy every morning.

I feel silly telling you about such stupid things as clothes, etc, etc. I really have many other things on my mind, but they are too deep and too complicated to discuss in letters. So, we just have to wait to have some real fun discussions. Can't wait to tell you. So much happening in this world of ours, so much to get involved in.

Love you – Elin

Downtown Odense

Odense, Denmark
August 1, 1968

Dear Bill

Well, you are now 31. I had two letters today - one was real fat and I was sure it had "news" in it, but alas, it was the paper and one had a picture. I loved both, really. Only by now I really thought I would get news of new station, and that you would get orders for your birthday.

Showed the two girls, Joan and Judy from Cambridge, Massachusetts, the town today. One comes from a resort hotel in New Hampshire, a "small" place consisting of 7,000 acres of hunting grounds, 5 small lakes, golf course, etc., and she is staying with her girlfriend in one of our small rooms for $4.00 a night. I have no complaints about it, and we will go to the beach tomorrow. We have an open invitation to drop in if we are ever in New England.

Went to the auction today, and got some old frames and an Egyptian piece of jewelry - old - the kind that is very "in" this year, hippy looking. I paid $2.50 for it so it was a good bargain. I'm not buying any more big things as I don't know how far we'll have to transport them.

Boy, I miss you something real bad. I dare not think about October because then the days will go too slow. I just muddle about each day. We are really busy here so we do keep active, and the weather is so lovely that it's hard to be too depressed. We hear little or nothing from Paris. I do hope they get going before too long. Seems like North Vietnam would realize they would be better off to negotiate than fight.

I love you dearly. I'm to send love from Mor and Far.

Love
Elin

Chu Lai, Vietnam
August 2, 1968

Dear Elin,

Got a nice long letter today with the picture. No exciting news from here. No word on assignment yet (there are a lot of other people in the same boat). Have been real busy in the office & the time goes fast - not fast enough though.

Well, yesterday we finally got authorization to hire hooch maids - something we'd (G1) had been working on for four months. Everyone was waiting for some luscious Asiatic beauties to make our beds & polish our shoes, well they came. In mine is an old MamaSan, about 60, no teeth & gumming betel nuts! The rest are about the same. They were all over the BOQ area today, walking into the showers & latrines really hilarious. Someone hired one for the General and he didn't know it. He went to his house at lunch time opened the door and the maid was sitting in the middle of the floor. "Who the hell put her there!!" could loudly be heard. Anyway, my area is clean for the first time in ages - glad to have someone pick up after sloppy me.

We're going to get a new thatched roof put on the officers' club. The present one has started to collapse. We got a Vietnamese contractor and he's going to start next week. Will take 20 days. He'll put in a larger, higher and nicer roof than the present one. Lieutenant Porta, the Club Officer, is going to Manila next week to arrange for the shipment of the Rattan furniture we ordered two months ago and is now ready. The bar has been completely refurbished and with the furniture and new roof will look great. Hope to get some glass fishing balls, jazzy lights, etc. to hang from the ceiling.

Well Honey love you. Only 65 days. See you month after next.

Much love & kisses & hugs- Bill

Odense, Denmark
August 2, 1968

Dear Bill

I've just sat here looking at all the pictures you have mailed me. I think I know every detail by now down to every freckle. I really love those pictures.

Sometimes I worry that I say something in my letters that you may misunderstand. Believe me, I have no complaints. I feel very close to you. I have gained much from this whole experience, and you are always in my prayers. I'm sure it's teaching you many things too, so don't ever look at it as a wasted year. Also, I feel that in the big picture of the world, the effects of Vietnam will pay off maybe more outside than right there. I'm sure it has had a needed deterrent effect on other Communist countries' filtration ambitions. At least that's how it looks. The importance of what's being done might be greater outside than inside Vietnam, sad to say, for those poor people who have suffered so.

My calendar reads 66. I guess yours does too. You always seem to be a couple of days ahead of me. Bill, if you come to Europe I would consider getting two Euro Rail passes, because we would really see more that way for less money. But it is really a little hard planning when I don't know where we are going. Two months cost $180.00, one month $110.00, and that is good all over Europe, except England (where we wouldn't go anyway).

How about it? Please let me know what you think tentatively so that I can start finding out about getting them. Jack could buy them for us, I'm sure - or Kirsten. I would just as well take the train as drive, it's less tiring, especially for you, and also we don't have a car here. One round trip to Rome is $100.00, so that one trip and everything else is gravy. What do you think? I need your passport number so please send it to me, that has to go on the ticket, so send it even though you don't know if you can come here. I'll have it just in case.

We got the last trip planned despite slow mail. I guess we will get this one planned too. You can count on me, I'll figure something out, only need to say where.

Love you deeply, sweety, etc., etc., etc.

Love
Elin

Odense, Denmark
August 3, 1968

Dear Bill

It's Saturday night and Mor and Far are visiting Nina and Poul Erik. I'm glad they get to go out a bit this summer. I always tell them to go as much as they want since I know they are tied down normally.

I had a wonderful letter from you today telling about the Smorgasbord. I'm so glad you enjoyed the goodies. Only sorry that's so hard to not say that it's almost impossible to get things from here to there now, that there is no point in mailing any more stuff. I got a box from Hong Kong today. It was one and a half months underway. I had ordered a petit point purse and it is really lovely. It is from a firm that is all right. I wouldn't order from that place that has been in the Stars and Stripes as a Communist front. But as long as the GI can go to Hong Kong on leave, I can spend $15.00 on a purse from there. It's very nice and I like it.

I enclose a clipping from Newsweek, because there are a couple of sentences in it that had me chuckling. I recall a lieutenant I knew who many years ago (at least 3) had an opinion that now is the lesson of Vietnam as seen by the second highest man in the nation. At times I don't think small people have a lack of common sense as might at times be assumed. I know you will recall the discussion.

Today I got that cocktail suit in all silver, in preparation for becoming "the wife" again. I really need something for evenings, so I figure I better get slowly ready for "normal" life again. I have been out three times in the evening this year. The celebrations when finishing school, and with my parents New Years Eve. I am totally unaccustomed to drinking anything harder than diet cola, so I feel I'll stay away from all alcohol in the future as it really puts on the pounds. I feel better when I don't drink. When I just have one I get like an allergy and really feel lousy.

I sun bathed today. The weather is still unbelievably nice. Last night the two girls, Joan and Judy, took me to dinner. We went to the beach that afternoon. One girl lives in an ultramodern home. When she described the house to me, I said that it sounded like something I had seen in House Beautiful. She almost died because that's the one it was! (Remember the one with the marble dining room table and slab floor?). We are invited to see it if we ever come to Long Island. Have you ever heard of the "Lake Tarleton Club" - I haven't but anyway we are invited there too.

Soon we only have two months. Are you sure they haven't lost your orders or something. I find it unusual that you haven't gotten orders yet. What about the other guys, have they heard? This is a crazy question because by the time you get this letter the question will have no relevance.

Next week I start my sewing course again so then time should really fly. Then I run my butt off for hooks, zippers, lining, etc. and will hardly have time to think. A very nice state of affairs under the circumstances. I'm sure you keep busy too. Just got to, and don't you get low now toward the end - promise. You really have done great, at least to judge from your letters. Never once a complaint. I'm really proud of my honey.

I just talked to an Egyptian guest who is staying here. They have wares for sale and she is telling me about how hard it is for thinking people to live under Nasser's rule. They think he is mad, and see their future as quite black. Denmark to them, is like a paradise. So many people live under impossible circumstances. One should be grateful for being free really, truly. They were only able to take 5 English pounds out of Egypt. They are teachers in agriculture, and they are here on a teacher exchange deal.

Well, I have not too much more to say tonight so I'll close for now.

Love Elin

HUBERT H. HUMPHREY: 'I MAKE NO APOLOGIES'

Of all the current candidates, Vice President Hubert Humphrey certainly enjoys the least freedom of movement—he is boxed in between loyalty and independence, between the past and the future, between the left and the right. But as he resumed his campaign last week after a bout of flu, Humphrey was talking almost as if none of these predicaments even existed. In midweek, the Vice President spent two hours with the editors of NEWSWEEK, discussing the Johnson Administration, Vietnam and the campaign. Some excerpts:

ON THE JOHNSON PRESIDENCY

I am not apologizing for our war upon poverty. We never had one until this Administration. I am not going to apologize for Project Head Start. I am not going to apologize for the aid to education that we have given to the millions of college students who received loans and scholarships and who never had a chance to go to college in my time. I am not going to apologize for an Administration that has done more for consumer protection than all the government administrations have done in the past. I am sure not going to repudiate what we have done in the field of civil rights. No Administration has ever done this much.

What we have done in these vast areas of social development at home is something to be proud of. Regrettably, they have been lost in the smoke, the smog, in the debates and charges and counter-charges of Vietnam. I believe history will judge President Johnson's Administration well . . .

I am going to take this message to the people, but I am not going to say that it is enough. This is what we have done yesterday. What I am going to talk about is what we can do for tomorrow.

ON THE LESSONS OF VIETNAM

One thing we learned is that the kind of military assistance that we started out to give to South Vietnam was totally unrelated to the problems of their security. We were training the South Vietnamese Army as if it were the army of Belgium, to fight on the plains or fields of Flanders, rather than . . . for the kind of infiltration and jungle warfare and guerrilla warfare which has come to be the pattern and the obvious facts of war in Vietnam.

Second, we gave it poor equipment. We gave castoffs. Only within the last year has that army been receiving the kind of equipment that was related to its security needs and its defense needs.

More importantly, we have always underestimated in our assistance programs overseas the necessity for political development, and the relationship of political development to economic assistance and military assistance. We have had a tend-

Humphrey in New York: 'Sort of old hat' but very much in the ring

ency—this is true not only of this present Administration or of any one in particular, but of all of us—we have had a tendency to think if you plow in the money that you can develop an economy . . . We didn't even help them develop political parties. We never even preached the necessity of it. We said that it was more or less their responsibility.

ON DE-ESCALATION

I am in favor of not only de-escalating the war, but . . . a cease-fire on both sides . . . I can make a very good speech about some of the possibilities of de-escalation on a unilateral basis, but I happen to know that that would not be of assistance to the men who are trying to get us peace in Paris. I think it would be a very detrimental thing.

If it means that I have to restrain myself as a candidate rather than trying to appeal to the popular view, then I will just have to do that. I will have to make that kind of sacrifice . . . I make no apologies in saying that I believe that one of my prime responsibilities was to try to be a loyal supporter of the Administration policy—once that policy had been arrived at—particularly if I did not have fundamental disagreement with it. I do not fundamentally disagree with the resistance of aggression in the north, our policy in Vietnam.

ON CAMPAIGN FINANCES

The financing of these campaigns for big offices and even lesser offices is getting to be a very, very serious matter. I think it is going to be the responsibility of you and myself in public life to try to do something about it. This business of panhandling around, of trying to raise the money that is necessary to conduct a

national campaign with unbelievable costs, is somewhat degrading.

ON 1968 POLITICS

What I have seen of the new politics is not very new . . . breaking up meetings, chanting, sign-carrying, walking out, being dogmatic, unwilling to listen, demanding an open convention when you have a closed mind. I don't consider that new politics. That is . . . as old as bigotry . . . itself . . . Storm troopers are storm troopers wherever you find them . . .

I believe that a very large element of the McCarthy supporters, an element of reason and tolerance, would be able to take a platform plank that would be designed by the Democratic convention. It would not repudiate the President . . . and would point to the future . . .

[But] there may very well be four parties in this election. We had that in 1948. It is not too dissimilar . . . Henry Wallace was a sort of poetical, kind, sweet, good Christian gentleman. He was a very fine man, and he had many, many people following him . . . Then there was another candidate—his name was Strom Thurmond, and he led the forces of segregation. We have got one like that and his name is Wallace.

Then there were two others, and neither one of them was looked upon as very good. They didn't enthuse people, and they were rather uninspiring. They were sort of old hat. They kind of had been worked over. One of them was Governor Dewey and one of them was Harry Truman. You know, Mr. Truman, that fellow that didn't enthuse anybody, that old hat—all he had was some twenty years of experience—he won that election. I kind of intend to follow in his footsteps.

Newsweek article – Summer 1968

Omaha, Nebraska
August 4, 1968

Dear Elin,

We finally arrived in Omaha, ugh. Saw the old house I lived in, the first house Tim & I had etc. etc. We saw all the first two days now I'm ready to go.

Houses are a riot. $35,000. is where they start, ones we're interested in. If this were California or out West we'd sink $35,000, but don't want to get tied down to Bellevue, Nebraska. Base housing is terrible, crowded, small, etc. etc. We are #2 on the list & should be in by 3-4 weeks. Schools are good. Going to buy a carpet etc. etc. to fix up the crummy quarters.

Lived in a motel 2 weeks, now moved into a small 2 bedroom apartment so we can cook. Motel was $17 a day plus all meals out. This is only $250 a month plus $88 to buy 5 pillows, 5 sets of sheets, 5 towels. Family Service is all out of everything except 6 plastic dishes & glasses. We bought a color TV yesterday. It's really fun to watch.

Haven't seen any riots. Everything seems quite calm on the home front. Tim's sister looks good considering. The Dr. said she'd be O.K. and live a long, normal life if she never drinks. Now, hope they can do this.

Let us know where you're going. More when I get going. More when I get settled (mentally settled too). All our love to Bill & your folks.

Love,
Buchers 5

Beth, Bill, Bob Bucher on a visit to the Ansgarhus Motel

Chu Lai, Vietnam
August 5, 1968

Dear Elin,

Received a nice long letter from you today, the one with Emma's & Mother's letters enclosed. Also a birthday card from Joan.

No orders yet.

It's been very humid. At night you get soaked through unless you sit in front of a fan.

This is what I plan to order before leaving in addition to the clothes (which are $260) - about $200 for things from the Japan catalog including a punch bowl, screen, double serving chafing serving dish & some odds and ends. Also I found a composite stereo set made in the U.S. & is $100 cheaper if I order it here. The tuner, turntable etc. are all compact. It has an FM/AM tuner, and a stereo cassette control which lets you either play, tape or record on it from a record or FM/AM radio with the flick of a button. Also comes with two separate speakers - $360. Delivered from New York. Very good firm and excellent equipment. If I order that, I'll pay for it & the stuff from Japan from advance pay in September.

I think I'll take a 5 day leave in September to Penang. Lieutenant Brown can get me on an R&R flight - it won't cost much and I'll just sleep late and be on the beach to get conditioned to leave. I really need a change of pace. I'll have enough money.

Honey I love you and miss you - only 62 days left.....

Bill

Odense, Denmark
August 6, 1968

Dear Bill

Today is another beautiful hot sunny day, I started my sewing course. Not much ambition in this kind of weather.

No mail today. I'm so excited every day for orders, but I expect that with the trouble around Da Nang it might be a week before I get news. I'll be all right. I already inquired about sending my things, and it is $27.50 per cubic meter. So I can probably get it all sent for $100 to $150. Not too bad, that is if we get to a coastal city. Otherwise, I guess I can't ship it. Only two more months to go. Boy, I'm really beginning look forward to a normal life again.

This is a short note during my lunch break. I only felt like writing you to tell you about my deep love. I always think of you.

Love Elin

Spokane, Washington
August 6, 1968

Dear Bill & Elin,

Your safety is on my mind so very much, Bill. I've been so very depressed & worried over the breakdown of everything in our country that I think it best not to write letters and spread my gloom, so I just work myself to exhaustion & then go to read. It frightens me to see the Communist undermining of everything and then so many, like Methodists & Presbyterians & some others, working blindly to help them - being misled by the World Council of Churches, etc.

Elin, I'm so glad you got to visit the Buchers. They enjoyed it so much. Did you enjoy all of your stay in Germany? The Buchers enjoyed their trip to Italy and then had the ordeal of packing & the farewells. They arrived in New Jersey and had to stay with Tim's mother until July 20 awaiting arrival of their second car. They are now in Omaha. We've talked on the phone several times , but I'll not see them until November. I'm cochair of our church bazaar in November.

My yard and garden are beautiful. I've just painted the outside of my fence.

Much love,
Hazel

Chu Lai, Vietnam
August 7, 1968

Dear Elin,

Boy, I had a surprise about an hour ago. Jean DeNio called me from Washington. He said he had checked with DA on my assignment - the officer responsible had my file on his desk. Nothing turned up yet, but it will probably be D.C. He said he was still determining exact assignments and that they would have it firm by the end of next week. Jean will let me know via USARV (he calls them every day). Also said he would write to you.

Well, anyway I'm all excited to find out for sure. I think D.C. would be exciting even if it's a rat race, but we'll get involved in all kinds of things. Won't speculate anymore until I get the final word. I'm really glad that Jean called because it will probably be September before actual orders come in. Jean said he will get a new job this month, and that they start moving into new house next week - are taking two weeks leave in between jobs.

Things are the same here but it looks like another NVA build up is imminent. It's been too quiet.

Honey I love you. Only 60 days left, it's going fast.

Bill

Odense, Denmark
August 8, 1968

Dear Bill

Yesterday I was so happy because I am so explosive – fantastic - overjoyed in love with you, and the 7th is kind of a marking day. I realized it was only two months, and that's really just like a Grafenwoehr separation. Only behind it all is the constant knowledge that this is a little different.

I stayed home to help Mor with the breakfast. The new class in the sewing school is slow and therefore boring. Maybe next week when we work independently, it will be all right.

One of the dresses I bought on sale doesn't fit. Typical, so I'm mailing it to Kirsten. Today the weather changed, and we have the first clouds in two weeks. These last few months, I'll be busy finishing all my started projects. I'd better not start any new ones until I finish what I started. Don't you think that is wise?

Mor gave me stunning earrings for my new silver suit, so now I'm really excited to show it off for my honey. Just can't wait to see my man again, but stick it out in good spirit please. We don't want to be wrecks OK - doesn't help anybody.

I love you as always
Elin

Odense, Denmark
August 9, 1968

Dear Bill

Had a nice long letter from you today. So you got a maid now. Well I'm glad, also for your fellow room mates. They must have suffered from your sloppiness as much as you yourself has suffered. I also take it as a sign that things must have eased up. I sure hope they check your maids out for possible sabotage.

The weather is still glorious here. A bit too hot for most people, it's fine with me, I love it. Enclosed is a picture of a dinner set Mor would enjoy having. Please order it and have it mailed to me at Kirkegards Alle 1719, Odense If you need, I'll mail a $50.00 check to you on 1 September, so please advise right now.

It's a mess that we don't know where you are going. How do we get paid in October? I would like to know. Will the whole salary go to Spokane, or just the $200.00, or what? Please find out soon, so I'll know in time.

Your last letter sounded cheerful. I'm so glad. We keep busy here, and are so excited about having you home soon. That's all we talk about. Mor and Far are also a bit sad to think I'll leave too, but that is life - the sweet and sour together.

Take good care.

Love
Elin

This letter has a funny tone to it, but I really am fine. Just my way you know.

Odense, Denmark
August 9, 1968

Dear Bill

As you can see in her letter of August 6, Hazel is still very upset about the situation in the U.S. I'm sure she needs the stabilizing influence that Strauss used to give to her. It must be hard to be by oneself. I feel like telling her that there are many ways to take care of the problems, but she would probably take that wrong, so I'll just wait until we see her. I do feel she is a bit too hysterical. What the U.S. needs is to realize that everyone has to have a better life, including the Negroes. This of course means some loss of some white privileges, and those are hard to give up for some with no foresight. But we have to survive.

I could go on philosophizing about the social needs of the world, but we'll just have to wait, and have some good long talks later on.

Love
Elin

Chu Lai, Vietnam
August 10, 1968

Dear Elin,

No mail for a couple of days seems like it's held up again.

The reason my writing is shaky is that I had a spill last night & dislocated my shoulder. Fell in an open, unmarked ditch about four feet deep in the dark and landed flat on my hand. Knocked the ball right out of the socket (right arm). Well, they took me to the hospital and gave me morphine (was really flying high on that!) & the orthopedic surgeon (he was a professor at Harvard and was drafted to be a surgeon in Vietnam) got it snapped back after some manipulation. Thing is, I've got to keep it immobilized for 4 weeks so it's in a sling. Even have to wear it in the shower, in bed - very limiting! So I'm doing everything left-handed, except this letter. I have to go back to see the surgeon in 4 weeks & he'll check it out. Doesn't hurt - just inconvenient. Don't worry about it. Maybe I'll become ambidextrous!

Otherwise, nothing exciting going on - just waiting for my orders next week.

11 August - *Sunday*

Today I got a nice long letter from you & a big box from Kirsten and Tom - all kinds of delicacies, smoked shrimp, smoked clams, goose pate from France, caviar, German dark bread, marzipan from Odense, candied fruit. Really fabulous! Now I can have another gourmet dinner. Will get some wine at the PX. They are really sweet to do that. I'll write them right after I finish this (I'm also going to eat some marzipan). It's nice and cool today, even spitting a little rain.

So my love, only 56 days left. I haven't got my approval for circuitous travel yet, but I got my visa pictures taken & the paperwork ready for them.

Give my love to Mor and Far.

Love Bill

Odense, Denmark
August 10, 1968

Dear Bill

Had a long letter today, with the letters from Mother and Margarete. I was sure this would bring news but no not yet - a little longer yet.

Went on a drive with an older American couple today. Quite boring as they are mostly interested in what they eat, and so disappointed that they can't have good sirloin in Europe. Why people like that waste the money on a ticket is beyond me. The countryside was lovely today, still such glorious weather. I so love this island. Tonight I'm visiting Gunhild on the farm, they are harvesting right now. Tomorrow I'll be the maid here at home, and next week sewing.

Time does go fast, and my little tape is in the 50s so can't be too bad. Only did hope for some news so I could make up a hundred different plans, but I'll be patient. Love you dearly hugs, kisses etc. etc. (I think the etc. etc. are the most interesting)

Elin

JARDINS DES TUILERIES

Paris, France
August 10, 1968

Dear Elin,

Arrived in Amsterdam Saturday afternoon after a miserable train ride with four changes. Spent a week there and loved it, and now we are in Paris for a few days.

When we remember our stay in Denmark, we think of the fun we had with you in Odense. Without the special interest shown to us by you and your family, we know that our stay in your town would not have been the same. We both look forward to hearing from you and Bill when you get to the States.

Joan and Judy

Chu Lai, Vietnam
August 13, 1968

Dear Elin,

I mailed you a birthday present today (for last year's birthday) Hope you like it.

No orders yet, but I found out today from Saigon today that my circuitous travel is being approved. I applied today for Indian and Pakistan visas. I should know in the beginning of September about what flight and when I'll leave Saigon for Karachi. We have to do some planning now on where to meet. I think Rome, however I do not know when I will get there, but could probably estimate within 2 or 3 days. Either you could go there to a pre-designated hotel around the beginning of October and I will get there when I do. Or, I can get there and call you in Denmark and you catch the next train. Whatever you think.

I think the Eurorail pass idea is good if Kirsten would get them for us.

Next month I am going to draw maximum advance pay around $3,500.00. I will keep some of this for traveling and put the rest in Spokane checking account. I'll leave the Soldiers deposits alone for three months after I leave Vietnam, you collect 10 percent interest 3 months after departure.

The arm is a mess, it is so hot and sticky with this sling and I cannot do anything. Bill Harris got me some zippers that lace into your boots, so that helps getting in and out of boots. It was taking me 15 to 20 minutes with one hand. It was a total dislocation and if I do not keep it immobile it will not heal properly and pop out again. Otherwise everything going fine. Hope all is well in Odense. Say hello to Mor and Far.

Much love
Bill **54**

Odense, Denmark
August 15, 1968

Dear Bill

I had hoped for a letter this morning, but no, but what there was a small consolation. Herr Maenner informed me that you will get DM800, and I will get DM1126. Nice huh. Now I only have to figure out what to do about having it mailed and if they will take my signature with you power of attorney. Otherwise it's only two months until we will be in Goppingen and rather than sending the legal papers to Vietnam and the chance of them getting lost, I'll either sign for you or wait. Boy, I had given up hope of ever collecting it for good, but leave it to "Mama" here! It sure comes at a nice time with moving expenses and vacation and all, but then I need $250 for my ticket, plus $150 to ship my junk, plus lots of other expenses so I guess the money will have legs and part.

I'm busy at the sewing school, mostly remaking old things so they are usable again. That too gives satisfaction. Made two skirts today to old suits and now can use them again. Also have finished one more embroidery. I'm trying to finish all projects that I started.

Mor and Far are out for an evening drive. They both said to send their love - we always talk about you. Kirsten wrote that she sent off a box of goodies to you, mostly canned stuff. Hope you get it on time for goodby parties for some of your friends. You know honey that I would mail stuff if it wouldn't take so long to get there.

Just rented a room to two young boys on bikes. They are coming from Flensburg, about 15. I remember when Kaja and I biked to Flensburg. Miserable - it rained. The Youth Hostel is full tonight, so they had to call home and say that they will run out of money and return sooner. Boy, I had to hide a smile - it all sounded so familiar.

No matter how one counts there still are 7 weeks yet. My mother thinks that's awfully short, but I think it's still an awfully long time to live without my love. The only good thing is that I am so busy to get to feel sorry for myself. So I only pray nothing will happen. The radio keeps scaring me when they talk of VC troop concentration around Da Nang. I hope it will fizz out like the attack they expected in Saigon. Maybe some of the things in the news are more for effect and used in conjunction with peace talks.

Bill, I think I'll save packing things until hear from you. I'm so anxious to share my work with you. All my work has been for you or for our home, the most beautiful there is. It's an idea and that is a true home. A home is not the physical plant, although that too is part of it. But a home is a spirit, reflecting a mental attitude, an institution with it's own air. Our home has a very special air - that of love. Can't wait to be home again. I know you feel the same.

I'll have to diet again, have lost nothing more. Will start exercises again on Monday and start a last campaign for the remainder of the time.

Will finish now. Honey I'm sorry I took so long to write this. It simply was an oversight, not lack of concern or love, only that the last three days went by fast.

Love you, love you, love you
Elin

Odense, Denmark
August 17, 1968

Dear Bill

Here I go, 1½ weeks without anything and then yesterday two letters and today one. By the envelope today I knew something was different, because you usually have a strong hand in writing. Dear Bill, how could you be so unlucky to land such, that it jerked the whole thing out? I know that it must have hurt awful. I really feel for you, and I can imagine the nuisance of having a sling in all that heat. Are you sure it doesn't hurt? Mor and Far send love, and hope for the arm to be fine fast. Can't they just ship you home? Why, with the right arm out of function you can't do much - or can you? I remember the trip to Grafenwoehr where you walked into a sump in the dark. Marked ditch or not you do have a bad sense of direction. But I so hope that it will set all right and not give you too much of a handicap. It will probably be a weak spot for the next couple of years. Did they say it can be worked up to be as good again as new? Now, take my back this year. It is as new again with the exercises, but that took 3 years to go into itself. I hope it will not give you too much trouble and pain, but I'm sure it will work out.

So you had a call from Jean. It was probably prompted by a letter to them in which I stated that we were frustrated that no orders were forthcoming. I never asked him to get involved, but leave it to Jean. Of course I'll appreciate to have him write me as it takes forever to find out the official way. Must be fun to get a contact all of a sudden from where you are. I wonder if he called Philadelphia.

How sweet of Kirsten and Tom to send that box. It also arrived at a good time when you needed to know that we loved you and think of you. They are real people - real gems. Kind of nice to be related to them. Kirsten is on a bus trip to North Carolina with her mother-in-law. Twelve hours by bus, and 104 degrees. She hates the heat but her sister-in-law's house is air conditioned. Her husband is in the Marines, just home from Vietnam. That whole family always feels for you and always asks how you are doing, and they haven't even met you.

Far is very concerned about your arm, he thinks it is terrible. Yes, now I think my guy should take a 5 day rest. Why not now when I'm sure it would do you good, and help the healing process. Anyway, you can do less at the office so you might as well take that leave.

I also like the stereo idea, but then go easy on the gifts. We really have so much, and if we go to D.C. we will need money for a house. In fact from now until December we need every penny as I foresee huge expenses.

I'm enclosing some things I have cut out that I think are nice. You do as you think, but I do think a little bit of money - and really, don't buy stuff for me. I know you love me and I have got so much already.

They have nice small pearl brooches for the grandmothers and Joan. They are $5.75 each. I have a ring for your Mother from Thailand, but you get her something if you want. It runs up fast.

Purse, Screen, Punch Set, China (Mor)

Our punch set 50.00, vase 10.00, 3 pins 20.00

That should be enough. We really have to get away from too many gifts. It seems I'm always buying stuff for other people. If the china is impossible to ship here, I guess we have to find another thing. My parents have really given me so much this year, I would like to give them a nice thank you gift. If the china won't work out, how about a cloisonne flower vase for $19.50, light green with cherry blossoms. But only if the china is impossible to get.

We are all fine here - all filled up still, and that does keep us busy and, I'm busy sewing. Please keep the spirit high despite your present handicap. Remember we love you and I in particular adore, admire and worship my honey.

Come home safe.

Love
Elin

Chu Lai, Vietnam
August 18, 1968

Dear Elin,

Got a letter from you today, with the letter from Hazel enclosed. This does sound a bit hysterical for Hazel - she was always so positive about life, but the events in the U.S. are shattering it at times to any thinking person.

I got a small gourmet package from the DeNios, so adding it to the box from Kirsten and Tom I've got enough to have a spread. Only problem so few people who would appreciate it. I found two bottles of Liebfraumilch back in a shelf in the PX the other day, so bought them to go with the goodies.

My arm feels a lot better - at least I can write better now. It's just inconvenient to have it wrapped up for three more weeks - especially in this heat. I guess I won't take any leave here now, not with an arm in a sling. Wouldn't be able to go swimming. Anyway, with time ticking away, I'll be leaving permanently - 49 days.

Still no orders, but hopefully some word will come back this week. On the dishes, you can't have them sent to a foreign address through the PX. So, I'll have them sent to Philadelphia and we'll have them sent on from there. I will have enough money to get them with the other stuff.

Well love, our hands are almost touching again.

Much love
Bill

Odense, Denmark
August 18, 1968

Dear Bill

It's Sunday, and quite an afternoon. We were full yesterday and almost again today. Still busy this morning. Mrs. Molgard, the one in the picture, came back after a European jaunt. Still bubbling and all that, at 75 - amazing. Also today on the radio they reported that the VC had attacked 20 towns and bases - could be the start of a new offensive. It seems like there is always bad news on Sunday. How I pray for that war to be over with.

I hope your arm is not making life too uncomfortable. Must be a mess in that heat to have it tied up all the time. Did anything chip or break? Did the doctor say it could affect the use of the arm later? How bad was it really? By now, I just want you home, but I'll keep the spirit high to the last, so you do the same OK?

I am still wondering about the best packing plans, but will just be patient a little longer.

Bill, please be careful about your arm, and about not falling again, that would be terrible. I so wish I could nurse my honey and be there to cheer you (you might get sympathy this time).
My calendar is at 50, so still get 7 weeks to go. When it's 30 you are really short.

I love you and pray for you
Elin

Odense, Denmark
August 19, 1968

Darling

I stayed home from school today to get some correspondence out, and much to my surprise here at 11 o'clock I received a box from you. A beautiful purse and lovely earrings. I absolutely love both. You are just the best husband anyone could ever want to have, but love my birthday was in December. Was that the morphine or what? I would have mailed a box to you, now I feel guilty & I didn't, but the long time it takes has discouraged me. Will you forgive me, and here your box took one week.

I wrote to Herr Maenner in Germany today. It took me over an hour to compose the letter. I'll have the money transferred to the Danish bank, so I have it here for the return trip to the U.S.

Bill, I miss you so and love you so, and I hope you feel I'm supporting you. I feel so helpless and I feel like if only I could do something for you. But soon my love soon I'll be there to take care of the little things, and you do know they mean a lot.

Love
Elin

Odense, Denmark
August 20, 1968

Darling

I was so touched by the box yesterday that I felt I had to mail some small thing in return. The big thing you'll have to wait for (I'm just too huge to ship!). I hope you receive this small box in the same loving spirit it was sent. One never knows how a person will look at something. Under the present circumstances, I'm forever worried that I'll say something in a letter that will be taken wrong, as I only love you and would not ever want to convey anything else. I'm very content in my every day life and only count the days. I know you must count them even worse.

I've started those exercises again. It feels great. I imagine you have to work up to work up the muscle and shoulder slowly again once it's all set. Please be very careful about it.

I still can't wear those lenses. Yesterday Mrs. Molgard wanted to take me out for dinner. She is 75 and speaks Danish real nice. So I wanted to make my eyes beautiful and in putting the eye shadow on I scratched my left eye. Boy did it hurt last night. I remember the one time it happened before, when I had my honey to lean on. Sure didn't hurt less, only made one feel better. I can't think too long about specific times before I get all melancholy, so I try to think ahead.

The way it looks now I'll never finish all my projects, which is good. It means staying active up to the last minute. I have a feeling those last days will be hard to take. You know how excited I get, so if one is all occupied I won't have time for a stomachache.

Bill, I love you so, and believe me anyone whoever meets me has to see the pictures of my handsome honey. They all think I'm a little nutty because no man is all that good - but mine is.

Love
Elin

Odense, Denmark
August 21, 1968

Dear Bill

I finished remaking an old skirt and started on a smock of Indian hand embroidered white wool - a gift from Gabby Zuschlag. I'll make a long skirt to go with it out of the silk you bought me. Should be nice for lounging or entertaining at Christmas time. I hate talking about all of these small things as they don't interest me that much, and they only serve to keep my mind from the troubles of the world. I only want you to know that I'm not absorbed in clothes and antiques. Only using them as outlets for my energies.

Mor gave me a lovely old Spanish comb today, and two serving spoons to go with the big spoon we have from my family. Yesterday I bought a brass ladle at the auction. In fact every day something is added to my collection. I really will have stuff to move once I pull out of here.

Bill, please tell me how the transactions will be in September and October. I plan to get the $200 in September. From then on I have no plans. Will you have advance pay, and if so, please don't have it flying around or carry it with you. It could go away so easily. Could it go to the bank? This is impossible planning, but I'll need a couple of hundred to go buy those rail passes, if you still want that, or if I go to the States I'll need $250 for a ticket if I go alone. If you come, maybe we can go space available. This get together will be planned like the trip to Thailand - lots of "ifs" and "buts" but it will work out.

I had predicted that I wouldn't hear about our new duty station until about 1 September, and so far, I am not too far off.

Today I got invited to Cairo to visit a schoolmaster and his wife, plus an Engineer and his wife. They have been vacationing here in the Motel and took a liking to me. One of the women knows of "an old Egyptian plant" that is sure to bring children. She wants me to use some of this herb, as they are very concerned that we have none. I said if I really felt it would help, I'll send for some. I was assured that it never fails to work. I really had to laugh at myself as I remembered how concerned the Lebanese were, really touching in a way. Maybe when you come home we can do something about that problem. I'm willing, how about you?

Enough of this before I get melancholy, and get you all worked up. I love you dear and I'm counting weeks. Soon I'll need only one hand to count on.

Love
Elin

How is that arm?

Chu Lai, Vietnam
August 22, 1968

Dear Elin,

Got two nice letters from you today. The news about Czechoslovakia yesterday was shattering. I can imagine what the reaction in Europe is. The whole "softening" of Soviet attitude over the past few years was too good to be true. The situation here looks glum too. All indications lead to another large offensive. Saigon got rocketed last night for the first time since the lull began.

No orders yet.

I've been "sidewalk superintending" the construction of the huge bamboo and thatched roof addition to the club by Vietnamese workers. It's really fascinating to watch the primitive, but effective methods used. The place will really be atmospheric when completed. Lieutenant Porta got back yesterday from Manila with the Ratan furniture. We haven't uncrated it yet, pending completion of the construction some time next week. Then we'll have a grand opening.

I haven't been doing too much work because I can't write too well & things are generally slow.

Much love Honey - also to Mor and Far
Bill

August 22, 1968
Philadelphia, Pennsylvania

Dear Bill,

Today I heard from Elin that you have injured your shoulder. How sorry I am and how concerned, also. You will have to be patient when you feel impatient so I found out several years ago. Why are we having falls? Are the stars against us? Do know we are all thinking of you and hope the pain has lessened. How can you carry on with your work or have your duties been assigned elsewhere?

As Elin told me that your "right wing" is involved, I won't expect you to answer my questions. In forty odd days I hope to hear them in person. At least some time following your start for the U.S.

Elin sent me a darling figurine, Royal Doulton, of a little girl. It is sweet and I love it. She also sent me something to embroider which pleases me a lot.

I took care of Jonathan for several days last week while Michael and Kathleen went on a small vacation (one overnight). He was great. He stands by his playpen and laughs. He is a happy baby and has won all our hearts.

Tomorrow Joan and I are spending a few days at the Ocean City apartment that belongs to Janet Carpenter. She insists that I go. It has been four years since I have been at the shore. They say it is hot there this year. We have had 90 degree plus weather almost daily since the middle of July. It is the hottest summer I can remember since you and Michael had the measles. Do you recall that misery?

Jack is trying to get used to McGuire Base but gets frustrated because they haven't let him bring in many planes as yet. After Thailand, he knows his experience is greater than many of theirs but perhaps they want him to go slowly on a new job.

Joan looks very well and loves New York for the position but hates the subways.

I hope you are assigned within reasonable traveling distance. I want to visit your beautiful home. If you are in the East, that will mean sending everything across the states again!

A package came for you and Elin from Captain Browning. I will hold it here.

I will pray for you that the shoulder knits as well as new. Did I ever tell you that my right shoulder was pulled out of place when I was a small child? Cousin Phyllis swung me around and it happened. I can't remember the incident!

My love always,
Mother

Chu Lai, Vietnam
August 22, 1968

Dear Mother,

Happy Birthday! Hope it is a happy one & wish I could be there to celebrate.

I still don't have my orders yet, with only 45 days left it's frustrating. The situation here looks glum, all indications are that a third large scale offensive after this long lull.

The reports from Czechoslovakia are extremely disturbing & I am sick about it. I vividly remember the wonderful reception and conversations I had with Czech students in Prague when I was there in 1964, and their fervent desire for individualism. Russia is still an ironhanded dictator despite the many reforms and softening over the past years.

My travel from here to Europe via India has been approved. That will complete my "around the world" travel. I'm greatly looking forward to getting started. Hope to meet Elin in Rome for an Italian holiday.

I did get a phone call from Washington two weeks ago (from Jean DeNio whom you met). He had checked on my assignment, and it wasn't made yet but they said they were attempting to get me to Washington D.C. I hope it pans out.

Say hello to Uncle Charlie, Mike & Kathy, Jack & Joan.

Much love,
Bill

Odense, Denmark
August 22, 1968

Dear Bill

Had a nice long letter from you today. From the looks of your handwriting it seems like you can at least use the hand. My poor honey in that heat, but for God's sake be careful that it sets right. It would be awful have a bum right arm, so please have patience now.

I have been so happy all day at the thought that my honey will meet me in Europe. Kirsten can get the rail passes easily. The only problem will be the payment. When will there be money in Spokane, and how much can I draw, or you too. It's real easy from here, so please don't have too much extra cash on your person as that can get stolen. I think it's fine to get advance pay, but how does it work exactly - how many months then until we get paid again? I don't ask to be nosy, only so we can make wise transactions as I foresee many large expenses all at once, and also large amounts of money floating around, so we have to make sure it doesn't fizz out. I should get the accident money too, and depending on those orders we will have to make a decision on a new car or a second car. It all depends on the new location. I favor one car - the old one but if you get D.C. we will probably need a new car for you. And then I might as well wait to get those rail passes until we know if we are going to buy a new car, and buying a new car will also mean going easy on the money.

I would rather see Europe by train than by car, and I'm sure you would much prefer to be free of the nuisance of driving. But I'll be able to decide when we get a little closer, and then we will just have to do like the Thailand trip and just tell each other what we are going to do as asking questions is silly. The answers might not arrive on time.

Tonight the guests have been real interesting. We have an Engineer from Bangkok, one from Cairo, and one from some place in Africa, plus various Germans and Americans - so international an atmosphere, I tell you.

Bill, believe it or not I keep so busy I doubt I'll have time to think from now on. I really am trying to wrap everything up, plus do all that I haven't done yet and I just won't get it all done - which is good. Now I can start planning a travel wardrobe. I have it all, only a matter of deciding what goes where - the eternal problem.

Mor and Far are very excited about your coming here - really. Far said he always knew you would get to travel that way. Of course I was not so sure. I'm never sure in this world as fast as it changes from day to day. Anyway, they are planning a warm homecoming for you. My mother joked and said, you couldn't even say "Come into my arms" at present, and my father said I had to treat you real gentle, as if I would hurt you. Mor didn't joke about your arm, she is very worried over it, but we hope it gives you less and less troubles. Will finish with love and kisses, and gentle hugs (I will have to sleep on my left shoulder, but that will do fine).

Love
Elin

August 22, 1968
Limeport, Pennsylvania

Dear Elin,

Time certainly does pass quickly. Here it is almost September. Before you know Bill will be with you again. Bet you are counting the days till he is there. We just heard that he hurt his arm by falling – hope that is O.K. by now!

How is everything in Denmark, and how are you doing? We hope that you are well!

Michael and I are fine. Our vacation has just ended and I'm recuperating from that (ha). We really had a lovely vacation. We visited with both sides of the family and took a trip to the shore (Ocean City, N.J.) for two days. Mother Fulmer watched Jonathan for us and they got along wonderfully. Also it was a good change for Mike and I.

Jonathan is really growing. He gets more interesting with every day. Now, he sits, pulls himself to a standing position in his playpen and crib, and he just started creeping pretty steadily now. Last week, in one day, he said Daddy twice, but hasn't said it since then. It is really exciting watching him grow and learn new things.

Along with this letter are three pictures of Jonathan. The ages are on the back. Do you notice that he had red hair on the earlier two and now is a blonde, which is good because Mike doesn't care too much for red hair. We had a small problem with his feet but they are corrected now, but he does still wear his special shoes.

We thank you so much for the little bell pull for Jonathan. It is really a very unique gift and I'm sure it is not every baby that has one.

Guess I'll be closing now. Take care and we hope to see you and Bill sometime after October and wishing you God speed.

Love,
Mike, Kathy & Jonathan

P.S. I am sorry about the note that I sent you a while ago. I didn't realize that I hadn't sent it air mail.

Note from Elin

August 26, 1968

Dear Bill,

Just got this today – is real nice – I wrote them right away – Jonathan looks like a real gem.

I'm watching the house today. Mor og Far are in Germany for a day trip. I'm all alone at present – have been for about 5 hours. Strange in such a big house.

Roskilde Domkirke is burning – the one we visited with your mother. Where all our kings are buried. I hope they save the treasures and stop the fire.

The weather is still fine and I'm glad about it. Makes one more happy.

How is your arm?

I have nothing new to report. I wrote yesterday. You know what? I've decided I only have about 30 more letters to write – or less – I don't mind writing, but will be nice to have a real talk.

Love,
Elin

Spokane, Washington
August 24, 1968

Dear Bill,

Will you ever forgive me for neglecting you as I have done? But I belong to a Prayer Circle & and I have you on my prayer list & and asked the others in the circle to pray for your safety too.

Elin says you have a painful injured arm. I am so sorry and I hope it is healing now.

World affairs, and especially those in our country have worried me so very much & and depressed me so I've felt it best not to write letters & spread my gloom. There are so many misled people that I fear what might happen to our country.

I'm anxious to know where your new orders will send you - wish it might be in the Northwest! Tim, Joan and the children are in Omaha, having a nice new home - 4 bedrooms & 2½ baths, etc., central air conditioning, etc. built. I'm so glad they decided they could not live in those crummy quarters at SAC. There are so many generals and full colonels there that all the lower ranks have to take terrible quarters. They hope to be settled by Christmas & I hope to go there then to see them. They are renting a small new 2 bedroom apartment until their house is finished.

Elin has sounded very happy to be with her parents again. They just must come to America later on to visit your folks and Kirsten's.

Evelyn Morgan called the other day. Gwyneth and Bill arrived in San Francisco the other day. Gwyneth had been quite ill. They were going right out to the lake house soon as they arrived so I have not called to see how Gwyneth is getting along. I've become quite good friends of Evelyn & Hadyn. They are very fine people.

I worry about all may happen in Chicago during the convention. It is too awful. I painted my house on the outside this summer. Some job!

Bye now Bill & bless you dear.

Hazel

Odense, Denmark
August 25, 1968

Dear Bill

It's Sunday afternoon and beautiful weather, but I doubt I'll get out in it. I don't have anyone to go out with, but soon I'll have beautiful Sundays again.

I'm trying on my contacts but it's no big success, and this morning I lost one and it's been found again. I wonder if I ever will ever be used to them. Yesterday I got my birthday and Christmas gift. A beautiful green (very green) suede coat. Mor had bought it for herself, but Far had vetoed it out because of the color. It was stunning on me, so now I'm the proud owner. Also yesterday I got word from Herr Maenner's office that the papers are sent to the insurance company, and that DM1926 will be transferred within the next three weeks, and if not to send him a notice. So, I guess it's not that important what amount is in Spokane, as I will use all of that money.

I guess I was right when I predicted it would be September before orders. So far nothing. I hate to plan anything until you know, but then I would really like to know soon. Could you maybe get Europe? As I told you, it would work fine as I could get plenty of stuff together to set up a household. You would only need the Texas shipment and your clothes shipped over. I say Europe due to the latest happening. Haven't heard any news about the U.S. reaction to troop movements in to Czechoslovakia, but I could imagine this could mean a build up in Germany, much the same as during the Berlin crisis. If that guess is right, people about to be transferred would be likely to be sent here. Therefore, my thought that you could get Europe.

I did a terrible thing - I cut my hair all short and now I regret it. My Mother said "Poor Bill, who has to listen to that complaining." It looks all right, but not as elegant as when long. I'm just not the cute type. I wonder how long it will take to grow out. It's not permanent, so it's not as bad as the last time. I still remember that horrible time, when I had had a permanent and my hair fell out, such trauma.

Bill, we are all fine here this week no news at all about Vietnam, so I wonder how things are going there. This thing with Czechoslovakia overshadows all other news for the time being.

Much love darling
Elin

Are you still going to Manila?

Chu Lai, Vietnam
August 26, 1968

Dear Elin,

How's my love today?

I got your sweet package today & it made the day. Tusind Tak for the nice letter & notes and "the lovebirds" & pack.

My arm feels OK - as you can see I can write better. I'm anxious to try to use it but must wait another week and a half before going back to the surgeon.

As you've undoubtedly heard in the news there's all kinds of action here in I Corps - we got hit on Friday and Saturday on the air strips. Nothing came into the Headquarters area - back to the bunkers again. The fighting is fierce all around our Division area though. We've got 4 NVA Regiments in our area but have been giving them hell with heavy ground action and bombs. Yesterday one of our units killed over 300 VC & NVA troops. The enemy is suicidal though, they don't budge even with overwhelming losses, etc.

I went out in a chopper on Saturday to three of our fire bases where the fighting is going on (mostly only at night). One is way up on a mountain top - only accessible by chopper. They were "dug in" bunkers and holes - very interesting. I was glad to get back!

Honey, I love you & thank you for your sweet attentions. Only 41 days (NO orders).

Much love
Bill

Odense, Denmark
August 28, 1968

Dear Bill

Had a letter from you yesterday and one today. But it's almost September and no orders. I never thought I wouldn't know by now. I even told your mother way last year that I might spend September in the U.S., depending on your orders.

We keep busy here. Have no guests, so Far and Mor are kind of vacationing. I'm sewing. I'm kind of bit by a bug I just can't go fast enough, but it does make the time fly. So you got two letters in one day. I wish they would come like I mail them about one a day or every other day.

Have not much news today - thought you would enjoy the enclosed note from the Buchers. Joan writes that they just bought a beautiful new house and moving in is a mess. But you know I am looking forward to that.

Yesterday the way you closed the letter was a most romantic way - touching hands soon. Just sounded so neat and sweet. It made me feel real good. I'm afraid my closings are not as poetic.

We had a famous painter stay here yesterday. His work is at the Modern Art Museum, National Gallery, etc.

My love be careful on the job. I don't like all those locals on the base. They could blow the whole place up. Are you sure they can't sabotage? As a Dane, I have great respect for what people can do on the sly. I pray you won't have any more heavy fighting or big attacks.

Regards from Far and Mor.

Much love,
Elin

Chu Lai, Vietnam
August 30, 1968

Dear Elin,

I held off writing for three days because I was so livid I couldn't think straight but after a delightful trip to Da Nang yesterday, I feel calmed down enough to write.

I got orders for Fort Sill, Oklahoma - totally unbelievable. Needless to say I don't intend to go there. I started by firing off the enclosed letter to the Chief of the AG Branch. I'm pretty sure it will do some good. Anyway this throws everything up in the air just when I wanted it to be so right. You can imagine how depressed I've been & not having you here to discuss all the ramifications or empathize. Sill is worse than Hood, & as I told someone who keeps telling me what "beautiful facilities" it has, the closest I want to get to Texas, Oklahoma or anything else in that area is 30,000 feet up in a jet on the way to the coast.

I'm still planning to come to Europe, even if I can't get anywhere here. Then we'll have to spend not as much time in Europe, and go to the Pentagon in person.

In a few days I'm going to get an advance pay (around $3,500) and deposit it in the Spokane checking account. I'll let you know exactly when & the amount.

My Hong Kong clothes came in and they are really sharp, except I couldn't try on the jackets because of the arm. Arm is bothersome I go to the doctor in 8 days. Imagine I'm going to have to use physical therapy for a while.

Did you ever get the letter where I asked you what your ideas were on how we should meet in Europe? Either you go to Rome to a pre designated hotel and wait, or, wait until I get there & I'll call. Problem is I won't be able to tell exactly when I'll arrive.

Honey, I know how upset you'll be after reading this. I'm confident that I'll get it changed - if not we may have to take some other action. You and I aren't going to stagnate in the middle of nowhere.

I ran out of money and had to cash a $10.00 check. But with the money I'll put in early September, it shouldn't be any problem.

Honey, I love you & hope you'll be optimistic about this.

Love
Bill

Chu Lai, Vietnam
August 31, 1968

Dear Elin,

36 TO GO

No mail today from anyone or any other word on my assignment. It will probably be about two weeks before I get a reply to my letter but I'm confident that they'll be changed.

We got in the new furniture for the club and the huge thatch roof is finished. Hurricane lamps on the tables. It looks terrific. Great atmosphere. The best in any club I've seen over here & especially out here in the boonies. Everyone is very impressed. I'm glad it got completed while I was still here. I'll take some pictures before I leave.

I was thinking why don't I come straight to Denmark. I can probably get a hop as far as Frankfurt & I really should go there first to arrange travel back to the States & see if you can go space available. Then we can relax for a while in Odense before going on a trek. That's what I'll do unless you think otherwise.

Next Saturday I go to the doctor & hopefully get out of the sling. However the arm is sore if I move it at all.

Take care I love you.
Bill

Say hello to Mor & Far

P.S. Maximum advance pay I can draw is $2,220. You pay it back in 6 months, which means half pay for 6 months (just basic pay).

Odense, Denmark
August 31, 1968

Dear Bill

Now we have 37 days until our 7th wedding anniversary, the day I have down for your end of the year.

Yesterday Nina and Poul Erik were here and we had a nice time. I like them a lot, she liked my short hair. I've decided not to go to school this next month, just too many other things to do, and this way I have more time to help Mor. Yesterday I found a large hammered copper platter for $4.00 for the wall. Really lovely. I have so much new stuff that I'm really looking forward to putting our home together again. It will be like a puzzle figuring out where things will go " here, no there - but dear that color just picks up that." Whatever one can say, it's not a dull place or it's not traditional things. It's a puzzle made up of components from life in many parts of the world, life lived at many times, changing times, under many different circumstances. The poor peasant's life, the rich life (the gold clock), the love (the statue), the hand work, the spirit of the art, etc.

We are still worried about the Communists in Czechoslovakia now - they are massing troops toward Romania. Doesn't look cheerful.

Bill, did I tell you I got notice from Herr Maenner that money should be on it's way, it should come to the bank next week. If not I should notify him. It's about $500, but we'll need every penny. I'm not spending my extra vacation money, I only buy a few cheap things. I have a feeling we will need a lot before we get everything together.

Bill, if you get Germany don't be upset - that will work out, and we will get so much help from here that we can have a "Walker" home there too without all of our stuff being shipped. I would cry over D.C. but I'll be happy to be any place just as long as it's with you.

I had the rice rubbing from Thailand framed - really lovely. Nonglare glass, gold with a wide orange wood frame around. The picture sits out kind of like you have always wanted for our paintings. The price was $8.00. I wish I had your pictures here to have framed.

We are fine here - no worries over us. Please know I have no problems, money or otherwise. Bill, we love you so. I can't believe I'm married to such a wonderful man. I really appreciate how good you are, and I'll spoil you rotten when you come home.

Love
Elin

Mor with Poul Erik, Bill, Nina and Elin in Germany - 1963

Odense, Denmark
September 2, 1968

Dear Bill

Here it is September and we still don't know where we are going. This last time sure will be hard if I still have to build air castles. I hate to plan when one doesn't know what one is planning for.

Rita is coming over to visit this afternoon. She will bring pictures from the times when they were at our house, and when we were at theirs.

Today I went out for a bit of shopping, and got some embroideries that were on sale, so I have some things to do next winter. I'm almost finished with a bell pull that goes with our new rug. It's really pretty and should be done this week. My mother says I've done enough hand work for a whole life time this year, but it does make the nights go faster.

I have no news to report, everything is going on normally, and we really hope for news and your arrival. My patience is being tried to the 9th degree but I'll last. How is my love? How is your arm?

Love you deeply
Elin

Odense, Denmark
September 3, 1968

Dear Bill

We still have this strange weather, it lays real heavy on top of your head. No mail from you today, but a bomb from Kirsten. After not hearing from them for 2 weeks she announced that Tom quit his job, and that they are moving from their apartment on October 1. He has this month to find a new job. She said that he was gone too much, and they were only together on Sundays. He often worked 60 hours a week, and they wanted a more normal life. So my poor Mother now has both daughters moving at the same time. Unsettling.

Today I got a box from Hanna with the stuff I bought. It will be a joke if we get sent to Germany. Forward and back are equally long.

I enclose two pictures for you that Rita gave me. One from Schwabisch Gmund in 1963, the other from Arhus in January 1968. If possible, I hope they don't get ruined. I have three more but you can see these when you return. We still don't hear a thing about Vietnam. News from Czechoslovakia comes first, then Biafra, which apparently makes Vietnam look pale. Millions are being forced into very small pieces of land and are starving. Then we hear about the U.S. comments about Czechoslovakia, the election, earthquakes in Iran, also terrible, but not one word about Vietnam in the last two weeks. Rather irritating.

Boy am I looking forward to having you home. Life is easier when one is two to share the worries and the happiness. There is no substitute for a happy marriage. Absolutely the best invention ever made.

Love you
Elin

Spokane, Washington
September 5, 1968

Dear Elin & Bill,

Now I'm wondering where your new assignment will be & when does Bill leave Vietnam?

My whole spring and summer have been depressing and not at all the usual. First, Sood's husband Dick went berserk at Easter & and I took them all in here. Then he tried to kill himself & I went to the hospital with him, & helped them all through a bad time & helped her with the divorce, etc. Then, my brother's adopted son, a brilliant schizophrenic was here twice for a week each time, then Malkait and Wilimina are having troubles, she seems to have gone haywire. I think it is from taking the pill plus diet pills. I've gone to Kellog to council them & Malkait calls me & comes here for days at a time, nearly out of his mind with worry.

Tim and Joan decided to have a nice house built. Four bedrooms, 2½ baths, etc. They hope to be settled for Xmas. They've rented a furnished apartment until then.

Things seem to get worse in our country - with the Commie agitated trouble, workers and dissenters. Let me know about your orders soon.

Much love,
Hazel

Alexandra, Virginia
September 6, 1968

Dearest Elin and Bill,

Surely hesitated on writing for I'm so disappointed in Bill's orders. Kept hoping you would write that it was D.C. after all. But haven't heard. Ft. Sill is a nice post (it was our first) but the southwest is the southwest!!! Can't understand it when so many try to avoid Washington. Do feel Bill will probably have an important , good job, & all you'll gain career wise. Received the stainless pieces. Many thanks. Shall settle our accounts when you come East for a visit in September? October? When?

We have had a frantic 3 weeks. All was well. Planned to move little by little and paint entire place in a week! But our air conditioner broke down in the apartment. Temperature was 96 degrees for a week. Former owners were from "Slobovia" so we had to scrub every wall, ceiling etc. with ammonia solution to cut grease to paint. Moved to Jean's mother's apartment to sleep. Finally lugged last belongings to house night of August 31st. Still not settled. We need you!

Jean returned to work only to have same old job & night shift! Darn. Kids are back in school and happy. Dog finally had to be told she was "A DOG" and hasn't had one accident in new house. I've been off at work since 17th and may not even have a job?? Had 4 moles removed and that vein on my leg injected yesterday at Ft. Belvoir (we're close to that now). So have total of 26 stitches and pain pain pain today.

Have another favor to ask. As you can see by the attached clipping the "Egg" chair is very valuable, but ours needs reupholstering badly. I was thinking of buying fabric to match sofa (we hope to buy) to have it redone. It's $13/yard. 54" wide. My new neighbor (an artist from San Jose California), who has an "Egg" suggested I ask you if I could buy new upholstery in Denmark precut? Also we have never had the cushion which I think would help on wear. So if you have time and energy would you look into this. I trust your judgment. The fabric I mentioned is white vinyl which looks like soft leather.

We will go to Philadelphia on September 26th, our first time since last year.

I know your parents will be sad to have you go again. If Kirsten is on the East Coast I imagine she is as unhappy as I am about Oklahoma but I am happy for you that separation is nearly over. Only days to go now.

Love,
Mel, Jean & D's

Odense, Denmark
September 6, 1968

Dear Bill

I have had such dreams of you lately. Boy I really miss you but only one month to go. I hope it won't be too miserable a month. In your letter you said you are back in the bunkers - ugh -- I do feel for you.

We called Kirsten today - they are fine. If you come over Europe they might come too and tour with us. Could be fun. I got the money from the insurance for the car accident. I got DM1126 and you got DM3800. I think that's DM3000 too much, and they are about to revalue the Mark, so it will be worth 10% more. I didn't know what to do. I put the money in a short time bank book and will wait and see what happens. The whole thing has always seemed fishy. Now it's in Danish Kroner so if they revalue, we may face a big mess if we have to pay back the DM3000. One would know it couldn't just go simply, but at least they didn't pay too little. I wish you had been here to advise me.

Any more about your travel plans? Please, what day do you leave Vietnam, or do you know? Needless to say, the excitement here is great, everything depends on you, Kirsten & Tom's trip, Mor's birthday etc. etc.

Love -Elin

Chu Lai, Vietnam
September 7, 1968

Dear Ein,

No mail for 4 days. Must be hung up again. No word from DA yet. Maybe next week.

Yesterday I got my arm out of the sling. It is quite weak. The doctor said not to lift anything or use it too much for 2 weeks. Then it should be healed. I can only raise it to my chest (can't salute which is awkward).

I bought a suitcase & am going to start to get things together & throw a lot out next week. I'm throwing out most everything or giving it away.

Got my visas for India and Pakistan the other day. I should find out what flight & when I leave around the 15th of September. Can't believe that it's finally going to be the time to leave - 29 days.

I got the letter with the pictures of Jonathan & Mike and Kathy - real nice.

Tomorrow I'll go to Finance & get advance pay. Then put most of it in Spokane except for a small amount of travel money. Then I'll send off the PX orders & write checks for them. I'll probably have to ship one box. Maybe I'll just mail one - don't have too much stuff.

Yates and Bob Dove & the bunch that came over early all left last week. My replacement, currently in a battalion, will probably come up in about 10 days. Maybe I can get in a couple of days on the beach to get well rested for the trip. It's been raining steadily for 4 days. Looks like it's clearing up today.

Honey - love you & am very excited about coming back to you and the world.

Bill

Odense, Denmark
September 7, 1968

Darling

"Keep your cool" as they say. Boy, what an assignment to come up with after Vietnam. Could it be an assembly point for the troops they plan to fly back to Europe? Wasn't Fort Sill the place they had Operation Big Lift from? If that's the case, I could take Sill if it's only a temporary deal to assemble troops for a further destination, but if your assignment is for two years, it would be a disappointment to say the least. But, I can take anyplace with you - especially after this year. In fact I'll do anything you want. Go to the poles if need be. I think your letter was wise and will bring some answer, at least I hope so. I'm sure everything is in a turmoil right now with the Russian mission, and all of the NATO Alliance is being reevaluated, it's hard to assess what's going on.

Tom quit his job and they might come to Europe, but it's hard with things up in the air the way they are.

I've looked into different travel schemes -

1. The train, round trip Denmark/Rome is $100 single.

2. Air is very high, $200.

3. Charter is from $90 air, room and board up to $200 depending on how much luxury you want. I've considered getting two $90 tickets. We could use the room, and both fly home to Copenhagen together. It's a cheap solution.

4. Could get Eurorail passes, but if you have a short vacation, would just get to use the amount and earn nothing on it.

My ticket to the U.S. is $252, then we have to ship my junk. Plus to find where to fly from I guess Frankfurt, and visit Emma and Tom before leaving for New York.

Kirsten and Tom would buy the Ford at December 1967 price if we want to sell it, but if we go to Sill I guess we'll keep it. If you get it changed to Europe, I guess we'll sell it.

As you can see, my head is opening with so many questions No, yes, if?

On Monday I'll get brochures of the cheap charter trips. Only two seats left for the October 5th and one double room. One week or two. All other trips booked solid. I will decide if I take those two tickets, then let you know the name of the hotel. Would be $180 for us both with the return to Copenhagen. If the hotel is undesirable, we can always go to another, but I doubt we will need to because we have always had good luck with the charter trips. We get breakfast and one meal, but no tours. Things will work out - be confident.

I'm sorry about your arm. All those gorgeous clothes and can't even try them on. Wouldn't need a "hot" wardrobe in Oklahoma, and we just got equipped, both of us. All my beautiful coats would be worthless there. Mor and Far hope you get it changed to Europe. I just hope you get it changed.
Will write more about Rome on Monday.

Love
Elin

Odense, Denmark
September 8, 1968

Dear Bill

Just called Kirsten and Tom. They probably will come to Europe since you are coming. He did quit and they sold the Porsche. They are moving out of the apartment on 1 October. They were very excited about making a trip with us, would be loads of fun. Whatever your assignment is, I refuse to let it spoil a beautiful reunion and vacation. I'm determined to have a nice month to get you relaxed in case you need it. I do too, for that matter. The nervous tension can get hard too. Find out about rail passes. When I know what's up will inform you. I favor meeting you in Rome, me being there before you arrive.

If all else fails you can always call Odense and ask Mor and Far what is going on, in case you haven't received final word. But it all will work out, also your next job.

Some guests just arrived, they spent 18 months at Fort Sill. They say it's one of the most beautiful posts in the U.S. Very old, with lots of history, nice houses too. Don't despair. It's not forever, any place you go. I'm not depressed anyway. I won't go to seeds any place. We can just start being artists. I'll write, you paint, and think positive. I must admit I would rather be someplace not 7,000 miles from everything, but then one can't have everything. Let's just for now look forward to doing Europe in a glorious way.

Mor wants to have a big family party. She will be 55 on October 26th. It's Sunday, and I'm baby sitting the house as usual. I think Far and Mor enjoy going out and not having to worry about the house.

Bill I'm about to burst with excitement, so is Mor. At times we don't think we'll last, but please promise to stay calm. Don't get upset, don't rant and rave. I don't either, but it will all work out OK. Don't ruin the vacation - OK. I'm cheerful so you can try to be too. Lawton is a lovely town with a beautiful residential area. The post has large quarters, and you and I will create our own culture and climate. If we don't like what we find, there is classical music on your new stereo. I'll even pose for paintings.

Love you forever
Elin

Chu Lai, Vietnam
September 10, 1968

Dear Elin,

Received two letters from you yesterday - one took two weeks to get here.

Saw "A Funny Thing Happened on the Way to the Forum" at the club last night (we're getting some good movies in for the first time) & and it was just as hilarious as when we saw it. Remember the little theater/restaurant in Carmel?

I've been so irritable and jumpy lately - everyone does when they get this short - 26 days. Even more so when I've got this assignment thing hanging over my head. If I don't hear anything before I leave, I'll call DA when I get to Germany.

Things are sort of quiet in the area right now. Arm is coming along, although I'm not using it too much. Just want to get it in shape to carry a suitcase.

Finally got some color Polaroid film and experimented today. It's a lot of fun.

Honey - love you.
- soon -

Bill

Oberursel, Germany
September 10, 1968

My dear Elin,

Tom and I have been in France for the last ten days and when we got back to Oberursel yesterday morning, we found the package with your very charming gift. You certainly are a <u>very</u> talented girl, and we do thank you so very much for sending us one of your embroidered pictures. It is already hanging on the bedroom wall, and I enjoy looking at it whenever I enter the room. It was so kind of you to send it to us, and I like it especially much because it was made by you.

Your news about poor Bill's injured arm was very sad, but we were so awfully happy to hear that he would be able to come to Europe in October. I can't think of a more exciting city in which to meet than Rome, and I know that you'll have a wonderful time there. The food is so good, and there is so much to see and do, that it's difficult to decide where to go first. You asked in your letter about hotels. Tom and I usually try to economize on hotel rooms so that we can "live it up" in other ways. When we're in Rome we stay at the Hotel Dinesen, Via di Porta Pinciana #30. This hotel was formerly owned by a Danish woman who wrote a book about her experiences as "an innkeeper in Rome". (She may still be alive, but she was quite elderly when we started going there twenty years ago.) The hotel is definitely second rate and is a little run-down, but we like the location very much. It's around the corner from Via Veneto where all the sidewalk cafes and the night life is located, but the hotel itself is much more quiet than the big places on Via Veneto. In back of the hotel is the big Pinciana Park and it's possible to walk to the Villa Medici and the area called the Pincio from where one has a wonderful view of all of Rome. You will be too far away to walk to St. Peters and the Forum, but you can take buses or go on a sightseeing tour. When we're in Florence we stay at the Hotel Berchielli on Dungarno Acciaioli 14. This hotel is also second class but the lobby was modernized after the November floods in 1966 and it looks quite nice now. The hotel is on the Arno River between Ponte Vecchio and Ponte S. Trinita. If you ask for a room facing the river you have a wonderful view, but there will be a lot of noise from the street, so we usually ask for a room toward the back of the hotel. Florence is small enough so that from this hotel you can walk to the Uffizi Gallery and the Cathedral and the Straw Market for shopping.

The weather should be just perfect in October – not hot and not cold, so it you take along a suit with both blouses and sweaters you ought to get along fine. The days ought to be sunny and warm but it will get cool at night.

I'm so very pleased that Bill can come to Europe, and you rally must stop at our house. We'll give you the bedroom; Tom will sleep in the "little room", and I'll take the living room couch. And please don't make a fuss about sleeping in our bed. After all, Tom and I have been together almost every night for twenty years, and we'll be more than happy to separate for a few nights while you are with us.

It will be so good to see both of you.

Much love,
Emma

P.S. I've been wanting to tell you that the yellow suit I bought when we were at the PX together is simply wonderful! I wore it almost every day in the United States and had it on all through France. Thanks ever so much for telling me to buy it. Also, did your pictures turn out all right from your last trip to Oberursel, and was there one of you and me, or of you alone, that you could have reproduced for us? My camera went on the blink while you were with us, and we don't have a single picture from your visit.

Note from Elin:

I'll meet you wherever you tell me. At this point it makes no sense since whatever is the easiest for you. Bill, I'll run off with this. Nothing new here.

Philadelphia, Pennsylvania
September 11, 1968

Dearest Bill,

If you only knew how often I think about you! I wonder how you are, what you are doing, if your shoulder is better, where you will be assigned, when you will reach home, et cetera, et cetera, et cetera. Then why don't I write more often? My days have not been too exciting and I have lacked interesting items to tell you. But fall is nearing Philadelphia and somehow or other I always feel happier in the autumn. It is my favorite season of the year.

First off, I should tell you that I have Charlie home. We brought him here two weeks ago after I ran out of money. I tried to enter him in a church home but he never joined a church! Then I tried other ideas for help but finally decided to see if Jack and I could manage here at home. He is better than before to my surprise but does sleep in the daytime and keeps awake at night. For instance, although he promises to stay in his room, I may waken and find him downstairs fully dressed! His mind is quite lucid but he gets mixed up with time. I think he is better than when you last saw him. Of course, I really believe he misses the "home". He was waited upon more than I can provide for him. But I do have a neighbor that has been willing to come in during the day to check and to give him a lunch. He surely loves the television!

Jack goes to work four days in different shifts and then has two days free. He is quite a fellow and I enjoy having him here.

Joan called last night and bemoaned the fact that if only she had her passport, she would be sent to Venezuela this week for Irish Airlines on a public relations fully paid trip of one week. She is getting her passport today in case they ask her to go another time. Of course she is definitely going to Ireland in a month or so for orientation. I feel she is in a great field with excellent opportunities and she seems very happy. There is one big drawback! The New York subways!

Elin sent me some beautiful needlework to do this winter and a lovely figurine for my birthday. It was very thoughtful of her. I can imagine how happy she will be to run her own household again with you by her side.

I do hope you are assigned to an area near enough for me to afford a visit. It will be seven years since you married and I've never been in your home. I think this next year will be different.

School has been in session two weeks and once again I am plunged into the world of boys and girls with not only their problems of study but their trials and tribulations of every day living. One boy today gave me a real bad time and his defiance was hard to take. I had him come for a conference at 3:30 and startled him by giving him the job of handling our electrical equipment. Then when he proved very efficient, I suggested we get along better at our next meeting. He agreed! "Catch more flies with molasses than vinegar."

What do the papers there say about our presidential candidates? Incidentally, how many have you ever voted for? Joan brought home this short joke:

"Knock knock"

"Who's there?"

"Spiro"

"Spiro who?"

"That's what everyone asks!"

I am not fond of either candidate but guess I prefer a Republican candidate this year even if it is Nixon whom I never liked.

Do take care of yourself and I hope the news of your next assignment has reached you by this time.

All my love,
Mother

P.S. I didn't thank you for my birthday card and letter and I truly enjoyed them both.

Philadelphia, Pennsylvania
September 11, 1968

Dear Elin,

I simply love the figurine you sent me and it was quite a surprise. I put "her" on the mantle next to the clock where "she" just seems to fit. Thank you so much. I also haven't thanked you for the needlework. I am glad you will be in the states this winter in case I get mixed up with arranging the book cover correctly. It surely looks interesting.

What a frustrating time for you and Bill to wait for news of reassignment! I never knew that the government kept one waiting so long. Every night I pray that it will be somewhere within a few hundred instead of thousands of miles. Probably you do know by this time.

Uncle Charlie has been home several weeks. The home finally proved too expensive for me to keep up. I often thought of your father's explanation of conditions in Denmark for the aged. If I remember it correctly, the government takes care of all expenses. Am I wrong? Here it is very different. The government only takes care of the very poor. But he is better than I thought and has been much clearer in his mind. But it complicates things here as you know.

Jack is a big help and provides the moral support that you gave me last autumn. He is very easy to live with and is quite a fine fellow.

Joan missed a trip to Venezuela this week because she hadn't applied for her passport. The airline was going to send her there on a public relations trip for a week. Today she is getting her application in case they offer a trip again. The orientation in Ireland is supposed to happen in another month or so. I feel she is happy in her work. When she was home last, she bought material for three outfits and is planning to make some clothes for fall. Of course "green" is the dominant color!

School is open again and I am in the midst of it all. This year I have a better homeroom class and look forward to having dramatics with them occasionally.

Do give my regards to your parents, and to you I send

My love,
Mother

Odense, Denmark
September 11, 1968

Dear Bill

Got your letter today about going to Frankfurt and then here to Odense. It would cause less complications for sure, then we both could take a week's jaunt to Rome, the Grand Canary Island or some other place. Trips from Copenhagen are cheap. That way we would have time to get organized first and could really relax after. But I would or could meet you in Frankfurt. I would like to be there when the plane comes in, or maybe that also is too complicated. Still waiting to hear if Kirsten and Tom are coming. Will fill you in, but it sounds right to come here first, then take a trip.

Your picture looks like you need someone to really love you and take care of you, my poor honey. I do hope your arm won't give you too many problems.

I love you dear and all will work out OK.
Elin

Chu Lai, Vietnam
September 13, 1968

Dear Elin,

Got two letters from you today - with pictures of you and Rita.

Would be great if Kirsten and Tom could come to Europe. I haven't gotten my port call yet, hope everything goes right. I'll be jumpy until I know exactly what flight and when, etc.

I got advance pay today, $1,950. I put $1,300 in the Spokane checking account & kept out $650 for trip (not to spend but I may get stuck somewhere and have to take a commercial flight & you know most places won't take personal checks).

I'll put in orders for the PX things. No stereo though. I don't want to spend that much until things are more definite.

My replacement comes in on Monday. I have one more project to complete so I hope to have some afternoons on the beach.

Arm is feeling better - more movement each day. I've started to throw out all of the smelly underwear & clothes & began giving away the few other things I had. I'm going to travel light.

Love you Honey
Bill

Chu Lai, Vietnam
September 15, 1968

Dear Elin,

Got two letters from you today. The first where you had heard of orders to Sill. They really cheered me up. But I am optimistic again & don't worry - nothing will spoil the vacation.

I've been so jumpy I can hardly stand it. My stomach has been upset & it's just nerves and excitement. Tomorrow my replacement comes in. Still no port call yet - but they said it would be after the 15th (today). Right now only 19 days left. But I could leave earlier, depending on when my flight leaves.

My arm feels pretty good unless I move it in certain ways. It would be terrific if Kirsten and Tom come to Europe - we could really have a ball.

It's taking your letters up to two weeks to get here, although once in a while I get one in 7 or 8 days.

17 September 1968

Two days later -- Yesterday I got my port call. I depart Saigon at 11:40 AM on a flight to Karachi, Pakistan on 3 October. From Karachi I'm on my own. Hopefully will be able to get on an embassy flight at least to Frankfurt - maybe even to Copenhagen. I think it best that you wait for me in Odense, unless I can find out a specific flight, time and place once I hit Europe and call you.

My replacement came in yesterday. I've got a lot to do to get ready - shots, shopping, shipping a small box etc. Got a letter from you yesterday that only took 5 days amazing!

Honey - love you. Maybe I'll get there in time for our anniversary.

Bill

Odense, Denmark
September 16, 1968

Dear Bill

The days here are rolling along. Nothing new. Haven't heard from Kirsten & Tom, or from you. I just sit here speculating on what will happen. It's all so exciting. I have constant ache, but know that will end soon and we will be together. I don't feel like writing long letters anymore. I'd rather wait until we can talk together. I still am busy embroidering. It is so soothing for the nerves and it keeps my mind occupied.

Love
Elin

Chu Lai, Vietnam
September 17, 1968

Dear Mother,

Received your letter today & was glad to hear from you. Things have been jumping, otherwise I would have written you earlier.

First of all, I got my assignment two weeks ago & have been fuming ever since - to Fort Sill, Oklahoma. I immediately fired off a letter to Washington asking for it to be changed - no reply yet. I was really disappointed in it & have no desire to go from here to the middle of the prairies.

Anyway I just have to wait for a reply. If I don't get one soon I'll go to D.C. when I get to the States & try to get it changed there.

I fly from Saigon on 3 October to Karachi, Pakistan. From there on it will be space available "hops" on embassy flights - probably to New Delhi, Saudi Arabia to Europe. I am going directly to Odense. After a rest, Elin and I will take a vacation in Italy or Spain for a few weeks. I'm taking 45 days leave so will stay in Europe for a while before coming to New York and Philadelphia. Depending if I can get my assignment changed to the East Coast will determine how long we stay in the East.

I've had an upset stomach all week because of the excitement of leaving and that I was approved to travel direct to Europe (just yesterday). My arm is out of the sling and I am using it sparingly. Still hurts if I move it certain ways. The doctor said it will be six months before I have full use of it again.

Kirsten and Tom may fly to Denmark while we are there & go on vacation with us. That would be great. It will be great to join the world again - & probably quite a jolt to leave this life in Vietnam. I'm packing, my replacement on board & in two weeks back to the world!

Much love to you & everyone.
Bill

Odense, Denmark
September 19, 1968

Dear Bill

Last night Kirsten called. They are coming next week, so there will be a grand welcoming committee waiting for your arrival. Now we only need to know where, when, how. They are leaving our car with Jack. I wrote a long letter of instructions to him, especially about the insurance. Kirsten and Tom might buy a car here. They wanted to buy ours, but without knowing where we were going, it was hard to decide on such things. Joan is also coming to Ireland. This is a traveling family. If only we can find ourselves in this huge world.

Mor has the basement almost cleared out. I have my stuff in one place for your inspection. If we go to Oklahoma, I might have to leave a lot here. I'm also trying to have my clothes and things in order so I can concentrate on you completely once you arrive.

We will have a big family birthday. Mor turns 55 in October. She is so excited to think the whole family will be together. We keep busy here.

I hope your arm is getting better and that these last days will go smoothly. We all know how hard and you have our greatest admiration. So do all the men over there. But when you come home I hope you can find peace, and forget about all the troubles in the world.

Love you deeply
Elin

Chu Lai, Vietnam
September 20, 1968

Dear Elin,

Well, my replacement has taken over the job so I'm just goofing off & getting ready to move out. Tomorrow I may go to the beach. On Sunday some of the my old 198th Brigade AG Section crowd are having a beach party & invited me, so I'll go to that too. I just check in at the office periodically to answer any questions that have come up.

Guess who walked into my office the other day? Les Hill, our Red Cross friend from Goppingen. We were both surprised to see each other. We met at the club for a drink later and reminisced. He received two promotions after leaving Germany & is now I Corps Field Director here. Joanna is living in Missouri. Also saw Woody Perham (now a Major) who as a lieutenant was in the 144th Signal Battalion in Goppingen with Mike Urette. He was just assigned to the Division. You may or may not remember him. It was great seeing Les - he said if we were still going to Oklahoma to plan & stay with Joanna in St Louis, which is on the way.

I packed one small box to mail. I didn't accumulate anything over here. Oh, I forgot to tell you that Tom Archibal from our career class (wife's name is Miriam) just arrived and is assigned to the AG Section. I still haven't received a reply to my letter to Colonel Myers. It's been 3 weeks.

The weather is beautiful right now. The oppressive heat is over & there is a nice breeze again along the coast. Beautiful crystal days. Vietnam is such an overwhelming beautiful country, it's such a tragedy that it's racked and scarred by this unending war.

Love you Darling

Bill (13 days)

GOING AWAY PARTY

The entire G1 staff held a going away party for Bill. It was in a warehouse with long tables. A lobster dinner was served, with drinks. The Officer and NCO Club Managers arranged to have a live Korean Floor Show perform. The G1 enlisted men presented Bill with an engraved Vietnamese swagger stick with the handle of a dragon. A great send off.

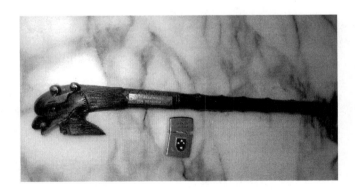

A Special Party Invitation

In September 1968, the Office of Public Affairs at the Division Headquarters invited our office to a "party." I received this 11" X 14" size, original (only one of it's kind) invitation by the illustrator for the Division newspaper, Southern Cross, PFC Dave McGowan. The "party" in actuality was just a bunch of guys drinking beer and having a barbeque!

Vol. 1, No. 1   CHU LAI, VIETNAM   May

AMERICAL ★ ★ DIVISION
SOUTHERN CROSS

THE SOUTHERN CROSS is an authorized publication of the Americal Division Information Office for all division units in the Republic of Vietnam. Army News Features, Army Photo Features, Armed Forces Press Service and Armed Forces News Bureau material are used. Opinions expressed are not necessarily those of the Department of the Army. Contributions are encouraged and may be sent to the Information Office, Americal Division, APO 96374, Tel Chu Lai 3212. The editors reserve the right to edit all contributions. Printed in Tokyo, Japan, by Image Public Relations, Ltd.

Major General S.W. Koster .... Commanding General
Major Gerald D. Hill, Jr. .... Information Officer
First Lieutenant Michael E. Wolfgang ...... Officer-In-Charge
Sergeant John Nicholson .... NCOIC
Private First Class Mike Kelsey .... Editor
Private First Class Bill Guerrant .... Photo Editor
Private First Class Dave McGown .... Illustrator
Private First Class Charles Gordon .... Reporter

"The Birth of Miracle Man" by Illustrator PFC David McGowan – Southern Cross, July 1968

DEPARTMENT OF THE ARMY
OFFICE OF PERSONNEL OPERATIONS
WASHINGTON, D.C. 20315

IN REPLY REFER TO

Dear Major Walker:

Upon receipt of your letter, we have reviewed our actions in assigning you to Fort Sill, and I have concluded that the assignment should stand.

You have a very good record, and we had you earmarked for possible assignment to this area. However, at the time, we had no high priority requirements open here, while we had a very real need for your services at Sill. You will not be assigned to the Training Center, but to the Artillery and Missile Center as Chief, MPD. Colonel Washburn was very thankful to get you, and I think you will agree, at least in future years, that this is a good assignment.

Don't worry — you'll get to Washington in due course —

Sincerely, and with best wishes

John W. Myers

Maj W. D. Walker
24 Sept 68

John W. Myers
Colonel, AGC
Chief, AG Branch, OPD

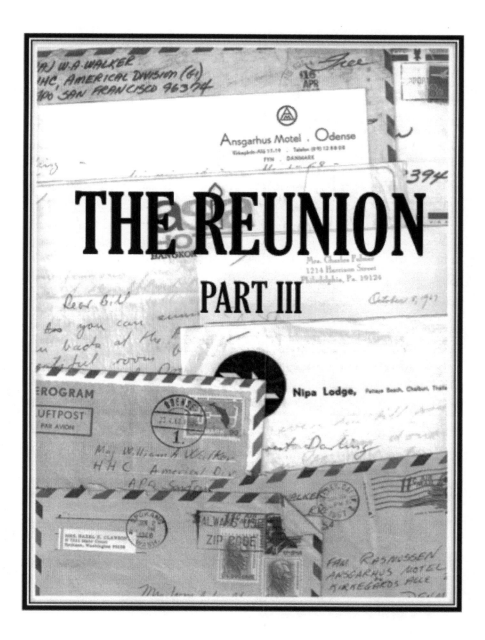

Back to Civilization

by way of….

India

Saudi
Arabia

Dhahran, Saudi Arabia
October 4, 1968

Dear Mother,

Half way around the world.
New Delhi last night. Tonight
Spain. Hopefully to Denmark
in two days,

Love Bill

Spain

*View from hotel room –
October 6, 1968*

The Reunion
Odense, Denmark
October 1968

Oct. 1968.

Dear Bill.

We wish you welome back safe after a
hard year. We respect your efford for the
sake of freedom. And a speciel welcome
home. This present is a delayed birthday - anniversary - and homecoming
present. We also wish you and Elin
a good time here as long as you can
stay.

Love.

Mor og Far.

Ansgarhus Motel
Odense, Denmark
October 8, 1968

Dear Mother,

I finally made it! Arrived here on the 6th from Madrid after the long trip from Chu Lai that took me through Bangkok, New Delhi, Karachi, Saudi Arabia, Madrid, Frankfurt. Hard to really believe yet that I'm away from Vietnam & here in Odense with Elin. Big welcome here as you can imagine. I'm sure you know that Kirsten and Tom are here.

On the 16th the four of us are going to Copenhagen for 3 days, then fly to Rome for a week. Elin & I will take a sentimental trip to Germany just before we leave for the States - sometime in the beginning of November. Will let you know the definite date when I find out.

My orders to Oklahoma still stand. I got a letter from Washington just before I left Vietnam. I'm not happy about it, but it's an important job so I can't complain much more. Say hello to everyone - anxious to see all of you in November.

Love,
Bill

On October 16, 1968, Elin & Bill and Kirsten & Tom went by train to Copenhagen to spend three days before flying to Rome. While in Copenhagen, Elin looked up friends living there who were classmates at Fyns Studentenkursus in Odense in 1958 and 1959 -- Thorkild Bog Hansen and Birgitta Juel Hillingso. They met Thorkild and some of his friends for drinks, and visited Birgitta and her husband, Premier Lieutenant Kjeld Hillingso at their home.

Lively Copenhagen was a refreshing change from Vietnam for Bill. However some of the Danes they encountered vocally expressed their opposition to America's war in Vietnam. A few of Elin's friends were more understanding.

Piazza di Spagna

Rome, Italy
October 23, 1968

Dear Mother and Uncle Charlie

Bill and I are at the top of these old stairs, it's very romantic. This morning we are going to an audience with the Pope. This town is overwhelming.

Elin

Rome is fabulous - tomorrow we're going to Naples for a day then back to Denmark on Saturday - then to Germany for 4-5 days. Expect to be in the States around 5-6-7 November.

Love
Elin & Bill

Rome, Italy

The Forum

Trevi Fountain

Bill and Elin at the Colliseum

The Vatican

Pope Paul VI at St. Peters

Pompeii

Bill with Ned Shivar and his wife at Pompeii

Ansgarhus Motel
Odense, Denmark
October 29, 1968

Dear Mother,

We're back in Denmark after a wonderful trip to Rome. We stayed in a very nice pension right in the heart of the city - within walking distance of some of the most prominent sights. We saw as much as possible within a week. Saw the Pope at St. Peters where he gave an audience to about 5,000 people. Elin and I spent two days in Naples visiting a friend from Vietnam who is stationed there. We went to Pompeii while there - quite a fantastic experience.

Kirsten and Tom are going to stay here until after Christmas. They're taking a trip to Tunisia during the month of November.

Right now we're packing up a lot of things Elin acquired this past year for shipment to the States. We plan to leave here in 4 or 5 days for Germany. Will visit friends in Hamburg, check on the flight in Frankfurt, and drop down to Goppingen to see some more friends.

I asked for a flight on either the 4th, 5th or 6th of November. It will land at McGuire AFB. If I find out soon enough exactly when, maybe Jack could meet us.

Hope everyone is fine in Philadelphia. We're looking forward to seeing all of you again.

Love,
Bill

Peace!
John & Peggy Burks
Hello out there — are you
two together again?
Come back & come see us.
Happy holidays & the
best for '69.
Love,
P.

Fort Sill, Oklahoma

Fort Sill actually turned out to be great. I was even on the board of directors of the Lawton Symphony. We got a mortgage to buy the house with no credit rating, just a handshake with a banker who wore a cowboy hat, and said my being a military officer made me credit-worthy. And of course, Eric was born there. We took college courses, Elin teaching, and me Art. I made wood sculptures for our garden (wish I had shipped them!).

Our home in Lawton

Wood sculptures in our back garden

Elin with Mother at Fort Sill

Visiting a Kiowan artist

Jack visiting Bill & Elin in their Lawton home

Mike, Kathy and Jonathan's visit to Oklahoma

"Wild West" Party

THE LAWTON PHILHARMONIC SOCIETY

BOARD OF DIRECTORS

Ed Dewey, President
Irvin Schmidt, Vice-President
Mrs. Gilbert C. Gibson, Secretary
G. Clifton Webb, Treasurer
Mrs. D. L. Wigington, Women's Ass'n.
Bill Crawford
Carey Johnson
Ben O. Key
Carmen Mercadante
Mrs. Ralph Newcombe
Wayne Smith
Miss Leta Mae Smith
Jack Storey
Frank Sovell
Major William A. Walker

HONORARY MEMBERS

Major General Charles P. Brown   Mayor Wayne Gilley   Dr. Don Owen

LIFE MEMBERS

American National Bank
Mr. and Mrs. John Bianco
Mr. and Mrs. James A. Black
Mr. and Mrs. Raymond Del Vecchio
Mr. and Mrs. Exall English
Dr. and Mrs. Gilbert C. Gibson
Home Decor and Air-Conditioning
Mr. and Mrs. C. P. Mercadante
Mr. and Mrs. Charlie D. Payne
The Sheridan Bank
Mr. and Mrs. G. Clifton Webb
Mr. and Mrs. W. F. Wulf

PATRON MEMBERS

Mr. and Mrs. Ed Dewey
Mr. and Mrs. W. Carey Johnson
Mr. J. R. Montgomery
Winston Raburn

SPONSOR MEMBERS

Mr. and Mrs. Alfred J. Ashton
Drs. Austin and Jolly
Mr. and Mrs. Bill F. Bentley
Edna House
Dr. and Mrs. F. David Kalbfleisch
Mr. and Mrs. Steven Kardaleff
Lawton Coca-Cola Bottling Co.
Mr. and Mrs. Charlie D. Payne
Dr. and Mrs. William L. Scearce
Mr. and Mrs. Irvin E. Schmidt
Dr. and Mrs. Lowell F. Thornton
Major and Mrs. James R. Wiltshire
Southwestern Stat'ry & Bank Supply
Townes' Men Store

GUARANTOR MEMBERS

AAA Glass
Academy of Ballet
Allen Home Lumber Co.
Amber Bottle Antiques
Dr. and Mrs. Charles E. Andrus
Mr. and Mrs. Ben Ansley
Mr. and Mrs. Dwayne Arndt
Mrs. Neil Ashlock
Dr. and Mrs. Byron W. Aycock
Rev. and Mrs. Richard M. Babcock
Dr. and Mrs. J. E. Barnes, Sr.
Mr. and Mrs. Elmer R. Bauman
Becker Funeral Home
Bill's Family Shoe Store
Business Bachines & Equipment, Inc.
Dr. and Mrs. Avalo Caldwell
Mr. and Mrs. Eddie Cordes
Col. and Mrs. Paul S. Cullen
Dr. and Mrs. Wm. E. Cunningham
Dr. and Mrs. Robert P. Dennis
Mr. and Mrs. John B. Doolin
First Federal Savings & Loan
Robert Giles
William Fletcher
Flowers by Ramon
Mr. and Mrs. B. K. Fowler
LTC and Mrs. Douglas M. Gaither
Mr. and Mrs. Richard Glenn
Mr. and Mrs. W. W. Godlove
Greenlawn Funeral Home
Greer's Flowers and Gifts
Col. and Mrs. Everett G. Hahney
Forest D. Harris
Kathleen Heinz
Dr. and Mrs. Bill G. Henley
Mr. and Mrs. John C. Hester, Jr.
Dr. and Mrs. J. T. Hicks
Dr. and Mrs. Robert P. Hillis
Col. and Mrs. James E. Holley
Theodore L. Horton
Dr. Bill Howard
Dr. and Mrs. Samuel C. Jack
Katy-K Meat Packers
J. C. Kennedy
Key Hammond Organ Studio
Mr. and Mrs. Vernon Klein
Lawton Band Instrument Co.
Lawton Funeral Home
Mrs. LeRoy Leister
Mr. and Mrs. Anthony Libro
Mr. and Mrs. Edgar Marburger
Mr. and Mrs. Richard M. Massad
Mathis Music Center (Baldwin)
Thomas O. McCollom
Jennie L. McCutcheon
Dr. and Mrs. Frank R. Michener
Mr. and Mrs. Graydon Miller, Jr.
Mrs. Clift Montgomery
Mt. Scott & Hankins Drive-In Thea.
Mrs. H. S. Neeley, Jr.
Mr. and Mrs. A. E. Newcombe
Mr. and Mrs. Ralph Newcombe
T. D. Nicklas
Dr. Donald E. Norris
OK Transfer & Storage
Dr. and Mrs. Norman O'Leary
Col. (Ret) & Mrs. Wilton K. Oneal
Parisian Stores
Dr. and Mrs. O. L. Parsons
Phillips-Aubrey Chevrolet
Pepsi-Cola Bottling Co.
Porter-Rhoads Construction, Inc.
Public Service Company
Rainbo Photo Color, Inc.
Mr. and Mrs. Jack Raulston
Rayl and Company, Inc.
Major and Mrs. Wayne R. Rickard
Dan Rudder Motor Co.
Sare's Printing & Letter Shop
Schubert Music Club
Sears Roebuck and Co.
Shwen-Davis Motor Service
Mrs. Robert P. Scott
Mr. and Mrs. Wm. H. Smisson
Mr. and Mrs. Arthur Duane Smith
Dr. and Mrs. George F. Smith
Miss Leta Mae Smith
Mr. and Mrs. Warren Smith
Mr. and Mrs. Frank C. Sneed
Storey and Barton School of the Dance
Mr. and Mrs. J. L. Stovall
Terry Lee Stovall
Walter M. Smith Agency
Mr. and Mrs. Dale Thompson
Tony & Fayrene Hair Stylist
Montgomery Ward
Dr. and Mrs. Daniel A. Woesner
Dr. and Mrs. Donald E. Wicker
Dr. and Mrs. Walter Wicker
Dr. and Mrs. Doug Wilson
Mr. and Mrs. Woody Wolverton
Mr. and Mrs. Lee J. Woods

The Lawton Philharmonic Society

presents the

ᏞAWTON PHILHARMONIC ORCHESTRA

NELS HARVELAND — Musical Director

with the

ᏟAMERON SINGERS

DR. GEORGE SMITH — Director

RHONDA WARD — Pianist

FRED FOX — Bass

Eighth Season, Final Concert
Saturday, 8:15 P.M., May 9, 1970
McMahon Auditorium

LAWTON, OKLAHOMA
DECEMBER, 1970

SORRY FOR THE LESS PERSONAL GREETING THIS YEAR — BUT WE'RE
JUST SETTLING DOWN AFTER SEVERAL TURBULENT MONTHS AND THIS
IS THE MOST EXPEDIENT WAY TO MEET THE "DEADLINE" FOR OUR
ANNUAL HOLIDAY CONTACT WITH YOU —

THERE IS NO DOUBT THAT OUR HOUSEHOLD HAS DRASTICALLY CHANGED
THIS YEAR — BUT SUCH A DELIGHTFUL CHANGE WITH THE ADDITION OF
LITTLE ERIC! AT 10 MONTHS HE IS QUITE THE LITTLE BOY WITH
HIS OWN HAPPY - AND VERY DISTINCTIVE - PERSONALITY - HE ALSO
MUST HAVE SET SOMEWHAT OF A TRAVEL RECORD FOR HIS AGE -
HAVING LOGGED IN ABOUT 25,000 MILES THIS YEAR!

IN MAY WE MADE A HAPPY TRIP TO THE EAST COAST WHERE THE
ENTIRE WALKER CLAN GATHERED IN PHILADELPHIA FOR ERIC'S
BAPTISM. THEN ON TO WASHINGTON D.C. FOR A FABULOUS WEEK
OR SO OF VISITS WITH FRIENDS AND SIGHT SEEING - FROM WASHINGTON
I CAME BACK TO BUFFALO COUNTRY ALONE WHILE ELIN FLEW
TO EUROPE TO SHOW OFF ERIC TO HIS DANISH GRANDPARENTS
IN A WONDERFUL MONTH-LONG VISIT.

FAMILY BACK TOGETHER IN LAWTON IN JULY - WE STIFLED THROUGH
AN UNMERCIFULLY HOT OKLAHOMA SUMMER - THEN IN SEPTEMBER
ELIN'S SISTER KIRSTEN AND HER LITTLE BOY JEAN CAME TO STAY
WITH US A MONTH WHILE HER HUSBAND TOM WAS WITH HIS FIRM IN
CALIFORNIA - NEWS FROM DENMARK IN EARLY OCTOBER SENT
ELIN, KIRSTEN AND THE TWO BOYS ON AN UNEXPECTED TRIP TO
ODENSE - ELIN'S FATHER WAS SUDDENLY STRICKEN CRITICALLY ILL
AND THE GIRLS WENT TO BE WITH THEIR MOTHER AT THAT TIME
(HIS CONDITION IS STILL CRITICAL BUT WE ARE PRAYING FOR RECOVERY) -

I DROVE EAST IN NOVEMBER - MET ELIN AND ERIC ON THEIR RETURN
FROM EUROPE - AND AFTER VISITS IN NEW YORK AND WASHINGTON WENT
TO PHILADELPHIA FOR THANKSGIVING AND TO PARTICIPATE IN MY
SISTER JOAN'S WEDDING. SO — HAVING ONLY BEEN HOME A FEW
DAYS WE'RE CATCHING OUR BREATHS — NOT QUITE PREPARED
FOR THE HOLIDAYS — AND PUTTING THINGS OUT OF REACH OF
TWO VERY BUSY LITTLE HANDS!

Bill

Eric

Have a Merry
and a Happy

Elin

Christening of Eric Halvdan Walker in Philadelphia

Mor and Far with baby Eric

Mother and Uncle Charlie with baby Eric

Kirsten with baby Sean

Joan and Patrick's wedding day

Joan with Best Man Terence O'Mara and brother Bill who walked her down the aisle

APPENDIX A

Special Orders – 4/27/1967

SPECIAL ORDERS   HEADQUARTERS,
                                                        DEPARTMENT OF THE ARMY,
No. 82   WASHINGTON, D.C., *27 April 1967*

*   *   *   *   *   *   *

84. TC 373. Fol ch dir. Rsn ABCMR. Auth 10 USC 1552.
    GARNER, KERMIT C., O70340 LTC TC Hq USCONARC Ft Monroe, Va 22351, act eff date temp to LTC AUS from 14 Dec 1966 to 30 Sep 1966.
    KILGORE, JEFFERSON G., O2326631 1LT MSC USAH Ft Gordon, Ga 30905, act eff date temp p.m to 1LT AUS from 1 Aug 1966 to 11 Jul 1966.
    KUTCH, ELZA L., O2326636 1LT MSC USAH Ft Ord, Calif 93941, act eff date temp prm to 1LT AUS from 1 Aug 1966 to 11 Jul 1966.

*   *   *   *   *   *   *

85. TC 300. DP fol detm affecting prm status indiv indic is ann. Comdr will ntfy indiv.

	Perm gr	Perm DOR	Basic date
HIGGINS, JAMES E., OF109829 JAGC	1LT	26 Sep 1966	26 Sep 1963
JONES, WALTER H., JR., OF109837 JAGC	1LT	27 Sep 1966	27 Sep 1963

1?1. TC 220. Fol rsg dir. WP. TDN. 2172010 01–2211–2212–2213–2214–2215–2216–2217 P 1422 S99–999. 2182010 01–2211–2212–2213–2214–2215–2216–2217 P 1422 S99–999. Scty clnc interim secret clnc. Resp comdr will comply w/AR 604–5, unoindc. Lv data 15 DALVP UNOINDC. Aloc student, UNOINDC. PCS (MDC) 2A. Sp instr: AD svc oblg incurred PRAP AR 350–100 par 20 AR 635–120 DA Pam 350–10 UNOINDC.

*   *   *   *   *   *   *

LEVITSKY, MARIAN M., N5407283 CPT ANC D–3442 US Army Hosp (6A–6003–06), Ft Ord, Calif 93941. Asg to Stu Det MFSS (MD–3410–02), Ft Sam Houston, Tex 78234 fpur atnd AMEDS Off Career Crs 6–8–C22 (QS 32–A) for a pd in excess of 20 wks. Rept date 3 Jul 1967. EDCSA 8 Jul 1967.

*   *   *   *   *   *   *

133. TC 220. Fol rsg dir. WP. TDN. 2172010 01–2211–2212–2213–2214–2215–2216–2217 P 1422 S99–999. 2182010 01–2211–2212–2213–2214–2215–2216–2217 P 1422 S99–999. Lv data 15 DALVP, unoindc. PCS (MDC) 2B.

*   *   *   *   *   *   *

MARTIN, ROBERT J., JR., MN2325725 2LT ANC 3437 Stu Det Fitzsimons Gen Hosp (MD–3412) Denver, Colo 80240, eff upon compl of neuropsychiatric crs. Asg to USAH (6A–6003–06) Ft Ord, Calif 93941. Aloc Sep–17. Rept date 20 Jul 1967. EDCSA 18 Jun 1967. Sp instr: AD svc oblg incurred AR 350–100 par 20 AR 635–120 DA Cir 350–46.
SAPOLIS, RICHARD J., MN5239598 2LT ANC 3437 Stu Det Fitzsimons Gen Hosp (MD–3412) Denver, Colo 80240, eff upon compl of neuropsychiatric crs. Asg to VFGH (MD–3416), Phoenixville, Pa 19560. Aloc Aug–2. Rept date 24 Jul 1967. EDCSA 18 Jun 1967.
SHONTS, MARILYN J., N5520864 2LT ANC 3437 Stu Det Fitzsimons Gen Hosp (MD–3412) Denver, Colo 80240, eff upon compl of neurospychiatric crs. Asg to USAH (6A–6003–06), Ft Ord, Calif 93941. Aloc Sep–16. Rept date 20 Jul 1967. EDCSA 2 Jul 1967. Sp instr: AD svc oblg incurred AR 350–100 par 20 AR 635–120 DA Cir 350–46.

*   *   *   *   *   *   *

140. TC 220. Fol rsg dir. WP. TDN. 2182010 01–3311–3312–3313–3314–3315–3316–3317 P 1433 S99–999.
    WALKER, WILLIAM A., O5208565 CPT AGC 2110 Hq USAG (6A–6003–05) Ft Ord, Calif 93941. Asg to USAG (4A–4005) Ft Hood, Tex, for further asg to 9th Spt Bn 198th Inf Bde upon activation. Aloc Jun–X–6148. Rept date NLT 15 Jul 1967. Scty clnc secret. Lv data 15 DDALV. PCS (MDC) 3A. EDCSA 1 Jul 1967. Sp instr: Prov of par 2a DA message 763677 6 May 1966 applies. Fld cmdr will amend DASO IAW par 38a(9) AR 310–10 as nec to incl restr clause cntn in par 7 DA Cir 614–8 as aprop.

*   *   *   *   *   *   *

218. TC 220. Fol rsg dir. WP. TDN. 2172010 01–2211–2212–2213–2214–2215–2216–2217 P 1422 S99–999. 2182010 01–2211–2212–2213–2214–2215–2216–2217 P 1422 S99–999.
    HORTON, CHARLES L., O78889 LTC Arty 1193 (0006) HHC 4th Bn 1st Bde (6A–6003–01) Ft Ord, Calif 93941. Asg to Stu Det Hq MDW USA (MW–7001–07) Tempo B 2nd and R St SW, Washington, DC 20315. Aloc Sep–M–1. Lv data 15 DALVP prior to TDY. PCS (MDC) 2A. EDCSA 2 May 1967. Sp instr: UP JTR M6453 and par 11c (7) AR 621–5 off permitted to pro on TDY to Univ of Omaha, Omaha, Nebr 68100, fpur fulfilling rqr for baccalaureate degree for pd approx 189 days to rept 9 Sep 1967. Compl w/par 11c (8) (9) (10) AR 621–5 rqr. No exp to the Govt WB incurred by reason of this TDY. Atch to Stu Det Fifth USA (5A–5002) Chicago, Ill 60615, for admin. Svc oblg 2 yrs is incurred UP AR 350–100 and DA Pam 350–10. Para 10a(1)(c) AR 635–130 applies w/ref to ret.

*   *   *   *   *   *   *

239. TC 240. Fol rsg dir. PRAP AR 55–28. WP. TDN. Indiv will send msg ntfy to CG USARV advising of ch in ETA when trans sed are ch at trans. shpmt or stopover pt fol dprt fr CONUS. Such msg WB given to CO of mil instl enr for xmsn. An ex bag alw of 134 lbs personal eff auth to acmp ea indiv while tvl by acft. Cncr tvl of depn and shpmt of POV not auth. Indiv will arr in Vietnam wearing khaki trousers and short sleeve shirt and will have in poss basic rqr khaki unif fatigues and cbt boots. Army tan and green unif opt for officers only. Dress unif not rqr. Summer clv clo desirable for off-duty wear. UP par 11 AR 40–562 plague imm are rqr tvl need not be delayed except for the first vaccine dose. Indiv needing corr eye lenses WB equip with mask protective fld M17 and nec corr eye lenses prior to dprt from CONUS. The introduction pur and poss of privately owned wpn is prohibited in the Republic of Vietnam. DA Msg 757912 dated 31 Mar 1966 applies. TDY enr to USA Atlantic Area Installation Cmd, Ft William Davis, CZ. PD (TDY) approx 2 wks. Crs Jungle OP (QS 09B). Asg to USARV Transient Det, APO San Francisco 96307. Lv data 30 DDALVAHP prior to TDY. UNOINDC. Scty clnc secret. PCS (MDC) ZZ. Acct clas for tvl costs to and PD at TDY sta only 2182020 32–28 P 2110–21, 22, 25 S99–999. For all other costs 2172010 01–4411–4412–4413–4414–4415–4416–4417 P 1444 S99–999; 2182010 01–4411–4412–4413–4414–4415–4416–4417 P 1444 S99–999. CIC 271A01. CIC 281A01.

*   *   *   *   *   *   *

CROSBY, CHARLES G., O5283489 2LT Armor 71203 (1204) Co A 4th Bn 41st Inf, Ft Ord, Calif 93941. Rept date (TDY) 15 Jul 1967. Cl No. 68–1 Aloc Aug–235 (IDC–2). Fur asg 11th Armd Cav Regt, APO San Francisco 96257. Aval date 3 Aug 1967 to arr OS dest NLT 6 Aug 1967. EDCSA 6 Aug 1967.

25

By Order of the Secretary of the Army:

HAROLD K. JOHNSON,
General, United States Army,
Chief of Staff.

Official:

KENNETH G. WICKHAM,
Major General, United States Army,
The Adjutant General.

DISTRIBUTION:
```
 2 - 1LT Elza L. Kutch, USAH
 2 - 1LT James E. Higgins, SJA Section
35 - CPT Marian M. Levitsky, USAH
35 - CPT William A. Walker, G-1 Section
35 - LTC Charles L. Horton, HHC 4th Bn 1st Bde
21 - CO, USAH, ATTN:  UPS
 2 - SJA Section
 2 - G-1 Section
 2 - CO, HHC 4th Bn 1st Bde
50 - AMNOR-AGPG
 1 - AMNOR-AGFW
 1 - EA: E2, E3, A47          [S.O. 82, 27 April 1967]
 1 - Post Locator
 1 - Post Central Clearance
25 - Officer Finance
```

A TRUE EXTRACT:

D. L. NEIL
Captain, AGC
Asst Adj Gen

Special Orders – 5/03/1967

HEADQUARTERS
UNITED STATES ARMY TRAINING CENTER, INFANTRY
AND
Fort Ord, California 93941

SPECIAL ORDERS   3 May 1967
NUMBER   123   EXTRACT

     8. TC 370. Fol orders AMENDED.

SMO: Para 9 SO 118 this hq CS.
Pert to: RSG of MC NITT, LANE W 05326441 1LT MPC 71542 293d MP Co (PCorS) to
          54th MP Co (Svc)
As reads: "Sp instr: Dy as Comd, Team AC Co Hq (MOS 9110)"
IATR: "Sp instr: Dy as Comd, 54th MP Co (MOS 9110)"

SMO: Para 140 DASO 82 CS.
Pert to: RSG of WALKER, WILLIAM A 05208565 CPT AGC 2110 Hq USA Gar (6A-6003-05)
          Ft Ord, Calif 93941 to USAG (4A-4005) Ft Hood, Texas for fur asg to
          9th Spt Bn, 198th Inf Bde upon activation
IATA: "Sp instr: CPT William A. Walker is rel fr dy at current unit and station
       and is assigned to USAG (4A-4005) Ft Hood, Texas for fur asg to 9th Spt
       Bn, 198th Inf Bde upon activation for fur move to a restricted area over-
       seas. Transportation of depn and mov of HHG auth to designated location.
       Movement of depn and HHG to vic of USAG (4A-4005) Ft Hood, Texas is not
       auth except as move to a designated place."

SMO: Para 123 DASO 50 CS.
Pert to: RSG of TOMLINSON, FRED B 088508 MAJ MC B3150 USAH (6A-6003-06) Ft Ord,
          Calif 93941 to WRGH WRAMC (MD-3401) Washington, DC 20315
As reads: "TOMILINSON, FRED B 088508 MAJ MC B3150****"
           "Lv data: 15 DALVP"
IATR: "TOMLINSON, FRED B 088508 MAJ MC B3150****"
       "Lv data: 30 DALVP"

     Para 9 to 50 inclusive not used.

          FOR THE COMMANDER:

                                    JAMES E. HENDERSON
                                    Colonel, GS
                                    Chief of Staff

OFFICIAL

DOROTHE CANTEBES
Act Adjutant General

SO 123 Hq USATC Inf & Ft Ord, California 93941, 3 May 67 (cont)

DISTRIBUTION
```
   E Less 7, 8, 24, 27, 30, 31, 32, 33, 34, 42, 55
   2 - 1LT Lane W. McNitt, 54th MP Co
  35 - CPT William A. Walker, dy w/G1 Sec
  35 - MAJ Fred B. Tomlinson, USAH
   2 - CO, 54th MP Co
   2 - CO, 293d MP Co
   1 - PM Sec
  15 - CO, USAH, ATTN:  Pers Sec
   2 - G1 Sec
   5 - CO, USAG (4A-4005) Ft Hood, Texas  (Airmail)
   5 - CO, WRGH WRAMC Washington, DC 20315 (Airmail)

SPECIAL DISTRIBUTION
   3 - TAG DA, ATTN:  AGPF-O
   1 - TSG DA, ATTN:  MEDPT
   1 - Director, OPD, OPAG
   1 - Director, OPD, OPMP
```

Adjutant General Officers Roster

ADJUTANT GENERAL OFFICERS ROSTER

HEADQUARTERS, 198TH INFANTRY BRIGADE (SEP)

RANK	NAME	BR	SERVICE NUMBER	DOB DOR	DUTY POSITION	WIFES NAME	ACC DEP	OFFICE PHONE HOME PHONE	ADDRESS
CPT	Walker, William A.	AGC	05208555	31 Jul 37 30 Oct 63	Adjutant General	Elin	0	5-3716 5-4661	BOQ 2210, Rm 17
CPT	Dove, Bobby Lee	AGC	05209489	7 Nov 32 31 Jul 64	Chief, PSD	Antonia	0	4135/3834 5-4659	BOQ 432, Rm 9
CPT	Payant, Kenneth A.	AGC	05318242	12 Jan 36 2 Jun 66	AG XO	Jutta	3	5-3716 KT75259	1305 S 23d St Copperas Cove
2LT	Yates, William Edward Jr	AGC	05537672	4 Feb 43 29 Sep 66	Chief, Pers Mgt Br	Penny	1	4135/3834 KT7-3695	2103 Crosten, Copperas Cove
2LT	Goertel, Michael W.	AGC	05537434	3 Jul 44 30 Sep 66	Chief, ASD	Sue	1	5-4231 ME4-2060	109 West Harriso Killeen, Texas
2LT	Brown, Otis, M.	AGC	05421874	21 Mar 43 4 Nov 66	Bde Postal Officer	Jane	1	6220/6416 ME4-1574	506 Joyner Circl Killeen, Texas
2LT	Bean, James W.	CMCL	05422811		Repl Det Cmdr				(ETA 15 Jul 67)
CWO3	Young, Wayne Lyman	AGC	W3150417	1 Dec 31 17 Jun 65	Chief, Pers Act Br	Ardith	5	4135/3834 5-4659	BOQ 432
CWO1	Harmon, Jesse T.	AGC	W3200913	27 Feb 36 4 Jan 67	Chief, Pers Rcds Br	Luise	0	4135/3834 5-4357	BOQ 430

Personnel Action – Quarters   05/15/1967

<table>
<tr><td colspan="2">PERSONNEL ACTION
(AR 340-15)</td><td>DATE
15 May 1967</td></tr>
<tr><td>REFERENCE OR OFFICE SYMBOL
AMNOR-A   WALKER, William A.
05208565</td><td>SUBJECT
Request for Continued Occupancy
of Government Quarters</td><td></td></tr>
<tr><td>TO:
Commanding General USATC, Infantry
ATTN: AMNOR-D
Fort Ord, California 93941</td><td colspan="2">FROM:
Captain William A. Walker 05208565
HQ USATC duty w/G1, Fort Ord, Calif.</td></tr>
</table>

NO. | PROCESSING ACTIONS

1

1. UP of Annex F, USATC & Ft Ord Reg 210-1, request that my dependent wife, Elin M. Walker, be authorized to remain in my presently occupied government quarters for a period not to exceed 90 days following my departure from this command on PCS.

2. I received DA orders on 4 May 1967 (copy attached), for reassignment to Ft Hood, Texas, for further assignment to Vietnam. Movement of dependents to Ft Hood is not authorized. Original reporting date at Ft Hood was 15 July 1967. This was ammended by DA per FONECON on 10 May 1967 to 15 June 1967. I will depart Ft Hood for leave and travel on or about 25 May 67. I have received information that I will depart Ft Hood for Vietnam on or about 31 August 1967. The requested extension of occupancy of government quarters would only be for the period of time that I am physically in the United States.

3. Because of the change in reporting dates, insufficient time remains to relocate my dependent before my departure. Our relocation plans were being based on the later departure date, and the present time-frame precludes completing proper arrangements for off-post rental, which would not be available until the first part of August 1967. Relocation at this time would present a hardship to myself and my wife; the requested extension would provide a reasonable time to relocate without difficulty.

4. My quarters address is 206 Rendova Road, Ft Ord, California, which is a two-bedroom duplex. My wife is my only dependent.

1 Incl
as

WILLIAM A. WALKER
05208565
Captain, HQ USATC duty w/G1, Ft Ord, Calif.

CONTINUE ENTRIES ON PLAIN WHITE PAPER.

DA FORM 1 OCT 55 **1049**   REPLACES EDITION OF 1 OCT 53, WHICH IS OBSOLETE   ® GPO : 1964 OF—715-938

2   AMNOR-DFH Walker, William A., 05 208 565 (15 May 67)
    SUBJECT: Request for Continued Occupancy of Government Quarters
TO CPT William A. Walker   FROM CG, USATC, INF and
    Hq USATC duty w/G1 Section   Ft Ord, California
    Fort Ord, California

    1. Your request to retain your present quarters until on or about
10 September 1967 is approved. No extensions will be granted as these
quarters are required to house permanently assigned personnel.

    2. In the event the need for these quarters develops, it may be
necessary for your dependent to make off-post arrangements in which case
your dependent will receive maximum notice and assistance to insure an
orderly move. This move would be made at government expense.

    3. At least one week prior to terminating quarters, you or your
authorized representative will report to the Family Housing Office,
Coe Avenue, to establish a definite "check-out" time and complete other
administrative actions.

wd all incl

                                    JOHN J. PAVICK
                                    Colonel, GS
                                    Deputy Post Commander

PP RUWPFO

DE RUEPDA 275A 1362038

ZNR UUUUU

P R 162030Z May 67

FM DA

****   ****   ****

RUWTULA/CGUSAG FTHOOD TEX

RUWPFO/CG USAG FTORD CALIF

****   ****   ****

BT

UNCLAS 08283 FROM AGSO-O

TC 370. BY ORDER SA FOL DA ORDERS AMENDED.

****   ****   ****

SMO; PARA 140 SO 82 HQ DACS (FT HOOD TEX). PERT TO; WALKER,

WILLIAM A 052085 65 CPT AGC 2110 HQ USAG (6A-6003-65) FT ORD,

CALIF 93941. AS READS; REPT DATE; NLT 15 JUL 67. EDCSA 1

JUL 67. INATR; REPT DATE; NLT 15 JUN 67. EDCSA 1 JUN 67.

BT

A TRUE EXTRACT

D. L. NEIL
CPT, AGC
Asst Adj Gen

DISTRIBUTION
   35 - CPT Walker, G1 Sec
   15 - Off Br
    4 - FAO, Ft Ord
    2 - G1
    2 - G2 Sec
    1 - Post Locator
    1 - Central Post Clearance

APPENDIX B

AMERICAL news sheet

Volume 1 Number 287   Thursday   February 1, 1968

MIRACLE WEATHER REPORT

Firday partly cloudy with early morning ground fog clearing by mid-morning. Winds will be northeasterly at 8-12 knots per hour. Friday's high 87. Low Friday night 70.

VIETNAM WAR NEWS

SAIGON (UPI) -- The Viet Cong launched their mightiest offensive of the war yesterday and sent thousands of troops smashing into dozens of towns and villages still celebrating the Lunar New Year cease-fire. They inflicted untold millions of dollars in damage but were defeated.

U.S. and Allied Forces canceled their part of the Tet truce and drove back the guerrillas in daylong fighting that ranged from house to house, from street to street. Seven major cities, and many U.S. military installations were hit.

First Time In 103 Yrs

WASHINGTON (AP) ---- Historic Ford's Theater reopened Tuesday night for the first time since President Lincoln was assassinated there in 1865.

Rain fell and anti-Vietnam war pickets chanted as Vice President and Mrs. Hubert Humphrey led an audience into the refurnished play house in downtown Washington.

The evening was dedicated to Lincoln, with

(Cont'd Page 2 Column 3)

CLEAN CUT: MURPHY

WASHINGTON (AP) ---- The U.S. Post Office Department, concerned about its own image and the morale of its regular workers, is preparing a set of regulations designed to clean up its newly hired hippie help.

Richard J. Murphy, Assistant Postmaster General in charge of personnel, said Tuesday he has received complaints from the public----especially in San Francisco----about letter carriers who wear "flamboyant and outlandish garb----bear coats and beads and bells."

Viet Cong Attack Chu Lai: Totalling 302 Enemy Killed

CHU LAI (AMERICAL IO) -- Enemy attacks on the Chu Lai Air Base and other division camps prompted quick reaction fighting that accounted for 302 enemy kills by Americal Division units in southern I Corps yesterday. Five U.S. soldier were killed and 23 infantrymen were wounded in day long fighting.

In continuous heavy fighting yesterday, units of Americal's 198th Brigade doggedly pursued enemy forces that staged a rocket attack on the Chu Lai Air Base Wednesday morning, and accounted for 137 kills.

The Air Base attack began at 4:06 a.m., with 48 enemy 122mm rockets fired. Although moderate damage was sustained on a number of the aircraft, the airfield was relatively unaffected. Shortly after the attack on the air strip an ammunition dump located about a mile south of the air strip was hit by rocket fire. A large explosion occurred and several secondary explosions followed lasting throughout the early morning.

"Brave and Bold" units began an immediate pursuit of the attackers in the early morning darkness. Flares guided the brigade gunships and at first light infantry companies moved out to intercept the escaping Viet Cong. As contact tapered off yesterday afternoon 198th Tactical Area of Responsibility (TAOR) units reported 72 enemy were killed.

In the largest contact of the day, an infantry company led by CPT Virgil Lee Con (Creedsmore, N.C.) set up a blocking position 20 miles south of here while gunships engaged an enemy

(Cont'd Page 2 Column 1)

Page 2   AMERICAL NEWS SHEET   Vol. 1   No. 287   Feb 1, 1968

AMERICAL (From Page 1)

force from the air. Forty-four enemy were killed in the hour long battle that began at 9:45 a.m., in the Operation Muscatine area.

In addition to the rocket attack at Chu Lai an enemy force simultaneously mortared and launched a ground assault on a small bridge force of military police and infantrymen guarding the An Tan Bridge on Hwy #1. During the heavy fighting the Viet Cong blew the center abutment causing the west span of the bridge to collapse. North-south traffic continued over the An Tan River on the east span of the bridge which was undamaged. Five Viet Cong were killed during the raid.

Later in the morning a brigade element operating south of here engaged more escaping enemy and killed nine Viet Cong. A brigade air observer

(Cont'd Page 3 Column 1)

"Shame and A Disgrace": Thurmond

WASHINGTON (UPI)—Sen. Strom Thurmond, Republican-South Carolina, shouting and clapping his hands in an almost empty Senate chamber Tuesday charged that the U.S. handling of the war in Vietnam was a "shame and a disgrace."

"How much longer are we going to wait?" Thurmond said in an extemporaneous 15-minute speech after he was advised Communist troops had attacked the U.S. Embassy compound in Saigon.

"How many more Americans are going to be killed before we take the firm, decisive action we should have taken long, long ago?"

Instructors Needed: CALL 251 NOW

University of Maryland Instructors: The Division Education Center has a continuing need for University of Maryland instructors. Personnel who have the time and interest for off-duty evening instruction should contact the Education Center (Chu Lai 251). Minimum requirement for appointment as an instructor, MASTERS DEGREE OR ITS EQUIVALENT.

LONDON (UPI)—Helen Vlachou, the Greek publisher, said yesterday she was unimpressed by the Greek government's amnesty offer Monday.

She said dismissal in an Athens court of charges against her "makes no difference to me at all. It's a clever little gimmick trumped up by someone seeking favorable propaganda. It changes nothing.

Ford Theater (From Page 1)

the First Lady of the theater, Helen Hayes, becoming the first player to stand on the stage since the President was shot nearly 103 years ago.

The theater, restored under a three-year project of the National Parks Service, was officially dedicated January 21. A galaxie of stars took part in the opening performance, televised on a special hourlong program broadcast nationwide.

------------------AMERICAL NEWS SHEET------------------
Major General S.W. Koster
Commanding General, American Division
Information Officer................MAJ Patrick H. Dionne
News Sheet OIC....................1LT Robert L. Brehm
Editor............................SSG Al E. Morris
Assistant Editor.................SP5 Washington Hardmon Jr
Telephone: Chu Lai 209 and Chu Lai 241
This News Sheet is published daily under the supervision of the IO, Americal Division as an authorized Army publication. This News Sheet is solely for personnel in the Americal Division and may not be duplicated or released to the news media. Opinions expressed in this publication are not necessarily those of Department of the Army.

Page 3   AMERICAL NEWS SHEET   Vol. 1   No. 287   Feb 1, 1968

AMERICAL (Continued From Page 2)

flying south of Chu Lai spotted an armed enemy force of 150 Viet Cong and directed artillery fire on their position. Five confirmed enemy kills were reported.

At 5 p.m., soldiers of "H" Troop, 17th Cavalry guarding the Binh Son Bridge south of here engaged a large enemy force. With the help of brigade infantrymen, the cavalrymen forced the enemy to break contact shortly before dark. The brigade has been the target of previous enemy attacks.

North of Tam Ky along Hwy #1 "C" Troop, 1st Squadron, 1st Cavalry and "C" Troop, 7th Squadron, 17th Cavalry engaged a VC force estimated at two battalions. Fifty-eight enemy were killed by "C" Troop, 1st Squadron, 1st Cavalry and 12 killed by "C" Troop, 7th Squadron, 17th Cavalry.

The action began early in the morning, when "C" Troop, of the 1st Cavalry came under heavy recoilless rifle, automatic rifle fire, and a mortar attack at their night position at Quang Tin Province Headquarters. The contact continued throughout the morning and ended early in the afternoon.

Sharp activity in Americal's 3rd Brigade, 4th Infantry's area of operation resulted in 66 enemy killed, seven suspects detained and the capture of four weapons.

At 3 a.m., yesterday morning, brigade artillery fired 247 rounds of 105mm at a large enemy concentration. Fifty-four enemy bodies were credited to the artillery fire. An additional 54 enemy kills were credited to the 2nd ROK Marine force located south of Hoi An who were conducting a joint operation with elements of the "Broncos".

An element of the 1st Battalion, 14th Infantry in several contacts killed seven VC and captured 400 pounds of rice, one M-16 and an anti-aircraft

(Cont'd Page 4 Column 1)

DATELINES -- (AP)

PALM SPRINGS, Calif. -- More than 500 golfers got in final practice shots Tuesday for the 122,000 dollar Bob Hope Desert Classic.

WASHINGTON--- The Internal Revenue Service has suspended all its activities directed at criminal prosecution for possession of unregistered firearms or for failure of gamblers to register and pay special taxes, the agency announced Tuesday.

EL TORO MARINE CORPS AIR STATION, California --Two Marines who escaped from the North Vietnamese last week after being held captive since Jan. 7 arrived here Monday after a 10 hour flight from Okinawa.

Six Killed From Explosion

PITTSBURGH (AP)--Six persons were killed and 17 others were injured Tuesday when an earth-- shaking explosion ripped apart a row of shops and apartments. Two others were missing.

The frame buildings were blown into a heap of burning rubble. Windows were shattered throughout the area in suburban Ingram.

The blast let loose as a 12---man crew from the Equitable Gas Company was digging up the sidewalk outside looking for a gas leak. Five of the dead were gas company workers.

The company said the crew was working on a four-inch gasline; and said that gas to the buildings was shut off.

"There is a lot of investigation involved," said a company spokesman. "Actually, the real cause probably will never be known."

Firemen also recovered the body of a woman. She was not positively identified immediately.

SEOUL---The North Korean military machine has been rebuilt into a much more powerful force than it was before the Korean War, according to South Korean military intelligence officials.

It is supplied, supported and advised by the Russians and the Communist Chinese but is moving closer to self-sufficiency, the officials said.

Page 4 .... AMERICAL NEWS SHEET   Vol. 1 No. 287   Feb 1, 1968

AMERICAL DIVISION NEWS (Continued From Page 3)

rocket and launcher. Early in the afternoon, a company of the 1st Battalion, 35th Infantry killed five VC and detained seven suspects who were hiding in a cave. Also discovered in the cave was one .38 caliber pistol. Another company of the 1st Battalion, 35th Infantry uncovered a homemade zip gun hidden in a hut.

Units of Americal's 196th Brigade killed 27 VC in moderate contacts in eastern portions of the "Chargers" area of operation in Operation Wheeler/Wallowa.

In the heaviest action of the day "F" Troop, 17th Cavalry engaged a large group of VC killing 12 and detaining 11. In a delayed report from Tuesday night "C" Troop, 7th Squadron, 17th Cavalry killed five VC and a company from the 2nd Battalion, 1st Infantry led by CPT John T. Thomason (Severna Park, Md) killed one VC they found hiding in a tunnel. The company also found one wounded NVA soldier hiding nearby. He had web gear and ammunition for an AK-47 rifle. He was evacuated for treatment at 2nd Surgical Hospital.

A small reconnaissance unit from the 3rd Battalion, 21st Infantry killed three VC they spotted fleeing from a hut. A small unit observed four VC with gray uniforms enter a hut. Artillery from the 3rd Battalion, 82nd Artillery was called in killing the four VC. A small unit from the 3rd Battalion, 21st Infantry observed eight VC moving down a trail. They called in artillery from the 3rd Battalion, 82nd Artillery killing two VC.

Two tactical air strikes were flown yesterday in support of the "Chargers". The missions resulted in two fortified structures destroyed, 10 meters of trench opened-up and two bunkers destoyed.

Operations in the Duc Pho area yesterday netted Americal's 11th Brigade's "Jungle Warriors" two VC kills and one suspect detained.

An element of the 3rd Battalion, 1st Infantry led by CPT Joe Rhinehart (Canton, N.C.) engaged two enemy soldiers nine miles west of Duc Pho. After a brief firefight one VC was killed and the other fled.

A helicopter from the brigade's aviation section, "Primo Aviation Limited", on a reconnaissance flight spotted two VC carrying weapons four miles southwest of Duc Pho. After an exchange of fire one VC was killed and two M-1 carbines with ammunition and miscellaneous clothing were captured.

INSTRUCTORS WHERE ARE YOU?

UNIVERSITY OF MARYLAND INSTRUCTORS: The Division Education Center has a continuing need for University of Maryland Instructors. Personnel who have the time and interest for OFF-DUTY evening instruction should contact the Education Center (CHU LAI 251). Minimum requirement for appointment as an instructor, MASTERS DEGREE OR ITS EQUIVALENT.

!!!!!!!!ZIP CODE!!!!!!!! Lest one of the 867 residents of Melcher, Iowa, forget his Zip Code, the number has been painted on the town's water tank in figures six feet high. DON'T FORGET YOURS!!!!!!!!

APPENDIX C

*Award of the Bronze Star for Meritorious Service
by Colonel Tixier, Americal Division Chief of Staff*

THE UNITED STATES OF AMERICA

TO ALL WHO SHALL SEE THESE PRESENTS, GREETING:

THIS IS TO CERTIFY THAT
THE PRESIDENT OF THE UNITED STATES OF AMERICA
AUTHORIZED BY EXECUTIVE ORDER, 24 AUGUST 1962
HAS AWARDED

THE BRONZE STAR MEDAL

TO

MAJOR WILLIAM A. WALKER, O5208565, ADJUTANTS GENERAL CORPS, UNITED STATES ARMY

FOR

MERITORIOUS ACHIEVEMENT
IN GROUND OPERATIONS AGAINST HOSTILE FORCES

IN THE REPUBLIC OF VIETNAM DURING THE PERIOD AUGUST 1967 TO SEPTEMBER 1968
GIVEN UNDER MY HAND IN THE CITY OF WASHINGTON
THIS   24th   DAY OF   SEPTEMBER   1968

CHARLES M. GETTYS
Major General, USA
Commanding

Stanley R. Resor
SECRETARY OF THE ARMY

APPENDIX D

WHO'S WHO IN THE LETTERS

William Alan Walker "Bill"

Bill is the eldest son of Elizabeth R. Walker (1908-1987) and William A. Walker, Sr. (1910-1949). Elizabeth's second husband was Charles B. Fulmer (1888-1977). He was called "Uncle Charlie" by his stepchildren. Elizabeth was a teacher in the Philadelphia Public Schools System for many years.

Bill was born in 1937 and raised in Philadelphia. He graduated from Temple University in 1959 with a BS in Communications and received an ROTC commission as an Army Second Lieutenant. His first assignment was the Recruiting Main Station in Spokane, Washington. His service included tours in Viet Nam, Turkey and Germany. He was retired as a Major in 1979. A second career followed as a Department of the Army civilian employee which included serving as Archivist of the Army from 1987 to 1995.

FAMILY MEMBERS:

Lillie M. Walker (1881-1972) - Fraternal grandmother
Beatrice L, Williams (1888-1984) – Maternal grandmother
Aunt Helen M. Hansen, nee Walker – Father's sister
Aunt Ruth E. Troxell, nee Walker – Father's sister

Siblings:

Michael L. Walker "Mike". Early in his career, Mike was pastor of a small United Church of Christ in Pennsylvania. He then trained in the Indonesian language, and he and his wife Kathy became missionaries in Borneo, Indonesia for eight years, where he taught English and practical religious subjects. He later became a linguist/analyst for the DOD, and for over 20 years had extensive field operational assignments.

John S. Walker "Jack" joined the FAA (Federal Aviation Agency) as an Air Traffic Controller after leaving the U.S. Air Force. He worked at various air traffic facilities, and in 1997 was appointed Program Director of Air Traffic Management, in Washington D.C. Since retiring, he became a founder of The Padina Group, an aerospace consulting company specializing in recommending standards for Unmanned Aircraft Systems. His wife Darlene is President of the company.

Joan Walker Miskell has had a variety of work experiences over the years in addition to raising her family. She retired from the IBM Corporation in 2007 after 20 years, then followed with six years with the New York Blood Center part-time as a donor relations associate. She is Registrar of her local DAR chapter and has self-published three family-related books: *Letters to Beth*, *Looking Back* and *Over the Spillway*. She and her husband Patrick reside in Beacon, New York.

Cousins:

Josephine F. Walker "Jo" had a career in education related positions. They included administration work at the Illinois Institute in Chicago, and a decade with the Radnor Township School System in Wayne, Pennsylvania. She later became Head of the Lower School of the Episcopal Academy in Merion, Pennsylvania near Philadelphia. Since retiring she lives in a Quaker Continuing Care Retirement Community outside of Philadelphia.

Edward S. Walker, Jr "Ned" is a former U.S. Ambassador to Israel, Egypt, and the United Arab Emirates. He was the Assistant Secretary of State for Near Eastern Affairs. After retiring he was the President and CEO of the Middle East Institute for over five years. He is currently holds a Professorship Chair at Hamilton College. He is married to Leslie.

Elin Rasmussen Walker

Elin is the eldest daughter of Ellen Rasmussen (1913-1998) and Bernhard Rasmussen (1912-1978). They were called "Mor" and "Far" which is Danish for mother and father.

Elin was born in 1939 in Odense, Denmark and attended schools there until the age of 16, when she received an American Field Service scholarship to spend her senior high school year as an exchange student at Acalenes High School in Lafayette, California. For the school year she was sponsored by Carl and Edna Kalbfleisch and lived with them and their daughters Ann and Peggy, in their home in Orinda, California. On graduating from high school, Elin returned to Odense and attended Fyns Studenterkursus. After matriculating in 1959, she received a scholarship to attend Washington State University "WSU" in Pullman, Washington starting in the fall semester of 1959. In 1959 she was a guest at the Kappa Alpha Theta sorority on the Pullman campus for the fall and spring semesters. During 1961, she lived with Dean Albert Thompson and his wife Edna in Pullman, until graduating in May 1961 with a BS degree in Hotel and Restaurant Management. After marrying Bill in 1961, she accompanied him in various assignments abroad and in the United States. When he retired they settled in Annapolis, Maryland. Elin became a US citizen in 1985.

FAMILY MEMBERS:

Aunt Nina and Poul Erik Andreassen. Nina was Elin's mother's sister.

Sibling:

Kirsten Rasmussen O'Donnell (1943-2001). After attending schools in Odense, Kirsten spent her senior year as an au pair for the McClure family in Princeton, New Jersey, and attended her senior year at Princeton High School. On her return to Odense she worked in banking. After her marriage to Thomas O'Donnell she lived most of her life in northern New Jersey. She worked for the Danish delegation to the United Nations, and later was the Vice President of a Travel insurance company in Manhattan. Tom O'Donnell had a career as a main frame computer technician.

FRIENDS

Ahlstone, Art & Ann
Ann is the eldest daughter of Carl & Edna Kalbfleisch. She was in college when Elin stayed in her parent's home, but was home for the holidays.

Art & Ann with granddaughter Daisey

Baretz, Roger M. Baretz (1931-2013) & Carol

Dr. Roger Baretz and his wife Carol became friends with Bill & Elin, in Germany when Roger was an Army captain and the head of psychiatry for the Fourth Armored Division in Goppingen, Germany. He moved to Valley Cottage with his family in 1964 and practiced psychiatry at Good Samaritan Hospital, Helen Hayes Hospital, in New York, and privately until his retirement in 2012.

Blohm, Jorgen & Rita (1939-1999)

Elin & Rita became friends in elementary school in Odense. They both joined a church youth group where Rita met Jorgen whom she married in the early 1960's. Jorgen taught Engineering at Arhus University. They exchanged visits with Elin & Bill often over the years, both in Germany and the United States.

Bill, Elin, Rita, Jorgen - 1963

Buchanan, Jerry & Nancy

Then Major Buchanan was Bill's section chief in the G1 office at Fort Ord, California.

Bucher, Tilman "Tim" K. (1926-2011) & Joan

Joan is the daughter of Hazel & Strauss Clawson. Tim was an Air Force Lieutenant Colonel. While Tim served at Da Nang Air Force Base in Vietnam in 1964 1965, Joan and their children lived with Hazel & Strauss in Wiesbaden, Germany. Tim was assigned to Lindsey Air Station, Wiesbaden following Vietnam in 1965-1968.

Joan Bucher – circa 1961

Burkhardt, Gunther & Lilo

The Burkhardts were German neighbors of Bill & Elin when they lived in Eislingen/Fils, Germany while with the Fourth Armored Division.

Burks, John

John Burks' career spanned magazines, newspapers, books and web sites, taking him from newsrooms to academia and back. He served as a Newsweek Correspondent, and was Rolling Stone's Magazine first managing editor, and Investigative Reporter for the San Francisco Examiner and Oakland Tribune. He established San Francisco Focus (now San Francisco Magazine. He is Professor Emeritus at San Francisco State University.

Ann, Elin, Bill, Peggy Burks
San Francisco Zoo, 2011

Burks, Peggy Kalbfleisch
Peggy is the daughter of Carl & Edna Kalbfleisch and was Elin's "American Sister" when they attended Acalenes High School together in California. Peggy, a member of The Board of Directors, Greenpeace Inc. 2002-2005, has over 25 years of nonprofit management experience. She served as executive director of the San Francisco Zoological Society from 1978 1996, and the Marine Mammal Center from 1996-2000. Her background in wildlife rescue, rehabilitation and animal care includes particular interest in conservation education and ocean health. Peggy has served on numerous advisory boards and task forces including the Oiled Wildlife Care Network, The Joint Use Task Force for Environmental Review of Oceanside Water Pollution Control Plants and the Salmonid/Pinniped Interaction Working Group.

Clawson, Strauss & Hazel
Hazel was a mentor to Elin in Spokane, Washington in 1960-61. Her husband Strauss was a Field Director for the American Red Cross. Hazel and Strauss remained close friends with Elin & Bill after Spokane in Germany where Strauss was posted in Wiesbaden, Germany as US Air Force Europe Red Cross Field Director, and later in America.

Hazel and Elin – Spokane, 1961

DeNio, Jean & Melva "Mel"
Then Lieutenant Jean DeNio was stationed at the Fourth Armored Division Headquarters in Goppingen, Germany when Bill arrived there in 1961. He and his wife Mel were sponsors of Bill & Elin and assisted them in getting settled at that location, and became close friends.

Farrington, Maury
Maury was an Army lieutenant stationed at the Recruiting Main Station in Spokane, Washington when Bill arrived there in 1959. He and Elin & Bill continued their friendship with Maury when he was stationed in Frankfurt, Germany.

Garcia, Gus & Maria

Elin & Bill met Maria when she was an au pair for a military family in Goppingen. Maria went to America with the family to Killeen, Texas. She stayed in Killeen where she & Gus opened a hair styling salon. They very kindly helped Bill when he was at Fort Hood, by providing temporary transportation.

Maria, Jimmy & Sophia Garcia

Hansen, Thorkild Bog

Thorkild was a classmate and friend of Elin at the Fyns Studentenkursus. He also was an American Field Service exchange student to the United States at a New York school. He and Elin sailed to New York aboard the Arosa Kulm in 1956. When Bill returned from Vietnam and visited Copenhagen with Elin in October 1968, they met with Thorkild. He became a Professor at the University of Copenhagen.

Thorkild – 2nd row, 2nd from left; Elin – 1st row, 3rd from left

Bill and Elin with Tom and Emma

Haynes, Tom & Emma Schwabenland

Bill & Elin became friends with the Haynes while at the Fourth Armored Division in Goppingen, Germany where Tom was working in the Staff Judge Advocate section of the Division Headquarters. Emma & Tom met during the Nuremberg Trials, November 20, 1945 October 1, 1946, where Emma was a translator and Director of the Defendant's Visitors Center. Tom was a court reporter at the trials.

Excerpts from Joseph E. Persico's book (pp 386-387).

Emma Schwabenland, an American civilian employee who managed the visitors' center, moved briskly, matching defendants with wives and children.   She admired the colonel for allowing the visits, but was disappointed that he had insisted on keeping up the mesh wire.   He had been adamant.   No touching, no kissing, no hand-holding.   This was how weapons and means of suicide were delivered.

With the visits over, a weeping Emmy Göring approached Emma Schwabenland.   "Do you think the court will send my husband to an island, like Elba?" she asked.   "Maybe I could join him there."

Hillingso, Kjeld & Birgitta Juel

Birgitta was a classmate and friend of Elin during 1958 at Fyns Studentenkursus. Birgitta spent the 1959 school year in Copenhagen studying privately with Princess Margrethe. Elin and Bill visited Birgitta and her husband Kejld during their visit to Copenhagen in 1968. Birgitta is a Godmother of Crown Prince Frederick, who was born in May 1968. Birgitta has worked for Christies Auction House in Copenhagen. Kjeld Hillingso is a retired Danish Lieutenant General. He became Lieutenant General in 1993, and Commander of Unit Command for the Northern Part of NATO's Control Region, while Chief of Operational Forces.

Elin and Brigitta

Brigitta Juel with Princess Margrethe – 1959

Brigitta's wedding – 1963

McClure, Donald & Laura Lee

Laura Lee was the Daughter of Albert & Edna Thompson. She was a Harpist. Her husband Donald, is a Professor Emeritus in Chemistry at Princeton University. He was a developer of color television in RCA Laboratories, 1955 1962. Elin's sister Kirsten was an au pair for the McClure family in Princeton in 1960, where she also attended Princeton High School.

Donald & Laura Lee seated across from one another

Mitchell, Lloyd "Mitch" & Monique

Then Lieutenant Lloyd Mitchell and his wife Monique became friends of Bill & Elin at Fort Ord, California.

Morgan, Hadyn & Evelyn

The Morgans were sponsors of international students in Spokane, where Hadyn was the manager of the Crescent Department Store. They assisted Elin & Bill in planning their wedding, and held the reception at their home.

Haydn Morgan, Bill - 1961

Morgan, Gwyneth

Gwyneth is a daughter of Evelyn & Haydn Morgan. Elin and Gwyneth saw each other during Elin's visit to Bangkok in 1968, where Gwyneth was staying when her husband, an Air Force officer, was stationed in Thailand.

Phenneger, Richard "Dick" & Claudia

Claudia the daughter of Evelyn & Hadyn Morgan is married to Dick Phenneger, a former Air Force pilot who after leaving the Air Force flew for Pan American Airlines. Dick is founder and President of Phenneger & Associates, Inc. In Washington State.

Reekie, Keith & Carole Eardley

Carol was a member of the Kappa Alpha Theta sorority at WSU, where she and Elin became friends. She was one of Elin's bridesmaids in 1961. Carol & Keith lived and worked in Germany and England in the 1960's where he was a reporter, and when Elin & Bill were living in Germany.

Carol Eardley, Julie Herrington, Susan Coffin, Evelyn Morgan

Romans, Tom & Barbara
Bill & Elin knew Tom & Barbara when he was a lawyer and Army officer assigned to the Fourth Armred Division in Goppingen. After returning to America, they were living in Pound Ridge, New York, where Elin & Bill visited them.

Ryans, Joe & Doris
Doris was an Administrative Assistant to the Fort Ord G1 when Bill was assigned to that office. She and her husband Retired Army Colonel Joseph Ryan, were friends of Bill & Elin.

Schmid, Margarete
Margarete was the Administrative Assistant and Translator for the Fourth Armored Division Adjutant General. She & Bill worked closely when he worked in that office. Elin & Bill became friends with Margarete when they lived off post in Eislingen/Fils where Margarete also lived.

Lovey Schuette, Bobbe Robertson, Jean Snow, Margarete Schmid

Schleicher, Juergen & Mary
Elin & Bill met Mary and Juergen while temporarily living at the Connally Apartments in Killeen, Texas in 1967.

Sternelle, Mr. & Mrs. Rudy
Mr. and Mrs. Sternelle were members of the church Bill attended as a youth. Mrs. Sternelle sent packages of home made cookies and fruit cakes to servicemen she knew when they were serving abroad. She generously did this for Bill over the years.

Thompson, Albert (1898 1994) & Edna
Dr. Albert W. Thompson was a professor of foreign languages at Washington State University and later served as Dean of the Humanities in the College of Science and Arts from 1953 to 1964. After retiring from WSU Dr. Thompson focused on Pacific Northwest history and published the book The Early History of the Palouse River and it's Name, in 1971. In 1972 the building on the WSU campus known as the Administration Building was renamed Thompson Hall for Dr. Thompson.

Edna Thompson pouring at Bill & Elin's wedding reception - 1961

Urette, Michael "Mike"& Karen
Mike was a lieutenant with the 144th Signal Battalion in Goppingen, Germany, where he & Karen became friends with Bill & Elin. After his active duty service he became a builder in Florida.

Welters, Warren & Marge
Elin met Marge & Warren when they stayed at Ansgarhus Motel while traveling in Europe with their American car in the 1950's. They lived in San Francisco, where Elin visited them while she was a high school exchange student, and in 1966 1967 when Elin & Bill were at Fort Ord.

Wolters, Curt & Sara
Curt was one of Bill's roommates in Spokane where he was in the Air Force at Fairchild Air Force Base. After leaving the Air Force he took classes at Washington State University (WSU). He took Bill to WSU to attend an International Student Club social event, which is where Bill met Elin. Curt was Bill's best man in 1961.

After marrying, Curt & his wife Sara went to Germany where he was a student at the University of Bonn. He later worked with the State Department in numerous assignments in Africa and the Middle East.

Curt, Bill, Elin - 1961

Zuschlag, Carl & Gabby
Elin & Bill met Carl & Gabby while visiting Beirut, Lebanon in 1965. They were from Hamburg, Germany. Gabby was originally from Lebanon.

GLOSSARY of ABBREVIATIONS

AG Adjutant General
AGC Adjutant Generals Corps
AFB Air Force Base
AFS American Field Service
ARC American Red Cross
BOQ Bachelor Officers Quarters
CO Commanding Officer
COMUSMACV Commander, Military Assistance Command Vietnam CG Commanding General
CONUS Continental United States
DMZ Demilitarized Zone
DOD Department of Defense
EL Elevated Train
FSB Fire Support Base
G1 Assistant Chief of Staff for Personnel
Hooch or Hootch Any living quarters as a barracks
KIA Killed in Action
LA Los Angeles
LST Landing Ship,Tank
LZ Landing Zone
MARS Military Auxiliary Radio System
MOS Military Occupational Specialty
NYC New York City
NV North Vietnam
NVA North Vietnamese Army
PFC Private First Class
PSD Personnel Services Division
PT Physical Training
PX Post Exchange
R & R Rest and Recuperation
RCA Radio Corporation of America
ROAD Reorganization Objective Army Division – 1963
SP4 Specialist 4th Class
TET Vietnam New Year
TWA Trans World Airline
USMACV US Military Command Vietnam
USAREUR US Army Europe
VC Viet Com
VN Vietnam
XO Executive Officer

WORKS CITED

"100,000 People March On the Pentagon". *This Day In History*. 15 August, 2015. Web. http://www.history.com/this-day-in-history/100000-people-march-on-the-pentagon

"Carol Doda". *Wikipedia*. 31 August, 2015. Web. http://en.wikipedia.org

Map of Chu Lai. 13 July, 2015. Web. www.weather-forecast.com

Map of Denmark. 13 July, 2015. Web. www.worldtravels.com

Map of Fort Ord. 13 July, 2015. Web. en.wikipedia.org

Persico, Joseph E. Nuremberg: Infamy on Trial. 01 August, 1995. Penguin Books, New York. pp 386, 387.

"San Francisco stripper famous for first ever supersized boob job busted on DUI". *New York Daily News*. 10 May 2015. Web.http://www.nydailynews.com/news/national/supersized-san-fran-stripper-busted-dui-article-1.1488334

"The Battle of Khe Sanh". *This Day In History*. 15 August, 2015. Web. http://www.history.com/topics/vietnam-war/battle-of-khe-sanh

"USS Pueblo Captured". *This Day In History*. 08 August, 2015. Web. http://www.history.com/this-day-in-history/uss-pueblo-captured

We Wrote Letters Then is the second collaboration for William Alan Walker, Jr. and Joan Walker Miskell. In 2014, they teamed up to publish *Over the Spillway*, the transcribed diary of their grandfather, Isaac Stanley Walker, who kept a journal of his life as a civil engineer and family man from September 1914 through January 1938.

**For more information on the content of this book
contact Bill Walker at**

wwalker7395@yahoo.com